Assault on the Soul: Women in the Former Yugoslavia

Assault on the Soul: Women in the Former Yugoslavia has been co-published simultaneously as *Women & Therapy,* Volume 22, Number 1 1999.

Sara Sharratt
Ellyn Kaschak
Editors

Assault on the Soul: Women in the Former Yugoslavia

Assault on the Soul: Women in the Former Yugoslavia has been co-published simultaneously as *Women & Therapy*, Volume 22, Number 1 1999.

Pre-publication
REVIEWS,
COMMENTARIES,
EVALUATIONS . . .

"**A** significant book and a true labor of love and justice . . . Necessary reading for all of us who have to face up to the human suffering and the political meaning of rape in our time."

Theodore Roszak,
Professor of History, California State University, Hayward
Author of America the Wise: The Longevity Revolution, The True Wealth of Nations, *and* The Memoirs of Elizabeth Frankenstein

The Haworth Press, Inc.

Assault on the Soul: Women in the Former Yugoslavia

Sara Sharratt, PhD
Ellyn Kaschak, PhD
Editors

Assault on the Soul: Women in the Former Yugoslavia has been co-published simultaneously as *Women & Therapy,* Volume 22, Number 1 1999.

The Haworth Press, Inc.
New York • London • Oxfo

Assault on the Soul: Women in the Former Yugoslavia has been co-published simultaneously as *Women & Therapy* ™, Volume 22, Number 1 1999.

The development, preparation, and publication of this work has been undertaken with great care. However, the publisher, employees, editors, and agents of The Haworth Press and all imprints of The Haworth Press, Inc., including The Haworth Medical Press® and Pharmaceutical Products Press®, are not responsible for any errors contained herein or for consequences that may ensue from use of materials or information contained in this work. Opinions expressed by the author(s) are not necessarily those of The Haworth Press, Inc.

The Haworth Press, Inc., 10 Alice Street, Binghamton, NY 13904-1580 USA

Cover design by Thomas J. Mayshock Jr.

Library of Congress Cataloging-in-Publication Data

Assault on the soul : women in the former Yugoslavia / Sara Sharratt, Ellyn Kaschak, editors.
    p. cm.
    ". . . co-published simultaneously as Women & therapy, volume 22, number 1, 1999."
    Includes bibliographical references and index.
    ISBN 0-7890-0770-3 (alk. paper). -- ISBN 0-7890-0771-1 (alk. paper)
    1. Feminist therapy. 2. Women–Crimes against–Yugoslavia. 3. Political refugees–Mental health. I. Sharratt, Sara. II. Kaschak, Ellyn. 1943- .
   RC489.F45A85 1999
   362.87′082′09497–dc21
                                                   99-28578
                                                     CIP

INDEXING & ABSTRACTING

Contributions to this publication are selectively indexed or abstracted in print, electronic, online, or CD-ROM version(s) of the reference tools and information services listed below. This list is current as of the copyright date of this publication. See the end of this section for additional notes.

- *Abstracts of Research in Pastoral Care & Counseling*

- *Academic Abstracts/CD-ROM*

- *Academic Index (on-line)*

- *Alternative Press Index*

- *Behavioral Medicine Abstracts*

- *BUBL Information Service, an Internet-based Information Service for the UK higher education community*

- *CNPIEC Reference Guide: Chinese National Directory of Foreign Periodicals*

- *Contemporary Women's Issues*

- *Current Contents: Clinical Medicine/Life Sciences (CC: CM/LS) (weekly Table of Contents Service), and Social Science Citation Index. Articles also searchable through Social SciSearch, ISI's online database and in ISI's Research Alert current awareness service*

- *Digest of Neurology and Psychiatry*

- *Expanded Academic Index*

- *Family Studies Database (online and CD/ROM)*

- *Family Violence & Sexual Assault Bulletin*

- *Feminist Periodicals: A Current Listing of Contents*

- *GenderWatch*

- *Health Source: Indexing & Abstracting of 160 selected health related journals, updated monthly*

(continued)

- *Health Source Plus: expanded version of "Health Source" to be released shortly*

- *Higher Education Abstracts*

- *IBZ International Bibliography of Periodical Literature*

- *Index to Periodical Articles Related to Law*

- *Mental Health Abstracts (online through DIALOG)*

- *ONS Nursing Scan in Oncology-NAACOG's Women's Health Nursing Scan*

- *PASCAL, c/o Institute de L'Information Scientifique et Technique. Cross-disciplinary electronic database covering the fields of science, technology & medicine. Also available on CD-ROM.*

- *Periodical Abstracts, Research I, general & basic reference indexing & abstracting data-base from University Microfilms International (UMI)*

- *Periodical Abstracts, Research II, broad coverage indexing & abstracting data-base from University Microfilms International (UMI)*

- *Psychological Abstracts (PsycINFO)*

- *Published International Literature on Traumatic Stress (The PILOTS Database)*

- *Sage Family Studies Abstracts (SFSA)*

- *Social Work Abstracts*

- *Sociological Abstracts (SA)*

- *Studies on Women Abstracts*

- *Violence and Abuse Abstracts: A Review of Current Literature on Interpersonal Violence (VAA)*

- *Women Studies Abstracts*

- *Women's Studies Index (indexed comprehensively)*

(continued)

Special Bibliographic Notes related to special journal issues
(separates) and indexing/abstracting:

- indexing/abstracting services in this list will also cover material in any "separate" that is co-published simultaneously with Haworth's special thematic journal issue or DocuSerial. Indexing/abstracting usually covers material at the article/chapter level.
- monographic co-editions are intended for either non-subscribers or libraries which intend to purchase a second copy for their circulating collections.
- monographic co-editions are reported to all jobbers/wholesalers/approval plans. The source journal is listed as the "series" to assist the prevention of duplicate purchasing in the same manner utilized for books-in-series.
- to facilitate user/access services all indexing/abstracting services are encouraged to utilize the co-indexing entry note indicated at the bottom of the first page of each article/chapter/contribution.
- this is intended to assist a library user of any reference tool (whether print, electronic, online, or CD-ROM) to locate the monographic version if the library has purchased this version but not a subscription to the source journal.
- individual articles/chapters in any Haworth publication are also available through the Haworth Document Delivery Service (HDDS).

Assault on the Soul:
Women in the Former Yugoslavia

CONTENTS

ABOUT THE EDITORS

Sara Sharratt, PhD, is Professor Emerita of Marriage and Family Counseling at Sonoma State University in California and has been actively involved in the development and application of feminist therapy since its inception. Born and raised in Costa Rica, she has also been active in multi-cultural psychology with a particular emphasis on Spanish-speaking clients in the US and in Costa Rica. For the last four years, she has focused on international human rights with an emphasis on the rights of women and currently resides in the Hague.

Ellyn Kaschak, PhD, is Professor of Psychology at San Jose State University in San Jose, California. She is the author of *Engendered Lives: A New Psychology of Women's Experience,* as well as numerous articles and chapters on feminist psychology and psychotherapy. She has had thirty years of experience practicing psychotherapy, is past Chair of the Feminist Therapy Institute and of the APA Committee on Women and is a Fellow of Division 35, the Psychology of Women, Division 12, Clinical Psychology, and Division 45, Ethnic Minority Issues of the American Psychological Association.

Preface

I am proud to present in the first volume of my new editorship this collection of writing on applications and intersections of feminist therapy, activism and jurisprudence with women and children in the former Yugoslavia. Focusing on the former Yugoslavia offers a look at applied feminist practice in a cultural context outside the American or Northern European. Nor is it the more usual milieu of working in the undeclared war zones. As many of the women writing in this volume have crossed man-made boundaries to honor the feminist connection of women, so I hope that this book can contribute to the project of making visible the still too often invisible connections between and among women in various cultural contexts. Sometimes even we do not know all the places in which feminists are practicing. To reach back and borrow a phrase from the sixties in the United States, "We are everywhere."

The writers in this collection are German and Dutch, Norwegian and Costa Rican, North American. They are therapists, lawyers and justices of the International Criminal Tribunal for the former Yugoslavia. All of them are struggling with the profound immorality of the circumstance, with keeping their vision and its applications culturally sensitive, contextually based and psychologically or legally useful. All have been profoundly changed by doing this work. A Serbian and a Croatian woman offer their perspectives on the situation, on the arrival of many of these women, foreign by official standards, to offer aid, to offer what skills they have, often inadequate in the face of the horrors with which they are confronted, to offer themselves in a struggle from which they could easily have turned away.

This material will never appear in official records, in the records of the United Nations or of the International Criminal Tribunal. It is women's psychology, women's history, women's geography, women's jurisprudence. It always has been and still is our work as feminists to make visible what patriarchy conspires to erase or confine to the margins. And so I hope that these writings will serve as part of the record of what women have done in

[Haworth co-indexing entry note]: "Preface." Kaschak, Ellyn. Co-published simultaneously in *Women & Therapy* (The Haworth Press, Inc.) Vol. 22, No. 1, 1999, pp. xxiii-xxv.; and: *Assault on the Soul: Women in the Former Yugoslavia* (ed: Sara Sharratt and Ellyn Kaschak) The Haworth Press, Inc., 1999, pp. xv-xvii. Single or multiple copies of this article are available for a fee from The Haworth Document Delivery Service [1-800-342-9678, 9:00 a.m. - 5:00 p.m. (EST). E-mail address: getinfo@haworthpressinc.com].

xiii

this war: this cadre of women, some crossing the borders, others working in the international courts of the Hague, still others from the war-torn territories, who offer their skills, their visions and their hearts without hesitation.

This collection, then, is also intended as an historical document, an assurance that both the plight of women and the role of women in bringing it to visibility, to the attention of the international community and the justice system, will not be erased. The official version will likely include "the facts"–who got tried and convicted, how many individuals were put in camps, tortured or killed, how many rapes were counted by the voice of authority. In these articles, the authors tell us what really happened to the most ordinary women and children. And to themselves. They recount a heroics of the ordinary.

This collection of articles includes three interviews with representatives of the justice system. They are not included to imply that women receive greater justice in the courts than in other social institutions, but that they receive greater justice when women are part of the decision-making process–not just any women, but those who are able to see with women's eyes, to notice the injustices that would simply have gone unnoticed except to someone who also lives life in a woman's body. Secondly, the intersection of justice and healing is a crucial one. Healing from such severe injuries inevitably requires an arena in which the truth is finally spoken and heard. The courts are only one possible arena for this to occur and it may be long overdue for feminists to devise others as part of the treatment of the effects of such atrocities. Here we visit some of the places where justice and healing come together.

What can happen when one female justice of the court decides to stay up all night looking for indictable instances of rape that she was told were not there? When a Serbian woman refuses nationalism for the connection of international feminism? When women already brutalized are willing to put themselves in further peril to testify against their torturers? When others living in relative comfort and safety are willing to place themselves in peril, to cross men's borders to offer their skills and compassion to other women trapped in the former Yugoslavia? And what happens when they return home too traumatized themselves to continue their previous lives?

Women go to war after war after war ministering to the wounded and the weary with the latest in psychological techniques. Many still use diagnosis and the DSM, for what tools and signposts do they have other than the woefully inadequate Post-Traumatic Stress Disorder (PTSD)? Would that in this world of postmodernism, declared postfeminism and various other posts, we might actually arrive at a time of post-trauma for women and children. Would that we really had more cases of post-trauma rather than chronic or repeated acute trauma. For as I have long argued (Kaschak, 1992), there is nothing *post* about trauma for women who continue to reside in the former

Yugoslavia and nothing *post* indeed for any women who reside in violent and damaging patriarchal societies even if they have not officially declared war on women.

And what of the idea that such trauma causes stress, a concept much too small to contain the multiple reverberations of ordinary life as a woman, much less the terror and grief, the shame and loss of being treated not only as the enemy, the spoils of men's wars, but not even as the enemy, instead as the battlefield itself. Women's bodies are part of the ground upon which war is waged; women's psyches and souls are damaged and compromised until feminist therapy must begin with reminding these women of their basic humanity. These women have committed perhaps the most ancient crime of all in patriarchal society, that of being women.

It is an artifact of the narrower lens of non-feminist psychotherapy that commitment is spoken of almost exclusively in the context of dyadic partner relationships and with a particular concern for its absence. For feminist practitioners, for those with a wider lens, the kind of commitment that these women demonstrate to the victims of this war, to the lived practice of feminism and to humanity is obviously one of the most profound kinds of commitment there is.

Still, how disappointing that, almost thirty years after the introduction of feminist theory and practice, there is still such need for us to continue to develop and apply feminist interventions for tortured and traumatized women. How disappointing that these immoral acts continue, that we have to go to war yet another time, that I have to repeat the very words that many of us spoke for the first time as we were developing the earliest feminist interventions almost thirty years ago. May all our practices in the name of damage to women's bodies, psyches and souls be rendered obsolete.

Ellyn Kaschak

NOTE

The editors wish to express their thanks to Gregory Kipling, who served as editorial assistant, and the Costa Rican agency Instituto Latinoamericano para Prevención, Educación y Salud (ILPES) for their cooperation. Assistance was also provided by the following University of San Francisco graduate students: Yolanda Briscoe, Roxanne Fowler, Margot Brown, Terry McClanahan and Shana Daronn.

REFERENCE

Kaschak, E. (1992). *Engendered lives: A new psychology of women's experience.* Basic Books: New York.

Introduction

Sara Sharratt

Our purpose in this special volume is to shed light upon women's wartime experiences, and to make sense of their coping strategies in the face of the innumerable atrocities committed against them. The war in question is that which accompanied the break-up of the Former Yugoslavia, and it is one with which I am all too familiar, having spent the past four years in Holland researching women's treatment at the hands of the International Criminal Tribunal in the Hague. Needless to say, exposure to the effects of war has provided both me and the contributing authors with a new perspective on the relationship between justice and recovery, and the impact of enormous and repeated trauma on helpers and victims. Moreover, one might argue that analysis of this conflict makes manifest issues that are of vital significance to feminist psychotherapists in particular, and to those working in the healing professions more generally.

Wars Make Visible the Declared and Undeclared Wars Against Women

Violence against women is magnified during armed conflicts, in the process exposing the artificiality of the boundary between "wartime" and "peacetime" violence. Indeed, one might even go so far as to say that attacks upon women in conflict zones are simply one more manifestation of the "undeclared" war upon women everywhere.

Challenging the Erasure of Women's Victimization in Wartime

To a large extent, war crimes committed against women have been marginalized, trivialized or ignored by the International Tribunals charged with

Address correspondence to: Sara Sharratt, PhD, P.O. Box 2292-1000, San Jose, Costa Rica.

[Haworth co-indexing entry note]: "Introduction." Sharratt, Sara. Co-published simultaneously in *Women & Therapy* (The Haworth Press, Inc.) Vol. 22, No. 1, 1999, pp. 1-6; and: *Assault on the Soul: Women in the Former Yugoslavia* (ed: Sara Sharratt and Ellyn Kaschak) The Haworth Press, Inc., 1999, pp. 1-6. Single or multiple copies of this article are available for a fee from The Haworth Document Delivery Service [1-800-342-9678, 9:00 a.m. - 5:00 p.m. (EST). E-mail address: getinfo@haworthpressinc.com].

investigating them. In this way, challenging the erasure of women's experiences is central to the political struggle against male violence, whether in the detention camps of Bosnia-Herzegovina, or in the suburbs of Los Angeles. At a personal level, I have found few things more shocking than the juxtaposition of clear evidence of atrocities committed against women on the one hand, and their absence from most accounts of the war in the Former Yugoslavia on the other.

It is generally accepted that the majority of casualties in armed conflicts are women and children. While not wishing to suggest that contemporary jurisprudence has suddenly broken with its misogynist past and prioritized the interests of these groups, attention is increasingly being focused upon the rights of victims (see Odio), with impunity seen as an impediment both to justice and to peace. This is an important point, and one which feminist therapists would do well to bear in mind: atrocities, including rape, need to be publicly acknowledged as war crimes and their perpetrators punished rather than the victims, as is usually the case in instances of sexual violence (see McDonald; Viseur-Sellers). Thus, it makes sense for us to work with institutions that punish crimes against women, and push them towards strong forms of redress and unequivocal condemnation of rape and other manifestations of male violence.

Wars Make Explicit the Links Between Treatment and Advocacy

Although feminist therapy and ethics have always placed great emphasis upon the integration of theory and practice, this becomes especially important in the context of armed conflicts such as that of the Former Yugoslavia. How so? In short, an activist stance in the fight against impunity may very well have a direct impact upon collective and individual healing, to the extent that feminists are able to persuade International Tribunals to recognize rape as the war crime and torture that it is. If we are successful in doing so, this could, as Nancy Kelley states, " . . . change things for women all over the world" (Chesler, 1996, p. 56), as well as helping us overcome powerful feelings of helplessness and despair (see Scheffler and Müchele).

War Crime Tribunals Force the Perpetrator to Take Center-Stage

By focusing attention upon those responsible for war atrocities, International Tribunals provide a basis for the public repudiation of perpetrators and the acts they have committed. In this way, justice becomes a way of expediting individual and collective recovery.

Wars Necessitate the Adoption of Broad-Based Models of Healing in Which the Search for Truth Plays an Integral Role

In the recent past, we have seen numerous examples of "truth commissions," such as those organized in South Africa or Guatemala, in which immunity from prosecution is traded for public admission of guilt. Whatever the strengths or weaknesses of such an approach, it does offer victims and families a chance to confront the perpetrator, and listen to him describe his crime and ask for forgiveness. Moreover, in Latin America in particular, there is also a tradition of victims coming forward to speak publicly about the violence committed against them, in the process breaking the silence and gaining the solidarity and support of other witnesses. Taken together, these approaches provide useful markers in helping us to find more communal ways of helping victims of violence, for example, by instituting "abuse tribunals" in which victims learn how to overcome self-blame and face those who victimized them in the first place (see McDonald; Viseur-Sellers; and Odio [interviews]).

War Alters Notions of Trauma

As one might imagine, not only does war trauma highlight the inadequacies of current psychotherapeutic theory and practice, but it also shows how our emphasis on the individual ignores the degree of traumatization within communities more generally. Moreover, given the magnitude of the suffering, it is difficult for some of us *not* to think politically, and see healing and recovering as possibilities *only* if existing social structures are radically transformed: there is no recovery from injustice that has not ceased; there is no healing when traumatization reoccurs on a daily basis. While such a perspective leads us, on the one hand, to make explicit the links between "wartime" and "peacetime" victimization of women, on the other it forces us to re-evaluate the interrelationship between the justice system in general, and psychotherapy in particular.

We must ask ourselves whether the justice available to war victims in the International Tribunals is therapeutic. If we answer affirmatively, does it not behoove us, as therapists, to expand our understanding of therapy when working with "peacetime" victims of violence? Indeed, one might even go so far as to argue that the judicial system, in championing reconciliation and the rehabilitation of victims, is introducing psychological and therapeutic elements into its mandate. In similar fashion, therapists would gain by learning and drawing inspiration from recent trends in jurisprudence, since both justice and healing are crucial if the victimization of women is to be effectively challenged.

Such a perspective, adopted by many of the contributors to this volume, demands that psychologists work with a far wider range of actors than has traditionally been the case (see Anderson). In this way, attention is shifted from individual women to the wider structures in which they are embedded, whether these serve to oppress and dominate, or to foster justice and peace to the world. Needless to say, at an individual level, this understanding calls for healing methods that are contextual and global, and focused on causes as much as effects (see Scheffler and Müchele).

Wars Highlight the Secondary Traumatization of Healers and Our Unwillingness to See Ourselves as Part of the Collective Damage

As I have suggested above, therapists working in war zones must reorient themselves from the intra-psychic to the social. Within that context, not only does our vicarious traumatization as healers become evident, but we are confronted with the impossibility of remaining neutral or detached from the sociopolitical forces that led to our clients' victimization in the first place (see Scheffler and Müchele). Obviously, there are certain dangers inherent within this state of affairs, including the likelihood that one will become caught up in the collective psyche of those with whom one is working (see Krämer; Scheffler and Müchele; and Foeken), and the risk that a colonial relationship will develop between survivors and healers on the one hand, and foreign and local professionals on the other (see Ostodic). As such, one of the recurring themes of this book is the danger of relying too heavily upon intra-psychic medical models in a war context. Needless to say, such approaches are naive at best, and unethical at worst. Indeed, I would go so far as to ask practitioners working in the "undeclared" war zones of Europe, North America and elsewhere also to reflect upon the ethics of de-contextualized interventions that do not take into account the institutionalized and systematic nature of violence against women.

Wars also serve to raise a number of other questions for feminist psychotherapists, including most notably those related to the existence of evil in our midst. How does it become so prevalent within a given social context? What happens to individuals who are witnesses or subject to evil acts? As one might imagine, these issues can only be addressed if we seek out the sources of the evil and learn how to face them in all their enormity and power. For the legal system in particular, this involves offering justice to the victims and punishment to the perpetrators, in the process rendering future conflicts and acts of vengeance less likely. Therapists would do well to learn from such an approach, and adopt a perspective that is sensitive not only to the suffering of individuals as a result of abuse, but also to the collective trauma that comes from living in a world filled with violence and despair. In short, Western psychotherapists tend to devote too much effort to the task of fostering intra-psychic recovery, and too little to that of restoring individuals at a community level, for example through victim testimonies, rape museums, public declarations of contrition by perpetrators or funds and monuments for survivors. While this is not to suggest that psychotherapy is superfluous or unnecessary, it must be accompanied by broader-based interventions as well.

There can be little doubt that the war has changed the perspectives of all those who have contributed to this volume, making us realize that, if we are to move forward in the treatment of rape victims, we must de-stigmatize the survivors while stigmatizing the perpetrators, both by accusing them publicly of their crimes, and by sending them to prison. Moreover, we have also learned that traumatization of those working with war victims is inevitable, not only from the perspective of countertransference, but also in terms of the war's impact upon the very essence of our being, causing us to question our existence, our choices, and what altruism and morality mean for ourselves and our communities. Thus, for the three interviewees in particular (McDonald; Odio; and Viseur-Sellers), they all make reference to a similar range of issues with which they have had to contend while working at the International Criminal Tribunal for the Former Yugoslavia (ICTY): evil, racism, sexism, and the trauma that comes from being exposed to war crimes testimony on a daily basis. In another instance, I asked one of the contributors why she had not gone for therapy in the two years since she had left the Balkans, despite suffering severe traumatization. In reply, she said, "I have been too incapacitated to do so." I then asked her how she would have reacted had one of her clients told her that. She laughed, and I joined her. In all too many cases, healers forget to take care of themselves while in the midst of looking after others.

In this collection, we gather together the voices and perspectives of a number of women whose work has brought them face to face with the hatred and violence of the Yugoslav conflict. They include a gender specialist and two judges involved in the ICTY in the Hague; a Serbian feminist and founder of the Women's Autonomous Center in Belgrade; the North American coordinator of Psychologists for Social Responsibility; a Bosnian psychologist engaged in research into the complexities of women's networking at an international scale; two Norwegians involved in the implementation and assessment of programs designed to help traumatized female survivors in Bosnia-Herzegovina; a team of German psychotherapists engaged in training activities for Bosnian para-professionals; a Dutch psychotherapist also involved in the training and supervision of local health workers; the German founder of one of the first treatment centers for women to be opened in Bosnia-Herzegovina; a Dutch social scientist offering advice and a new vision on treatment interventions; and finally the special editor herself, who conducted the interviews, gathered the voices and bore witness to the women's testimony.

All of these individuals are intrinsically connected to one another. As a scholar researching the activities and mandate of the International Tribunal, I developed a relationship with the three women interviewed for this volume. I met Anne Anderson in the Hague when she took part in one of the consultation sessions organized for the Tribunal by Psychologists for Social Responsibility. As for Edita Ostodic and Gabriele Krämer, I got to know them through my friendship and close collaboration with one of the founders of Medica Mundiale. This latter individual also introduced me to Sabine Scheffler and Agnes Müchele who had previously provided training to Medica personnel. She also served as a point of contact for Berit Schei and Solveig Dahl, whose team was also based in Zenica and often collaborated with Medica. Turning to Ingrid Foeken, I had been friends with her in Holland many years ago, and we reestablished our friendship when I returned to the country. As an individual closely associated with the activities of Admira in the Former Yugoslavia, she is an especially well-qualified contributor to this publication; she is also the one who recommended her friend Anja Meulenbelt. Finally, the circle closes with Lepa Mladjenovic, who agreed to participate in this project after approaching Ingrid for help and support, who subsequently put her into contact with me. While I do not pretend to suggest that the views of these authors are necessarily representative of all those who have ever worked with war survivors in the Former Yugoslavia, they are nonetheless women who care deeply about other women, and who found themselves in a foreign land or with foreign visitors at a time of profound horror and devastation.

REFERENCE

Chesler, P. (Winter 1996). *On the issues: The progressive woman's quarterly*, p. 56.

Feminist Psychology and Global Issues:
An Action Agenda

Anne Anderson

SUMMARY. Highlighted in this article is a call for feminists to expand their level of intervention to include global awareness. Several projects are described as examples of feminists working as positive facilitators of change for victims and survivors of war. *[Article copies available for a fee from The Haworth Document Delivery Service: 1-800-342-9678. E-mail address: getinfo@haworthpressinc.com]*

KEYWORDS. Peace psychology, feminist psychology, global awareness, Psychologists for Social Responsibility (PsySR)

Anne Anderson, MSW, is Coordinator of Psychologists for Social Responsibility and in practice with the Washington Therapy Guild in Washington, DC.

The author thanks Susan McKay, Martha Mednick, Bianca Cody Murphy, and Mike Wessells for their valuable comments and suggestions.

Consultants included: Anne Anderson, MSW, Coordinator, Psychologists for Social Responsibility; Leila Dane, PhD, Director, Institute for Victims of Trauma, McLean, VA, who was particularly instrumental in developing the first draft; C. J. Frederick, PhD, UCLA/VA Medical Center, Los Angeles, CA; Mary Harvey, PhD, Director, Victims of Violence Program, Cambridge Hospital, MA; Kathleen Nader, DSW, Director of Evaluation, UCLA Trauma, Violence and Sudden Bereavement Program, CA; Shana Swiss, MD, Director, Women's Program, Physicians for Human Rights, Boston, MA; Janet Yassen, MSW, Boston, MA.

Address correspondence to: Anne Anderson, Psychologists for Social Responsibility, 2607 Connecticut Avenue N.W., Washington, DC 20008, U.S.A. Electronic mail may be sent to: psysrusa@interserv.com; Website: http//www.rmc.edu/psysr.

[Haworth co-indexing entry note]: "Feminist Psychology and Global Issues: An Action Agenda." Anderson, Anne. Co-published simultaneously in *Women & Therapy* (The Haworth Press, Inc.) Vol. 22, No. 1, 1999, pp. 7-21; and: *Assault on the Soul: Women in the Former Yugoslavia* (ed: Sara Sharratt and Ellyn Kaschak) The Haworth Press, Inc., 1999, pp. 7-21. Single or multiple copies of this article are available for a fee from The Haworth Document Delivery Service [1-800-342-9678, 9:00 a.m. - 5:00 p.m. (EST). E-mail address: getinfo@haworthpressinc.com].

Feminists have long been active in the peace movement. Early Western feminists often made a connection between militarism and sexism and were active opponents of war (Brock-Utne, 1985). Today many feminist peace psychologists and other mental health professionals (Van Soest, 1997) are working on global issues to respond to violence and to build peaceful communities. Traditional peace psychology, informed by feminist perspectives (Murphy, 1995), addresses not only issues of war, international and inter-ethnic conflict, but also has expanded to include "the elimination of coercive systems of interaction as a basis of interaction between individuals and groups" (McKay, 1996, p. 94). The multiplicity of manifestations of structural violence, violent conflict and oppression that afflict our world calls for multi-level, multifaceted interventions.

Feminist psychotherapists, by definition, are familiar with this type of analysis and are working with their clients "towards strategies and solutions advancing feminist resistance, transformation and social change in daily personal lives and relationships with the social, emotional and political environment" (Brown, 1994, p. 22). But the press of individual situations and cases can often cause us to lose sight of the larger picture. We overlook our capacities to participate at several levels of intervention well beyond the confines of our office walls. With this report I hope to stimulate the creativity, passion and hope of feminist therapists to expand our horizons and find ways to support, extend and multiply the work of our colleagues around the world.

We find feminist psychologists in a variety of settings–from working with individuals in the treatment room, to performing community-based interventions, teaching psychology, pursuing action research, providing policy analysis, and initiating political action. This article discusses several projects as concrete examples of the multi-leveled interventions being undertaken to support women and foster peaceful, sustainable societies around the world. These projects were chosen because they adhere to the following feminist principles:

1. They contextualize individuals in their societies;
2. They are aware of and alert for gender differences in experience;
3. They analyze power relationships relevant to situations;
4. They use a range of empowerment models of therapy;
5. They use collaborative processes to accomplish goals;
6. They listen and learn from others, across cultural and language barriers;
7. They are based on an ethical, non-neutral stance regarding social justice, equality and misuse of power.

Many of the programs described in this article were developed by members of Psychologists for Social Responsibility (PsySR) or have been supported by PsySR members. PsySR is a United States-based international network of psychologists and other mental health professionals who draw upon the research, knowledge, and practice of psychology to promote durable peace at the community, national, and international levels. Members work to: (a) apply the growing body of knowledge about conflict resolution and violence prevention, (b) facilitate positive change for victims and survivors of personal, community and civil violence, (c) advocate for basic human needs–including actions which decrease poverty, ensure ethnic and gender equity, increase work opportunity, promote healthy and sustainable environments, and achieve wiser balance between human needs and military budgets, (d) ensure that relevant information from psychology is used in local, national and international public policy. The first project we look at facilitates positive change for victims and survivors of war.

WAR TRAUMA AND RECOVERY BROCHURE

In 1992, when the stories of mass sexual assault and rape began to break from the territories of the former Yugoslavia, PsySR realized that women would be needing psychological services but that many would not have access to them. Few services were available and there was little social support for seeking mental health therapeutic help. With Irena Sarovic, M.A., originally from Croatia, as our principal author and translator, we consulted with a number of mental health professionals with particular expertise in dealing with the aftermath of sexual violence and trauma and developed a self-help psychoeducational brochure for use throughout the region. Several principles guided our process: the information was to be drawn from the best that feminist psychology had to offer at the time; the product needed to be short and inexpensive–easy to reproduce, transport and distribute in a war zone; the brochure needed to be "user-friendly," offering its help in a culturally acceptable way. For instance, since rape carried such social stigma, the subject needed to be approached in the larger context of the trauma of war. The resulting brochure recognizes the social context of trauma experienced by individuals and their communities. It gives information on normal human reactions to experiencing trauma, includes paragraphs on rape and torture, and provides some concrete suggestions for self-care and support. Recognizing that many people would be experiencing chronic stress because of the continuation of the war, self-care suggestions focused on maintaining as much control over one's life as possible, deciding carefully, for instance, about who to talk to about what and when to do it. There are versions printed in both the Latin and Cyrillic alphabets, so that all sides of the conflict are able to use it.

Well over 15,000 have already been directly distributed by grassroots women's groups working in all parts of the former Yugoslavia, by U.S.

mental health professionals providing workshops and other support there, and in asylum countries for use with refugees. Since people are encouraged to copy the brochure, and the brochure has been reprinted in some handbooks, it is impossible to say how widely this resource has been distributed.

Anecdotal information as to its usefulness has been forthcoming from a number of sources. For instance, mental health professionals have found it most useful as a conversation starter for groups of refugees and some have used it as training materials for paraprofessional volunteers. Women's knitting circles, developed by displaced women as a way of making warm clothes and providing a support system for themselves, have used the brochures as a way of helping members of the circle to deal with their experiences. Women for Women, a U.S.-based non-profit organization that hand delivers funds and sponsors microenterprises for women in Bosnia, distributed the brochure and reported that children as young as ten were able to read it out loud without difficulty. The brochure is now also available in a more generic form in English and continues to be distributed more widely.

TRAUMA, TESTIMONY AND SOCIAL MEMORY

Inger Agger, a psychologist from Denmark, has been instrumental in creatively addressing issues of appropriate treatment for women and girls who have experienced gender-specific human rights violations. She was responsible for the Psycho-Social Projects of the European Community Task Force during the war in the Former Yugoslavia and subsequently was Psycho-Social Advisor at the OSCE Democratization Branch in Sarajevo. She has been a strong advocate for taking "an ethical non-neutral stand" (1995, p. 35) when working in therapy with women who have survived sexual assault, torture and other human rights abuses. " 'Mixing therapy with politics' is in fact unavoidable in psycho-social assistance to victims of political conflicts. If aid workers do not take an ethical stand against injustice they are still acting politically, because they are joining the conspiracy of secrecy and silence which maintains the traumatizing and oppressive power of shame" (1997, p. 123).

In her research project interviewing women from 10 different countries in the Middle East and Latin America (Agger, 1994), Agger used her office as what she calls "a ritual space" in which women could tell their stories "so that people in asylum countries would know more about the human rights violations which take place against women" (1995, p. 37), to contribute to social memory. She used a tape recorder to record their testimony so that the woman knew "that her voice and her name could be heard" (p. 37).

Agger describes this extension of the traditional therapeutic hour this way:

> . . . I attempted to unite my experience from the use of testimony in the consciousness-raising groups of the women's movement with experi-

ences from my therapeutic training and my work with testimony as a trans-cultural therapeutic method. This method implies that the research process and therapeutic process are not separable. For victims of human rights violations, testimony has a special significance, because it becomes a documented accusation and a piece of evidence against the perpetrators. 'Testimony' as a concept has a special, double connotation: it contains objective, judicial, public and political aspects, and subjective, spiritual, cathartic and private aspects. (1995, p. 37)

Agger is very concerned about "the major contradiction between the psychological processes involved in reconciliation and those involved in social memory. Reconciliation involved recreating trust between people who are divided by hatred and fear of each other; social remembrance and testimony require keeping all that happened–both the good and the evil–in the collective memory of these same people" (p. 38). The term reconciliation has many meanings. At one end of the spectrum we see that when a conflict has terminated there is social pressure on people to come to some accommodation with the former foe, to "live and let live," or "forgive and forget," so that some order and stability may return to the community. Galtung probably expresses the most ambitious end of the spectrum best when he describes reconciliation as using "creative, positive conflict transformation . . . not only to avoid violence . . . but to increase the entropy [of peace] by emerging from that phase of conflict with more mature selves and more mature social formations . . . " (1996, p. 272).

At the same time there is a need for recognition of and restitution for the suffering experienced by both sides, and for social memory to act as a preventive to "never again" let such atrocities happen. Of particular concern for feminist therapists is the fact that women's experiences are often lost in the social memory, that the underlying structural issues which fostered the conflict are not addressed in the aftermath, and traumatized individuals are caught in the middle. If they go along with the reconciliation then they contribute to the sense of community, feeling connected again, but are in danger of denying their own reality. On the other hand, if they maintain their insistence on publicly remembering their experiences they are in danger of remaining outside the community and stigmatized when their society wants to forgive and forget. Issues involved in both effective reconciliation leading to durable peace (Lund, 1996) and accurate and inclusive social memory need to be addressed in the "search for new methods and aims in trauma therapy" (Agger, 1995, p. 39). This is an area that requires much attention and creative innovation, with feminist therapists uniquely positioned to bring their considerable insights and experience to bear on this problem.

CONSULTATION WITH THE INTERNATIONAL
CRIMINAL TRIBUNALS

In 1994, in my role as PsySR Coordinator, I was contacted by an international women's rights Non-Governmental Organization (NGO), The Coordination of Women's Advocacy (CWA), for help with their process of consultation with the International Criminal Tribunals for the Former Yugoslavia and Rwanda (ICTY/R), which is based in The Netherlands, at The Hague. CWA began its work as a group of women from 10 asylum countries in 1993 and has since organized a number of consultations with institutions of the United Nations system. These have focused primarily on the question of gender-specific war crimes against women during the war in the former Yugoslavia, and more recently, also in Rwanda. CWA has consistently called for prosecution of rape as a war crime, has advised the Tribunal on ways to reduce retraumatization of women survivors who agree to provide evidence, how to best support witnesses in the process of testifying, and has called attention to the problems of witness protection.

For instance, when the Tribunal was deciding on whether or not to require public disclosure of witnesses' identity in open court, the prosecution staff asked for expert opinion on the issue. The Tribunal needed to balance the defendant's right to know the identity of his accuser against the right of the witness to protection from physical and psychological harm and intimidation. The PsySR network was able to provide the Tribunal prosecution staff with background psychological information on the probable chilling effect of allowing public identification of witnesses testifying in cases of sexual assault, especially given the very serious stigma attached to rape in their society. This contributed to the Court's decision to allow anonymity of witnesses.

My fellow CWA consultants have been working with refugees, potential witnesses, and survivors of war crimes, both in therapeutic situations and in other advocacy and service roles. Their dedication and concern for maintaining the dignity of their clients, empowering their recovery and providing the best they can offer to the ICTY/R in its quest for some measure of justice is palpable whenever they gather in consultation. They maintain a clear-eyed view of both the limitations of international institutions to make real differences in individuals' lives, and also the power of reaching international consensus on such issues as declaring and prosecuting rape as a war crime.

Former Chief Prosecutor Justice Richard Goldstone, said,

> The role of gender-based war crimes in the former Yugoslavia . . . is of much greater importance than we originally expected. . . . The question of rape in Rwanda and the frequency of crimes of sexual assault point to the need for more focus there. . . . You may not realize how important your inputs have been all these years. The Tribunal has carefully lis-

tened to your recommendations and it has responded to the quest for solutions in many of the areas which you brought up with us. (CWA, 1996, p. 12)

The consultations have also contributed to successful political action. We developed a draft resolution which was adopted by the European Parliament, which increased the budget for the protection and support of people testifying before the Tribunal. CWA provided a whole list of suggested psychosocially informed support systems and improvements in the treatment of female witnesses interviewed by Tribunal personnel (CWA, 1996). For instance, we have recommended that all witnesses be allowed to bring a support person with them, with their travel also funded by the Tribunal, that interviews be held in the mother tongue of the witness, that translators, when used, be trained to handle testimony about traumatic events sensitively, and that asylum countries (where many potential witnesses currently reside) be called upon to offer increased witness protection. With the increased funding, the Tribunal should be able to implement at least some of the improvements in their support of witnesses. The most recent Consultation considered how witnesses are faring back in their communities. A questionnaire is being developed for use with the now hundreds of people who have been interviewed by the ICTY/R, to give them a voice and an opportunity to affect the future workings of international tribunals through the telling of their experiences as people who testified for the ICTY/R. These practices, established at the international level, can also be used, eventually, as models for women activists striving to improve treatment of women in their own countries.

WOMEN AS PEACE BUILDERS

Women in roles as peace builders are often invisible. "Women have a long history of negotiating conflicts and creating compromises in the private sphere and at the community level. Yet rarely is this ever called upon in situations of armed conflict and war" (Bunch, 1997, p. 7). To shed some light on this critical aspect of women's lives, a multicultural research project has been developed by another PsySR member, Susan McKay of the University of Wyoming, and Cheryl de la Rey of the University of Cape Town, South Africa. McKay notes:

. . . we think that women work in ways that are distinct from men's but these have not been documented. It is interesting that several peace building projects are presently occurring . . . and I am not free to give any details because of concerns for women's safety. [Women] tend to work quietly and at community levels, building coalitions and networking for proactivity. . . . We think we can start to learn more by asking women themselves, women who do this work. (McKay, personal communication, 3/12/98)

The project, based in South Africa, consists of two parts:

1. A workshop which will bring together women leaders to discuss peace building processes within the context of their own organizations and culture and to describe women's approaches (Phase I). The workshop will be held during a two-day period and will be dialogic, a model traditional to South African culture. Participants will be 15 to 20 women in South Africa who represent diverse ethnic, racial and geographic perspectives and who are leaders within governmental, nongovernmental and grassroots social movements.
2. An implementation phase (Phase II) which will utilize workshop proceedings as a foundation for developing a program model and researching peace building training for emerging women leaders. McKay again comments on this work in progress:

One of the problems we think occurs, and I have discussed this with very experienced people, is that there seems to be a trendiness in doing peace building training and it is a quick affair without extensive and ongoing capacity building (capacity building is key in peace building work) which we see as critical. So a central question is how to develop woman-centered programs to build women's capacities in peace building. (McKay, personal communication, 3/12/98)

In another example of ways in which small projects relate to wider levels of intervention, McKay also notes the direct connections between this project and one of the goals specified in the United Nations Beijing Women's Conference Platform for Action (United Nations, 1996), that of increasing women's capacities for peace building. Included as part of this goal is the development of policy recommendations for governmental and nongovernmental organizations about best practices and training models which can help facilitate sociopolitical and psychosocial reconstruction processes (McKay, personal communication, 2/6/98).

Community-Based Intervention–Angola

Psychologists and other mental health professionals are increasingly called upon to treat the survivors of the chaos that is unattended to in our cities, our rural communities, and in war-torn countries. And yet, often those programs are designed and implemented without tapping the local knowledge and resources, often held by women for their communities. The project described below is an attempt to correct those problems.

Carlinda Monteiro, an Angolan psychologist in Luanda, has been leading an all-Angolan team of mostly women, under the auspices of Christian Children's Fund, on a seven-province project to assist war-affected children. Since over half the population of Angola is under 15, and includes many child soldiers, the problem is immense and cannot be addressed through traditional Western-based individualized treatment for PTSD and other related diagnoses. For one thing, there are very few trained psychologists available and Western interventions must receive appropriate cultural tailoring in order to be effective. But more critical to the situation is the fact that "the psychological wounds are communal and cannot be addressed effectively at the individual and family levels" (Wessells, in press).

One of PsySR's past presidents, Michael Wessells, has been working with Monteiro and her team in an effort to bring an effective blend of Western psychological expertise and traditional methods to bear on the problem. Using a "train the trainers" approach, the team has been conducting seminars with groups of people from around the country who have been nominated by their communities as trustworthy and effective in caring for children. The team's process has been effective in eliciting traditional views of what children need to grow up healthy, as well as community assessments of the problems children are facing today. For instance, in 1995 the team

> conducted a study of a nonrandom sample of 200 unaccompanied children who had come to the capital city, Luanda. . . . Although it was a worst case analysis, the results were shocking: 27% had lost their parents, 94% had been exposed to attacks, 66% had witnessed mine explosions and 55 had been victims thereof, 36% had lived with troops, 33% had suffered injuries by shooting or shelling, 65% had escaped death, and 7% had fired guns. These experiences had a powerful psychological impact on the children who exhibited trauma symptoms such as fright and insecurity (67%), disturbed sleep (61%), intrusive images (59%), frequent thoughts about war (89%), and sensory-motor disturbance (24%). Moreover, 91% of children in the sample exhibited three or more symptoms of trauma. (Wessells and Monteiro, in press)

The team has also been able to teach basic Western-based psychological perspectives on child development, and has developed culturally appropriate techniques for helping children work through the trauma they have experienced and for helping restore spiritual harmony. For instance, in Angola,

> . . . traditional Bantu societies place a strong emphasis on extended family and community, which includes both the living and the spirits of

the ancestors. . . . The spirits of the ancestors protect the living community, which is an extension of the ancestral community. If the ancestors
are not honored through the teaching of traditions and the practice of
appropriate rituals, their spirits cause problems manifested in poor
health, misfortune, social disruption, and even war. (Wessells and Monteiro, in press)

Given that the children experiencing the trauma described above are also
part of the Bantu culture, these spiritual, communal issues must be part of the
process of healing.

Participants in the project have been using art, dance and music as vehicles
for the children to address their distress. They have also worked with traditional healers to handle the difficult problems of people not having been able
to bury their dead properly, and in arranging for the proper cultural rituals
that will allow child soldiers who have killed to reenter the community and be
reunited with their families wherever possible. These last two factors could
not have been addressed without a willingness to listen respectfully to all the
voices with an openness to understanding the meaning and significance of the
issues being brought forth. It also required respect for local cosmologies.
While there are many traditional African cultural practices that are harmful,
especially to women, the team is committed to gender equity and believes
that the process of listening with an eye for healing and prevention of future
problems can only help with the change process in the long run.

This particular project, while still in progress and therefore not fully assessed, has had good interim results in reducing problems of children's flashbacks, sleep disturbances, aggression and social isolation, while improving
child-child and adult-child interaction and helping to mobilize communities
around children's needs. Working with local helpers, the team is document-
ing ethnographically traditional healing ceremonies and their impact. The
project activities have also been helpful for primary caregivers, most of
whom are women, who themselves have been strongly affected by 35 years
of war (Wessells, personal communication, 2/2/1998).

UNITED NATIONS FOURTH WORLD CONFERENCE
ON WOMEN–BEIJING, 1995

PsySR and the APA Division of Peace Psychology, under the auspices of
Women for Meaningful Summits NGO status, sent a delegation of psychologists to the NGO Forum that accompanied the official UN Women's Conference in Beijing. A major concern for the delegation was to strengthen the focus
of the Conference on peace issues and how they affect women's lives. The
delegation led open dialogues on conflict resolution processes in different

cultures, women's experiences of human rights violations and the role of forgiveness in conflict resolution. Upon their return, psychologists gave over 100 presentations to community and student groups who were interested in the Conference. They reported on the forum and educated people on the significance of the world-wide consensus reached on a number of issues critical to women which appeared as the Platform for Action (United Nations, 1996).

The President's Interagency Council for Women was charged with the official U.S. follow-up of the Platform for Action and invited continuing consultation with NGOs. PsySR participated in the nationwide conference televised through satellite down-links and provided analysis and suggestions both at the roundtables and through written responses. As peace psychologists, PsySR especially emphasized the lack of attention to issues of peace and war in the follow-up agenda. Recently, the Council published its report, "America's Commitment: Federal Programs Benefiting Women and New Initiatives as Follow-up to the UN Fourth World Conference on Women" (1997). A second report, "Building on Beijing: United States NGOs.Shape a Women's National Action Agenda" (Stanley Foundation, 1997), is a compilation of the suggestions from many NGOs, including PsySR, who contributed to the dialogue.

Even a cursory look at the sections of the Platform highlights how far the United States has to go in meeting these international goals within our borders. Feminist mental health professionals understand that public policy decisions affect the health, mental health and well-being of the people with whom we work. For instance, social policy in the United States is inextricably tied to the policy priorities that place continued high military spending as a given and also require a balanced budget. Those same policies support continued sales of conventional arms to almost any country who pays for them, exacerbating the tensions in that area and turning simmering conflict into lethal violence. That lethal violence is then used as a rationale for continued high military budgets. Then, to complete the vicious circle, high military budgets mean decreased resources available for health care, job training, child care, environmental clean-up, etc.

It is in our best interests, as feminist psychotherapists, to use our expertise to advocate for governmental policies that will alleviate and prevent the devastation we see every day in our offices–to help meet the real human needs of the women, men and children of our world. And, we need to advocate not only for the physical human needs of people, but also for those psychological needs with which we are most directly familiar–"the equitable satisfaction of human needs for security, identity, well-being and self-determination" (Christie, 1997, p. 329). The implementation of the Platform for Action is a unique opportunity to focus attention on the full range of human needs with a feminist lens.

ADDITIONAL RESOURCES

The projects reviewed in no way encompass the breadth and depth of the work being pursued by feminist psychologists around the world. Although this article cannot even attempt to be fully inclusive, there are several good resources that can add significant analysis and suggestions for action.

The United Nations Report on "The Impact of Armed Conflict on Children" (1996), led by Graca Machel, former Minister of Education and First Lady of Mozambique, must be mentioned here. It highlights the need for psychosocial interventions at the community level which include supporting and caring for the women who often end up being the sole caretakers of our world's future generations. Machel brings the point home that prevention of violent conflict must become a priority for the international community and provides a number of specific suggestions for changes in policy. Feminist mental health professionals will find much in this report to support arguments for reductions in conventional arms sales, support for psychosocial services, and shifting resources to meet human needs.

A recent book, *Myths About the Powerless: Contesting Social Inequalities* (Lykes, Banuazizi, Liem, & Morris, 1996), provides a powerful analysis of ways that Western psychology has been misused in the assessment and treatment of "other" populations. As feminist psychotherapists participate in the facilitation and development of more cross-cultural connections, cross-fertilization, partnerships, support systems, research projects, and practice alternatives that match the cultural milieu in which they are to be carried out, we need to tread with care. Banuazizi points out that,

> . . . the potential role of a culturally sensitive psychology within an interdisciplinary approach to problems of development in the Third World can be quite significant . . . collaborative efforts between Western psychologists and their Third World counterparts in recent years cannot help but broaden the horizons of both groups. (1996, p. 192)

AN ACTION AGENDA

The global feminist coalition for women's rights as human rights has proven extremely effective in advancing our cause on a global level. Those activists have chosen an issue and pursued it from the grassroots level up to the largest global arena they could find. We, as feminist mental health professionals, need to do the same thing. I'd like to propose a framework within which we can work together, bringing our many strengths, talents and interests together to focus on a specific vision–building sustainable, peaceful communities. This vision encompasses a vast array of issues from the most local and individual to the global and international. For instance, the projects mentioned above all contribute to the development of such communities. Feminist psychotherapists can provide psychological perspectives to existing programs and projects or develop their own. I suggest the following strategies as a sampling for your consideration, in the hopes that they support and encourage your own thinking and action.

1. *Foster prevention.* My own personal view is that we need to place prevention of all kinds of violence and oppression at the core of our work. Albee and Gullotta note that "no mass disorder afflicting humankind has ever been eliminated or brought under control by attempts at treating the affected individual" (p. 19-20). And yet, most therapists spend most of their time working with individuals or small groups. Gather together and think with your colleagues what policies and programs you want to develop and support in order to prevent the kinds of devastation you see everyday in your offices. As Agger did, we can consider the work we do with individuals and, moving with appropriate care for the dangers of innovation, continue to develop creative responses that empower women and men to make societies more just and equitable.

2. *Focus on one aspect of the system.* Since the issues are complex, multi-faceted and structural, no one intervention will cure a problem. By the same token, any intervention can affect the system. So choose one you know about, you feel passionate about, and can do something about.

3. *Raise questions.* Questions are powerful, easy to ask, and give lawmakers important information about the concerns of their constituents. For instance, one does not have to be an expert on a particular issue to ask one's Congressman or Senators the simple question: "What effect will this proposed law have on the lives of women in the U.S. and around the world?" Treat lawmakers and their staff like regular people; use your listening skills when you are talking about an issue with them.

4. *Join together as mental health professionals.* Become part of networks that address global issues and add your perspective and expertise. For instance, PsySR is developing such a communication system called "International Practitioners' Network: Building Cultures of Peace." The mission of the Network is to promote holistic, equitable, culturally appropriate applications of psychology for building peace at all levels. As the membership in the Network grows, practitioners with similar interests from different cultures will be able to collaborate and support each other in work which can often be very isolating and overwhelming. This form of collaborative partnership can serve as a model for the peaceful societies we are attempting to build for women, men and children around the world.

REFERENCES

Agger, I. (1994). *The blue room. Trauma and testimony among refugee women: A psycho-social exploration.* London: Zed Books.

Agger, I. (1995). Trauma, testimony and social memory, in I. Agger, S. Vuk & J. Mimica (Eds.), *Theory and practice of psycho-social projects under war conditions in Bosnia-Herzegovina and Croatia.* European Community Humanitarian Office.

Agger, I. (1997). The clean and the unclean, in E. Richter-Lyonette (Ed.), *In the aftermath of rape: Women's rights, war crimes and genocide,* pp. 119-123. Givrins, Switzerland: Coordination of Women's Advocacy.

Albee, G.W., & Gullotte, T.P. (Eds.) (1997). *Primary prevention works.* Thousand Oaks, CA: Sage.

Banuazizi, A. (1996). Psychology, the distant other, and the dialectics of change in non-Western societies, in M. B. Lykes, A. Banuazizi, R. Liem, & M. Morris (Eds.), *Myths about the powerless: Contesting social inequalities.* Philadelphia, PA: Temple.

Brock-Utne, B. (1985). *Education for peace: A feminist perspective.* New York: Pergamon.

Brown, L.S. (1994). *Subversive dialogues: Theory in feminist therapy.* New York: Basic Books.

Bunch, C. (1997). Women's rights as human rights in war and conflict, in E. Richter-Lyonette (Ed.), *In the aftermath of rape: Women's rights, war crimes and genocide,* pp. 3-8. Givrins, Switzerland: Coordination of Women's Advocacy.

Christie, D.J. (1997). Reducing direct and structural violence: The human needs theory. *Peace and Conflict: Journal of Peace Psychology,* 3(4), 315-332.

Coordination of Women's Advocacy. (1996). Witness Protection: Third consultative working group on gender-specific war crimes between the International Criminal Tribunal & the Coordination of Women's Advocacy. Givrins, Switzerland: Author.

Lund, M.S. (1996). *Preventing violent conflicts: A strategy for preventive diplomacy.* Washington, DC: United States Institute of Peace Press.

McKay, S. (1996). Gendering peace psychology. *Peace and Conflict: Journal of Peace Psychology,* 2(2) 93-107. Mahwah, NJ: Erlbaum.

Machel, G. (1996). Impact of armed conflict on children: Report of the expert of the Secretary-General, Ms. Graca Machel, submitted pursuant to General Assembly resolution 48/157. United Nations (A/51/306, 26 August, 1996).

Murphy, B.C. (1995, June). Ecological feminism and peace psychology: A natural connection. Paper presented at the 4th International Conference on the Contributions of Psychology to Peace, Capetown, South Africa.

Psychologists for Social Responsibility. (1997). Psychologists for Social Responsibility: Using psychological knowledge to build a peaceful world. Washington, DC.

President's Interagency Council on Women. (1997). America's commitment: Federal programs benefiting women and new initiatives as follow-up to the UN Fourth World Conference on Women. U.S. Department of State, Washington, DC.

Richter-Lyonette, E. (Ed.) (1997). In the aftermath of rape: Women's rights, war crimes and genocide. Givrins, Switzerland: The Coordination of Women's Advocacy.

The Stanley Foundation. (1997). *Building on Beijing: United States NGOs shape a women's national action agenda*. Muscatine, IA: Author.

United Nations (1996). Platform for Action and the Beijing Declaration. New York: UN Department of Public Information.

Van Soest, D. (1997). *The global crisis of violence: Common problems, universal causes, shared solutions*. Washington, DC: NASW Press.

Wessells, M.G., & Monteiro, C. (in press). Culture, healing, and post-conflict reconstruction in Angola: A community-based approach to assisting war-affected children, in U. Gielen, J. Fish, & J. Draguns (Eds.), *Culture, Therapy and Healing*.

Interview with Gabrielle Kirk McDonald, President of the International Criminal Tribunal for the Former Yugoslavia

Sara Sharratt

SUMMARY. This frank interview with the President of the Tribunal explores the issues of social power and the historical dehumanization of women during times of war and civil unrest. Gender bias as it relates to sexual assault in the context of a war is considered along with recent legal attempts to broaden the scope of war crimes to include rape. Judge McDonald discusses her personal and professional experiences as a civil rights lawyer, a judge and an African-American woman. The intersection of justice and healing is considered. *[Article copies available for a fee from The Haworth Document Delivery Service: 1-800-342-9678. E-mail address: getinfo@haworthpressinc.com]*

KEYWORDS. Race, gender, rape, war crimes

SS.   We talk of ending impunity so that the victims can heal. As a therapist, I hear the implicit connection of justice and healing. There is no

Gabrielle Kirk McDonald, LLB, is currently the President of the International Criminal Tribunal for the Former Yugoslavia.

Address correspondence to: The Honorable Gabrielle Kirk McDonald, International Criminal Tribunal for the Former Yugoslavia, Churchillplein 1, 2517 JW, The Hague, The Netherlands.

[Haworth co-indexing entry note]: "Interview with Gabrielle Kirk McDonald, President of the International Criminal Tribunal for the Former Yugoslavia." Sharratt, Sara. Co-published simultaneously in *Women & Therapy* (The Haworth Press, Inc.) Vol. 22, No. 1, 1999, pp. 23-38; and: *Assault on the Soul: Women in the Former Yugoslavia* (ed: Sara Sharratt and Ellyn Kaschak) The Haworth Press, Inc., 1999, pp. 23-38. Single or multiple copies of this article are available for a fee from The Haworth Document Delivery Service [1-800-342-9678, 9:00 a.m. - 5:00 p.m. (EST). E-mail address: getinfo@haworthpressinc.com].

peace without justice. Can justice be a form of psychotherapy? What can we do to heal such enormous wounds?

GKM. Well, I guess there are two schools of thought, though there may be several. Some say talking helps to heal and some people believe that if you talk about things, you risk opening up additional wounds and perhaps have further need for a psychologist. I am not a psychologist, but this is my opinion. But having sat through the Tadic trial, I do not really know whether it is one or the other. I don't know how to judge whether it helped or exacerbated the situation for the witnesses because we did not do any follow-up.

I think just generally, though, based on my own life experiences, that it is better to talk about something because when you keep something inside you do not have a discussion with anyone except yourself, and you get only what you give back. So generally I believe in talking things through.

SS. Have you ever been in therapy yourself?

GKM. My ex-husband and I went to therapy when we were going through our divorce. We so frightened this white Anglo-Saxon male therapist. He was so shocked [laughs] that we had been yelling and screaming in front of him that he wrote us a letter saying something like "I can see you have very difficult issues to resolve and you must resolve them for the sake of your children." He was not used to black folks. We were married 18 years and they were long tough years. I also went to therapy with my son when he was having some problems, and later I went for help myself.

SS. Did you find it helpful?

GKM. No, I didn't. When I look back upon it, I think some of the problems I had should have been identified and acknowledged. She may have known what they were and simply not acknowledged them. But I do not know enough about psychology, and I think some psychologists believe that they should not tell you things, but instead let you find out yourself. So maybe that was her approach. The therapist and I became friends afterwards because she was an African-American woman who belonged to the same club for middle-class African-American urban professionals.

SS. But she did not give you much more than silence?

GKM. Right. For a long time she just sat there while the family was in need of help and I was having problems coping with all the pain. But that is my personal situation and I tell you that only because it gives you a certain perspective on what I perceive as a judge.

SS. How did that experience influence your work as a judge?

GKM. I think it makes you more sensitive because I recognize vulnerability in myself that I had never seen before. I had always been, as I found out, a human who was "doing" rather than "being." I thought I could conquer the world and I have always been very cause-oriented. I was a civil rights lawyer and when you give me a cause I'll take it on and I go with it until the end. I believed that I just could take on anything and nothing would stop me and I think that, for the first time, I was going through something that I could not control and could not change. That made me more sympathetic and empathic to vulnerability and to people caught in a situation that they cannot get out of.

Also, I think it has made me more aware of my own feelings, allowing me to respond more naturally to situations. I was much more guarded before and made sure that my emotions were always under control. So in some respects it made it more difficult for me because as I would be sitting there, listening to the testimony, and I would want to cry. I have, in a sense, lost some of the control that I used to have over myself, and so it was more difficult for me, as a judge, to exercise self-control.

I was a judge in the United States for ten years. The pressures were enormous. People expect you to have a greater degree of control and wisdom and that you are always right. As a judge, you do not have the luxury to admit that you do not have all the answers. So what can happen is that you end up transferring this belief into your personal life. I was also isolated as a judge, particularly as a Federal judge in the States. When I became one in 1979 through 1988, I could not keep the relationships I had in the community because I was now part of a white institution that I had always challenged as a civil rights lawyer. That forced me to divorce myself from my whole way of life. I was under constant strain. So what I learned through therapy is that I do not have to have all the answers and that it is all right not to be responsible for everything.

SS. As psychologists, we learn to protect ourselves. As a judge you have been listening to horrific testimonies of cruelty. How did you protect yourself?

GKM. I didn't. I don't . . .

SS.   During the Tadic case. Some of the cases . . .

GKM. No. I was fortunate to have two judges with whom I was very close. I mean we did not have any conflicts with each other. There was a sensitivity that we had for one another. It is amazing because I was the presiding judge, the youngest, African-American and a woman. But I believe I was respected by both judges. One is ten years older than me, the other 20. Yet they respected me and told me how quick I was and how much control I had over the trial proceedings. I asked one of them when we were assigned another case, "Why don't you take the position of presiding judge?" "No," he answered, "you are doing a good job, just keep doing it."

Also, I think it was a good experience for one of the judges because he has five daughters. Although we never talked about it, I knew his daughters were very active with feminist and human rights groups in his country. I believe he is a rather conservative person in many respects, and so I think it was an eye-opener for him to see a woman in a position of power, who, if I may pat myself on the back [chuckles], did well in a way that didn't make him feel uncomfortable. He was at ease and did not feel bombarded by my style. I wouldn't give myself an A, but I think I did well under the circumstances. My other colleague had tremendous respect for me. His wife is a lawyer so he sees me from a different perspective.

Also, when the judges were working on the rules, some were not vocal when we were addressing the issue of sexual assault. There were others who were. But the experience of working with a woman they respected enabled them to at least camouflage their perspective. However, it's the little experiences which change people for the better. I remember one incident in the Tadic case. A witness testified about reportedly being raped. It was so horrendous, one rape after another. My colleagues were visibly moved and very disgusted by it. I bet if we had considered the rules on sexual assault after hearing this testimony, some of the judges would have had a different attitude. There were a couple of days when I was really upset.

SS.   By the testimony?

GKM. Yes. Mostly by the magnitude of it and sometimes I still choke up when I think of it. It was not just the graphic nature of it, although there was some vivid testimony. Mostly what affected me was the loss. When you hear people like this woman, let's call her Natasha

K, who testifies that she has lost 35 people in her family, and then the prosecutor asks her to look at photo after photo, and she says this was her husband, this was her uncle, and this was her father-in-law . . . You listen to that kind of loss and it's just unbearable.

I read an article by one writer who said that while listening to the testimony, he saw me visibly grimace on one occasion. My face is very expressive, so I probably did. For example, a witness testified that he was at Omarska [detention center and site of numerous war crimes]. One son had already been killed on the way there. He and his other son went to Omarska together. One day he was asked to go and get his son. So he called him and he came out and said, "Father, take care of my family." And he testified that he never saw his son again. I can see this man. I can still see these people.

SS. So what did you do?

GKM. I read mystery books by the ton. Because you can just lose yourself. I also talked a lot with my own son. He and I are very close. There is a group of African-American women here and we get together every now and then. After the Tadic verdict, I was telling them how upset I was. I stayed up the night before writing, trying to figure out what I would say to this man, and I wrote what I then read the next day. I read it and when I got to the point of reading about the conflict with the Muslims and why did he do it, I said: "Why? Why?" Elizabeth [Judge Odio Benito, the only other female judge] thought I was going to cry. I was nervous, but I was also upset. I was not trying to be dramatic because I am not a dramatic person. I asked "why" but I did not expect an answer. But it was the question that stuck with me throughout the proceedings.

And then I said, "It came to pass" and I had written that. And when I said it, it was like, "Oh God"; it came to pass because before then there were thousands of Muslims in the area and afterwards there were only about 300. So again I was touched by the loss, by the magnitude of it. It is not just one individual doing horrible things to another. It is absolute inhumanity to man, as we say.

SS. Do you think that evil is inevitable? Have your perceptions about people or the world changed?

GKM. No, no! Because what is happening here is, in a sense, what I have seen as a civil rights lawyer, only that it is happening on a much larger level. Racial intolerance and hatred has not, in my lifetime, risen to this level of destruction. Slavery happened a long time before I was born. But it has changed me in large and small ways. For example, although I was never much interested in "action" movies, I now cannot bear to watch violent films at all. They just make me grimace.

SS.   You say it has not changed your perceptions about people.

GKM. I do not think so.

SS.   You were the first African-American judge to sit in the federal bench. . . . and the third African-American woman in the United States . . . Are there parallels between what happened to African Americans in the USA and ethnic cleansing in the Former Yugoslavia?

GKM. Well, it is all based on intolerance and a lack of respect for difference, and also a failure to resolve what has happened in the past. Many people in the United States say, "What's the problem? We have the Civil Rights Act and you are equal. There is no problem." But you just do not beat someone for ten years and then stop and say, "Well, I stopped. What is the problem?" I want you to know that you have beaten me for ten years. I want you to acknowledge the horrific experience of slavery, the complete destruction of a culture. President Clinton said last year that there should be a dialogue and an acknowledgment of what happened. A more direct acknowledgment.

SS.   You are talking about a more direct acknowledgment. What kind do you have in mind?

GKM. I do not know. I do not know that you can have it on a mass level. I look more to individual human relationships.

SS.   But the French apologized to the Jews and I thought Clinton at one point was suggesting an apology.

GKM. I do not know what form it would take. I suppose it helps [pensive]. I guess it would affect individual relationships. Sometimes you do not want to even bring up race. I have many white friends, but I do not even want to bring up the topic of race with them.

SS.   Why not?

GKM. Because, well . . . It depends. If they are not close friends, if they are business acquaintances, I know they believe it is all over and happened a long time ago, so let's not talk about it. So you do not want to destroy that kind of relationship. You want to be accepted. What is good about me being here [i.e., Europe] is that I do not have to face this race problem that has pursued me my whole life. That is why I went to Law School.

My mother was half Swedish and half African-American, but she looked white so there were many instances where we had problems. She was lighter than I am, very light. As a single example, once in New York I made an appointment over the phone at the same beauty parlor where my mother has her hair washed and cut. However, when I arrived, I was told right to my face that they did not do "that kind of hair," even though my hair is not that different from my mother's.

It is a relief to be in Europe. It is less personally agonizing. When I sit on the bench, I am used to, not to the horrible atrocities, nobody can get used to that, but I am used to the concept of people being intolerant to each other. At the Tadic trial, I asked a principal, "How can you explain these atrocities when Muslims, Croats and Serbs had gone to school together, lived together, intermarried with each other?" Now, I asked him this question because I wanted to know about the conflict, but also because I wanted to know for myself. How can you explain this important battle for desegregation in the 1950s and it's now thought that everybody is going to go to school together and supposedly everything is okay, yet it is not. There is re-segregation and there is intolerance on a different level.

I was once having dinner with an African-American woman at a Thai restaurant in The Hague. I told her, "You know, if I were in the United States right now with this slow service I would put on my NAACP button and think it was racism. But it's just slow service." People like Americans here. So it feels like a burden has been lifted from my shoulders not having to expect a daily affront.

SS. Are you saying they like African-Americans?

GKM. Americans. Period. I think the Dutch love Americans. I think they look upon me as an American and not as an African-American. For the first time in my life, I do not have to face it. So it might have been easier for me, but it also hurt more because I saw it happening again. So when I asked "Why?" I was trying to get an answer about this conflict, but I was also trying to get an answer for myself. Why do people do this to each other?

SS.   Have you come up with an answer?

GKM. No [emphatic]. The principal answered my question by saying that he did not know, that a madness had just taken over. So in effect you had these latent feelings, similar to those existing in the United States, these old wounds dating back from World War II or maybe even from 1389 when the Ottoman Turks defeated the Serbs. They held onto these feelings and passed them down from generation to generation. Then, you have a group of power-hungry politicians on both sides who are feeding and fueling these old wounds and old grievances that have never been resolved. Of course, I do not expect the same thing to happen in the United States, but there are similarities.

SS.   I want to go back to something. You said that maybe there should be an apology to African-Americans, that more needs to be done. I was thinking in terms of race and in terms of women here. Should there be a monument for rape victims? Should we have international declarations of repudiation of rapists? Should we do more or do things differently?

GKM. I was talking to Elizabeth [Judge Odio Benito was also interviewed in this volume] just this morning about the number of rape Indictments. Yes, there should be a monument, but before you get one, you have to be seen to deserve it. The way that you do that is to get the story of rape out. We know it happens in war all the time but what we hear is, "Oh, I guess boys will be boys."

        I recently confirmed an Indictment and rape had not been charged. There were one, two, three Indictments, major Indictments and while rape had been charged in one Indictment, but it was not charged in the major one. As soon as I looked at the Indictment, I called the prosecutor assigned to the case and asked him about it and he said, "We do not have any statements. There is no support for it." So I said, "You know me. I am going to go through every single page, every single page of this material, and if I find something, I am going to tell you." I worked through it all and I found numerous statements referring to rape. One of the physicians who had treated rape victims had not even been contacted to find out whether there were any who would want to talk about it. In the statements, the women said that they would be willing to testify. It was not like they were saying, "This happened to me and I don't want to talk about it." That is usually the excuse given, that they do not want to talk about it. If they do not want to, that is another story.

I called a legal assistant and I said, "We have some problems here and I need you to help me." We prepared a whole list of references to rape in the material. So when I confirmed the Indictment I said, "Now I want to get into something else. Rape has not been charged. Let me go through what I have found." I went through it affidavit by affidavit. I turned each page and just kept on going, affidavit by affidavit. Then, in one Indictment, rape was charged on the basis of an affidavit that had been redacted; they had deleted all the names and everything about the woman that would identify her. In another Indictment, the whole affidavit was in there but was not redacted. Right there in the material. The prosecutor was not even charging rape. They were shocked by that. So I say that before you get a monument, you have to earn it, meaning that rape has to be charged; it has to be brought out; it has to be a part of the trial. So far, this has not happened. The numbers are certainly there: 20,000 or more women have been raped in this war. You do not get a monument unless there is an acknowledgment that you are a hero or a heroine.

SS. So you are saying that there are not enough indictments?

GKM. Yes. I saw the prosecutor a couple of days later at a party and he came over and said, "Gaby, I am sorry." He acknowledged it, and was personally committed to charging rape as a war crime, yet since he left us there has been no movement on this front. This case has gone on and there is no word of rape. They charged rape in the biggest of the cases and I bet they do not have more evidence than was available here.

There is a danger, in my estimation, of running away from the issue. It can be very difficult to identify with women's issues, for men because of their position of power, and for women because some may be reluctant to be identified as women. They want to pretend that they are equal and that they made it on their own. When we talk about sex crimes, sex and gender are important. Many women do not want to acknowledge gender or race. Yet in this way the former Chief Prosecutor was an exception, he was committed to the cause.

SS. You said race . . . And that is true, too.

GKM. All through my life it has always been race first and gender second, and when I became a judge there were some women's groups who said, "Look, you haven't been active in women's groups." I said, "I have filed lawsuits against every major corporation in this area and all the petro-chemical companies." You can only take on one cause at a time and I have taken on the women's cause. I mean on the rape issue, I participated in the First National Women's Political Caucus, spoke on the same panel with Sarah Weddington of Roe vs. Wade. But in my experience it has always been race first.

SS.   Has it shifted?

GKM. Yes, it has shifted. It has shifted particularly in the Tribunal because rape has been used as a weapon of war and therefore gender issues have become very important. It is more obvious to me now.

SS.   I am wondering, do you think that your election as President of the Tribunal represents a turning point?

GKM. Yes, I suppose so. I have already given one interview to Human Rights Watch who were doing a study on rape. I told them, "Rape has been used as a weapon of war in this instance in the Former Yugoslavia, and for the first time it is specifically listed as a crime. We should treat it like any other new weapon. If there was a new rocket that was devastating in its destructive capacities, wouldn't we want to focus on it and make sure that we stopped it before people started using it all the time?" Rape does not only destroy women, it destroys the family.

SS.   In the States, many women don't want to testify because they feel they are being violated again by the system. Is, for example, cross-examination unfair?

GKM. Yes, that is true. Our rules establish the principle that consent is not a valid defense and also that prior sexual conduct is inadmissible. So our rules are very far-reaching in this respect.

SS.   But it does depend on who is the presiding judge. I have seen judges here in the Tribunal who do not exercise sufficient control, resulting in the abuse of the victim.

GKM. I wouldn't have allowed that to happen to any witness but obviously I have more sensitivity because of who I am. As a woman, I can feel the act of rape. I can empathize with it. Men look at it differently, if they are sensitive. It is almost as though they see themselves in the shoes of the perpetrator, and they see more the damage that can be wrought because they could be a perpetrator themselves. I feel, as a potential recipient, that I can feel the pain more. I don't want to be too graphic, but I can feel it in my body more than they can.

SS. Because cross-examination is so much a part of the common law system, many women in Europe are shocked that rape victims are subjected to this process. They see it as extremely violent. Are we, for historical reasons, placing too much emphasis on the rights of the accused, and not enough on the rights of the victim?

GKM. Certainly the rights have to be balanced, particularly at the ICTY, because our statutes direct the judges to provide rules for the protection of victims, and especially victims of sexual assault. No other system has a similar provision.

In the United States it is horrible because women are put on the stand. I mean they are put on trial. For example, the whole business with Mike Tyson, the discussions that I have had with my son who is not at all sexist. The frequent arguments that my daughter and I had with him about why she went to Mike Tyson's room. She went to his room, but that doesn't mean she was going to consent to sex, and even if she went there thinking about it, she still had the right to say "No" at any particular time. I can go up there to have drinks or whatever, but I don't have to have sex. I can change my mind and say, "I don't want a drink anymore."

SS. I wonder if, as a North American, your sense of justice has changed since being here?

GKM. I suppose so. The trials we've held are not just about individual accountability, although that is our primary goal. There has to be individual accountability so that there won't be group stigmatization. We also have to record what has happened so that it won't happen again. Never again. So, I look upon justice now in a somewhat broader fashion.

SS. What do you mean by group?

GKM. We don't want to stigmatize a whole group of people, but it is a major problem. It is not just one man killing someone, or one man killing several people. It is the question of why did he do that? What was the cause of this? What was the role of the media? What was the role of the politicians? What were the group dynamics? Not that you blame all Serbs, Croats or Muslims in the group. During the Tadic trial there was evidence which suggested that these politicians had completely taken over the media, and look what happened. Although we talk about individual accountability, there is more to it than that because it is a community problem. It is a community problem because of the attitudes that people, as a group, have for one another. However, that doesn't mean that when a Serb is tried the whole Serb nation is on trial. But in a sense it does go beyond the individual, because you need to look at what caused the individual to act in the way he did, so that you can hopefully avoid repetitions in the future.

SS.   When you looked at Tadic what did you feel?

GKM. I used to look at him a lot and I kept him with me a lot. Maybe I became a little obsessive. I kept testimonies in my head because I had to concentrate so much. I'd look at him sometimes and just try to figure out what was going through his head and what kind of a person he was. And the key thing for me was when he said, "Nobody else seemed bothered about what was going on. I don't think anyone is guilty." That kind of thinking is probably what allows him, and other people, to keep their sanity. They feel that what they were doing was all right because everyone was doing it. I'd look at him and I'd catch him looking at me and it was really a strange kind of a relationship that developed.

SS.   A relationship?

GKM. Yes. I'd often look directly at him and he'd look at me. I think that he knew that I carried clout and if he could convince me, I would be sympathetic. He picked up on things when I asked questions, and he pointed out loopholes. He had already seen them. He would then look at me and volunteer the answer to a loophole that I had mentioned during the trial. I don't know. It was a strange relationship.

SS.   Were there times when you liked him? Liked him in the broadest sense of the word?

GKM. No, though I know what you mean. It was not liking so much as he became part of this court family almost. You sit in that room, that little tiny room, week after week, month after month. We went through 73 trial days and he was a major part of the process. I was very conscious of the fact that he was there, very conscious of him. He became a part of my life, really, for a long time.

SS.   Do you still think about him?

GKM. No, I have moved on to other things now. We've got other issues. And I am very busy as president and see the issues from a broader perspective.

You are talking about the tremendous personal impact that these experiences have and how there is no way of going through them without having them affect your life. I remember when I went back to the States one year, and I was angry that most people knew almost nothing about Yugoslavia. I really get angry about that. I speak to Americans and I tell them, "Americans are not interested because Yugoslavia is thousands of miles away and the people have these funny names you can't pronounce. Why should you care? Because it is important in a moral sense. How can anyone not care about the destruction of humankind?"

SS.   If you are going through a rough time, they often say it means that you are not strong. No, it means that strength encompasses vulnerability.

GKM. Yes, that's true, and being able to acknowledge pain.

In the past there was a commonly heard phrase, "blacks and women," and Alice Walker asked, "What about black women?" There were black people, mainly men, and there were women, mostly white. Black women were totally out of the picture. For many African-American women, there has been a struggle to identify with feminism. What I gathered from what you were saying before is that for you it had to be a split.

I was in the South and the same women who were feminists were either married to white men who were racist or racists themselves. You see, racism was so dominant in the South that I had a difficult time connecting with them, especially because I was suing their husbands, or men who looked like them, who were heads of corporations. We are talking about the early 1970s. I went to Houston in 1969. I once saw an article in the *New York Times* that said that most of society has always looked at black men to speak about black issues, and at white women to speak about women's issues. Where is the black woman? She is not in the equation. If we look at my daughter, she is just as ardent as a feminist as I was in my work in civil rights. She just reminds me so much of myself and she is very active in women's groups, AIDS and other issues. She is an ardent feminist because times have changed. We don't have the same types of race issues, though I still believe that white women have benefited more from the civil rights movement than black people have. You see more white women in managerial positions in the United States than you see blacks in those positions. In Europe I don't see that, so it is so nice that one doesn't have to be concerned with race issues on a personal level.

I am now at a point in my life where I am more conscious of the fact that I am a woman who is faced with different issues than the men here. More than being a black person, I feel that I am a woman, and this awareness has allowed me to focus on my gender and what it means in my relationships.

SS.   Does it surprise you that the men in the Foca Indictment have not been arrested?

GKM.   When I met with the Minister of Justice in France, who is a woman, I made specific reference to that Indictment even though I have as President said that I was not going to talk about Karadzic and Mladic by name. But I bent the rules a little bit and talked about it and sent her the Indictment. I also spoke with the French Foreign Minister and told him about the case. I told him, "Let me show you on the map where Foca is." He said, "Let me see that map." He gave it to an assistant and told him to make a copy. I said that I would send him the Indictment in French. It will certainly be on their minds.

SS.   You are saying that because Foca is in the French sector. The Indictment is all about crimes committed against women. Do you think that has got anything to do with it?

GKM.   I have no idea, but there is an attitudinal crisis that makes it seem like it's okay. "These men are under strain and, after all, they have only raped." I still think they've got the mentality that "Boys will be boys." I remember reading about an Allied military commander in the Second World War who was questioned about this issue and he said, "In times of war this will happen and you can expect it of our troops." You hear rumors about UN troops themselves. That they were implicated in raping also.

In rapes, in forced prostitution. So, it brings up a whole range of issues that I don't think they want to face. We are not talking about women like you or me. We are just talking about women in general. In the one case that I confirmed, this woman was held for weeks on end and was raped repeatedly by group after group. It would just turn your stomach.

However, they will not find it as justifiable when you talk about it in terms of enslavement. It presents an entirely different dimension of what is acceptable in times of war. If men were held and became victims of sexual assault, of course they would want to punish the perpetrators. In Tadic, the testimony about biting a testicle was sensational. That's all they talked about. So if they can talk about that, why can't they talk about rape? I guess I am contradicting myself when I said people don't want to talk about sexual occurrences.

SS. Thus, what is clearly seen as torture when it happens to men is not as easily seen as such when it happens to women. Most of the women who are writing for this volume went to the former Yugoslavia. My sense through my contacts with them is that they are traumatized.

GKM. Well, maybe I am traumatized and I don't know it. It will take a long while for me to feel the full effects of this experience. It was horrible. I couldn't sleep during the Tadic trial. I think it is still inside me and sometimes when I start to talk about Tadic, I feel tears welling up, I think perhaps because I did not have the luxury of doing so during the trial. Judges don't cry, so you just have to sit up there. When I came back after we finally sentenced this man, I felt like I could just let it all out, and I really did cry. I really did, but it's still inside me, so when people ask me "Why?" I find I get really upset, and then I start asking about how can people do that to each other? But I have to let go of the question "Why?" It happened and I don't have to solve it.

SS. You're a judge and I am an expert in human behavior, and I have no idea. I don't know. I don't understand. I don't know why. I know that soldiers who do that aren't human.

GKM. One woman judge I know, who was strongly affected by some of the testimony, said that maybe she was not cut out to be a judge. I replied that "Maybe it is the opposite. Maybe it's because you get emotional and you feel it, that you should be a judge." If you don't express your emotions, you go crazy. The problem, as I've said before, is that I've learned as a judge to control it. But I've suffered on account of this. I mean you control it all and then, when you finally release it, you sometimes do so in what is not necessarily the healthiest fashion.

SS. I just talked to a Holocaust survivor in Costa Rica, and I asked her about what kind of support she received from her husband when she talked about her experiences in the camps. She said that she never discusses it with him. I know, it doesn't surprise me.

GKM. How could you not?
      You know that in the United States in 1957, Central High School

in Little Rock was desegregated and, in order to do it, President Eisenhower had to send in troops. In Brussels, there is a sister of one of the "Little Rock Nine" and another black woman who was actually one of the "Nine" now lives in Holland. These are all black women. They had a 40th anniversary recently and they got together. All these people are my age and so their children are in their 20s. For the first time, the children heard about these things because their parents had never talked about them before. I have read about what went on in that high school and I can understand why. You read it and you see the humiliation that you were put through, you were kicked and spit upon, and books slammed and all kinds of death threats. You want to fight back.

SS.   Yes. Thank you for giving me a chance to talk with you. It was very moving for me.

Interview with Elizabeth Odio Benito, Justice of the International Criminal Tribunal for the Former Yugoslavia

Sara Sharratt

SUMMARY. This interview is with a previous Justice of the International Criminal Tribunal for the Former Yugoslavia and current Vice-President and Minister of the Environment of Costa Rica, Elizabeth Odio. Such issues as women's rights as human rights, the relationship of justice and recovery and the nature of evil are considered, among others. *[Article copies available for a fee from The Haworth Document Delivery Service: 1-800-342-9678. E-mail address: getinfo@haworthpressinc.com]*

KEYWORDS. Human rights, women's rights, rape, torture, genocide, Costa Rica

SS.   What is important for us to know about you?

EOB.   Perhaps the most important thing to know with respect to my job here is my past experience working in human rights. I came to the

Elizabeth Odio Benito, Lic. in Law, was a Justice of the International Criminal Tribunal for the Former Yugoslavia and has returned to Costa Rica to fill the elected position of Vice President.

Address correspondence to: The Honorable Elizabeth Odio Benito, Office of the Vice-President of Costa Rica, Apartado 2292-1000, San Jose, Costa Rica.

[Haworth co-indexing entry note]: "Interview with Elizabeth Odio Benito, Justice of the International Criminal Tribunal for the Former Yugoslavia." Sharratt, Sara. Co-published simultaneously in *Women & Therapy* (The Haworth Press, Inc.) Vol. 22, No. 1, 1999, pp. 39-52; and: *Assault on the Soul: Women in the Former Yugoslavia* (ed: Sara Sharratt and Ellyn Kaschak) The Haworth Press, Inc., 1999, pp. 39-52. Single or multiple copies of this article are available for a fee from The Haworth Document Delivery Service [1-800-342-9678, 9:00 a.m. - 5:00 p.m. (EST). E-mail address: getinfo@haworthpressinc.com].

Tribunal from this field and not from any background as a judge or criminal attorney. Human Rights started to become prominent after the Second World War, following the horrendous ways in which human rights were violated during that conflict. I am not suggesting that human rights were invented after the war but rather that the International Declaration of Human Rights of 1948 projected onto the international community what had traditionally been handled by different States at the national or regional level.

Thus, it was only in national legal systems that protection of human rights was encoded. After the Holocaust and genocide of World War II, there was tremendous pressure to internationalize the protection of human rights. Nevertheless, it is obvious that since that conflict there has not been a true synthesis between this preoccupation and the protection and punishment of individuals, which remain the responsibility of the nation state. We did not create supra-national organizations which could truly protect human rights and punish its violations.

SS.   How did you become involved with Human Rights?

EOB.   I was interested since my early life as an academic and practicing attorney. I became aware then of the tremendous discrimination and inequality faced by women in the judicial system, and started, together with other women, to try to change some of the laws that worked against us. That was a time in my life when I believed that changing the laws would change the world. Afterward, I realized that nothing was ever that simple and that it is much easier to change the laws than to change human attitudes and behaviors. In 1978, when I became Minister of Justice of Costa Rica, I focused my attention on the problems of political refugees from Argentina, Uruguay and Chile seeking asylum in large numbers in Costa Rica. Shortly thereafter, I became a member of a United Nations Committee which handles funds to rehabilitate victims of torture during armed conflict. Since then I have been working with projects to help rehabilitate people who have suffered torture and/or inhumane and degrading treatment during national or international conflicts.

SS.   You have been talking about discrimination against women and human rights. When did these interests converge?

EOB.   In a way they were always connected but there has certainly been lots of development in my thinking. When I started participating in human rights work, I did so in a genderless fashion. I developed a gender perspective some time later, I would say in 1986, when it became obvious to me that violations against women were more serious because they were being committed against women simply on account of the fact that they were women. My gender perspective was clearly a lens through which I have looked at the world since then. It became clear to me also that international humanitarian law and international public law did not have the mechanisms to demand individual accountability of those who violate human rights laws. It is important to remember that violations of women's human rights occur outside what might technically be called the context of armed conflict. Violence against women is clearly a manifestation of the same phenomenon, with domestic violence, street violence, sexual harassment at work, and violence during war conflict all being manifestations of power differentials and inequality. What became more evident and painful was the realization that there was in the international community neither the mechanisms nor the political will to hold responsible those who violate women's basic human rights.

Since I started my work in the Tribunal for the former Yugoslavia, it was immediately clear that there had been heinous, massive violations of human rights and women's rights in particular. The situation for women has been especially painful because one sees a new component: the use of rape being as part of ethnic cleansing. In this war, we have begun talking about ethnic cleansing just as we did after World War II. Our challenge from the beginning, and in this I was accompanied by both Judge McDonald, Patricia Sellers from the Prosecutor's office and with the support of Chief Prosecutor Judge Goldstone, was to make sure that the serious nature of the crimes against women was acknowledged, investigated and prosecuted.

SS.   You were the judge who confirmed the petition for a deferral in the case of Dusko Tadic and you publicly appealed to Judge Goldstone when you said, "Do not forget the women." This was broadcast by CNN and other media worldwide. That was an unusual step for a judge. What was the reaction? Did you receive support or not?

EOB.   From the perspective of a traditional judge, I guess it was unusual. But remember that I told you that I did not come to the Tribunal as a judge or academic. I was not a professional judge and I think it is true that they have a different attitude. I came as an activist who expresses concern for the violation of human rights and does not think it may have a negative impact. I guess it was the gesture of a novice.

SS.   Do you regret it?

EOB.   No, not at all. On the contrary. If I had to do it over again, I would do it even more forcefully than the first time.

SS.   Are you saying that you were criticized or did not receive support?

EOB.   I was not criticized directly but I was told in the Tribunal of the "concern" expressed by some judges. However, I never received any criticism from my two colleagues. They did not say anything. I found out later from an old friend of mine that there has been a great deal of discussion about the proper behavior of a judge with the clear implication that I had fallen outside of those parameters. It was felt that I was pronouncing judgment ahead of time. I thought I was doing that in terms of the application of norms. I was expressing my own worries about the Tribunal's political future and legal work.

If we had started working on cases from an armed conflict in the former Yugoslavia where the United Nations legal documents documented massive rape of women and there was not a single mention of rape in this indictment, I thought I had a very valid reason for expressing my concern. I was worried that once again we were going to invisibilize what had happened to women with the pretext that we did not have any evidence or that no one was talking about rape. However, I also received support: I found out that it was extremely important for many women to hear my intervention, and that it continues to be important for them to know that there is a supporting presence within the Tribunal.

SS.   You were in Vienna in 1992 for the International Conference on Human Rights. Women from all over the world organized a mock Tribunal, of which you were one of the judges, to hear testimony from women about violations of human rights. After hearing wrenching testimony, you said with tears in your eyes that maybe you were not made to be a judge. Now, you have been a judge. Do you still feel the same way?

EOB.   [Laughs] We had a very different situation in Vienna. In the first place, I did not really have much idea about what that Tribunal would be like. In Vienna, we had acts of profound solidarity where we created what we called the "Tribunal of Conscience" in order to hear the testimony of women who had suffered, in a number of contexts, heinous violations of their basic human rights. As I said before, we were trying to link the different kinds of violence under the same umbrella. We were struggling to ensure that everyday and "exceptional" violence against women would be recognized as human rights violations and help extract them from the private sphere where they had been kept hidden for centuries. In the Tribunal, we heard testimony from women who had been battered at home, survived incest, had been tortured by police while under arrest or raped during an armed conflict. It was very moving, especially to hear women from the former Yugoslavia, Muslims, Croats and Serbs, talking about what they had gone through, and what they expected to go through in the future. At that time it was still in the middle of the war. All of this took place in one session. I was not prepared to hear about that much indiscriminate, unjust and painful violence. I felt totally overwhelmed and publicly said so. I did not feel I could be impartial in the context of so much violence committed against women.

SS.   How does one prepare for such an event and do you think it is possible not to have a multitude of feelings?

EOB. It is very difficult. I have felt similarly in this Tribunal. I feel this solidarity, which instinctively links me with those who have suffered atrocities and, if anything, I feel even stronger about it than before.

   Seeing at close range the tremendous pain and agony of women and men caused by war has only strengthened my commitment to fight against the violation of anybody's human rights. I have seen the violence suffered by civilians who have nothing to do with the political games of these wars. I have seen them and I shudder.

SS.   As I listen to you, it reminds me of my work as a therapist where I learned to protect myself in order to maintain some professional distance, even though I knew it was impossible to avoid having feelings.

EOB. Exactly. That is the way it is. It is not possible to separate feelings and thoughts. I do not believe in that. In my own case, my feelings are right there and are part of what I listen to when I am paying attention to the testimony. I have also learned that the accused is protected by the presumption of innocence and is also a human being. One has to be very careful. As judges we evaluate the evidence with freedom of conscience.

SS.   Would you then say that you are cut out to be a judge?

EOB. I would say that my words in Vienna were said in a different context and my experience here proves that I can be a judge.

SS.   Do you think that it would make you a better judge?

EOB.   Yes. One can be a better judge if one has direct experience with the victims, as happened to me in Vienna.

SS.   It has been over four years since you made your remarks in the Tadic deferral hearing. Did your fears prove to be justified?

EOB.   I would say yes. In spite of my remarks and Judge Goldstone's efforts, the indictments that followed did not reflect the crimes committed against the women. I was responsible for confirming the first formal indictment after that, namely the Nikolic case. In that indictment, there was no mention whatsoever of crimes or sexual abuse committed against female detention camp prisoners.

SS.   Could he have been implicated?

EOB.   Yes, because in the United Nation's report by the Special Rapporteur, that was one of the regions where massive rapes were reported to have occurred. I was told, because I asked, that it had not been possible to gather evidence. After that, both Judge McDonald and myself had to really struggle to ensure that what happened to the women would be reflected in the indictments. Therefore, my concern was quite valid.

SS.   In another historical case, the equivalent to a trial in absentia of Karadsic and Mladic, it was obvious that you were spearheading with our colleagues the struggle for rape to be considered one of the weapons of ethnic cleansing. That became part of the official record when the conclusions were read. That was a historical first. You are currently one of the judges in a trial where rape has been charged as torture and two female witnesses have testified in court about their own rapes with the alleged rapist in the courtroom. That is again unprecedented in the history of International Tribunals. In spite of all the obstacles, it is obvious that women can have a tremendous impact. Did you believe that before?

EOB.   When the Tribunal was created, all the official United Nations documents mentioned crimes committed against women, especially the massive rapes of women of all ages. Nevertheless, the first unpleasant surprise came when only two women got elected to the Tribunal out of a total of 11 judges. To me that was a bad sign because I had hoped that if more women were part of the Tribunal, their presence would serve to make these crimes more important in the proceedings. The two of us have had a long difficult struggle, although we were supported by some of our colleagues. I imagine Judge McDonald would feel the same way. But the need for more women has been painfully evident during these years. During the next four years, there are only two women again. Always two.

SS. Was it lonely?

EOB. Yes. It was true in the beginning and I think it continues to be true today that women's organizations and Non-Governmental Organizations (NGOs) have not kept as close watch over the proceedings as they should have, especially in the very early stages. I think the lack of vigilance was a mistake on our part, and we should have actively supported the Tribunal rather than remaining silent. Also, we should have given more publicity to the Foca indictment. There was almost no reaction when it came out; virulent criticism would have been preferable. When something important happens, we should make it known worldwide. There must be an echo of women's voices so that each time these voices get louder and more difficult to ignore. If they are transformed into isolated screams, if there is not a universal cry, we will have a hard time getting to where we want to go.

SS. You are currently involved in a case against three Muslims and one Croat. What do you feel when you look at them?

EOB. I have been really sorry and angry at the irony of life that has made me one of the judges in the only case where the accused are Muslims. They suffered the highest number of casualties in what had been recognized as numerous crimes against humanity; women were massively and systematically raped as part of an ethnic cleansing strategy; their monuments were bombed with the sole intent of destroying their culture. So it is ironic that three out of the four accused are Muslim. It is very painful to realize and I have often asked myself how people who know suffering can become victimizers of others. What happens to solidarity and empathy?

The four men are human beings. When I worked with inmates in Costa Rican jails, I learned very quickly that what separates the perpetrator inside from the one outside has a lot to do with chance and politics. What makes an individual commit an offense is quite complex. I have often met in jail individuals who I would say are very good people, who were helping other people in jail adjust and change. Often the older folks would be worried about the younger ones and advising them on how to stay out of trouble. Lots of them wanted to better themselves and lots of them did. For these reasons, the four in front of me are not any different. How people got caught up in Milosovitch's perverse and criminal discourse is something for all of us to think about. But one thing is for sure: the consequences will be hard to erase.

SS.   You were not reelected in the last elections. When I talked to women's groups in the United States, I was told that they were not informed that the election would be taking place that day. Were you disappointed?

EOB.   I was very disappointed and disillusioned, especially with my own government which did nothing to promote my candidacy. They did not care essentially because I am a member of the opposition party. It also showed a total lack of interest in what is happening at the Tribunal.

But I was also very disillusioned because I felt alone. I felt that my friends in struggle from Vienna had disappeared. It is true that the election was not publicized, but it was public. It was known that national governments were making their moves within the United Nations and those who work or lobby there knew very well what was happening. It was known that my candidacy was going to be submitted and I did not get one word of support from any of the women's groups, including those in Costa Rica. As a candidate from a small country, I would have needed a great deal of support from the women's community. Yes, it hurt me and I hope it never happens again.

SS.   Do you think it has something to do with the way we are politically organized? Is that why we often do not follow through or give support at crucial times?

EOB.   I am sure we are not very well organized at all. We must organize globally in order to change the world. Like the old Marxist saying, "proletarians of the world unite," I would say "women of the world unite!" My vision of Yugoslavia strengthens my conviction that we women have to change the world, because men are not really interested, as much as they say they are or as much as they call themselves feminists. We always leave each other alone, almost as if we felt that once we win a battle, everything is accomplished and the women who scored a victory should be able to make it on their own. If we are left alone, our chances of success quickly diminish.

SS. You have been a strong supporter and defender of the Tribunal. You have repeatedly said that there cannot be peace without justice and that we must put an end to impunity. Do you think getting justice helps with recovery?

EOB. Justice is not the only means to achieve peace. But let's understand justice in its broadest sense: as something that transcends tribunals and as encompassing the need to somehow redress what happened to the victims. Let's give victims of the conflict an opportunity to be heard, to be supported, to be valued and respected in their grief and loss. Only then will we be finding paths towards justice. Without justice, vengeance is given center stage, and vengeance is violence and violence begets more violence. In order to put an end to this downward spiral, victims have to be heard, respected, valued and seen. I also believe that is important to punish individually all or at least some of the direct instigators and perpetrators of these crimes. I believe in individual responsibility for one's actions and that is why I believe in tribunals; they are the only mechanism available to punish the perpetrators while giving them a fair chance to prove their innocence. In this regard I'm wary of the notion of collective guilt because it includes not only the perpetrators, but also the innocent ones and those who actively tried to put an end to the atrocities. Collective guilt can also lead to revenge, whereas individual guilt confronts the perpetrator with his actions. This is also why I support the creation of a permanent international criminal court. History has taught us that we must fight with all our might against impunity.

SS. You have also been a great spokesperson for the rights of the victims. You come from a juridical system where there is no cross-examination. What is your experience with it, especially with regard to victims of sexual assault?

EOB. In general, I think it is an inadequate mechanism. I say inadequate because during cross-examination the intent is to impeach the witness and not to seek the truth. This is personally very distasteful to me because it often ends in the humiliation of the witness, and the public exposure of their weaknesses simply because they have come to testify. I find it offensive, especially when it happens to victims and witnesses of rape and sexual assault. It is very cruel and painful to watch, since what the defense is looking for is impeachment and, if this is the case, there is an absence of empathy, respect and human compassion.

SS.   What would be the alternative?

EOB.   What exists in continental law. The witness is not cross-examined but re-questioned which is different as the intent here is to seek contradictions within the witness's testimony. Her personal life, habits and weaknesses are not used to impeach her. And, in the case of rape victims, previous sexual behavior is often used as a way of discrediting her.

I was a practicing attorney for many years and I can think of many instances where it emerged that the witness was lying using their own testimony. I did not need cross-examination nor did my colleagues in Costa Rica. Really, I find North Americans go to frightening lengths to defend their "right" to cross-examine.

SS.   Anglo-Saxon law also has the principle of the right of the accused to face in court his accuser. Do you think that it is an absolute right?

EOB.   No, no. I do not believe in that either. Anglo-Saxon law is based on some old and worthy principles which grew out of the need to protect the rights of the defendant against institutional abuses. The obvious example is the Inquisition, where the accused had no right to know who the accuser was or what the charges were. That was a horrible travesty. However, the right to a fair trial does not automatically imply cross-examination or the right to face the accuser in court. In my opinion and that of others, the defendant should even have the right not to appear during the trial, so long as they are represented by an attorney. I also believe, again contrary to the tradition of Anglo-Saxon law, in trials in absentia. Hence, I do not feel there is a need for the defendant and the victim to face each other in court, especially in cases of sexual abuse.

SS.   Are you suggesting that the rights of victims may have been violated?

EOB.   I would say that primary importance has not been attached to them. However, it's a very delicate situation as a careful balance must be established between the rights of all parties. However, in many instances the rights of the defendant have come first, often at the expense of those of the victim.

SS.   Justice can be puzzling. I have heard that there is a higher probability of going to jail for stealing items from a store than for committing genocide. Do you agree?

EOB. I am absolutely in full agreement with that. North Americans' obsession for serial killers is absurd if we compare it with the absolute indifference they have shown towards those who are responsible for the genocide in Rwanda or toward what is happening to women in Algeria and Afghanistan. That is another real genocide. But very few citizens of the world worry about that.

SS. Do you think Costa Ricans worry more about these genocides?

EOB. I would say that because the United States is the most powerful country in the world, theoretically it should be the most informed. I have learned that this is not the case. In Costa Rica, we are also more preoccupied with individual crimes and with what happens in our cities than with international atrocities. In that way, we are very similar to Americans.

SS. One parallel is that in war most of the atrocities committed are against civilians and most of these are women and children. In civil society, crimes against women are often ignored, dismissed or trivialized.

EOB. I agree. It is mostly white men who run the world and make the political decisions. Most victims are women and children and since we lack representation in the halls of power, there is little concern for developing mechanisms to eradicate systematic violence against us.

SS. Even though crimes committed against women were instrumental in the United Nations creating the Tribunal in the first place, it has often been my experience, especially in the early years, that we as women did not exist.

EOB. Yes, it was profoundly mystifying and agonizing. Crimes against women are hidden. They disappear when one reads accounts, number of indictments, legal decisions, press reports. I would go back to what I said before: we needed more gender-sensitive women. Given that the ratio of men to women was so uneven, crimes against men were what predominated in all the discourses and concrete actions.

SS. What has been the price of being involved in the Tribunal for the past four years?

EOB. One pays many prices. One suffers a lot . . .

SS.   Why does one suffer a lot?

EOB.   Because one's identification with human suffering becomes sharper and more intense. I also now have a total incapacity to tolerate violence. I shudder at the slightest hint of it on television or at the movies. I deliberately avoid violent shows. They hurt me at a level which is almost unbearable. That is a price. On the other hand, I also think I have developed a deeper maturity which comes not only from aging.

SS.   What do you mean by maturity?

EOB.   Let's say a greater capacity for empathy, for understanding, for solidarity with others. A profound feeling that I am part of a wounded humanity.

SS.   Can you say more about that?

EOB.   In my previous work with victims of torture, I had identified with their suffering and had seen the devastating consequences in their lives. I had learned that torture was the most perverse punishment inflicted upon a human being. It is more perverse than murder because if one is murdered at least at some level the suffering ends. Torture tries to destroy the person, physically, emotionally and psychologically. It also tries to destroy the victim's family and all that was associated with that person.

Interestingly, though, during all those years nobody talked to me about rape as part of torture: neither the men nor the women. It was only in this Tribunal that I became aware that rape is the most heinous form of torture. I started looking at the four articles of the Tribunal [i.e., crimes against humanity, genocide, war crimes, and violations of the laws and customs of war], and I knew we had to include rape in one of them, and not only if it was massive and systematic as it is the case in crimes against humanity. This is the only place where the word "rape" appears in our Statute. This is a legal point but a very important one. I remember feeling it very poignantly: rape is torture and must be made a crime if only a single woman is raped during an armed conflict. Its intent is to destroy the person, and is an evil act.

SS.   When you spoke of your previous experiences in South America, rape, which we must infer happened, was never spoken about and now it is almost as if your work in the Tribunal has brought you closer to the cruelty and pervasiveness of violence against women.

EOB. That is true. I have a much keener sense of the enormity of violence against women. By comparison, my previous experience had been focused on individual torture victims. I had worked with them as people, trying to help them overcome some of the post-traumatic stress they all suffered from. But the war victims are so numerous that the whole experience has magnified the context into a universal one of perversity and evil aimed explicitly at women, and this I find very heartbreaking.

SS. What do you do with this?

EOB. I have been very fortunate to have a close intimate support network which has allowed me to survive and to process, as you therapists say, these experiences. Had I not had this support, I think I would have given up earlier and the personal price would have been much higher. This confirms my profound conviction that we need emotional support and kindness to live. Without this type of support, it is very difficult if not impossible to live through these kinds of experiences.

SS. Has your impression of people changed?

EOB. The daily contact with evil and wickedness was very intense. I am a natural optimist. I believe in human kindness and that there are millions of people who are kind and good. Sometimes when I get depressed I wonder if we are not fewer in number and less powerful than the evil ones. Yet, those moments of despair have also made me want to renew my efforts to get the good people of the planet to join forces. This is why I ask women of the world to unite. I believe a great many of us are on the side of humanity, peace and solidarity. It is not that we do not have problems. The choice before us is whether we are going to use wickedness to resolve them, or whether we are going to use kindness and solidarity.

SS. I am hearing you say that, in having closer contact with evil, it has also put you in closer contact with purity and human kindness.

EOB. Yes. Otherwise, I would want to shoot myself.

SS. Thank goodness you had emotional support. What did you do to have fun?

EOB. [Laughs] Go to museums. Art is the most sublime manifestation of human kindness. Many artists dedicated their lives to the creation of beauty and I have a great deal of admiration for that.

SS.   After you lost the election to the Tribunal, you have been elected Vice-President of Costa Rica and appointed Minister of the Environment. What do you see in your future?

EOB.   A new opportunity to set new goals and engage in new projects. This is very gratifying for me because it was a team effort and intended to make my country a more just and equal society. I am a great believer in teamwork. Now I have been given the additional opportunity to work in a different context which involves seeing the environment as an integral part of the human development equation. The challenge is not only how to work for nature's preservation but how to become a harmonious part of that nature. This is one of life's curious ironies that I end up working in an area that has been called the third generation of human rights: the right to breathe fresh air; the right to a safe habitat; the right to clean water. We are talking about the right to live in societies which co-exist harmoniously with and within nature; the right to use natural resources without destroying them; the need to replace them responsibly. This is what we are talking about when we discuss the rights of people to sustainable and harmonious development. I am very enthused about this new direction.

SS.   I think it is most fitting that you get a great opportunity to focus on life, human kindness and solidarity. It is about time.

Interview with Patricia Viseur-Sellers, Legal Officer on Gender Issues

Sara Sharratt

SUMMARY. In this interview such issues as morality and integrity, the meaning of rape in various social contexts and the demand for justice from the international community are discussed. In addition to her role in the legal system, Viseur-Sellers discusses her experiences as an African-American woman in the social systems of Europe, the United States and Latin America. The personal effects of this work on her are also explored. *[Article copies available for a fee from The Haworth Document Delivery Service: 1-800-342-9678. E-mail address: getinfo@haworthpressinc.com]*

KEYWORDS. Gender issues, sexual violence, trauma, war crimes

SS. Could you share with us some of your personal and professional background?

PVS. I am a US citizen and an African-American. Originally, I am from Philadelphia, but have lived in Europe for about 13 years and have been working in The Hague at the War Crimes Tribunal for the Former Yugoslavia for close to five years. I was a Public Defender in

---

Patricia Viseur-Sellers is Legal Officer on Gender Issues, Office of the Prosecutor of the International Criminal Tribunal for the Former Yugoslavia. She also functions as a prosecutor for certain cases dealing with sexual violence.

Address correspondence to: Patricia Viseur-Sellers, Office of the Prosecutor, International Criminal Tribunal for the Former Yugoslavia, Churchillplein 1, 2517 JW, The Hague, The Netherlands.

[Haworth co-indexing entry note]: "Interview with Patricia Viseur-Sellers, Legal Officer on Gender Issues." Sharratt, Sara. Co-published simultaneously in *Women & Therapy* (The Haworth Press, Inc.) Vol. 22, No. 1, 1999, pp. 53-78; and: *Assault on the Soul: Women in the Former Yugoslavia* (ed: Sara Sharratt and Ellyn Kaschak) The Haworth Press, Inc., 1999, pp. 53-78. Single or multiple copies of this article are available for a fee from The Haworth Document Delivery Service [1-800-342-9678, 9:00 a.m. - 5:00 p.m. (EST). E-mail address: getinfo@haworthpressinc.com].

Philadelphia. Then I worked in the field of human rights in Latin America at the Ford Foundation, after which I worked in foreign affairs at the European Union before coming to the Tribunal, where I've been working almost since its inception.

SS.   You came as a gender legal specialist?

PVS.   Yes, as a legal advisor on gender issues, for both Rwanda and Yugoslavia.

SS.   Why a gender specialist?

PVS.   The sexual violence and rapes that occurred during the Yugoslavian conflict were not only too egregious to ignore, but were the focus of the human rights community, and the women's community in particular. It certainly was known that countless rapes and other forms of sexual violence took place. The Secretary General incorporated rape into statutes related to crimes against humanity, and stated in his report that sexual violence was considered a serious violation of international humanitarian law. Therefore, Judge Goldstone and Graham Blewitt [Chief Prosecutor until 1996 and still current Deputy Prosecutor, respectively], asked me, soon after I arrived, to be the legal advisor on gender-related crimes since they were to be an important area within our investigations, our evidence and eventually the prosecutions.

SS.   My sense was that Judge Goldstone's previous work in South Africa was important.

PVS.   Coming out of South Africa, I think Judge Goldstone had an ease with which to understand different types of prejudice and oppression and how law could either support that oppression or assist in redressing it. He applied this awareness directly to issues related to sexual violence during war time, making it something that he wanted his office to actively pursue.

SS.   Was he supportive of you?

PVS.   Yes, he was.

SS.   How?

PVS.   He was supportive by creating and then asking me to occupy this position. The fact that he placed me and the issue of gender at the cabinet level of the Office of the Prosecutor made it possible for me to intercede in investigations and speak with investigators and lawyers horizontally. This was a tremendous help, and I'm sure if his support was not there from the beginning our ability to address gender issues would have been compromised.

SS.   Where else did you find support?

PVS. Within the Tribunal we sometimes underestimate the staff that have professional backgrounds pertaining to sexual violence. There are several attorneys who have worked with sexual violence, including child abuse, within their careers. There was also quite a bit of support from lawyers who studied international law and understood the importance of this issue. I think also many women in the office made an attempt to integrate gender policy internally in order to support and accelerate our gender policies in the investigations and prosecution of sexual violence. They were very supportive, and caught the connection between their everyday life as women and the possibility of sexual violence during armed conflict.

We moved into the second stage under Judge Arbour. Now our policy and operations concentrate on normalizing the inclusion of sexual violence under our mandates [Judge Arbour is the current Chief Prosecutor. She is from Quebec, Canada]. The subject has become more like the air we breathe; it's no longer disquieting, shocking, intrusive or invasive. We have developed a legal framework, an investigative methodology. Moreover, we understand how great an impact the gender of the interpreter can have on our sexual assault investigations.

SS.   That was not taken into account in the beginning?

PVS. Perhaps not consciously. Most of our interpreters are female. When we developed internal expertise, we started examining and understanding more deeply the role of the interpreter; the gender of the interpreter; the age of the interpreter and the nationality of the interpreter. As we analyzed our internal teams, we looked for the best strategy to investigate evidence of sexual violence. How should an investigation team be configured? How should we amass the evidence? Should we separate sexual violence out from other crimes? Or integrate sexual violence into other crimes? There has been much internal evaluation and, after pointed debate, we decided to have mixed gender teams.

SS.   What are the differences that you have found?

PVS.   A major difference is that, in the context of a war, the crime of rape is no longer "just" rape. It's a crime against humanity manifested through sexual violence. It's a war crime in which one side is a non-combatant, and the other is party to the conflict. Just having those distinguishing legal elements removes rape from the realm of "non-consensual sexual penetration,"a definition more appropriate to the prosecution of rape within a neighborhood in Brooklyn. Also, one has to remember that rape is generally not the only crime inflicted against that person on that day. Often in wartime you might have a victim or witness who has been shot, has seen family members killed before their eyes, been detained, starved or tortured, in addition to the sexual violence inflicted on them. So rape during war is not an ordinary crime. War crimes by themselves are serious violations of international humanitarian law and as such cannot be considered ordinary crimes.

SS.   In addition to the multiplicity of crimes, what is the difference for the rape victim in Brooklyn as opposed to the former Yugoslavia?

PVS.   Rape in war is connected to a much larger political content. Of course, this is not to say that rape in Brooklyn is not connected to the policies and the politics of patriarchy or the policies and politics of urban poverty. But the sexual violence that occurs during an armed conflict is distinctly related to the political and the societal upheaval that has led to war in the first place. Societies don't usually have temporary detention centers where segments of their population are interred and guarded by soldiers on a random basis. There is a parallel, but also a pronounced difference between detention during war and "peacetime" incarceration.

SS.   Or detention centers where women are raped constantly.

PVS.   That's right, it's not as formalized. Although you might have sexual violence in US prisons, it's not the same political context where you have a reckless society "breaking down" in the midst of an internal or international war.

SS.   Do you think the trauma would be any different?

PVS.   I think that is a very difficult question. Most of the psychologists I have talked to acknowledge that during war, trauma is multi-faceted. Some trauma is related directly to the sexual violence. One always has to ask when precisely the sexual violence occurred in the midst of the traumatization of a given person. Was it the first traumatic act or did it occur after a series of ten acts?

I think we have to start looking at the context of war-related trauma, and broadening it so that it encompasses trauma from sexual violence either as a victim or witness, or as someone who has had to incorporate the fact that their daughters, sons or wives were raped. Thus, I think we have to look at post-traumatic stress in war-like situations, whereby sexual violence is certainly a part but not necessarily the entire trauma.

SS.   I have heard expressions like "collective damage" to the community, or to the soul or to the country.

PVS. Both would work. While the trauma does remain very individual it also becomes part of the community trauma. This strikes, as I suggested earlier, at the very heart of the political context in which war-related sexual violence occurs. In municipal or domestic situations, you do have a community that is perhaps affected on a certain level, with all women being aware that one shouldn't walk through dark parking lots at night because we know there is danger. I don't think it's the level of traumatization, but we have a sense of what is dangerous. Moreover, there is a community reaction in terms of the domestic rape situation. So it is not contradictory or surprising to think that there is going to be a communal reaction to war-time sexual violence in addition to the reaction of an individual person who has experienced sexual violence or post-traumatic stress reaction.

SS.   We've also talked about atrocities. How has that impacted you personally?

PVS. I can't even bear the thought of going to see a violent movie. When I see a movie advertised with Sylvester Stallone or Bruce Willis with a gun, I block the poster right out. I couldn't even tell you what the name of the movie would be. I know from myself personally that when I started doing this work I didn't go back to my gynecologist for two years. I'm sure that was part of my reaction to the sexual violence.

Another reaction is that I find myself crying over things that are not really that important. Over a soapy television commercial, for example, or when I go to my son's basketball ceremony and they're handing out medals to these eight- and nine-year-old kids. They all think they're going to be the next slam dunk champions and I get all weepy. I know that it won't last for very long but for ten seconds it can be realized. It's so nice to be able to look at a kid and enjoy them in that way. I know it's related to these horrendous things and hearing how families are destroyed. I wasn't crying over those basketball medals. Instead, I was realizing that, "O.K., I can exhale for a second."

SS.   Innocence . . .

PVS.   All of a sudden the innocence came back. At least I think I am being very honest with myself: This is when it comes out and I'm happy it can come out. On the other hand my reaction to the sexual violence from work, as with most people, could appear in the form of vicarious trauma that might not show up for years. Ten years from now while walking down the street something might click a memory that I hadn't even been aware that I had suppressed.

SS.   Were you prepared for it at all? Did anything in your background prepare you for this?

PVS.   Not really, but perhaps. I think maybe the time I spent living in Latin America helped, since Brazil was just coming out of a dictatorship at the time. There were certain narratives about torture in Latin America and there were certain situations where you saw people who had gone through politically traumatizing situations, sometimes related to sexual violence. But nothing could have prepared you for this. Unless you were an investigator from, say, Guatemala, I would challenge anyone in this building to say that they were prepared. Thank goodness you don't have to walk around being prepared for these kinds of stories in your life.

SS.   What did it do to you?

PVS.   In many ways it made me understand better the multiple ways in which people try to destroy each other. Often, whether from a right or left perspective, we allow violence to be seen as heroic. I mean the violence that was used to overcome: oppression, nationalism or colonialism. One takes up arms and you've got this very nice, idealized "everyman" who is pictured defending the homeland, or whatever. However, when that same violence strikes an individual, it is a ghastly dehumanizing thing. There are very few ways to shoot someone nicely, and there is absolutely no way to rape someone and be a hero. The Quakers say that if violence is part of the manner in which you gained or you have acquired your society, violence is already integral to that society. When part of that violence incorporates sexual violence, one really has to question the validity of any violence whatsoever, no matter how romantic. And I admit to not being completely clear and sure on this issue.

SS.   What issue?

PVS.   On the issue that all violence is bad. Yet, I still have certain romantic notions of violence, as we all do. The Amistad movie has just come out. I haven't seen it yet. It might be too violent for me to see. I'm not too sure that I want to see it. However, I'm sure that it is about people fighting off chains of repression, a slave woman fighting off a man who might be trying to rape and kill her. That is all violence that one "should be in agreement with." What I'm saying is that violence is horrid. It's horrible.

SS.   Are there connections between the former Yugoslavia, slavery in the US, Rwanda and other ongoing struggles?

PVS.   Well yes, but I don't think one can compare these struggles in a straightforward fashion. If you look at slavery in the Americas, that was institutionalized torture for a period of two hundred years. One recognizes that this institution provided economic benefits, and de-culturized large regions of the Americas. Not even to talk about the genocide committed against Indigenous Americans, we had institutionalized sexual violence that is reflected in the legacy facing African-American women and Brazilian women today. In the make-up of the African-American community, part of our legacy, our differentiations of color, are associated with past rapes that occurred during slavery and the blood has descended down through the generations.

Now, is that comparable to the psychic damage of sexual violence that occurred in Yugoslavia? There might be some parallels. However, I have never lived in a war situation; I am talking about six generations after slavery and how does that feel, compared to someone else who is talking about three or four years after an armed conflict, and their legacy of rape. In Rwanda, the sexual violence that occurred during the genocide, is that related to an African-American sense of slavery? I don't know. I haven't thought about it that much, but what I will say is that there will be a psychic legacy in Rwandan society due to the sexual violence. Why should individual psychic scars and societal scars be anything new? I think it's normal.

It derives from patriarchy and it is part of the legacy of sexual violence.

SS.   Is it easier to live in Europe than in the USA?

PVS.   No, I don't think so. I think that anyone who is really dealing with their life is dealing with it no matter where they live. I'm not living in Europe because I think it is less racist. I am in Europe because this is where my husband lives and we decided to live here. I think that Europe has a lot of its own problems and legacies. They have plenty of stereotypes of black women. Where I used to live in Belgium, men would stop me because they thought I was a prostitute on the street. I had to tell them, "No I'm not a prostitute but if you are looking for one, come with me, maybe I can help you." Then I would say in a loud, public voice, "This man needs a prostitute. Does anyone know where he might find one?"

They see a tall black woman and from their colonial legacy of Zaire the only black woman that they imagine is a sexual partner. And thus they act surprised and devastated when I tell them I am not a prostitute. I am American, an educated American, and they don't have anywhere to fit that in psychologically because it's not a part of their worldview in Europe. I think Europeans need to truly deal with their own colonial legacies and sexual myths associated with this legacy.

SS.   To go back to something that you were talking about before, about support for people who are involved in your line of work, have you ever felt like talking to a psychologist and have you?

PVS.   I think many of us have talked about this and I think we should have an in-house psychologist who will assist the staff, whether the people who input the evidence into the computers to interpreters, attorneys, investigators, guards and supervisors. We must not underestimate how traumatic each person's job could be at any step of the way. The bailiff who is calling out the case, listens to that testimony everyday. What is their reaction? What about the guards who are sitting next to the accused? I wouldn't underestimate anyone's need to speak with a psychologist to express their feelings. However, it would have to be user-friendly enough that people would feel comfortable. But the need comes and goes. That is one excellent thing about working in the Tribunal: You don't feel victimized because you have identified a problem and you're actually doing something about it. If it doesn't always give you the illusion that you are contributing to the common good, it does allow you to control the trauma in a different way.

SS. They may need to go to somebody sometimes but not all the time, that is what you are saying.

PVS. Yes. I don't think people necessarily go around denying that. I mean no one is keeping a stiff upper lip. At times a little stress is going to have to come out, and it is probably good that it does.

SS. What shocked you the most so far?

PVS. Sometimes the extent of barbarity within the witness statements affects me. I also have been pleasantly shocked, for example when reading the *Golden Notebook* by Doris Lessing. She describes the beauty of a little blade of grass coming up amongst the cracked pots. Sometimes you're shocked by that little blade of grass and you walk over to protect it. Sometimes you are amazed and shocked by the tiny heroism that, had someone not been interviewed on a side issue, you may never have seen this. My God, when humanity grows it can bloom wonderfully, to the extent of shocking you.

That stands in sharp contrast to the barbarity, the banality of it all. I think those of us who work here all the time put up certain defense mechanisms. We all get into this nice, water cooler type of gossip, right next to the horrendous things that a witness is saying. Or you declare that I've just had it, I'm not taking it anymore. I'm not taking what? You shock yourself at your own pettiness [Laughs].

At the same time you have to understand these are normal non-war folks who have come to work at the War Crimes Tribunal. So, there is a whole part of "normal" society that continues to exist alongside of these traumatic war scenarios.

SS. There must be an impact. There is no way of going through it without changing something about your views of the world and people in it.

PVS. I would say yes, but sometimes I ask myself whether those views would not have been changed anyway. The work probably accelerated the change. I am much less inclined to underestimate people. I think that people are capable of everything.

SS. You don't underestimate anyone?

PVS. I don't underestimate anyone, to the extent of how barbaric or how heroic they could be. I think also that it is very important to have morals and to know yourself.

SS.   I am very interested in morals. Tell me more about morality.

PVS.   I really had to question myself here. What do you value in life? What is your self-integrity? What are your values in terms of human beings? Who can be used? Who is the throw-away population? Can you ever pre-judge who that throw-away population might be? I mean the more you start looking at people . . .

SS.   You are assuming that there is a throw-away population.

PVS.   Well, I think we have to assume that no one can be thrown away. Does that mean the perpetrators are good or that there is some redeeming quality in them? I don't think you can throw them away either because people can change. How one is treated is how one will treat someone else. I think of that when I look at that blade of grass or hear about the men who go in and instead of raping say, "Hey, don't say anything let's just sit here for 10 minutes, but don't say anything when we go out either." I mean that person is someone who had some moral integrity.

SS.   Where did you go with that?

PVS.   Where you go with that is the recognition that it is important to have some values, and that there are some things you are not going to do. Would you do them if someone had a gun to your head? I don't know, everyone likes to think that they are heroic, but you do need to have some values. When you have no values you can commit any act, any crime. I think people reflect the integrity they have about themselves and others. People with less morals always assume that no one else has any morals either. Why would you kill children? Why would you kill children if they're not armed?

SS.   You qualified your words by saying, "if they were not armed," because you know what is happening in the world.

PVS.   Right. Although I really think it is important for people to have values and morals, at the same time I have a lack of understanding and disdain for what my value judgment refers to as stupid nationalistic morals. I believe that people can go through a nationalistic phase and then move onto an international level. I think particularly after you emerge from a colonial situation, you go through a nationalistic phase. It's a way of saying, "I'm okay, I'm good, my culture's fine." But just don't get stuck in nationalism. When that happens, you think your country is the best, your way of doing things is the best, and eventually your way of seeing things is the best. Eventually no one else's way is valid and they have to be eliminated because all you are doing is preserving the "true view," whether some type of absurd Aryan race ideology, or an equally absurd middle kingdom notion coming out of China.

When you think that there is only one way of ever doing something, and you don't allow any competing values, it lets me know that you are not quite secure in your own way. So I think you have to go through nationalism in order to get to internationalism. I think that if we have so many absolutely demonic-like perpetrators it has a lot to do with their value structure, not just as individuals, but also as societies.

No country has a monopoly on justice and freedom, and that's made it very hard for me to live in the USA. Of course, this is also something that American lawyers working here have had to learn, along with the fact that there isn't a single law system in the world. There is also a civil law system which has been around for two thousand years. I think that the difference with the United States is that we have much more legalistic values in our culture. Why do we put on all these court-room shows on TV which are a combination of entertainment and civil value lessons, whether it be Night Court or anything from the comic to the very serious? They do influence us. Thus, Americans seem to have more of a sense that they have legal rights in their everyday life. In civil law countries, they do not have such exaggerated notions of individuals' legal rights. Legal notions are things you get around or avoid, and you certainly would never go to court to sue, to vindicate your rights, because you don't have this particular legal concept embedded within your worldview. Americans often run to court too quickly, but it is ultimately because you have a notion of an individual life backed by law. There should be a middle way between the civil and common law poles. However, I don't necessarily think that common law soldiers perpetrate less violence during war-time than civil law soldiers.

SS.   What would be the evidence?

PVS. I don't see any evidence for that. So what is the value of all of those legal systems during an armed conflict? Maybe we need to incorporate values as to how one should act in war-time, but I'm inclined to agree with the Quakers who say that war should simply be eliminated. Why don't we just start incorporating values where raping someone is not seen as a solution to anything?

SS.   Are you a Quaker?

PVS. No, I am not. I come from Philadelphia and I have been influenced by Quaker values. I participated in Quaker missions and sat on their boards. They first came to the United States with a vision, I guess as outcasts, as many European immigrants did, but they have been very vociferously non-violent, against war, for three hundred years. They have influenced and affected me.

SS.   Have they become more relevant now?

PVS. I was more involved with them before in Philadelphia. I readily relate to their religious values and vocabulary. They have said a couple of things that have really influenced me: As I have mentioned a couple of times now, the values that you put in your society at the beginning will flourish, whether violence, patriarchy, racism, or homophobia.

SS.   Maybe that is why there is so much need for the Tribunal. There has to be some justice, otherwise we will be recreating the pain in Yugoslavia in twenty years.

PVS. I think so, too, though I don't know if we can necessarily talk about justice. Maybe we can talk about some deterrent and small instances of individual injustice. But until the international community is committed to demanding justice and establishing institutions to do so, passing out justice by calling upon some witness, victim or survivor, to testify will not be sufficient. We must get to the point where we see Yugoslavia as part of an international community, and that everyone is equally outraged at what has occurred.

SS.   It is pretty arbitrary as to who gets brought in.

PVS. It's arbitrary in a sense. But those who are indicted are the only ones who risk being arrested. The Office of the Prosecutor represents the international community. The Tribunal was set up by Security Council on behalf of the international community. I would really like to see people in every part of the world, from Argentina to the most far-flung island in Norway banging their shoe on the table, demanding that the perpetrators be brought to justice.

   In other words, we need more outrage in the international community, and once we start to feel the same way about the horrific acts that have been committed in Angola and Guatemala, then we may get to a different level. When the international community says there is absolutely no room for sexual violence, then justice will be served. You can still have legitimate killings during war, you can still have legitimate bombardments of our civilian population, but there is no reason why there should be any sexual violence in war whatsoever. While this is a women's issue, it's also an issue that affects everyone: women, children and men.

SS.   Yes. I would also like to talk about some of the rape victims that I have heard testify and I am wondering how you feel about cross-examination? Is it fair?

PVS.   Really, I think it is too early to judge that. When you look at the cross-examination of the sexual assault evidence related to the Tadic case, I don't think it was unfair for the women who testified about their own rapes as part of the evidence in support of wide and systematic violations. In truth, there was very little cross-examination in that case. However, I do think that the cross-examination in the Cellebici case was the worst. I certainly hope it will be the exception. Your cross-examination has to be bound by the fact that you are dealing with a crime against humanity, and questions about prior sexual conduct are not permissible. Indeed, for anyone who is sexually violated in wartime, prior sexual conduct has to be absolutely unrelated, even if sexual conduct occurred the night before in a detention center.

SS.   You know that they brought up such issues as one of the women having contraceptive pills in her possession. Why should we keep cross-examination?

PVS.   Well, I think we have to keep cross-examination in terms of a fair trial procedure. Under civil law you have a form of questioning and, under common law you have another form which is more abrupt because the two parties are to eventually bring out the truth with their astute questioning. With civil law, the judges play a more active role. In these cases, you have three parties that are bringing out the truth. The system in the Tribunal is evolving. It is not quite civil law nor common law. Cross-examination is expected to clarify and bring out some truth yet judges' questions will also serve to bring out the truth. I've seen the cross-examination at the Rwanda Tribunal as well as at the Yugoslav Tribunal, and sometimes you do have what might be termed "pointed" cross-examination.

SS.   It still depends on the judges.

PVS. Yes. It is much more tri-party here. It is not just the two sides as in common law or the judges playing the central role as in civil law jurisdictions. That type of cross-examination would not develop here.

SS. It still does amaze me how much it takes to recognize rape as a war crime.

PVS. I think in most people's minds killing remains the worst crime. Male-oriented investigation and prosecution has highlighted that, not to say that there hasn't been evidence of sexual violence as well. Also, people feel that once we have identified who killed who, we were just about finished. Only then can we address such questions as who raped who, who burned what, and then finally who stole the cows. This has been the norm until women declared, "Hey, I'm part of the international community, what about the other 53 percent of the world's population?"

SS. Not as many women in the international community before . . .

PVS. Yes, completely. I think that when people begin to partake in civil society they need to have much more of a voice to say "as a member of society, this is unacceptable." So this is part of the process that is going on right now. In addition, we are still rather parochial. We think that things like war won't happen again. However, when war returned once again to civilized Europe, Europe was in a state of shock. I can almost hear people say "I can deal with rapes when they happened in the past, or when they're happening in Bangladesh, but I can't believe that it's right now in my own backyard." Well, hello! You, too, are being called upon to join the world and make it move forward.

SS. You have a very global outlook, which I appreciate. I remember a saying: "Think globally, act locally." Should it also be the reverse?

PVS. Both at the same time, yes.

SS. When I was planning this special volume, I was asked if it was going to be relevant to American psychologists. What would you have said to someone who asked you that question?

PVS. I would have said, "Take off your sunglasses, honey, you look a little ridiculous. The sun shines on you too. There is no place to run; there is no place to hide and you wouldn't want to run and hide, not from this stuff."

SS.   It's happening everywhere.

PVS.   That's right. Take for example the domestic violence issue, which is something we talk about a lot in the States. How you see women in your civil society and how you are going to treat them when you're at war and the structures suddenly break down are closely related. If we permit domestic violence, incest and all this stuff, why should we be shocked when rape is committed in war-time?

SS.   We will publish a summary of the Foca indictment. It is a historical indictment and you were instrumental in making it happen. Before you got it confirmed, what was it like? What did you have to do?

PVS.   Well, before we could have the indictment confirmed it had to follow the path of all indictments: an investigation, followed by a legal analysis of the statements, and then we had to draft the indictment and finally go through a very interesting process here. The team that conducted the investigation, together with their legal advisor, drafted the indictment.

  After that, all of the attorneys in the Office of the Prosecutor are invited to participate in an indictment review. Every attorney can critique or support that indictment in a way that they feel is justified. Foca, an indictment which was based almost entirely if not solely on sexual violence, went through a rather lengthy indictment process. We must have had three or four indictment reviews.

SS.   Is that unusual?

PVS.   I wouldn't call it highly unusual. It went through that process not just because of the complexity of some of the legal arguments we were putting forward, but also because it was the first time that we were charging torture and discussing how to group various rapes together on such a large scale. We decided to place many together under one count and not one count per rape, as that would have been too unwieldy. It just took time. People gave us their time and I think the investigative team and the lawyers were quite patient. When you go into an indictment review, you have someone who knows nothing about your case. That person will ask the hard questions that the judge might ask or that the defense attorney might ask. The team is already convinced because they have been living with the investigation for a year and a half. They have seen the faces. The person who has been working on a completely different indictment comes into your indictment review and has to be convinced that there is evidence of a prima facie legal case.

SS.   What was the most agonizing question?

PVS.   Let me give you an example, not of a question that was asked, but of a decision that had to be made. How does one charge all these rapes? When you look at indictments from the Rwanda Tribunal you might have 8,000 killings in one indictment. We can charge that as one count of extermination under crimes against humanity. For example, in one Rwanda case, we had several rapes, fifteen or more, and they were charged as one count of rape under crimes against humanity. The Foca indictment has numerous rapes. Therefore, we had to ask ourselves whether we should count the rapes and give each rape one count, or should they be pleaded as one count of crime against humanity. Our solution, when we presented the indictment, was to plead separate counts of rape for each defendant. That was a very difficult charging decision, and is one of the reasons why, when you read through the indictment, it is impossible to know how many rapes occurred just by adding up the counts.

SS.   You make it sound so easy.

PVS.   [Laughs] Is that so easy?

SS.   It never happened in the other International Tribunals.

PVS.   In Foca, the indictment deals with events that happened during the takeover of the town. The charges in the indictment involved sexual violence during interrogation, sexual violence during detention, sexual violence during military and paramilitary maneuvers. The evidence is unfortunately abundant. I think that perhaps in Nuremberg and Tokyo the intent was missing and while they had evidence of sexual violence, they did not pursue it in a diligent fashion. I think that the intent to follow through is precisely what distinguishes the Second World War trials from the current ad hoc Tribunals.

SS.   You obviously had the intent.

PVS.   Yes. The re-drafting and re-writings are part of my job, and very important to the workings of the Tribunal. The team worked very hard on the investigation and the indictment. While I think most teams feel very attached to their own investigations, people understood there was something even more special about the Foca investigation. We understood that Foca was going to be a ground-breaking prosecution. We wanted to be cautious. We wanted to be prudent, so that people would not be able to criticize this indictment for being less rigorous or not providing sufficient evidence.

SS.   It always pains me how much harder we women have to work. Two weeks ago [March 98], one of the defendants unexpectedly surrendered. There was going to be a Foca trial. How did you react?

PVS. I think everyone was elated. The fact that he surrendered was also unexpected. But that was almost immediately overridden by the fact that he pleaded guilty. Guilty pleas, cases to prosecute, sentencing, all this has to start becoming normal. We should be able to look up at a court docket and say to ourselves, "Okay, what do we have today? Looks like a couple of murders, some sexual violence, nudity and other standard war crimes." We want to be at that stage.

SS.   Which I think, as you and I have discussed before, is a very strange and bewildering honor.

PVS. Yes it is, but when we get to that stage then we can really start comparing the early indictments with the later ones. Then we can start fine-tuning the process and seeing what we've been doing right and what areas still need more work.

I had never been in a court where an accused pleaded guilty to rape even though he has now pleaded not guilty. He was obviously pleading guilty to something. It felt like a relief for me to be looking at a rapist and not an alleged rapist. What was very surprising was that there was no indication, at least not to the Judges or prosecution, that this plea would be entered. His attorney probably knew that he was going to plead guilty. I have never seen this scenario at an initial appearance.

SS.   Here you were one of the attorneys also.

PVS. I remember Hildegard [She is the German co-council for the prosecution] and I just looked at each other. I said, "What do we do now?" It was really quite funny. We had no prior contact with the accused nor his attorney, except to shake hands. We had just assumed that there would be a "not guilty" plea and we would proceed to the next status conference.

SS.   One often hears that women who have been raped need special protection. How do you feel about that?

PVS.   In the Tribunal's experience, it depends very much on the individual cases. Usually in situations of physical perpetration between the defendant and the witness, anonymity is almost impossible because you are dealing with an identification issue. The defendant will need to know the person who is accusing him. However, most witnesses request confidentiality, which means that the public does not know their identity. The defendant might know, particularly if he is the physical perpetrator anyway, but the public has no interest in knowing the identity of the witness. Meanwhile, some women want to be identified and seen, not only by the defendant but also by the public. "What do I have to be ashamed of and why should I hide?" they might ask. Others have a very different sense of privacy and don't want to be identified. So the prosecution, in almost all of our cases, files motions for witness protection during the pre-trial preparation phase of a case. Then, as we move into the trial phase we talk to the witnesses in order to establish what the reasonable risk or fear for the safety of themselves and their families is. For sexual assault witnesses, it suffices that they are survivors. Those confidentiality motions have been very favorably received by the court.

SS.   When I hear that rape victims will not testify I wonder who is it that doesn't want them to testify, because I think that a lot of them want to testify.

PVS.   I am very curious also about who does not want them to testify, because that hasn't been the Tribunal's experience so far.

SS.   That's right, but it's said consistently all over the world that women do not want to come and testify.

PVS.   Yes.

SS.   I am just as mystified because when I talk to women they are all willing to come. Maybe they do not want their names to be shown or maybe they do not want their faces to be seen, but they are willing to come and testify. In the one particular case that we talked about before, two women who were raped came and accused one of the defendants directly.

PVS.   Yes. They didn't even request any confidentiality.

SS.   They didn't ask for anything.

PVS. The same scenario happened during another trial. A woman came who was raped five times. She testified very openly, over two days. It is all part of the public record. There is a fear among some NGOs with regard to some witnesses testifying. But the real question comes down to the individual women when it is time to testify. Do they want to come forward or not? I don't think that you can necessarily generalize how they are going to feel at the moment of decision, either from your own feelings or from a group's stand on testifying. What I am trying to say is that we tend to ignore that there are women who are willing to come forward.

SS.   Yes. I think a lot of the claims the women do not come forward is fear or projection.

PVS. There has been a lot of criticism of the media for trying to find rape victims for the evening news: "Just tell me who raped you, how many times, where, who was watching?" And then after the interview, after they've used her, they leave her. Rape and testimony in general raises the issue of the protection, physically and psychologically, of witnesses, and as you know I have been very critical of the protection offered by the Tribunal which has shown almost no willingness to be proactive in addressing the issues of victim and witnesses.

SS.   That is a question all the International Tribunals in the future are going to have to really address. What does witness protection mean in different stages of an investigation? What is the responsibility of the Tribunal? What is the responsibility of the nation state? What are the responsibilities of the transiting-state?

PVS. I think the Tribunal is set up in very practical terms. I don't think that it is just because the witness unit has ten people or fewer that this determines the type of services offered.

SS.   It is severely under-staffed though.

PVS. I don't think that any international body like this Tribunal can go into Tuzla or Sarajevo and give private police protection to a witness. At this point we have to tell the witness: "What is your reasonable risk or fear for your safety? If you come to the Tribunal protective confidentiality measures can be taken that will ensure that your neighbors do not know that you have come to the Tribunal to testify. Transit to The Hague can be kept confidential. When you return to your town you say nothing." That might be the best method of protection at this point in time. On the other hand, you have to understand that witnesses are going back to areas that are not completely secure, areas of high criminality, of increasing crime.

SS.   What kind of services are offered then?

PVS.   When investigators in the field interview someone or contact a potential witness who is in a bad psychological state, they will usually attempt to put them in contact with local social services.

SS.   But you can't predict it.

PVS.   No, you can't. At this stage some people will say that they don't need social services, including mental health care.

SS.   And then they will . . .

PVS.   When you return and you speak to witnesses who are closer to the trial stage, you might find that those who were stable at an earlier stage now require social or psychological services. So you try to locate the resources within the community, near the person, because local care is where they can build up a relationship with the provider and where there is a language compatibility. Then, when they come to The Hague to testify, they have access to medical and psychological services here. When they return home there has to be follow-up. The person still needs services and they need to have access to that local NGO. That is the real productive partnership between witnesses and civil society.

SS.   It has not been done.

PVS.   It has been done.

SS.   It has not been done in lots of other instances.

PVS.   In a lot of other instances people have said they don't want to, they don't need to. Some people have support from their families and some people have fallen through the cracks. Now, that is also related to people not identifying themselves as a witness when they go back. Some interviewers could be handling people who were witnesses but who chose not to say anything. We have told witnesses that they do not have to identify themselves, because it could be a security risk.

SS. At the same time we know that the more we ask them to keep secrets the longer it is going to take them to heal and we also know that it is important that they talk about it.

PVS. I think this is true but then you get caught in a bind: security and the secrets. Some people feel much more comfortable telling certain members of their family, letting part of the secret out. That can facilitate some of their recovery. At the same time, they can go for psychological assistance, not necessarily identifying themselves as a witness.

The idea I had about a protection unit goes beyond getting witnesses to The Hague, getting them into a hotel and then transporting them back. We were fighting over the availability of funds for rape victims to bring in a therapist or not being able to secure a bus trip for witnesses stuck alone in The Hague giving testimony. I also felt that sometimes you have an obligation to the witnesses to follow through and help them with the next step. We must talk about re-building civil society, as that is the only way that witnesses will ever have long-term psychological protection.

SS. We have to de-stigmatize rape in civil society. We have to take that stigma away because otherwise she will get victimized again. The rapists are not on trial and she continues to be. I think that is part of the problem. Maybe you can't just solve it by having them come here, if they will have to go back to a disaster back home.

PVS. I agree completely. I agree that the Tribunal is only a small part. The impact will be magnified and scrutinized but the real work will go on in civil society.

SS. That's right, and also we really have to put rapists on trial. In some ways these are related. For example, the Vatican just came out with another attempt at an apology to the Jews. Clinton has talked about an apology to the African-Americans.

PVS. There was an apology and compensation to Japanese Americans.

SS. Compensation, yes, but I don't think they apologized. Do you think there should be an apology to African-Americans in the United States even though it is not only the United States that is responsible for this institutionalized torture as you called it?

PVS.   Yes, but you should get all the countries that were involved in slavery and the slave trade to apologize. African-American literature speaks of redemption. The perpetrator must seek redemption through an apology to the victim/survivor. It helps when say you are sorry. But only when the apology is sincere. You have to acknowledge guilt in relation to the problem that you caused. Some people want to measure that sincerity in terms of income or compensation. So yes, I think that apologies, like guilty pleas, do help but they have to be sincere and followed by concrete action. In the Vatican's case, I heard it was an apology but it took a step back from saying that they had any impact on racist attitudes towards Jews. I mean the Vatican can't have it both ways. Then I'm wondering if we should also do something more in civil society for our rape victims?

SS.   Why not have a monument?

PVS.   A friend said they would probably desecrate the monument!

SS.   That would really show that society wasn't ready to show honor.

PVS.   But there is something we need to do to really de-stigmatize rape. It is very interesting. I gave a speech in Washington in the fall, and I mentioned our indictments, saying that in the future we will know all the names: Foca, the Bungalow, Omarska [an infamous detention center]. A member of the audience approached me afterwards, and said, "You recite the names of those places as if you were referring to Gettysburg, as if they were monumental." And I replied, "Yes, I am, because this is exactly what they are."

   I am certainly not suggesting, for example, that we will have, a year from now, a Foca fund for any person, particularly women, who have been sexually violated during an armed conflict. Or will we? Who knows, we are not doing any of this now.

SS.   You work for both Tribunals. What are the differences for you? There have been allegations of racism by the international community when looking at the Rwanda Tribunal.

PVS.   Well, I think that one can look at the facilities, the physical buildings.

SS.   The amount of money.

PVS.   No, it's not the money. It is a very strange situation to a certain extent. The Rwanda Tribunal is funded at a comparable level to

Yugoslavia and their trust fund has even more money in it than Yugoslavia. Thus, one might ask oneself whether it is a question of administration. One might ask about the location: Was the building housing the Rwanda Tribunal readily convertible from its former use to its present one? One might ask oneself about the impact of the local skills and local goods that one had to use. However, setting up an organization like the Rwandan Tribunal in Arusha sends a political signal. This is the center of the East African community and there was a good political reason why the Tribunal needed to be there, just as there were good reasons for the Yugoslav Tribunal to be here in The Hague. If, however, both Tribunals were situated in New York, with the Rwandan Tribunal on the third floor and the Yugoslav one on the fifth, my guess is that they would look identical.

SS.   So you haven't felt any differences?

PVS.   Sometimes people would like to say that since it looks poorer and it's in Africa, there must be racism. I think that when people say things like that, the real question is whether Rwanda is a kind of second cousin to the Yugoslav Tribunal. Much of this has to do with our impression of the importance of the Rwanda genocide as opposed or compared to the importance of the Yugoslav conflict. However, you've got to ask yourself who is it important for. To the Western world? To Africa?

SS.   Do you think the Western world, where there was hardly any interest in Yugoslavia, can get interested in Rwanda?

PVS.   If you read Western newspapers on any given day, you will see more interest in Yugoslavia and western countries in general. Although there's been war in Angola for the past twenty years, it doesn't make the papers on a daily basis like Northern Ireland. Somewhere in the back of many Western minds, there is the idea that wars and genocide always happen in Africa and that this is not news. When you look at Yugoslavia, people were shocked that the war took place on European soil, where it wasn't supposed to occur. As for women and issues of sexual violence, we can turn to the Rwanda Tribunal for important advances in the prosecution of sexual violence cases. Rwanda has been the first to prosecute genocidal sexual violence. Rwanda is the first Tribunal that had a group of six women come forward and testify about their own sexual violence in the Akayesu trials, and in other cases, men described sexual violence committed against women that they witnessed.

SS.   Were they raped?

PVS.   Yes, the women were. I think Rwanda is a place where we have already offered in evidence various forms of sexual violence, not just rape, but also sexual mutilation, impaling of the vagina or slicing of genitals as a method of killing. It is very important to view both Tribunals jointly in terms of sexual violence.

SS.   Has all of this made you less sexual?

PVS.   That is an interesting question. I don't know whether it is the sexual violence or it's just that I'm getting older, period [laughs].

SS.   There are too many variables!

PVS.   There are so many variables, but, I don't think so. I think I now appreciate sexual integrity much more. I mean it is a wonderful part of a human being.

SS.   Yes, sure. But we are talking about perversions . . .

PVS.   You know, it becomes clearer and clearer that violence has very little to do with sex. Yes, it does have a lot to do with sexuality. But these acts are connected to aggression, to war and not to how one feels about oneself in terms of being sexual. It does not make you responsible for any of the acts that could ever have happened. You could have dressed like a nun and you could have been the most absolutely neutered person, but if you were to be sexually assaulted in these wartime situations, it was going to happen. None of the witnesses that I know spoke of being "sexually attractive," or inviting in any way. While some of the perpetrators supposedly chose beautiful women, most, however, were people who were running, were scared. They were frightened. They were nasty. They were dirty. They were starved. I'm sure that they all had bad breath. I mean this has nothing to do with sexuality.

SS.   I notice that when I read a lot of rape testimony, I get very edgy. In fact I was walking down the beach yesterday and I noticed three heterosexual couples. All three men were playfully pushing the women into the water. It just hit me.

PVS.   When I look at some of this in terms of non-war situation sexuality, I think of the names we use to describe why men rape: power, entitlement, violence. You can see how these might be part of everyday sexuality. However, when you have a war, if men really deep down believe they are entitled, powerful and so on, they will act out. Not all men are rapists in war which is very important to bear in mind. It's a question of morals. But we have to understand how sexuality in a non-conflict situation could reveal characteristics related to war-time acts.

SS.   I don't think that I have any more questions. I wonder—we have talked a lot—do you have any reflections?

PVS.   One thing that I was thinking yet have never articulated was the passage of African-American women through institutionalized sexual violence and raping, and the question of how this is related to Yugoslav women or Rwandan women today. In many ways, and for very good reasons, we tend to focus a lot within the women's movement on the question of rape. But I think sexual violence is so much broader. Violence in general often occurs prior to the act of rape.

With slavery, it goes much further than that. Breeding was sanctioned; forced birthing was sanctioned; selling of children was sanctioned. What about forcing someone to be a wet nurse? What about the master or the state owning your breasts and you don't own the liquid in them? That is sexual violence, yet it is not rape.

SS.   Yes, which is what these Tribunals can truly accomplish.

PVS.   If the Tribunals can accomplish just that, it would be a great step.

SS.   What does it feel like to be part of history?

PVS.   I feel like I'm part of the path of history. You feel a wonderful obligation and a very intense privilege.

SS.   Do you feel very proud?

PVS.   Yeah, I feel very, very proud.

SS.   You did it.

PVS.   Thank you. It is extremely rewarding, and when people say, "My God, how could you get up so early in the morning and do all this?" I think to myself that I'm descended from women who had to get up at the same time, if not earlier, to go pick cotton. This is not hard. It's a real historical challenge.

SS.   You are saying something that I strongly believe in, namely that the presence of women can make a difference in the world. I am amazed by that and also amazed by the way that some of their male colleagues take the ball and run with them.

PVS.   Like you cannot imagine.

The Foca Indictment
by the International Criminal Tribunal
for the Former Yugoslavia

Sara Sharratt

SUMMARY. The following is a brief summary of the main implications of the Foca indictment of the International Criminal Tribunal for the Former Yugoslavia. This case is mentioned in the interviews with McDonald and Viseur-Sellers. It is of central relevance to the concept of justice in relation to women's issues. *[Article copies available for a fee from The Haworth Document Delivery Service: 1-800-342-9678. E-mail address: getinfo@haworthpressinc.com]*

KEYWORDS. Foca, International Criminal Tribunal for the Former Yugoslavia, rape, war crimes, Grave Breaches

On June 26, 1996, the International Criminal Tribunal for the Former Yugoslavia made history with the "Foca" indictment against eight Bosnian Serbs for the rapes, gang rapes, sexual assaults and sexual enslavement of women and girls living in this town in the southeast of Bosnia-Herzegovina. Muslim women and girls were detained in a number of sites, including houses, sports halls, detention centers, apartments and the Foca High School. They were raped, gang raped, tortured, enslaved, forced to perform domestic chores and sexual services on behalf of allies and friends of the perpetrators. In several instances, they were sold for profit by their masters. These crimes

---

Address correspondence to: Sara Sharratt, PhD, P.O. Box 2292-1000, San Jose, Costa Rica.

[Haworth co-indexing entry note]: "The Foca Indictment by the International Criminal Tribunal for the Former Yugoslavia" Sharratt, Sara. Co-published simultaneously in *Women & Therapy* (The Haworth Press, Inc.) Vol. 22, No. 1, 1999, pp. 79-81; and: *Assault on the Soul: Women in the Former Yugoslavia* (ed: Sara Sharratt and Ellyn Kaschak) The Haworth Press, Inc., 1999, pp. 79-81. Single or multiple copies of this article are available for a fee from The Haworth Document Delivery Service [1-800-342-9678, 9:00 a.m. - 5:00 p.m. (EST). E-mail address: getinfo@haworthpressinc.com].

were carried out with either the active or passive knowledge of a number of individuals in positions of power, including paramilitary leaders and Dragan Gavovic, Foca's Chief of Police. In the indictment, they are charged with crimes committed against at least 14 victims, some of whom are young adolescents. Meanwhile, the eight perpetrators remain at large.

This is the first indictment in the history of International Humanitarian Law in which an International Criminal Tribunal has indicted male perpetrators for war crimes committed exclusively against women and girls in which all of the charges are related to sexual offenses. In turn, this means that there has been no "mainstreaming" of the war crimes committed against women.

Of course, this is not to say that the present Tribunal has never before charged a perpetrator for rape. But this is the first time that rape has not been bundled with several other charges or used as a means to achieve other ends. In short, the gendered nature of these crimes has been made entirely explicit: these are acts committed by men, in wartime, against women and girls because of their sex. Moreover, these crimes must be understood to be gender-specific because they are committed disproportionately against women, because they are women.

Yes, men do get raped, but it is mostly by other men and it happens less frequently than is the case for women. Yes, men are also enslaved, but usually it does not entail limited or unlimited sexual access to their bodies or forced impregnation.

Also to be stressed in this regard is the fact that such acts have neither the same attribution nor meaning for women and men, and thus the gender specific aspects of the same "act" must be carefully analyzed and understood. Quite simply, the narrow view that crimes committed against both women and men cannot, by definition, be considered gender specific overlooks the fact that women are routinely persecuted because they are women, whereas men are not persecuted simply because they are men. Moreover, when women are raped, the institutional and structural consequences are radically different than they are for men: the latter are not cast away by their wives; they are not seen as having dishonored their partners or families; they are not deemed to be unmarriageable; questions are not raised as to whether or not they were consenting, and so forth. As well, the implications of forced/ unwanted impregnation must be considered: death, botched abortions, sterility, horrific traumatization, unwanted children, abandoned children, stigmatized children, etc. For women in general and those living in the Former Yugoslavia in particular, we must look very closely at the intersections of class, religion/ethnicity and gender: women and girls were persecuted as Muslims, Croats or Serbs and as females. Men were persecuted as Muslims, Croats or Serbs. The crimes were directed principally against Muslims. However, in the case of rape, the problem is that women often suffer subsequent persecution at the hands of their own families and societies.

Also important in this indictment is that rape is typified as torture, both under Crimes Against Humanity and under Grave Breaches. However, there is continuing disagreement among legal experts as to whether the incidence of rape and enslavement must be massive and/or systematic to be considered Crimes Against Humanity, or whether it is sufficient that the rape itself be massive in its violence. There is no such debate in relation to Grave Breaches: *one* crime of rape, committed by *one* individual against *one* woman or girl *once* is deemed to be a serious war crime. The dualistic thinking that rape is bad when massive and/or systematic in scale but not as bad when sporadic must be overcome. Describing it as torture also labels rape for what it is: torture and as such a serious war crime.

This is the first time that an International Criminal Tribunal has charged perpetrators with the sexual enslavement of females. This highlights once again the gender specificity of slavery, with women and girls forced to per-form household duties, while their bodies become sexually accessible to their masters and their masters' associates.

It is hoped that this short summary of the main implications of the Foca indictment will prompt the feminist community to pay more attention to the significance of what has been happening at the Tribunal, particularly in relation to women's issues. We must insist that all indicted criminals be brought to trial and, if the political will continues to be lacking, then we must also ask that these eight perpetrators be subjected to the Tribunal's Rule 61, allowing the prosecutor to present further evidence against them and issue international warrants for their arrest. This will ensure that, if they are found guilty, they will become the international pariahs that they are. It will also ensure that we, as women, will get a chance to speak. Let us work towards this goal.

Beyond War Hierarchies:
Belgrade Feminists' Experience
Working with Female Survivors of War

Lepa Mladjenovic

SUMMARY. The experience of a Belgrade feminist now defined as Serbian by a government that she rejects is explored in this article. The organization, Women in Black Against War, of which she is a founding member, works to help women regain a sense of dignity as they move from victim to survivor. Other goals include strengthening women's rights and training paraprofessionals to participate in the healing process by witnessing the women's retelling of their experiences. The solidarity and connections that have developed among women in the Former Yugoslavia and with other women around the world is an important aspect of this process and one which undermines nationalism. *[Article copies available for a fee from The Haworth Document Delivery Service: 1-800-342-9678. E-mail address: getinfo@haworthpressinc.com]*

KEYWORDS. War crimes, trauma, Belgrade, Women in Black Against War

For the Former Yugoslavia, 1992-93 was marked above all by the ascendancy of fascist power and the mobilization of patriarchal violence in pursuit of a demonized Other. The presumed ethnicity of an individual's name or her street address determined her destiny, whether it was life, death, rape or

Lepa Mladjenovic is a Belgrade feminist and founding member of the organization Women in Black Against War.

Address correspondence to: Lepa Mladjenovic, Women's Center, Tirsova 5A, 11000 Beograd, Serbia.

[Haworth co-indexing entry note]: "Beyond War Hierarchies: Belgrade Feminists' Experience Working with Female Survivors of War." Mladjenovic, Lepa. Co-published simultaneously in *Women & Therapy* (The Haworth Press, Inc.) Vol. 22, No. 1, 1999, pp. 83-89; and: *Assault on the Soul: Women in the Former Yugoslavia* (ed: Sara Sharratt and Ellyn Kaschak) The Haworth Press, Inc., 1999, pp. 83-89. Single or multiple copies of this article are available for a fee from The Haworth Document Delivery Service [1-800-342-9678, 9:00 a.m. - 5:00 p.m. (EST). E-mail address: getinfo@haworthpressinc.com].

displacement. What was done to protect that individual's rights and liberties? For many, nothing. Thus, Serb security forces were able to run concentration camps in Bosnia according to a particularly twisted logic: men, as potential soldiers, were killed; women, as potential sexual objects, were raped. The regime currently in power in the state in which I live was responsible for these war crimes. What does it mean politically and professionally to us, as feminists living and working in Belgrade?

At the very beginning of the conflict, in October 1991, a group of us founded a pacifist organization called Women in Black Against War, under whose banner we held weekly vigils in Belgrade. We felt that it was imperative that we go out into the street in order to communicate our message to the public at large that we opposed the Serbian regime, its involvement in wars in Croatia and Bosnia, and that we opposed militarism and violence against women. Each Wednesday I would get up and think of the clothes I would wear. By choosing black in a time of war, we hoped that part of our sense of helplessness would be transformed into strength and action. So it continued, standing on the street in black and in silence, season after season, for all the years of the war.

Needless to say, the latest news from Kosovo hints at more ethnic cleansing on the part of the Serbian regime. In the face of this threat, Women in Black are currently in the process of planning the forms which our opposition to the fascist regime will take.

By 1993, our commitment to feminism had led some of us to travel between Zagreb, Belgrade and Zenica in order to gather and focus support for women raped in war. These efforts culminated in the creation of the Autonomous Women's Center Against Sexual Violence in Belgrade, which offers psychological and social support to women traumatized in this way. Thus, while volunteers visited hospitals to talk to physicians about the issues at stake and the Center's work, we devised and put into practice a counseling program. Throughout this process, we received the support of many women, who offered books, funding and their own time and energy. We were often struck by the incredible lengths to which women would go to help us and, in truth, it was these interventions that sustained us on a day-to-day basis.

Having been part of both these groups during the war, in the pages that follow I will seek to summarize what I believe to be the essence of our experience.

WHAT DID WE LEARN?

Women Are the First Enemy of Men

The SOS Hotline for Women and Children Victims of Violence was founded in Belgrade in 1990 as a service provided by women for women. As the war in Bosnia and Croatia progressed, we began to hear from women who had never contacted the Hotline before. Particularly significant in this regard were calls made at the very beginning of the war, at the same time that the regime was televising daily propaganda broadcasts in which scenes of mutilated corpses were accompanied by an emotive voice-over. Clearly, the regime's purpose was to rouse the population into a frenzy of nationalism and lust for revenge. However, the broadcasts also had another, unintended effect. Men who watched the programs would become agitated and angry, and start hitting their wives or children as a proxy for the "enemy" that was far away and not as easy to reach. For many of the women it was the first time they had been struck by their husbands, and they would call SOS asking, "What happened to him?" We named the condition "post-TV news violence syndrome." Needless to say, these incidents only serve to confirm the view that the enemy of first resort is Woman; ethnicity comes in a distant second.

Misuse of Women Raped in War by State Institutions

Seeking to make contact with female war survivors, the Autonomous Women's Center Against Sexual Violence approached numerous medical facilities in the Former Yugoslavia. However, as we undertook this task, what immediately became apparent to us was the fact that the regime was exploiting women's suffering for its own ends, identifying those with Serbian names in order to provide evidence of war-time atrocities committed against Serbs. To cite but one example, in 1994 a psychiatrist working in a Belgrade area mental health center provided a foreign journalist (known to us) with the medical histories of women who had been sexually abused during the war. Thus, not only was this hospital breaking the first principle of medical ethics in the name of nationalist politics, but the women themselves were being treated as any other mental health patient, while being forbidden from meeting with the representatives of feminist NGOs.

It should be noted as well that there was a general reluctance on the part of medical facilities to collaborate with the Center, a reluctance that was in all likelihood due to our strong disavowal of Serbian nationalism. In this way, state-run health care institutions proved themselves to be more interested in serving the nationalist cause than serving the needs of the women under their care.

Rape in War Is Part of a Continuum of Male Violence Against Women

Although the Center has evidence to show that women from all ethnic groups–Serbian, Croat and Muslim–were raped during the war, most of our work was with women possessing Serbian names, simply because they were the ones who felt safest in Belgrade. At the same time that the Center denounces the Serb regime and its genocidal policies, war rapes must be understood in the larger context of male violence. In short, we believe that atrocities committed against women in wartime are driven by the same dynamics that have resulted in so many women calling the SOS Hotline after having been raped, battered or humiliated by their husbands or boyfriends.

WHAT DO WE DO? WHAT ARE OUR POLITICS?

Enhancing the Dignity of War Victims

Humiliation is intrinsic to every war crime. Thus, in our work, we have sought to create the conditions necessary for women to regain their sense of dignity, a journey which takes them from victim to survivor, and possibly to transformation of the social conditions that led them to be victimized in the first place. Central to this process is the development of spaces of dignity, through the establishment of non-hierarchical relationships and respect for women's bodies and otherness.

Strengthening Civil Rights

Wars, by their very nature, circumscribe the rights and lives of those who are forced to live through them. Our experience has been no different, and to survive under these suffocating conditions we have engaged in a number of strategies. These include working with women from the conflict zones, publishing statements denouncing war crimes and their perpetrators, holding weekly peace vigils, and promoting nonviolent means of conflict resolution. We also sought to undermine the nationalist agenda by exchanging letters with friends across the front lines, and ensuring that women's NGOs were places where women of all ethnic names could gather in dignity and solidarity.

Witnessing Pain

If one is to work with female survivors of war, one must learn to listen, to act as a witness for the pain they have suffered. In this capacity, we have sought to provide women with support that does not categorize, question or judge their experiences. Of course, there are many other feminist groups in the region that played a similar role, each of us bearing witness at both the political and personal level.

Undermining Nationalism Through Personal Narratives

Over the years, the regime in Belgrade has been unswerving in its efforts to arouse hatred of the other nations in the war, while hiding from the popula-

tion the fact that these "others" have also faced great suffering and deprivation. Given this lack of knowledge, we have learned that a single person's
story can have an enormous impact upon people's perceptions, and break the
cycle of ethnic chauvinism and hatred. Thus, we have devoted considerable
energy to the task of bringing the Other into our communities, through the
publication of life histories, the production of film documentaries and the
organization of face-to-face encounters. To recount one particularly telling
example, the political views of many Belgrade women changed abruptly in
1995 after the Center screened documentary footage from the massacres in
Kozarac and concentration camps in Omarska.

BEYOND THE HIERARCHY OF DISCRIMINATION

If one accepts that the production and reproduction of hierarchies plays a
key role in sustaining patriarchal power, one will not be surprised to learn that
we were faced with many such hierarchies in our work with female war
survivors.

Hierarchy of Pain

Each region in the war was left with its own legacy of trauma and pain,
and individuals laden with so much suffering of their own that they had little
capacity left to feel empathy for others. It is important for those working with
women war survivors to recognize and understand the implications of this
process, which typically involves the creation of a circuit of blame and guilt
whereby women from one region ask those from another, "Where were you
during the shelling?" Needless to say, the effects of such questioning are
highly pernicious: women who live outside of the war region feel guilty;
women who have had only one family member killed feel guilty; female
refugees who return home are made to feel guilty, as are those who do not go
home. The cycle is never-ending, with patriarchy being the only real benefi-
ciary of this process. If we are to avoid falling into the circuit of blame, we
must all try to come to terms with our own guilt feelings.

Hierarchy of Rapes in War

Although some feminists distinguish between "ordinary" and "genocidal" forms of wartime rape, there are others, myself included, who would
argue that any such distinction is dangerous, since it posits a rape hierarchy
that places the violation of nations ahead of that of women. Whether one sees
such rapes as instruments of war or of genocide, they are all acts of torture,
war atrocities, and crimes against humanity.

Hierarchy of Rape in War and Rape in Peace

We know that men have been raping and abusing women continuously over the past three thousand years. We know that the trauma suffered by war survivors is very similar to that experienced by women who have been battered or sexually abused by their partners. Finally, we know that an invisible war has been waged by men against women from the origins of civilization until the present. Given that we know all these things, why is male violence against women not considered a war crime? Clearly, there is ample scope for feminist jurisprudence to intervene in this area and lay the groundwork for a new understanding of war atrocities.

Hierarchy of Rights in Wartime

In times of war, there is usually room for only one human rights issue, namely that of who is to live and who is to die. While it is by no means surprising that this is the case, one of its consequences is that other forms of rights, along the lines of gender, ability, sexual orientation or race/ethnicity, are all too quickly forgotten or subsumed under the individual's will to survive.

Although it was not uncommon for human rights organizations, along with the peace movement in general, to fall into this trap, it was important for those involved in Women in Black Against War to avoid reproducing this hierarchy of rights. As such, we devoted considerable energy to the task of ensuring that the rights of all women, whether older or younger, lesbian or heterosexual, Roma or Serb, were respected and cherished.

Solidarity with Women Across the Front Lines

Throughout the war years, feminist groups in Belgrade were in constant communication with their counterparts in Croatia and Bosnia. We sent news, food and books, as well as making the journey ourselves across the front lines in order to meet with our sisters face-to-face. Building solidarity with women across the lines was both a personal and political objective, and remains a priority today in face of growing tensions in Kosovo.

International Solidarity with Women Around the World

In September 1992, we welcomed three women who had come to Belgrade from the small Italian town of Mestre in order to visit the SOS Hotline for Women and Children Victims of Violence. They knew no one here, had never been to Belgrade before, yet, because of their work against the war in Iraq, had decided that they should show their solidarity with women who were facing a similar prospect in the Former Yugoslavia. At the time, we did not really understand why they had traveled 14 hours by train in order to bring us chocolate and soap, visit with us, and then get on the train again to go back to Italy. Of course, at the time we also did not know what the war would entail nor the true meaning of women's solidarity in wartime. Only later did we come to understand these three incredible women. They were the first angels of support who would be followed by many others in the difficult years that followed, all of whom made personal sacrifices for our sake.

After five years of war there are many of us here who can say that women's solidarity in war has profoundly influenced our work and lives as feminists. We have welcomed countless women into our midst who have come to the Former Yugoslavia on their own initiative, using their own savings, to offer us support at both a material and emotional level. At the very beginning of the war, women from The Netherlands and Germany provided us with training in crisis intervention. Women from Austria gave lessons in self-defense, while women from Lausanne showed us how to take and develop photographs. A group of women drove trucks laden with foodstuffs all the way from Great Britain; these we distributed among women living in the refugee camps. Women from Seville and Madrid traveled to Belgrade in order to ask how we were and to mount an impromptu Flamenco show. Women from Freiburg sent us our first computer. Women in the United States sent us care packages which we gave to female refugees who were in need. Women from Australia sent us glittering paper stars that would reflect the sun if hung from the window. A few of the women who came decided to stay on in Belgrade, and are with us even now.

However, of all those who provided assistance and support over the years, few had a greater impact than the sixteen women from Switzerland who visited in December 1992 and told us, "Set up an organization for women raped in war and we'll provide you with the necessary financing." This is how the Autonomous Women's Center Against Sexual Violence came into being, and is what gave many of us a chance to become political activists in the full sense of the word. In this way, the solidarity that was part of our everyday lives during the war became inscribed in our minds and souls, and as such will remain with us for the rest of our lives.

Confusing Realities and Lessons Learned in Wartime: Supporting Women's Projects in the Former Yugoslavia

Ingrid Foeken

SUMMARY. The personal experiences of the author working with women's organizations in regions destabilized by war is the focus of this article. The author summarizes the results of a report commissioned by the Dutch government to analyze the state of para-professional work, describes her own work in the Former Yugoslavia and makes recommendations for the training of Western feminists to work in war regions. She also examines the effects of the trauma of doing this work on her own life. *[Article copies available for a fee from The Haworth Document Delivery Service: 1-800-342-9678. E-mail address: getinfo@haworthpressinc.com]*

KEYWORDS. Trauma, refugees, feminist counseling, nationalism, AD-MIRA

INTRODUCTION

Professional and Personal Motivation

When the war started in the summer of 1991, I had been working for ten years in the treatment of sexually traumatized women, including many with

Ingrid Foeken, MS, is a Dutch psychotherapist and social psychologist, specializing in lesbian feminist and international issues in private practice and with a Regional Institute for Mental Health in Amsterdam.

Address correspondence to: Ingrid Foeken, Okeghemstraat 16/ii, 1075 PM, Amsterdam, The Netherlands.

[Haworth co-indexing entry note]: "Confusing Realities and Lessons Learned in Wartime: Supporting Women's Projects in the Former Yugoslavia." Ingrid, Foeken. Co-published simultaneously in *Women & Therapy* (The Haworth Press, Inc.) Vol. 22, No. 1, 1999, pp. 91-106; and: *Assault on the Soul: Women in the Former Yugoslavia* (ed: Sara Sharratt and Ellyn Kaschak) The Haworth Press, Inc., 1999, pp. 91-106. Single or multiple copies of this article are available for a fee from The Haworth Document Delivery Service [1-800-342-9678, 9:00 a.m. - 5:00 p.m. (EST). E-mail address: getinfo@haworthpressinc.com].

histories of rape or incest who were suffering from dissociative problems or identity disorders. I had also engaged in research on the impact of confrontation between incest survivors, perpetrators and other family members. Thus, I felt that my experience, both as a psychotherapist and as an educator (in which capacity I have trained shelter and crisis hotline volunteers), could prove useful in the war-ravaged region of the Former Yugoslavia. In addition to the symptoms of post-traumatic stress disorder per se, I was well aware of the long-term dangers inherent in denying or repressing trauma experiences, and of the importance of real contact, of being there to listen to survivors talk about the atrocities committed against them. There have been many times that I have witnessed "wars" within families, so that I knew not to be surprised at the sadistic, impulsive and unpredictable behavior of which men, and sometimes women as well, are capable. I knew that dissociation, denial, hostility and scapegoating should not be seen as pathological reactions on the part of victims, but rather as normal responses in the face of unbearable life circumstances.

Societies have been all too willing to ignore the importance of grief and collectively acknowledging war injustice, and the Balkans are no exception, as is attested to by the perpetuation of revenge sentiments from one generation to the next. Thus, in deciding to work in the region, I not only hoped to gain some insight into the war situation itself, but I also wanted to help its victims, most of whom are women and children.

A good friend and psychologist from Belgrade phoned me one day just after the war started in 1991. She said, "I am no longer seen as a Yugoslavian feminist, but as a Serb, a citizen of the criminal nation that started the war and all these atrocities. As you know, I never chose this political system and I hate the politicians it's produced. I still think of myself as a Yugoslavian woman and an international feminist. Please be my witness. I need friends here who believe in the work we're doing, like that of the 'Women in Black' who protest every Wednesday in the center of Belgrade, as well as the SOS hotline we're running for raped and sexually abused women and girls. I need the warmth of friends from abroad to help energize me and keep me focused on the anti-war cause." For my friend, the war engendered feelings of helplessness and uncertainty. When she called, I was suddenly brought face-to-face with these feelings myself, and I was left with the sense that the only way forward was to try to transform my sense of powerlessness into concrete action.

Dutch Policy in the Wake of Publicity About Mass Rape

Prior to disbursing funding in support of women's projects in the Former Yugoslavia, the Dutch government commissioned a report analyzing the state of para-professional and volunteer organizations working with traumatized or war-raped refugee women (Foeken and Kleiverda, 1993). Gunilla Kleiverda, a gynecologist, and I spent three weeks in the region in September of 1993 gathering data for this report, which we subsequently presented to our government. A summary of our findings follows.

INTERVENTIONS

Most refugees were sheltered by their relatives, with only five percent in Serbia and thirty percent in Croatia housed in refugee camps. The principal problems they faced included lack of contact with family members who had remained in Bosnia-Herzegovina, tensions with host families, little opportunity for meaningful activities, uncertain prospects for the future, and poor mental health, itself the product of such traumas as the loss of home, family members and personal belongings. In the camps, mothers' wide-ranging responsibility for the care and education of their children would exacerbate feelings of apathy and depression, making them less likely to set limits upon the aggressive behavior of their offspring, angering camp leaders in the process. Children would latch onto teachers and other adults, making burnout that much more likely among these latter groups. As for more complex psychiatric problems, outside professionals visited the refugee camps whenever possible. For example, a Bosnian psychiatrist based in Zagreb organized regular group sessions for adolescents, ex-concentration camp prisoners, and women from different ethnic communities. However, she admitted to us how difficult it was for her group of professionals to integrate questions about rape, even if participants had no problem in discussing other violence-related issues. There was simply too much shame, and raped women were at risk of being driven out of their community if they were found out. Despite these difficulties, the group was very interested in receiving training in this field.

At a more general level, state mental health agencies were overwhelmed by the demands placed upon them, particularly in an environment in which lack of funding delayed or stopped altogether the payment of salaries. Indeed, many female professionals decided to leave their posts in order to work, on a volunteer basis, for feminist NGOs providing health services in the region.

The Implications of Nationalism

For many refugees who were forced to relocate for economic reasons or because of their ethnicity, retraumatization was a daily occurrence. Anti-Muslim sentiment ran so high on the Croatian coast, where refugees were housed in empty hotels, that some police agents would simply tear up the documents of Muslim individuals whom they encountered. The politically neutral stance of United Nations agencies and foreign NGOs was interpreted by many as evidence of anti-Croatian sentiment. We had occasion to experience this hatred directly, when stones were thrown at our vehicle when we were traveling in a United Nations car. In short, it was widely believed that the United Nations coddled the Serbian and Muslim refugees, providing them with two meals a day while many local people were forced to go hungry. It was also reported to us that there were cases of refugees being raped and beaten up by members of their "host" families. Needless to say, the level of general aggression in these societies had increased enormously over the war years.

It was also in this region that we encountered, for the first time, strong nationalist feelings, even among women. In one particularly telling incident, a leader of the Women's Association of Bosnia-Herzegovina grew angry with me when she heard of our plans to meet with feminists in Belgrade. In her view, Serbian feminists had no value, since they had betrayed their sisters elsewhere in the Former Yugoslavia, had done nothing to prevent the war, and had been shielded from the sexual attacks suffered by Croatian and Bosnian women. When I asked her what possible influence she thought Serbian feminists had over their government, she had no response.

As it was almost impossible to visit or send money to projects in Bosnia, and Serbian feminist organizations received little sympathy in any case, Croatian projects benefited disproportionately from international funding initiatives, with the Center for Women War Victims in Zagreb being an especially notable case. Individuals working at the Center were receiving salaries that were considered extravagant by local standards. Not only did this serve to engender widespread jealousy among area residents, but it led many non-feminist women to become involved in the project only because of the wages.

Meanwhile, in our hotel in Split (Croatia), pornographic pictures were shoved under our door and we received obscene calls during the night. We assumed that the hotel's owner was responsible. However, despite the crudeness of his acts, he was not alone in showing hostility to us. In several cases, professionals accused us of only wanting to work with Bosnian women, and of underestimating the suffering of Croatians. Obviously, it was all too easy to go astray in this nationalist minefield, and we were left with the sense that ADMIRA's philosophy of promoting transnationalism (see discussion below) by its insistence that support be given to women's groups regardless of ethnicity was more a case of wishful thinking than a reflection of actual conditions.

Politics served as a constant interference in the handling of the mass rapes. Politicians from all sides wanted gory accounts of rape and sexual abuse that they might present to the international community as evidence of the barbarity of their foes. Of course, in doing so, they showed themselves to be all too willing to sacrifice women's emotional recovery on the altar of political expediency. While these incidents served to underscore the extent to which nationalism and health care were working at cross-purposes to one another, they also highlighted serious problems among health workers themselves, including feminists, many of whom were competing to be first to exploit the stories the victims told.

Of course, foreign journalists were not blameless in this regard, fueling this exploitation by offering money to raped women who were English-speaking. Western governments' policy of making raped women a priority in aid programs was in many cases counterproductive, since it served to down-play the seriousness of other war crimes committed against women. In the end, I was left feeling very confused, since I had expected the issue of rape to be treated in a careful, respectful manner, only to discover a reality in which callousness and insensitivity were the norm.

Consequences of Rape

Although the number of women seeking abortions has doubled since the beginning of the war, hospital staff never ask why the abortion is being sought. While this is in part due to the fact that the procedure is generally far less controversial in Eastern European countries than it is in the West, it is also the case that many physicians did not want to know the answer. What would they do with the information? Also, we know of at least one incident where a colleague was raped by her husband who had come home drunk from the war zone. As one might imagine, such an attack was even more shameful for the victim than one inflicted upon her by the enemy.

In our workshops for mental health professionals and volunteers, the issue of sexual violence was ever-present. Participants often asked us if we thought it wise to ask clients directly whether or not they had been raped. In one scenario described to us, a 16-year-old girl was placed in care in a psychiatric hospital for refusing to speak and severe anorexia. She was the daughter of a Serbian father and Croatian mother and, over the course of several weeks, was subjected to multiple rapes by her father and his friends. She hated herself for being Serbian, and her revenge was to attempt to starve herself to death. Faced with these circumstances, we argued that it would be impossible to talk about the rapes at this point; of far greater importance was to make contact with her in a manner with which she could identify. The psychologists attending the workshop were relieved, as they had the idea that Western psychotherapists always address the issue of rape explicitly, without taking into account the particulars of a given case.

Other participants asked us to comment on the accuracy of their guesses regarding signs of sexual violence among concentration camp survivors. As an example, they referred to instances where mothers would adamantly declare that only they had been raped and their daughters had been spared, whereas the girls themselves showed signs of depression, recoiled at every touch, suffered from vaginal infections and spent long periods of time under the shower.

We suggested that the daughters could also be protecting their mothers. Women would often claim that they were forced to undress, but that they had been too skinny to be raped, or that they were spared because of their period. Everyone understood what it meant when a Bosnian woman arrived in the camp dressed in Croatian clothes, or when a woman hated and neglected her newborn child. Everyone knew, yet no one challenged the stories told. Thus, we agreed that all of the signs touched upon above could be indicative of a rape experience, and we supported them in integrating questions about rape into their discussions with this individual.

We also sought to emphasize the importance of seeing denial and repression as necessary survival mechanisms rather than pathologizing them. Interestingly, most workshop participants appeared not to be familiar with this perspective. Thus, we suggested that rape was one of many traumas where women should be encouraged to verbalize their feelings in order to overcome the sense of shame within them.

Issues Raised by Staff During the Consultation

Guilt feelings for not doing enough and individuals' sense of powerlessness in the face of so many multi-traumatized people were other areas touched upon during the workshops. We shared with those present the helplessness which we so often felt during the course of our own working lives, and noted that things must be far more difficult in a war situation. We stressed the importance of boundary issues and the need for self-protection. Although participants recognized immediately the risk volunteers ran of becoming entrapped in the "rescue triangle," we realized that further training about this issue would be needed.

During consultation, participants would often be left feeling drained and overwhelmed, so we would also ask them to share with us their successes as well as their problems. On one occasion, we suggested that we should try to find at least one funny thing in the midst of the misery. Several group members came forward to share humorous anecdotes, with one refugee describing, all the while laughing out loud, how she had seen a woman in Sarajevo rushing out of her house the moment a mortar exploded nearby to lock all of her doors and windows. The smoke blowing around her body while she was doing this gave her the appearance of a ghost. Having heard the story, all the participants burst out laughing.

In conducting workshops and consultations throughout the region, we were generally very impressed with the educational background of professionals working in the field, whether psychologists, psychiatrists or social workers. Some had been trained in the diagnosis of post-traumatic stress disorder. Thus, in many cases we were simply providing participants with information on recent theoretical advances in the field or giving them concrete suggestions that might prove helpful in their counseling work. At the same time they were very interested in learning about other countries' experiences in refugee counseling, indicating that there had been no local research done in this area, and that they believed that the extent of sexual violence during the war was unprecedented in their society. One woman went so far as to suggest that the latter may be due to the intrusion of Western capitalist values into the region. Incest was another area where information and training were lacking. However, volunteers were beginning to be faced with it more and more often, perhaps because women felt at greater ease talking about sexual violence than they had prior to the beginning of the war.

Although we found women's volunteer projects to be in a pioneering phase, with enthusiasm and willingness to learn new techniques and approaches, most were also in severe need of organizational support. The majority were being sustained through the charisma of their managers and the strong commitment of the volunteers.

Founding of ADMIRA

Presented with our recommendations, the Dutch government initiated funding of ADMIRA for three years, which it subsequently extended until 1999. Members of this new foundation included women's organizations working in the field of sexual violence, along with the Mental Health Institute for Refugees (Pharos) and a research center studying the sociological and psychological impact of the Second World War.

The Aim and Policy of ADMIRA

The purpose of ADMIRA was to provide information, advice, support and training for NGOs in the Former Yugoslavia working with multi-traumatized women from different ethnic and religious communities. However, following implementation of the Dayton peace accord, the emphasis has shifted somewhat toward the provision of support to key organizations, which would then be in a position to train other women's groups, networks of care providers and professional mental health agencies working with sexually traumatized refugees, women and children.

In order to carry out this mandate, eight trainers with a background in refugee counseling and sexual violence were dispatched to the region. The group was divided into four teams, each consisting of a specialist in one of the two areas. I was selected as one of the teacher/trainers. To participate, organizations had to have a policy of anti-nationalism and be willing to work with women and children of all ethnic and religious backgrounds.

My Experiences as a Trainer

Workshops were developed that focused upon the recovery process and staff empowerment. However, once the workshops were underway, we found that issues related to leadership, task management and delegation of responsibilities were just as important in many women's organizations as trauma counseling.

Developing Knowledge from Experience

The concept of experience-based knowledge is central to women's therapy. In short, insight into a particular problem is gained by analyzing one's own feelings, cognitions and conclusions, together with the reactions and responses of others. In the example below, I seek to illustrate what I mean by discussing a guided fantasy I used with workshop participants.

First, I asked group members to focus on their childhood and think of a secret that they had not shared with their mother or caregiver. Then they were to write down the reasons why they had not been able to tell their secret and what would have been necessary for them to do so. In sharing and analyzing the range of responses that this exercise engendered, the group learned that it is "normal" not to reveal a secret, how secrets isolate individuals, and how shame or fear of punishment prevents people from opening up. The exercise was also useful in establishing a connection between participants' childhood experiences and those of girls or women who have been sexually assaulted, in the process blurring the boundaries between "us" (the care providers) and "them" (the clients).

Along similar lines, emphasis was also placed upon the contradictions inherent in the mother-daughter relationship. For example, although men's violence is a given, it is seldom presented as an inevitable part of marriage. However, when daughters verbalized different, more romantic expectations of the men in their lives, mothers blamed them for being naive or stupid. Another issue that was frequently discussed in the workshops was the problems associated with men's inability to perform sexually, causing them to be rejected by their mates. As a number of women laughingly put it, "no fun, no marriage." I suggested that the increase in alcohol consumption by male war survivors may partially explain this problem, as would war traumatization itself.

Differences in political ideology were also a source of difficulty for many workshop participants, particularly among those who were Serbian. That is to say, parents would often accuse their daughters of disloyalty when they voiced their hatred for the war or indicated their preference to be identified as feminist rather than Serbian. After sharing these views, volunteers who worked on crisis hotlines (such as the SOS Telephone Hotline for Sexually Violated Women and Children in Belgrade) found it easier to understand their irritated reactions when listening to women who expressed nationalist sentiments, many of whom were members of the same generation as their mothers.

Learning Techniques for Counseling Clients

Although some techniques were readily adaptable to conditions in the Former Yugoslavia, others had to be modified somewhat. On the one hand, participants welcomed information on strategies to avoid feeling overwhelmed, such as self-protection measures which involved thinking about happy memories before sitting down with an individual suffering from severe trauma. On the other hand, techniques focused upon the development of a "safe place" in one's mind were generally less well-received. For example, our suggestion of imagining a forest caused one woman from Sarajevo to experience unpleasant flashbacks to the time she had to flee through the woods to escape the fighting. The suggestion of a beach was painful for many Serbian women because they were barred from traveling to the Dalmatian coast at that time. Faced with this situation, we asked those present to take a moment to comfort each other. At this point some group members criticized us for placing so much emphasis upon fantasy when the real world was so hard and cruel. We agreed whole-heartedly with this assessment, and argued that it was for precisely this reason that fantasy might play a useful role in helping them to cope. Another woman came forward to tell us that she had been living a fantasy life in Sarajevo the last few years, and was fed up with the need to do this. We indicated that we respected her position. We added that we had come to the Former Yugoslavia from a country that was at peace, and asked what we could do that would be preferable from their perspective. Needless to say, this experience taught us that we must be careful not to assume that strategies that work well in one context are necessarily the most appropriate in another.

In other cases, the women were so tense that conflicts within the group manifested themselves, making it impossible for us to relinquish a measure of control. Indeed, it was precisely in this context that we brought up the question of safety, stressing the importance of always maintaining self-control in dangerous situations, either by means of a pause for self-reflection or by focusing on one's breathing and physical feelings. Interestingly, once group members began to use these techniques themselves, their capacity to address other difficult issues was enhanced.

Techniques to Encourage Cooperation Among Participants

Personal conflict within organizations was identified as a problem that was becoming increasingly serious. As one might imagine, lack of communication was one of its root causes. Thus, considerable energy in the workshops was devoted to communication training, stressing the development of listening skills, distinguishing between feelings, opinions and intuition, giving positive feedback, being honest with one's emotions, and curbing destructive behavior such as projection. Generally speaking, participants found it extremely difficult to express their anger in a self-reflective manner and avoid scapegoating others. To make sense of this anger, we would first interview all of the individuals involved in a given organization, then analyze and categorize the different responses. In most cases, problems were due to one or more of the following reasons: the structure of the organization itself; the nature of its work; poor communication among staff members; lack of clearly defined roles; and issues related to leadership style or personality. Once we had undertaken the analysis, we would share the findings with all members of the group, and then help them work through the problem areas, thereby lessening the level of mistrust and facilitating communication.

While these exercises did not differ significantly from those we had previously undertaken with volunteer groups in The Netherlands, our efforts to help women's organizations in the Former Yugoslavia move toward greater professionalism and transparency were met with a markedly different reaction. Our attempts to encourage group members to invest in the development of their agency's organizational structure engendered considerable opposition, albeit at an unconscious level. At first we did not understand why participants were responding in this way, but it soon became obvious that the problem was in large part due to the fact that many were faced with such uncertainty in their own lives that long-term planning meant little to them. As several women asked us, why should they think of the future of the organization when it was what they were doing right now that was important? There was also significant resistance to the models of coordination and leadership we presented. Probing participants' feelings in this regard, we were told of the deep distrust, fear and anger that welled up inside them whenever they thought of the politicians who had brought so much grief to their country, both before and after the fall of communism. They tended to associate leaders with manipulation, deceitful power games, and only being interested in helping their cronies at the expense of all others. This in turn meant that women who attempted to assume a management position were also looked upon with suspicion or contempt by other members of the organization. However, after we discussed these issues in the workshop, the groups generally became more open to new models of coordination and task delegation. In our view, the disappearance of communism had left something of a vacuum where new forms of democratic governance needed to be developed.

Boundary Issues

As trainers, boundary issues often proved problematic for us. In one case, a para-professional asked me if I would be willing to meet with her for a private consultation in connection with a couples counseling issue. I agreed, and also accepted her choice of translator. In the meeting, she indicated to me that she was fearful she was taking sides in her work with a particular couple, and I helped find a solution to the problem with which she seemed happy. However, as I walked out of the room at the end of the session, the translator turned to me and said that the couple in question was her and her partner. I felt manipulated and asked them why they had not told me earlier; they replied that they thought I had known all along.

Boundary issues were also complicated by the war situation. Volunteers resented the fact that they were not being paid, and all the more so because of the long hours they worked, and the apparent lack of appreciation for their efforts on the part of the refugees. Meanwhile, the professional staff would become defensive and blame them for not setting limits or establishing clear boundaries. As one might imagine, communication group work was extremely helpful in addressing such conflicts.

Interdisciplinary Work

In our training workshops, we also encountered significant problems in the area of interdisciplinary cooperation. Although we offered facilitation to help work through these issues, there was great resistance to our interventions, particularly within those organizations dominated by physicians. In these instances, psychologists would generally serve as the survivor's advocate, defending her right to remain silent in the face of physicians' demands that she immediately reveal the details of her assault to the police or other state official. However, as the groups became sensitized to their colleagues' perspective, they were more likely to engage in cooperative behavior and support each other's interventions.

Among the other issues raised by workshop participants in this regard, many wanted to hear about the working relationship between gynecologists and psychologists in the West and what I, as a psychotherapist based in The Netherlands, thought gynecologists in the Former Yugoslavia should know. Interestingly, it was precisely in this context that cultural differences between the trainers and the participants arose. My partner, herself a gynecologist, suggested that physicians may wish to give a small mirror to patients during the course of a gynecological exam with the aim of familiarizing women with their bodies and giving them a greater sense of control. When she said this, all those present started to laugh and suggested that the patients were more likely to use the mirror to look at their hair. However, the next day one of the physicians did offer a mirror to a patient, who was curious enough to use it in the proposed manner. As long as one is in a position to make one's own choice, the chance to act in a novel or unconventional way can be refreshing.

Hate and Guilt Divided Feminists

As one might imagine, we were particularly interested in working in Serbia, as this would give us the opportunity to hear the perspective of the war's "perpetrators." At the beginning of the conflict, the guilt feelings of the Serbian volunteer staff were overwhelming, causing them to feel torn between their sense of shame and their belief that Serbia was being unfairly demonized by its neighbors and the international community. However, the wish to help former friends and refugees from all ethnic communities was great. In the words of one Serbian woman, "The war is the most awful and shameful experience of my life, but I also want to do what I can for the refugees and other traumatized women." Many volunteers kept in regular touch with their old friends in Sarajevo, sending them letters and care packages, as well as crawling through a tunnel under the city's occupied airport in order to visit them in person.

The multi-ethnic professionals working for Medica Zenica emphasized to us the importance of personal friendships in preventing the perpetuation of hatred. For example, when Bosnian Croats rampaged through villages in the northeastern region of Bosnia-Herzegovina, burning houses and killing people, one of the organization's Croatian staff members felt ashamed because she knew that her colleague's parents lived in one of the affected towns. She did not dare speak to her friend, fearful that she had lost all respect in her eyes. However, the Bosnian staff member sought her out and said, "I need your friendship now more than ever before; otherwise I'll start hating all Croatians and I don't want that." In this way, not only did the friendship survive, but it helped each of them avoid generalizing their hatred to an entire nation. At a broader level, it is clear that feminists, both locally and internationally, have invested a great deal of effort into bridge-building between communities split by war and hatred.

The Psychological Power Balance and Internalized Oppression

In order to gain a deeper understanding of difference and the unconscious mechanisms which serve to discipline and control marginalized groups, we asked the participants of a large workshop to write down on a piece of paper the various "majority" and "minority" groups to which they belonged. We all have mixed identities, and group members mentioned many of them: ethnicity, class, religion, (dis)ability, age, sexual orientation, gender, marital status, among others. We collected all of the responses, divided them into "majority" and "minority" categories, and proceeded to discuss ways in which power differentials among women might be reduced or overcome. One suggestion involved always endeavoring to be honest and listen carefully to the words of others without interruption. To illustrate the importance of this type of healing work, a disabled woman suffering from muscular dystrophy was asked to describe some of the challenges she faced in her everyday life. She touched upon a range of issues, including the tendency of some to question her in a highly offensive way. Most of the women present had never realized how one's unconscious actions help to reproduce oppression and injustice. In another exercise, we asked two women, one lesbian, the other heterosexual, to engage in a role play. Their interactions gave the group considerable pause for thought, with one lesbian woman describing the intense loneliness she had felt her whole life, along with the forms of discrimination she has faced. The support the women gave each other and me in this session was very useful in promoting healing and countering internalized oppression.

ADMIRA's Dutch Trainer Group

As trainers, we held regular meetings in order to share experiences and discuss logistical or administrative issues. However, in spite of our best intentions, differences of opinion often arose during the course of these meetings. For example, several organizations asked for training that did not comply with ADMIRA's criteria for inclusion in the program. While a strict interpretation of our policy demanded that they be excluded, extenuating circumstances often made us reluctant to take this step. In one particularly telling case, a Croatian women's project that was characterized as nationalist by international feminists, had applied to participate in the training. We were forced to weigh their nationalist designation against the fact that they reached many Bosnian and Croatian rape survivors and ex-prisoners from concentration camps. Although there was a heated debate among the trainer group, in the end ADMIRA agreed to the NGO's request. In another instance, the Belgrade Mental Health Institute submitted an application to us. None of the trainers was willing to become involved with this organization because it was both Serbian and non-feminist. However, because of its background in providing support to many survivors of sexual violence, we added two new educators to the group so that we might offer the Institute the training it had requested. In this way, we sought to make use of pragmatic means of dealing with the challenges at hand.

Related to these problems was the fact that trainers found it difficult to stay aloof from the ethnic conflicts that surrounded them. In several cases, educators became partisans of the community from which "their" project had emerged, resulting in considerable rivalry among the trainers. However, we were for the most part successful in keeping this rivalry in check during our meetings.

CONCLUSIONS

The realities of working with women's organizations in a region destabilized by war make it impossible to plan exhaustively or place cast iron limits upon the scope of one's activities. In the context of ADMIRA's work in the Former Yugoslavia, we were often forced to change our agenda in the face of cuts in staff or exhausted personnel. Moreover, competition among international organizations, national agencies and women's NGOs proved to be a significant obstacle to cooperation and coordination. Finally, all of our interventions took place against a backdrop of growing nationalism and ethnic cleansing, which in some regions continues to this day. As Western educators are still asked to share their knowledge with local groups, it behooves the latter to sensitize themselves to local contexts and to recognize that not all nationalisms are alike. That is to say, one should not attempt to equate any and all verbal expressions of hatred with the National Socialism of Adolf Hitler (Pusic, 1994).

Because feminist organizations tend to identify less with particular ethnic communities and more with a transnational sisterhood of women, many female refugees avoid seeking help from agencies characterized as feminist. Thus, by distinguishing between the different forms of nationalism as Pusic (1994) suggests, one is placed in a position where one can engage in meaningful collaboration with the wide range of organizations that work with severely traumatized women, yet do not have a clear feminist perspective.

RECOMMENDATIONS FOR TRAINERS

Many of the Western trainers who take it upon themselves to work in areas affected by war are motivated by their own personal histories and traumas, such as rape, incest, sexual assault or victimization in a previous conflict. Although they are able to deal with the effects of these traumatic experiences in their home countries, being exposed to the legacy of war can be exceedingly disturbing in its own right, and thus it is important that individuals prepare themselves for this eventuality.

In a somewhat different vein, although burnout prevention is an issue that receives considerable attention in training sessions for field staff, I would argue that secondary traumatization is inevitable for all those involved in such work, including the trainers. In short, not only is there a tendency to make the unconscious distinction between "us" and "them," recreating confusing or dysfunctional patterns of interaction in the process, but individuals' exposure to a multiplicity of extreme traumas necessarily affects their ability to function. To counter these problems, training must include the development of a system whereby care providers can express their innermost feelings and emotions. In parallel fashion, a similar system must be put into place in the trainers' home country if the latter are to avoid burnout or the adoption of unhealthy coping mechanisms. Steps must be taken to address the "mirroring" phenomenon, which causes outsiders to lose their detachment and become party to the conflicts of their host country. This was seen within the team of Dutch trainers, who were at times indistinguishable from the warring communities of the Former Yugoslavia. Thus, rather than merely focusing upon what the trainers can do for those they will be working with, adequate attention must be paid to the "mirroring" issue and the best means of avoiding it.

Shame is another problem with which trainers must contend. Labeled "experts," we arrive in the region only to discover that we know far less than we thought. This in turn leads to feelings of powerlessness and lack of confidence in our own abilities, reactions that are themselves part of the secondary traumatization process. In this way, trainers become indirect victims of the war.

One must also be sensitive to the fact that not all theoretical insights that are useful in the West are readily transferable to other cultural and sociopolitical contexts. Post-traumatic stress disorder is a case in point. Given that individuals' trauma in the Former Yugoslavia is rooted in the political structures and conflicts of the region, post-traumatic stress is a misnomer, since the violence and hatred are ongoing. Thus, trainers' focus must be changed so as to incorporate peace work into their interventions. Similarly, even as one acknowledges the usefulness of physical exercises, guided fantasies and other creative techniques in the training workshops, one must also be wary of using symbols or images that may trigger unexpected flashbacks related to the war.

Finally, it is important to recognize the key significance of feminists' efforts to build ties and friendships that transcend the bounds of nationalism, helping to break them down in the process. In my view, one of the most valuable aspects of our work in the region has been the contacts and connections it has helped to engender between women of diverse cultures and backgrounds.

Still, there can be little doubt that the time I spent in the Former Yugoslavia, along with the fifteen years I had spent as a psychotherapist before that, has taken its toll on me. I returned to Holland experiencing many of the same symptoms described in this article: exhaustion, shame, confusion, anger and a profound sense of powerlessness. Faced with these problems, I decided it was in my best interest to take a year of medical leave. I started taking art courses, visiting museums and focusing on the beauty of life. It has been a long journey, but I have slowly recovered my sense of joy and optimism.

REFERENCES

Foeken, I. and Kleiverda, G. (1993), *Missie naar voormalie Joegoslavie: inventarisatie van mogelÿkheden tot ondersteuning van hulp aan verkrachte en getraumatiseerde vrouwen*, Utrecht: ADMIRA.
Pusic, V. (1994), *Uses of nationalism and the politics of recognition*, Erasmus, Zagreb: Gilda, pp. 3-21.

Traumatized Women Working with Traumatized Women: Reflections upon Life and Work in a War Zone

Gabriele Krämer

SUMMARY. In this article, the author shares both her personal and professional experiences in working with women and children who have been subjected to soul-destroying violence in the Former Yugoslavia in recent years. *[Article copies available for a fee from The Haworth Document Delivery Service: 1-800-342-9678. E-mail address: getinfo@haworthpressinc. com]*

KEYWORDS. Bosnia, Tuzla, trauma, women's projects, refugees

Although one might argue that there is nothing unique or novel in the kind of soul-destroying violence that has killed so many in the Former Yugoslavia in recent years, what is remarkable is the fact that it took place in the heart of Europe, less than one hour by airplane from Germany. Also extraordinary is the solidarity shown by women from all over the world with their counterparts living in the war zone. In this article, I would like to share with you my own experiences in this regard.

Gabriele Krämer, PhD, is a clinical psychologist in private practice specializing in working with women and children.

Address correspondence to: Gabriele Krämer, Prinz-Friedrich-Karl-Strasse 34, D-44135 Dortmund, Germany.

[Haworth co-indexing entry note]: "Traumatized Women Working with Traumatized Women: Reflections upon Life and Work in a War Zone." Krämer, Gabriele. Co-published simultaneously in *Women & Therapy* (The Haworth Press, Inc.) Vol. 22, No. 1, 1999, pp. 107-120; and: *Assault on the Soul: Women in the Former Yugoslavia* (ed: Sara Sharratt and Ellyn Kaschak) The Haworth Press, Inc., 1999, pp. 107-120. Single or multiple copies of this article are available for a fee from The Haworth Document Delivery Service [1-800-342-9678, 9:00 a.m. - 5:00 p.m. (EST). E-mail address: getinfo@haworthpressinc.com].

THE CONTEXT

"Just start at the beginning," was the answer I received when I said that I did not know how to begin or what to write. But when did it all begin? I became aware of the escalating violence in the Former Yugoslavia in 1991, at the same time that Germany was reeling from a wave of neo-fascist militancy, characterized by numerous attacks upon immigrants and asylum seekers. Taken together, these events conjured up for me images of the Second World War, the stories my parents had told me, the flight of my mother and sister, and my shame and guilt for being German.

It was in this frame of mind that one day I visited some old friends from Kurdistan, and well remember my sense of anger and helplessness when I saw the fear in their eyes and the knives they kept on hand should skinheads attempt to burn down their home. It was precisely the same feeling that swept over me when I first read of the mass rapes being committed in Bosnia. Will we never learn anything from history? Is humankind fated to repeat the same mistakes over and over again until finally there is no one left to kill?

With these thoughts in the back of my mind, I did not hesitate for a moment when a friend asked me to become involved in a woman's aid project she was in the process of developing. It was no longer enough merely to attend demonstrations or engage in intellectual debate; the time had come to do something, and three of us, three women, sat down in order to plan what this would be. However, it soon became obvious to us that we would not be able to determine what was needed by Bosnian women and children so long as we remained in a living room in Germany. Instead, we would have to travel to the region and ask the women themselves what they needed and what they wanted us to do.

Thus, in June 1993 we set out for Tuzla (Bosnia). We had decided on this destination for two reasons, first because of the political situation–the town was under the control of a coalition (non-nationalist) government–and secondly, because we had a number of local contacts. However, our journey was not an easy one. In the first instance, we had to struggle to obtain a permit from the UNCHR headquarters in Zagreb to enter Bosnia. They asked us for evidence of support from an international aid organization, and smiled when we told them of our plans to implement a women's project in the war zone. In the end we did obtain the necessary permits, though only thanks to the timely intervention of DHH, a German humanitarian organization engaged in work throughout the region.

The next stage of our trip was equally harrowing. Landing in Sarajevo in the midst of shelling, we were transported by armored car to a United Nations base in Kiseljak, and from there by jeep to Zenica. This is where the waiting began, since Tuzla was being blockaded at the time and the main road was impassable due to fighting in the area. Eventually, we were able to secure a ride with a supply convoy organized by a group of ex-soldiers from Britain. Traveling along small mountain tracks with the sound of shelling and machine gun fire in the distance, we were very glad when we arrived safely at our destination. We were immediately struck by the apparent lack of life: no cars, no noise and no electricity. However, the town was not lifeless. Children were playing in front of their homes, and it seemed that every open area–even balconies and terraces–was being used for growing fruits and vegetables. Meanwhile, walking into the hotel lobby was like entering a man's world of Bosnian soldiers, UN personnel and French Legionnaires with rifles slung casually over their shoulders, talking with one another or sipping drinks at the bar. Everyone appeared to be astonished by our presence, and by the fact that we had come all the way from Germany to find a project or agency to which we could lend our support.

Although the level of need in Tuzla was obviously immense, most of the organizations that were active in the town were either strongly nationalist in character or only interested in providing support to maimed or injured combatants. We spent two months in the region evaluating the needs and wishes of local women, in the process meeting a wide range of individuals, from refugees and displaced persons, to politicians and psychiatrists. While area residents were clearly trying to lead as normal a life as possible under the circumstances, there was no doubt in our minds that the war was taking a dreadful toll upon their minds and bodies. The local hospital, for example, was chronically short of basic medical supplies, with doctors and nurses forced to work long hours under the most primitive conditions imaginable.

If this were not shocking enough, refugee camps in the vicinity of Tuzla were characterized by even greater deprivation. Hundreds of women, children and elders crowded into a large hall, without any privacy and everything they owned sitting in a cardboard box under their bed. "What do you want?," they shouted at us during our visit to one of the camps. "Did you just come to stare? Either go back home, or tell the world about us!" Their anger was palpable, as was their pain in the face of the terrible losses and atrocities inflicted upon them.

In the end, having consulted widely, and profoundly moved by the suffering around us, we decided to focus our energies upon the development of a center that would provide psychotherapeutic counseling to traumatized women and children. Although we envisioned ourselves playing a key role in its genesis and early growth, it was to be a project that would be run by Bosnian women for Bosnian women. We returned to Germany in August 1993, and I spent the following months writing proposals and searching for funding bodies willing to support our initiative.

We made our next trip to Bosnia in December of the same year, after having secured our first funding commitment from a women's organization associated with the German Evangelical Church. However, their support was conditional upon one of us overseeing the implementation of the project in the field. Needless to say, we were all aware of the living conditions in Tuzla at the time, and we were all afraid. I, for one, spent long hours deliberating whether or not I should accept the assignment, and finally decided to do so during the course of our visit to a women's project that was already in place in Zenica. We spent five days here before traveling on to Tuzla, where the situation had clearly deteriorated since our last visit. It was winter, mortally cold, and we heard numerous reports of people dying of hunger or killing themselves. Still, we had much with which to busy ourselves: renting a building; preparing contracts and meeting with the local women who would work on the project with us.

I made one final trip to Germany before relocating to Tuzla on a more permanent basis. It was at this time that I quit my job as a hospital psychologist, as well as engaging in fund-raising and other tasks necessary for project implementation. When I was finally ready to set out in March 1994, I was fortunate enough to be able to take advantage of a new air service operating between Sarajevo and the American Air Force base outside of Frankfurt. As one might imagine, this cut down considerably on my travel time, allowing me to arrive in Tuzla while still in relatively good spirits. In possession of one lap-top computer and limited financing, the two Bosnian women and I began work immediately on the new Center. Looking back on these early days with the hindsight I now enjoy, I would say that I was strongly motivated, but very, very naive.

THE PROJECT

As previously stated, the aim of the initiative was to provide counseling to women and children traumatized by the war, regardless of their ethnic or religious backgrounds. In embarking upon this task our first priority was to establish a center that would function as both a hospital and women's shelter. Given the degree to which women were being re-traumatized on a daily basis, it was critical that a safe environment be created; only then would recovery become possible. When the center opened in June 1994, it became home for 18 women and 40 children, with the average length of stay being approximately eight months.

Once this phase of the project was operational, we turned our attention to two further areas of intervention. The first of these was centered upon the creation of a mobile unit of psychologists who would provide individual and group therapy, as well as support the development of self-help groups in the refugees camps surrounding Tuzla. The unit visited its first camp in August 1994, with an average of 90 women receiving counseling on each occasion.

In 1995 the unit was provided with an ambulance, so that medical care could be offered alongside its counseling services.

Our third priority was to furnish the women who came to the Center with the means to become self-sufficient afterwards, so that they would not have to return to the refugee camps. To this end, we acquired three houses (with a total capacity of 40 women and 90 children), each offering its own distinct range of services. House objectives are summarized below:

1. Women living in the first house were interested in enhancing their educational credentials while organizing their own lives. A coordinator was hired in October 1994 to oversee project implementation, with psychologists and social workers available on call.
2. Opened in March 1995, this house was geared towards women who wished to live independently yet have ready access to support services should the need arise.
3. Centered around an agricultural initiative, women living here were given the chance to become involved in an income-generating activity. This house opened its doors in the summer of 1995.

All of the women involved in the project were integrated into a therapeutic model comprised of the following elements:

Medical care (somatic interventions and psychotherapy)
Therapies (psychotherapy, body therapy, art therapy, among others)
Social work (counseling by a social worker; help in searching for missing family members; assistance in planning life goals)
Education (day care services; training in literacy, sewing, computers and languages)

As much as possible, we attempted to involve everyone in the day-to-day operation of the houses and the Center. For example, residents were expected to help prepare meals and work in the garden, as well as being responsible for the upkeep of their own room. In the later stages of the project, once we had acquired sewing machines and looms, the women were also given the opportunity to make clothes or carpets during their spare time. Finally, staff and residents would assemble every week for a general meeting, in which disputes would be resolved, proposals tabled and schedules drawn up.

By the end of 1994, the project employed a total of 30 staff members, drawn from all ethnic communities and encompassing a wide range of competencies. Moreover, personnel were divided into four separate teams: Technical/administrative support, Therapies, Medical care, and Education. General staff meetings were held once a month, while therapists met on a weekly basis. I served as project coordinator, meeting with team managers on a regular basis in order to address key issues and engage in strategic planning.

Of course, in assessing the project's structure and objectives, it bears emphasis that our original plan, when we first set out for Bosnia in June 1993, was more narrow in scope than that upon which we subsequently agreed. How so? In short, while we had intended to focus our efforts solely upon those women who had been raped or sexually assaulted, it quickly became obvious to us that women in Bosnia were being victimized in any number of ways, sexually, physically and psychologically. Although it was this awareness that prompted us to refer to our project as a psychotherapeutic center for traumatized women and children, we were also aware of the dangers inherent in such a name, most notably that of obscuring women's suffering on account of rape and other forms of sexual violence. In the face of this risk, we have made it a priority to bring the issue out into the open whenever possible, both with the women who were taking part in the project and the public more generally.

When we first began work in the Tuzla area, we did not have a clear sense of how many of the women who came to the Center or whom we visited in the camps had been raped. We did not ask, though in some cases they would broach the topic themselves; in others we would simply guess. However, as we became more and more familiar with local conditions, we were left in no doubt of the full extent of women's victimization. Quite simply, not only had almost all of the women living in the camps been forced to flee their homes, but most had also witnessed the torture and killing of family members. Indeed, we know of several cases where individuals had lost 30 or more male relatives, including husbands, fathers, brother and sons. If this were not traumatic enough in itself, many women were subsequently raped and tortured by militia forces, as well as being subjected to psychological humiliation by government officials and others.

Given this context, it is not surprising that the women bore terrible scars, at both the physical and psychological level. Among those who came to the Center, their symptoms were usually quite similar, encompassing loss of self-esteem, depression, mood swings, somatic illnesses and flashbacks, to name but a few. While in some instances we also encountered individuals with a distorted perception of reality or suffering from dissociative identity disorder, in all cases the scope for destructive behavior was considerable: many were addicted to one or more pharmaceutical drugs, while outbursts of extreme anger toward their children or other residents were not uncommon.

Although we had hoped at the outset to focus much of our attention upon the recovery of women and children traumatized by war, we soon discovered that the need for crisis intervention was such that at least some of our energies would have to be reoriented in this direction. Not only were there relatively few relief agencies operating in the area, but the refugee population was immense, consisting of roughly 300,000 individuals (predominantly women, children and elders) living both in camps and in the town itself.

THE REALITY

I spent my first three months in Tuzla engaged in a frenzy of activity: obtaining permits, hiring staff, arranging for telephone and electrical hook-ups, buying furniture and countless other tasks. It was also at this time that I became aware of the size of the challenge that lay before me. Not only were bribes routinely demanded of us by public officials anxious to enrich themselves at our expense, but we were initially faced with considerable hostility on the part of refugee camp administrators, who were either unwilling to let us into the camps in the first place or insisted that any woman who returned with us to the Center would immediately lose all of her rights as a refugee. Needless to say, this placed us in a difficult position, which we only managed to resolve with the assistance of Tuzla's mayor.

In the end, the Center welcomed its first residents on June 15th, 1994. The initial complement consisted of 18 women and 40 children; all were from the region surrounding Srebenica and most had lost the majority of their male relatives. From the very first day of the Center's operation, the work was at once difficult and empowering. Most of the staff had other jobs, and thus would spend part of the day working elsewhere, and part of the day at the Center. However, for all those whom we hired, the hard currency they earned played a crucial role in helping them meet their families' basic needs.

In light of the working conditions, not to mention the anxiety which many staff members experienced when thinking about their children at home or family members in other parts of the country, it should come as no surprise that we were forced to contend with interpersonal conflicts within the organization, either between myself and employees, or between employees and residents. As one might imagine, language differences were especially problematic in this regard; only three staff-members could communicate in English or German, and my own language training was proceeding at a frustratingly slow pace. Thus, not only was it impossible at first to engage in casual conversation with employees (since a translator was necessary for interaction to occur), but the risk of misunderstanding was omnipresent. However, the situation improved substantially once we began to offer personnel foreign language training, and once I became more confident about my own language abilities.

As I have already suggested above, the relationship between residents and staff members also proved to be problematic. In large part, this was due to the fact that most of our employees were from cities or towns, whereas the overwhelming majority of refugees, including those taking part in the project, had lived in rural areas before being displaced by the war. On the one hand, this meant that there were significant cultural differences between the two groups, with city-based women generally having far more scope to travel, obtain an education or pursue a career than their rural-based counterparts. On the other, the Bosnian countryside suffered disproportionately from the war-time violence, causing many of the refugees to resent city dwellers for escaping relatively unharmed, with their homes intact and their family members alive.

Psychotherapy is a relatively new field in Bosnia. Individuals who wish to specialize in this discipline must travel either to Zagreb or Belgrade for the necessary training. As such, I had absolutely no luck in finding psychotherapists living in the Tuzla area who would be willing to become involved in the Center's work. In order to overcome this difficulty, I located a number of psychologists, social workers and educators and told them that I would help train them providing that they were willing to learn, and would be supportive of the life contexts of those with whom they would be working.

The first therapy session took place shortly after the Center opened. Needless to say, everyone involved was anxious and insecure, ensuring that we had plenty to discuss during our initial staff meeting. However, despite the fact that I was taking part in these meetings every week, it took some time before I realized that many key issues related to the work and the patients were simply not being addressed in an adequate fashion. It took even longer before it dawned upon me that I was part of the problem. Quite simply, the therapists were struggling with a number of challenges, the risk of secondary traumatization not least among them, and they needed a safe place where they could work things through without constantly feeling the need to prove themselves (as they did when I was present).

However, even as I acknowledged the importance of providing the therapists with adequate support and positive reinforcement, I lost touch with my own needs and boundaries. That is to say, I was so absorbed in fulfilling my responsibilities to the project–as coordinator, fund-raiser, psychotherapist, referee and resident strong woman–that I ignored the warning signals my body was sending me. In the end, it took a series of setbacks, including a medical operation in Germany and an attack by six soldiers in my home in Tuzla, before I started asking why I was not taking better care of myself. Although this awareness did not lead me to make an immediate change in my lifestyle or activities, I began to devote more and more time to writing in my journal, as well as making a number of weekend trips to the coast in order to visit with a friend from Germany who was working with another organization. Also helpful in this regard was the decision to restructure the work teams, with the art and physiotherapists transferred from Therapies to the Education and Medical Care teams respectively. In so doing, the therapists were placed in a position where they could meet as a small group every week in a closed session, and discuss work-related problems, as well as other pertinent issues. Finally, it was also roughly at this time that I organized a "self-experience" retreat for all staff members in a Tuzla area hotel. It proved to be a good experience for all of us. Not only did the change in venue make it easier for people to open up and be frank with one another and me, but the exercise helped to engender a new atmosphere of mutual respect and understanding.

Needless to say, it was largely this atmosphere that provided the basis for the project's success and growth over the first two years of its existence. Not only did the purchase of an ambulance substantially increase our capacity to serve the needs of refugee camp residents, but we started increasingly to plan and implement new initiatives, such as computer and language training for the women living at the Center and in the houses. However, at the very moment we were registering these successes, the political situation in the region was becoming increasingly unstable, with the kidnapping of United Nations peace keepers, NATO air strikes against Bosnian Serb military targets, and, in July 1995, the capture of UN safe havens in Srebenica and Zepa by the Bosnian Serb militia. In all, 40,000 people were forced to flee, of which a significant proportion ended up in the Tuzla area.

As the new refugees arrived, we began to make arrangements to accommodate additional residents at the Center. However, we were immediately struck by the fact that these women had substantially different psychological profiles than those who had fled to Tuzla previously. Although many had emerged from their ordeals severely traumatized, having been subjected to rape and other forms of physical and psychological torture, the memories were so fresh in their minds that they had not had time to repress them. Given this finding, we launched into counseling as quickly as possible, and found that, for a significant number of women, a series of regular meetings for debriefing proved quite helpful, obviating the need for long-term therapy.

However, as horrible as the attacks upon Zepa and Srebenica undoubtedly were, the real turning point in the conflict was not until December 1995, when the Dayton peace agreement was ratified by the warring parties. Although the refugees and residents of Tuzla were happy that peace was at hand, the vast majority were exceedingly disappointed by the terms of the Dayton accord, most notably its willingness to recognize Serb sovereignty over the Srebenica region. In effect, this meant that the bulk of Tuzla's refugee population would never be able to return home again.

While the Center's social worker continued to devote much of her energies to the task of locating missing family members on behalf of residents, others' husbands began slowly to trickle into the Tuzla area, many having not seen their wives for well over two years. Not surprisingly, this was often the source of considerable tension, since both wives and husbands had undergone significant traumatic experiences, and many women were loathe to give up the relative autonomy and independence they had enjoyed during the war years. In this way, spousal abuse rapidly became a serious problem within refugee families, as men sought to compensate for their low self-esteem by assaulting, raping and sometimes even killing their marital partners.

In the midst of these developments, we continued to carry out the mandate of the Center to the best of our abilities. Moreover, we were particularly gratified to learn that a German organization had agreed to provide specialized training to our therapists during the first half of 1996, as well as offering body therapy to Center residents. Finally, it was also at this time that we started to prepare for my own departure from Tuzla in February 1996. Having originally planned to stay for one year, which was subsequently extended to two, the time had come to step out of the way so that project staff could take charge themselves. However, we agreed that I would continue to serve in an advisory capacity from Germany, and would endeavor to ensure continued funding for the project until such time that it became wholly self-sufficient.

THERAPY

When I first arrived in Tuzla, I was simply too busy with project logistics to spend much time thinking about the implications of undertaking therapy in an unstable environment in which traumatization was ongoing. Moreover, even when I did become sensitive to this issue, there seemed to be little that could be done. I was immersed in a cultural context with which I had little familiarity; my colleagues were for the most part inexperienced and not confident; and there was essentially no scope for bringing in outside experts so long as the town was under a state of siege. Thus, we had no choice but to attempt to find our own way of working with clients and overcoming the challenges inherent in the environment in which we found ourselves.

As one might imagine, these difficulties were themselves exacerbated by problems in adapting therapeutic approaches to the life contexts of clients. That is to say, whereas the therapies had been designed for work with individuals who were well-educated and lived in a Western industrialized country, the women involved in the project had little formal education and emerged from a cultural background that was at once highly traditional and patriarchal in its orientation. Sensitive to these differences, the challenge we faced was one of making contact with the women while at the same time resisting the urge to force our theories, structures and techniques upon them.

Given my own background as a German woman who had no previous work experience in the Former Yugoslavia, I found this to be particularly difficult. In short, not only was I forced to modify many of my expectations and assumptions, but it also became clear to me that I would have to have the courage to leave the "normal" structure of therapy if I was to reach the women with whom I was working. This latter point was brought home to me in particularly stark terms in August 1994, when the husband of one of the residents returned to Tuzla, having managed to escape from a Serb-run concentration camp. His description of the atrocities committed there left all of the other women in a deep state of depression (as many had relatives who were being held in the same camp), and there seemed to be no way of making contact with them. At wit's end, I decided spontaneously that I would organize a special evening of music and dancing, having noticed previously how much the women appeared to enjoy singing and listening to the old traditional songs. The evening proved to be a remarkable success, with everyone–even those who had until that point been entirely non-communicative and apathetic–taking part in the festivities. For me, the night also brought understanding, highlighting as it did the extent to which something as seemingly mundane as music could bring the women back to their roots, and give them the sense of being on common ground.

After this evening I began to notice myself interacting with the residents in a different way, as I placed more and more emphasis upon uncovering their feelings, relationships, and ways of understanding the world around them. For example, in the sessions I held with women living in one of the Center's houses, I suggested that we rearrange the meeting room, replacing the tables and chairs with pillows on the floor in traditional Bosnian fashion. Having done so, everyone felt more at ease, and increasingly willing to talk about their lives prior to the war, whether their childhood, their family, or their first contact with men. Like the music and dancing, storytelling offered the women a means of regaining a lost sense of identity and stability.

Still, this is not to suggest that the latter was the only therapeutic technique used in the sessions. On the one hand, we engaged in a number of exercises involving imagination and dreams, though I was always careful to avoid references to images (such as forests) that might bring back unpleasant memories of the war. To the extent that I was successful in doing so, participants found the exercises to be quite helpful, particularly those involving the seaside and inner helpers (e.g., wise women). On the other hand, I also made ample use of drawing and painting as a way of helping the women to come to terms with their pain and shame, feelings that had led many of them to abuse or mistreat their children. Needless to say, this latter behavior was especially disturbing in light of the fact that the children were often severely traumatized themselves, forcing us to devote considerable energy to the task of working through this issue with both parties.

However, regardless of the therapy used, it quickly became apparent to us that the degree of traumatization, among both women and children, was immense by any standard. Indeed, many could only make sense of their suffering by placing it within the context of a plot designed specifically to punish them, at a personal level, for misdeeds which they had committed in the past. In other words, they were incapable of grounding their trauma in the wider political and social structures of which they were part. Thus, our aim in working with the women was to help them overcome their sense of helplessness and guilt. However, as strenuously as we tried to empower and reenergize them, we were often unsuccessful. In these cases, we simply attempted to provide the women with a set of structures around which they could organize their lives, and support them step-by-step in their journey towards independence and autonomy.

Of course, an important element in this regard was the fact that we were there to bear witness for them, and to affirm them in naming those who were responsible for their suffering. This was neither the time nor the place for neutrality; the crimes were too horrible, and the women were simply too much in need of someone who would be there for them and believe in the stories they told. However, this is not to suggest that the therapists were unaware of the dangers of transference and counter-transference, leading them to pay particular attention to boundary issues in the sessions they held with the women. While it was vital that staff members protect themselves from the effects of secondary traumatization and burnout, it was also important that they assist the clients in recovering a sense of control over their everyday lives, for example, by showing them how to manage traumatic memories in a constructive fashion.

Reference has already been made to the problems inherent in attempting to provide therapy in a context where one's clients are being re-traumatized on a daily basis. Almost all of the women taking part in the project had been forced to flee their homes, taking only what they could carry with them, and most had missing family members as well. Needless to say, this made it very difficult for them to acquire a sense of closure, and all the more so because their lives continued to be circumscribed by the violence around them. Obviously, this presented us with a serious challenge, made that much worse by the fact that many of the women were not willing to accept closure in any case, since this would entail admitting to themselves that there was no hope of returning to their old homes or old ways of life.

Indeed, from this perspective it must be acknowledged that much of our work in Tuzla was focused upon crisis intervention and supporting women as they struggled to regain their will to live. As such, we encountered many individuals who were suffering from symptoms akin to dissociation or psychosis, as well as many others who had adopted highly destructive coping mechanisms. For example, it was not uncommon for survivors to engage in a form of projective identification with the perpetrators, seeing them as essentially good people who were merely punishing them for evil acts they themselves had committed. To cite one particularly disturbing case, a woman who was suffering from profound guilt and shame from a previous rape experience was attacked once again by the same group of men. However, on this occasion she had her period, and they told her that she was so dirty and worthless that they would not even bother to rape her. Afterwards, she was so traumatized that it almost came as a relief when she started to articulate her hate and rage by means of self-injury. Although her anger was directed towards the inner enemy rather than the outer and real one, it provided an opening through which she could vent her pain and, in so doing, avoid going insane.

CONCLUSION

As I have endeavored to make clear in the discussion above, the overwhelming majority of female refugees whom we met during the course of our work in the Tuzla area had been subjected to extreme victimization at the hands of militia forces and others. Moreover, as a therapist myself, I could see how their suffering, along with the stress of living in a war zone more generally, was having an effect upon my own well-being. Although I tended not to experience any ill-effects while I was in Bosnia, as soon as I returned to Germany for a holiday I would immediately become physically ill, all the while suffering from nightmares, insomnia and a deep malaise. Needless to say, these symptoms were warning signs from my body, informing me of the dangers of working in an environment where relaxation was at a premium and constant vigilance a necessity.

In the event, I left Tuzla in February 1996. Upon my return to Germany, I devoted several months to the task of finding new sources of financial support for the project, since the organization with which we were originally involved was in the process of winding down its commitment to the Center. Although it was clear by July that sufficient funding would be available to ensure that the project could continue to operate for at least another year, I remained actively involved in the Center's work until early 1997. At this time, I decided that it would be in everyone's best interest if I stepped back and let others take my place.

However, this is not to say that I have become disengaged from the vision that drove me to Bosnia in the first place. I continue to work with refugees, many of whom are from the Former Yugoslavia, and many of whom bear scars remarkably similar to those which I encountered so often in Tuzla. I also continue to get angry, angry at the individuals who inflicted such suffering upon my clients, angry at the ritual of humiliation which asylum seekers must endure before they are allowed to stay in this country, angry at the War

Crimes Tribunal in The Hague for failing to provide adequate protection to witnesses and their families. It was precisely this same anger that drove me, along with two other women, to take action in 1993 in the face of the unimaginable atrocities being committed in the name of ethnic nationalism in the Former Yugoslavia. That had not changed.

War, Life Crisis and Trauma:
Assessing the Impact of a Woman-Centered
Training Program in Bosnia

Sabine Scheffler
Agnes Müchele

SUMMARY. This article presents a woman-centered approach to healing that is necessitated by trauma inflicted by armed conflict. The authors present a historical context within which they depict many of the daily consequences that citizens experienced. A training program was developed during a trip to Bosnia in which sixteen women, among whom were social workers, psychologists, physicians, teachers and one Islamic theologian, participated. This program was comprised of five training modules: introduction to basic concepts and issues, the social psychology of war, the counseling process and techniques, social work in a wartime environment, and termination. *[Article copies available for a fee from The Haworth Document Delivery Service: 1-800-342-9678. E-mail address: getinfo@haworthpressinc.com]*

Sabine Scheffler, PhD, is Professor of Social Psychology, College for Applied Sciences and Co-Director of the Zentrum für Angewandte Psychologie und Frauenforschung (Center of Applied Psychology and Women's Research) in Cologne, Germany. Agnes Müchele, PhD, is Co-Director of the Zentrums für Angewandte Psychologie und Frauenforschung (Center of Applied Psychology and Women's Research) in Cologne, Germany.

Address correspondence to: Dr. Sabine Scheffler, Zentrum für Angewandte Psychologie und Frauenforschung (Center of Applied Psychology and Women's Research), Fridolinstrase 27, D-50823 Köln, Germany (e-mail: zap.frauen@t-online.de).

[Haworth co-indexing entry note]: "War, Life Crisis and Trauma: Assessing the Impact of a Woman-Centered Training Program in Bosnia." Scheffler, Sabine, and Agnes Müchele. Co-published simultaneously in *Women & Therapy* (The Haworth Press, Inc.) Vol. 22, No. 1, 1999, pp. 121-138; and: *Assault on the Soul: Women in the Former Yugoslavia* (ed: Sara Sharratt and Ellyn Kaschak) The Haworth Press, Inc., 1999, pp. 121-138. Single or multiple copies of this article are available for a fee from The Haworth Document Delivery Service [1-800-342-9678, 9:00 a.m. - 5:00 p.m. (EST). E-mail address: getinfo@haworthpress inc.com].

121

KEYWORDS. Woman-centered training, trauma counseling, training program, feminist training, psychoeducation

THE HISTORY OF THE PROJECT

When the war in Bosnia began, we were living in Vienna, Austria. Thus, it was very much a conflict in our neighborhood and, as such, awoke many of the old feelings of fear and anxiety that we had experienced as children, either as a three-year-old forced to flee with her parents through large parts of rural Germany, or as a young girl immersed in the tension of the immediate post-war era, when many thought another conflict was imminent. Dulled by time, these fears were roused once again in 1956, when the Hungarian Crisis burst upon our consciousness.

From the beginning, events in Bosnia filled us with rage. The power politics of the governments involved, their actions designed to sabotage any hope of a negotiated settlement, together with the empty rhetoric of the European "community" more generally left us feeling helpless, yet determined to contribute in some small way to the cause of peace. It was at this time that feminist groups from various countries began to make contact with local women's organizations, providing support and assistance that went mostly unnoticed by a mainstream media narrowly focused upon government-sponsored aid programs. Moreover, it was also in this context that we embarked upon our first intervention in the region, offering training courses in Zagreb and Split (Croatia) in an environment that might be characterized as one of collective shock and emotional desensitization (Scheffler and Müchele, 1996). Without wishing to downplay the difficulties and challenges we faced, this was preferable to the sense of powerlessness we had previously felt in Austria.

Planning for the project was undertaken in 1994/95, and the work itself was carried out over a three-year period, from 1995 to 1997. Our objective was to provide woman-centered training in therapy and socio-therapeutic counseling, with a total of 16 women taking part, among them social workers, psychologists, physicians, teachers and one Islamic theologian from Bosnia. All were involved in the activities of NGOs working in the region.

As one might imagine, our work in Bosnia and Croatia was motivated and underpinned by our own political commitments and consciousness. In short, it is our position that the attacks carried out against women during the conflict were part of a deliberate strategy that is reflective of the gendered nature of the societies in which we live. Through our intervention, we sought to contribute to the healing of those who had suffered violence, while helping to build capacity among women of the warring region.

ORGANIZATION AND FINANCING

Project financing was derived from the following sources: German People's Aid (coordinated by Karin Schüler); Norwegian People's Aid (coordinated by Liv Bremer); Caritas Leverkusen (coordinated by Friedel Herweg); personal donations by women psychotherapists at the Fritz Perls Institute, Dusseldorf, Germany; and Women's Association of Split (responsible for project logistics in Split). Translation services were provided by Lejla Derzic. Our co-trainer in two courses was Angela Reinhardt. Planning, management and implementation were conducted by Dr. Sabine Scheffler and Dr. Agnes Müchele.

PROJECT DESIGN

If our initiative was to be successful, we deemed it vital that we make a preliminary trip to the region; not only would this allow us to gain some insight into the day-to-day challenges faced by the women themselves, but we would also be in a better position to tailor our training program to the needs and requirements of participants. Setting out in August 1995 (during the time of the Krajina offensive), we visited several women's projects being implemented in Tuzla and Zenica (Bosnia). On the one hand, our trip was useful in forcing us to question our assumptions and become more realistic in our goals and objectives. On the other, it served to strengthen our resolve to carry out the training program in Croatia, and not in Bosnia as some participants had originally wanted. In our opinion, a relaxed environment is critical for meaningful learning to take place, and the atmosphere in Bosnia was anything but relaxed at that time. Finally, on a more mundane level, our journey to the region gave us an opportunity to discuss the aims of the project with our local partners and to assess local working conditions. It should be noted that this aspect of the trip was of particular symbolic importance to our partners, who took it to be indicative of the non-hierarchical nature of the project.

Assumptions

Throughout the planning and implementation stages of the project, we were guided by the premise that, for healing to occur, women's suffering must be understood within the broader politico-historical contexts of nationalism and patriarchy. That is to say, women who are victims of war cannot be expected to regain their dignity and self-esteem unless the processes and events that led to their victimization have been acknowledged and exposed for what they are (Laub and Weine, 1994; Graessner, Gurris, and Pross, 1996).

Injustice Against Women During the Injustice of War

At a personal, social and historical level, war means something different for women and men. Thus, while dominant discourses (including those of the mainstream media and the state) are focused narrowly upon the "organization of war" and issues of concern to men (e.g., battles lost and won; number of personnel injured, missing or dead), the violence experienced by women is targeted and total, and is used as a way of sapping the morale and weakening the resolve of men. Objectified and subjected to torture, humiliation and violence, the destruction of women's dignity undermines and destroys the social bonds and values of the culture in which they live. However, in spite of these attacks, women struggle continuously for their dignity and freedom, both in the face of wartime atrocities and the daily humiliation and violence of life under a patriarchal social order. Indeed, in this regard one might argue that the public response to violence is equally as important as the psychological resources available to an individual who is setting out on the path to recovery. Recognition of the truth must precede the victim's recovery, as Judith Herman (1994) has so aptly noted.

Of course, the wartime victimization of Bosnian women is an atrocity that has been largely ignored by the international community and mainstream media, which is reflective of the taboo nature of the topic itself. For example, it was only in the early 1990s that German feminists were able to initiate a public discussion of the atrocities committed against women during the Second World War (Sander and Johr, 1992). In a similar fashion, Austrian women had a very difficult time indeed convincing the Minister for Women's Affairs in that country to accept rape in war as a basis for political asylum. While by no means wishing to suggest that either Austria or Germany has gone far enough in addressing the issue of violence against women in war, they are sadly two of the more "progressive" cases. In many other countries, there is absolutely no interest in the issue, which serves as a shameful testimony to the willingness of societies to accept male violence and its pernicious effects upon women's lives.

Aware of this situation before we had even embarked upon the project, we arrived in Bosnia expecting to be confronted with women whose socialization into a patriarchal, conservative culture would leave them feeling ashamed of their victimization, as well as causing them to suppress its effects. However, as we began the training courses, we were reminded of the fact that talking leads to recovery, and that joint responsibility in combination with the women's own coping strategies would provide the basis for them to overcome their suffering. Significantly, these findings are confirmed by scholars examining healing processes in the context of women's shelters (Brückner, 1997; Walker, 1979).

A Woman-Centered Approach to Healing

That violence toward women is grounded in patriarchal relations of power is well-established, and is equally the case for Bosnia as it is for Austria or the United States. However, it was our hope in intervening in the manner that we did to contribute to a process of change whereby Bosnian women were able to make gains similar to those achieved by women in other countries. Of course, there is a long tradition of solidarity among women in the face of domination and violence, and we have shown our power to overcome the latter in order to begin life anew. Drawing upon the legacy of women's projects the world over, one might identify the following premises upon which to ground our anti-violence work. In particular, there is a need to: acknowledge injustice and injuries; find a language to describe the act; become responsible and bear witness; reestablish individual and collective self-esteem; promote self-confidence; and achieve balance between dependence and independence.

Needless to say, these aims require facilitators to establish active contact among all members of the group. Our strategy in this regard involved taking the skills and competencies of participants seriously, and using them as the starting point for a two-way learning process. On the one hand, this demanded that we focus continuously upon the group and group events. On the other, we had to resist the temptation to take charge, since it was critical that members find their own solutions to the issues they were facing. Our role was to offer support, stimulation and knowledge in a manner that would be helpful in developing self-confidence and confidence in others.

The Concept

Aims

Focused on the development of professional skills in social-therapeutic work with female war victims and refugees, the training course was designed especially for the women who would take part, among whom numbered physicians, psychiatric nurses, teachers, social workers and psychologists. Moreover, we identified three areas in need of priority intervention: Enhancement of theoretical knowledge; Counseling methodologies; The work context.

At a theoretical level, the course dealt with such issues as the psychodynamics of trauma, diagnosis of post-traumatic stress disorder, sociodynamics of war, models of crisis intervention and trauma counseling. We also dealt with a number of general concepts, including: Contact and relationships; Defense and resistance mechanisms; Transference and counter-transference; Group settings; Counseling techniques and media (creative media and dreams, role-playing, body techniques and exercise-centered work). Of course, in dealing with all of these issues we also emphasized the importance of focusing, identifying one's strengths and weaknesses, taking care of oneself, and strategies to avoid burn-out.

Structure

The meetings we held with prospective participants during our preliminary field visit were useful in familiarizing us with one another, as well as helping all concerned finalize their decision as to whether or not they would become involved. From our perspective, it was important that the group be heterogeneous, since we wanted to bring together a wide range of experiences, while at the same time fostering networking opportunities.

The course itself lasted two years, and was divided into six modules, consisting of 40 units (each unit was 45 minutes in length) spread over the course of five week-days. The modules may be summarized as follows: Introduction to basic concepts and issues related to work with war and trauma victims; Establishing group strengths and weaknesses; Social psychology of war and violence; Deconstructing gender roles and relations; Counseling techniques and the counseling process; Social work during and after a war; Completion of counseling processes; Discussion of the case studies; Conclusion.

At the end of the two-year period, all participants were expected to document a counseling experience, as well as describing their application of methodologies we had discussed in the training. Finally, it should be noted that we are currently in the process of planning a seventh module, scheduled for September 1998, when we will have returned to the region in order to take part in the day-to-day counseling work of project participants.

Principles of Evaluation

Seeking to engage with our own assumptions in planning and carrying out the project, we distilled a number of key questions from the training material, our progress reports and evaluation exercises. These may be summarized as follows:

1. Is there any evidence of change in the language used in our reports to describe the women, interpersonal dynamics and course contents?
2. In what ways does our attitude and working method change according to the degree of acceptance by participants of the course's goals and objectives?

3. What unconscious processes and dynamics become visible as issues around violence and traumatization are raised and discussed?

4. With respect to the last point in particular, we engaged in a deliberate attempt to interrogate and question our intervention strategies, so that they might be rendered appropriate to the contexts in which we found ourselves (The Adjectives);

5. Moreover, we also sought to relate these questions to our course objectives, which are summarized below (The Concept);

6. Enhance and systematize participants' understanding of the long-term effects of traumatization and individuals' coping strategies;

7. Identify and discuss means of strengthening the working relationship with women who have been traumatized or are in crisis;

8. Identify and discuss alternative intervention strategies (i.e., use of media or creative material);

9. Contribute to participants' understanding of the dangers inherent in burnout and secondary traumatization, identify and discuss professional coping strategies;

10. Facilitate the development of woman-centered approaches and methods, paying particular attention to such issues as violence against women in wartime, the socio-political context underlying women's exploitation and humiliation, and the effects of wartime experiences upon women and men's post-conflict relationships.

However, while these objectives informed our interventions in the training courses, it should be noted that we placed particular emphasis upon group work (e.g., dream work, role-playing and sculpture work), as we were concerned that we might exhaust ourselves if too much time was spent in individual sessions, and all the more so because participants were dealing with the legacy of their own war-time experiences.

Challenge # 1: The Way from Dependence to Independence

Before the training courses began, we assumed that those taking part would be cooperative, appreciative and motivated to learn as much as possible within the existing time constraints. However, once the project was underway, we were forced to revise our expectations somewhat. Although the participants were prepared to accept our leadership, even in the face of difficult or provocative topic areas, it became clear to us that they were anxious, and would become silent and introverted whenever we pushed them too far. This response, together with the chatting, loud laughter and somewhat frantic attitude during leisure-time activities suggested to us that we should reduce the intensity of the sessions and provide more release mechanisms.

Challenge # 2: Acknowledging the Needs of Those Traumatized by War

When we made our first trip to Bosnia in 1995, we were immediately struck by the looks of exhaustion on the faces of our colleagues, and by their willingness to accept whatever we offered with the words, "It would probably be useful." We interpreted their wariness as indicative of the traumatic experiences they had undergone, experiences that made them fearful that the training course would lead to nothing but the repetition of their wartime humiliation.

Faced with the exhaustion of the individuals with whom we had come to meet, along with that of the country itself, we felt an enormous pressure to give something of ourselves, to present a token of our solidarity. However, we soon realized that solidarity, professional support or money was not what was required here. Instead, what our partners needed above all was recognition of the humiliation and injustice they have suffered, and so to bring an end to their sense of shame and isolation. Needless to say, this presented us with a significant challenge, since on the one hand, we hoped to validate and acknowledge their grief and, on the other, we wanted to ensure that they learn to act by themselves and overcome their sense of humiliation. Thus, we sought to provide constant support and positive reinforcement, so that the women began once again to appreciate themselves and to develop the self-confidence necessary to make use of their skills and talents. However, by no means do we wish to downplay the difficulty we experienced in negotiating this knife edge between over-identification and the need for distance; all too often we were left feeling overwhelmed and tempted to give up.

Challenge # 3: The Ambivalence Inherent in a Solidaristic Relationship

From the moment that we first set foot in the Former Yugoslavia, we were faced with a discernible gap, between us–foreigners, prosperous, our lives in no direct danger–and those with whom we were working, women grounded in a mixed socialist-Islamic culture heavily oriented toward family. Needless to say, we often asked ourselves "What are we doing here?" as we nursed our self-doubts. "Are we good enough? Do we have something useful to offer? Are we imposing our Western feminist values upon participants (which we were communicating unconsciously to them in any case)?" As for our partners, they confronted us with their attitudes towards children and men, testing the limits of our tolerance, although soon warming up enough to share with us their cordiality, directness and charm. It should also be noted in this regard that the gap appears to have reproduced itself among the participants themselves, as they went about their work with female refugees who had come down from mountain villages in the Bosnian hinterland.

We strongly believe that our relationship with the participants was a special one, characterized by a deeply hidden intensity of emotions on both sides. From our perspective, we interacted with the women in a way that was reflective of our own sense of sympathy and solidarity, our fury at the horror and injustice of the war, and the ambivalence of participants who were forced to make do in a highly precarious, dangerous environment. This ambivalence was evident in the conflicting messages they sent us; at one moment they would be serious, highly productive and creative, and the next this would be replaced by avoidance, regression and a tensed silliness.

Thus, as facilitators, we could only give of ourselves, our sympathy, solidarity and knowledge, while acknowledging that these were merely a symbol of our belief in the injustice of the war. In other words, we were forced to accept the fact that participants' behavior in the course was only tangentially related to our own motives, desires and expectations. Of course, relinquishing control in this way was difficult and often painful, and at times we would seek to regain our sense of power by pushing through difficult topics.

The issues touched upon above encapsulate our experiences during the course of the training project, and, paradoxically enough, they help to explain its success as well. That is to say, not only was the latter due to the particular manner in which we approached the participants and the issues addressed, but it also depended crucially upon the women themselves, who engaged in their own interpretations of the material, which provided the basis in turn for its incorporation into their personal and professional lives.

Evaluation Strategies

External Standards

This would include the trip made by the project coordinator to assess its impact. She carried out interviews with participants concerning changes in their work lives. Also relevant in this regard is a women's shelter being planned for the Tuzla region by some of the women involved in the training course.

Internal Standards

Falling in this category would be the participants' assessment of the project; the case studies, which were presented and discussed at the end of the course; and, finally, our own evaluation reports. It is our position that the evaluation reports provide an especially powerful lens through which to assess the relative success or failure of the project. In short, they reflect the complexities inherent in communicating, in a theater of war, topics related to trauma and crisis, but they also lay bare our own engagement with the women and the topics covered, summarized as follows in the form of two key questions:

How does the language of the reports mirror and reflect our attitudes and prejudices towards the participants?

How do we describe and reflect upon our experiences?

The reports also include references to our fantasies, our prejudices, our likes and dislikes. In the pages that follow, we analyze this material, in its entirety, in order to shed some light upon that which is usually unconscious, in the background, the gestalt. In so doing, we hope to show that our facilitation of the training courses was informed throughout by our positioning within a complex web of social relations and structures (Benjamin, 1990; Nadig, 1992).

The Evaluation Questions

As the preceding discussion suggests, our evaluation strategy is part operational, part discursive. In this regard, we would argue that the context of the project, i.e., the fact that it was undertaken in a post-war environment, the war-time experiences of the women themselves, along with the professional demands placed upon them in terms of the lack of preparation for the type of psycho-social problems generated by the war, together served to create what one might call a special learning situation. How so? Consider the following points: The energy and tension engendered by the crisis were given concrete manifestation in the training seminars through the actions and reactions of participants. The relationship between participants and facilitators was characterized, on both sides, by ambivalence and resistance. On the one hand, we were the conveyors of skills and knowledge, and they the receivers. On the other, we were women outside of our own cultural milieu, interacting with individuals who were on their home turf, albeit one shattered by the effects of war. In this way, the evaluation reports offered a means of working through the implications of being immersed in a special learning environment by giving us the opportunity to reflect upon the events, the participants, and the ways in which we dealt with the process.

EVALUATION PROCEDURE

Group-Centered Interventions

We scrutinized the evaluation reports in search of examples of interventions that were related, at an operational level, to the project objectives.

Having identified relevant cases, we then assessed participants' responses to our interventions, and registered their effects. We discuss our findings in detail in the paragraphs that follow.

The Adjectives

We extracted all the adjectives contained within the reports and divided them into categories. In doing so, it was our contention that an activity as complex as "working with traumatized women" engenders reactions at the psychological, somatic and social levels, thereby influencing behavior, perception, sensation, cognition and affect. It was also our belief that these coping mechanisms would be changed, emphasized, corrected and extended as we pursued the training objectives over the course of the project.

Adjective Categories

In total, we identified 968 adjectives in the six reports, not including those used in the assessment circle undertaken in the final training module. Although we discuss each of the adjective categories below, the reader should bear in mind the fact that equivalent words do not always exist in English and German. However, we have endeavored to ensure that our translation is as faithful to the original as possible.

Category 1: Modifiers

Adjectives which intensify, increase, underline or make more extreme.
Examples: very professional, very slow, tiny deviations, only German women, little courage, lots of fear, very silly

Category 2: Value Statements

Words that judge, value or rate.
Examples: good answer, wrong, bad, morally, nice, professional, lazy, good attitude

Category 3: Body Sensations

Adjectives which describe an individual's condition at a sensuous body level.
Examples: wrinkled-up nose, ill, wounded, shitty, strong

Category 4: Activity

Descriptors of initiative, vitality, vigor (or their opposites).
Examples: exhausted, explosive, powerful, quick, slow, tough, vivid, politically active, sexual

Category 5: Relational Statements

Words that imply or describe a relationship.
Examples: keen, empathic, polite, social, open, erotic, present, reserved, competitive, lonely, affected, appreciative, together

Category 6: Emotions

Examples: anxious, guilty, happy, furious, pissed off, desperate, sad, funny, proud

Category 7: Cognitive or Technical Terms

Adjectives related to cognition (i.e., perception or thought).
Examples: pensive, resigned, perplexed, disappointed, vague, impressed, clever, traumatic, depressed, hysterical

Category 8: State of Being

Any word that implies an assessment of one's state and that cannot be categorized under Emotions, Cognitive or Technical Terms or Body Sensations.
Examples: apprehensive, pleasant, satisfied, finished, comfortable, strange, diffuse, cheerful, quiet

Principles of Evaluation and Group-Centered Work

As we have already made clear, our interventions in the training course were group-centered. That is to say, we placed particular emphasis upon group development, seeing it as a way of building self-confidence among participants. The following example illustrates the precise means by which we accomplished this.

During the second morning of the first module, we asked participants to describe their moods and dreams. Having spent the first day in small groups, punctuated by a number of mini-lectures, this was our first real opportunity to perceive and appreciate the women and their feelings. After the session, one of the group members approached us and asked if she could introduce a rule, namely that participants should avoid speaking, discussing or interpreting when another woman is making a statement. We took this as a reaction to the experience of having to deal with such a diverse group, as well as an attempt to provoke us into setting group norms and rules of behavior.

In our evaluation report, we described the group's mood as "immediately tensed" after the participant voiced her request. We responded to her by noting that there are as many opinions and perspectives on a given problem as there are women in the group, and thus that it behooves each member to decide for herself what feedback is helpful and what is not. Following this intervention, a conversation ensued regarding the distinction between what might possibly be manipulative and what it means to be a mutual influence. The discussion became increasingly confused until there was no longer any scope for understanding. It was at this point that we decided to end the session: it was time.

In the seminars, participants continually expressed their disappointment with the fact that we were not more forthcoming with advice and opinions, and that all of our attention was directed towards their knowledge, their views and their possibilities. Even when we were engaged in dream work, the focus was always on the group's feelings, fantasies and associations. Thus, we were pleased when, during the course of the final module, several participants came forward to express their surprise at how far they had come in perceiving and appreciating their fellow group members, and how much they had learned from them. These comments were especially gratifying in light of the self-doubt, counter-transference and mood changes we had recorded in the evaluation reports, all of which we took to be indicative of our fear that we would be unable to meet the needs of participants. Of course, to a large extent we were merely reflecting the emotions of the group, who were constantly expressing their desire to "consume" our authority.

This meant, in effect, that we were often faced with participants who perceived our knowledge as more important or significant than that of the other group members, a problem that was especially marked during the supervisory elements of the course. Moreover, this in turn was exacerbated by the fact that we were not always successful in stimulating the women in their activities and reflections. We often reminded ourselves in the evaluation reports not to use the group like a stage (in the manner of gestalt therapy), but rather to focus upon developing a group-centered position. In the end we were somewhat successful in this regard, as attested to by the fact that the women were becoming increasingly active in their statements, in their personal presence, and in setting themselves apart from one another. We will relate another example in order to illustrate the dynamics of this process.

Relatively early on in the course, when we were at an emotional low point, both from trying to come to terms with a culture other than our own and worried that the project would fail to meet its objectives, we embarked upon a guided fantasy exercise to enhance personal power (Pendzik, 1996, p. 104). After spending a period of time in small groups painting and visualizing, the participants reassembled, each identifying with the role of an imagined wise woman, so that the group became an assembly of wise women. At that moment, a shy, anxious group member came forward to take over the leading role, and initiated a feedback and sharing exercise. The group followed her in this, rendering our instructions and guidance superfluous. We had not expected this woman, generally tradition-minded and reserved, to take charge in the manner that she did. As we stated in our evaluation report, playing the role of the wise woman, she became iridescent and seemed to grow, adopting a tall, straight posture and occupying more physical space.

Evaluation Principles and the Use of Language

From Dependence to Independence

Participants' development in this regard can be traced through reference to the adjective categories "activities" and "emotions," with attributive descriptions changing as individuals' capacity to act and become more differentiated grew. In other words, our descriptions became less polarized (e.g., irritated, harassed behavior) in a manner that was reflective of growing self-confidence, competence and control on the part of group members. As is made clear in Table 1, this change was especially evident in the final module, when the score for activity statements (21.53 percent) was far higher than that registered in any of the earlier sessions. What makes this all the more remarkable is the fact that we had described the final weekend of the course as "rather sluggish," with the topic "suicide and prostitution" proving too much for the women, although they had been in favor of including it in the syllabus.

As for adjectives related to "state of being" and "body sensations," we understand these to be indicative of the women's socialization and identity formation, with the body in particular becoming a container for tensions and conflicts. Thus, while the first module was rife with negative attributions (e.g., broken, exhausted, muted, scared), a discernible change was already evident by the time of the second (e.g., safe, well, contemplative, comfortable, relaxed), with the sense of release becoming even more palpable later on (attested to by the use of such adjectives as witty, humorous and silly).

From Needs to Resources

Along somewhat different lines, we also registered significant growth in the use of cognitive adjectives over the course of the training (from 7.1 percent in Module 1 to 15.38 percent in Module 6). As one might imagine, not only was this due to the development of a shared reference system, but also to the project's role in stabilizing participants' capacity to classify and regulate events, so that they no longer felt overwhelmed by them.

Significantly, change was also apparent in the use of adjectives denoting emotion, particularly at our final meeting and in those modules that dealt with self-experience. We would argue that this was suggestive of participants' growing ability to perceive and accept their own emotional state of being.

TABLE 1. Adjectives Used: An Overview

Categories		Modules					
		I	II	III	IV	V	VI
Modifiers	quantity	61	43	36	35	38	11
	%	24.11	29.45	26.0	18.81	20.0	16.91
Value statements	quantity	22	14	15	29	10	3
	%	8.69	9.58	10.87	15.60	5.26	4.62
Body sensations	quantity	30	13	19	18	27	2
	%	11.85	8.90	13.76	9.67	14.21	3.07
Activity	quantity	26	17	20	27	19	14
	%	10.27	11.64	14.49	14.51	10.0	21.53
Relational statements	quantity	38	11	14	21	24	10
	%	15.01	7.53	10.14	11.29	12.64	15.38
Emotions	quantity	21	17	9	11	21	12
	%	8.30	11.64	6.52	5.91	11.05	18.46
Cognitive or	quantity	18	16	6	19	26	10
	%	7.11	10.95	4.34	10.21	13.68	15.38
technical terms	quantity	10			11	13	
	%	4.9			5.91	6.84	
State of being	quantity	27	16	19	15	12	2
		10.67	10.96	13.77	8.07	6.31	3.08
TOTAL		253	146	138	186	190	65
Body sensations and state of being	quantity	57	29	38	33	39	4
		23.45	19.86	27.53	17.74	20.52	6.15

Meanwhile, attributions denoting anger, aggression or annoyance were reflective of the women's ambivalence and frustration as they entered into the training course, feelings which were themselves derived from fears of helplessness and powerlessness, and guilt that their own lives were better than those of the refugee women with whom they worked.

Needless to say, we had prepared ourselves for the outward surge of emotions (remembering the phases of the mourning process) by maintaining a measure of distance between ourselves and the group. To our mind, the manifestation of greater emotional openness served as confirmation that our resource-oriented work had improved the participants' capacity for control, thereby reducing the anxiety they felt in being honest about their emotional state.

The Ambivalence Inherent in a Solidaristic Relationship

In this section, we address the use of adjectives falling under the categories of "relational statements," "value statements" and "modifiers." As Table 1 shows, the frequency of relational adjectives in particular was subject to considerable fluctuation over the course of the seminars. Not surprisingly, they were especially common during the first module, when we were struggling to make contact with participants, and the atmosphere was one of affection and dependence on the one hand, and criticism and claims-making on the other. In one case, a participant who was a physician was asked for her professional opinion on an issue that had just been raised. She refused, saying that she was there to learn.

The group was surprised and taken aback by the manner in which we sought to guide them, give instructions, and introduce order into the chaos. Of course, our purpose in acting this way was to serve as models and to set boundaries, with the latter being particularly important in crisis management. In subsequent modules, our description of the relationships became increasingly varied, itself a function of the growing salience of the supportive element in our interactions. Still, it should be emphasized that our leadership position was never called into question, except for challenges related to our seeming failure (in the eyes of participants) to set limits or cut off discussion. As we already suggested, the pressure upon us to set limits was closely related to group members' desire that the "other one" regulate and impose conditions on their behavior.

Meanwhile, our use of modifiers and value statements in the reports serves to underscore very well the pressure and drive we were feeling from the group. Often during the breaks we would argue among ourselves concerning the "right" procedure or intervention, as the group listened with perked-up ears. Underlying these arguments, of course, was our sense of horror and fury at the injustice of the war, combined with feelings of self-doubt and unworthiness. Thus, it is not surprising that we tended to rate the working conditions as poor and the women as naive and non-feminist. However, even as we became increasingly morose in the face of our exhaustion and hopelessness, we sought to overcome our self-doubt by endeavoring to find value in the situation. The evaluation reports were of significant assistance in this regard, both as a way of protecting ourselves and helping us to avoid feeling overwhelmed.

Still, despite this sense of unworthiness, the modifiers used in the reports made clear "how very much," "how completely" and "how deeply" we identified with the project and its objectives, even if this identification was severely tested by the participants, the "others" who were judging us and our work. They were individuals with lifestyles very different from our own: heavily family-oriented, subject to a highly patriarchal gender order, and leading lives circumscribed by the needs of their children, husbands and relatives. It was only because of the war that they had become conscious of patriarchy's deleterious effects, forcing them to come to terms with disillusionment and disappointment. Needless to say, it took considerable energy and flexibility on our part to move away from our understanding of emancipation to the possibilities which they were willing to consider. We sought to highlight and discuss our differences, but at the same time we tried to encourage them to remain assertive and to retain the sense of power they had gained during the war. Moreover, it was precisely in this context that a space began to open for participants to give voice to their alternative biographies. For example, when one woman told the group that she lived alone, unmarried and without children, she was not criticized by other participants, but rather appreciated for who she was. Meanwhile, another woman came forward to say that, although her father had died during the war, she was not sorry and would never forgive what he had done to her family while he was alive. Finally, a widow was able to talk to group members about her secret lover without risking their judgment. The time for secrecy was past; the creativity inherent in alternative life arrangements was exposed for all to see.

CONCLUSION

In this paper, we have used self-evaluation as a lens through which to assess the impact of a feminist training project we carried out in Croatia in 1995-97. We wanted to share with the reader the difficulties inherent in undertaking such a project in a country still reeling from the effects of war and deprivation. Of course, part of our purpose in going to the region at the time that we did was to bear witness to all that had happened during the war, though this was not our only reason; we also wanted to assist in the skill enhancement of local professional women. In either case, the building of trust was crucial to the success of the project, and we believe that a feminist psychotherapeutic approach provided an appropriate basis upon which to initiate change and recovery.

This view was confirmed by the case studies submitted at the end of the training course, in which participants documented their use of the course material in their own work lives. In a particularly telling case, one of the women reported that "I felt changes in myself and my attitude towards other women. To show weakness is human and helps to build rapport." She went on to describe the process which led her to this insight: Everything that came out of the group was important. Each woman was part of the process. The group had its own strength and energy; it was weak at the beginning, but grew increasingly capable of self-reflection.

Meanwhile, another participant commented, amazed, that topics were developed through body work and relaxation. "After the war, relaxation is a novelty." Needless to say, these statements by the women in their case studies have provided us with important feedback, all the while underscoring the fact that we were able to succeed in our aims, despite being "strange, foreign, feminist women."

While many of the topics that had been raised in the seminars came up in the case studies as well, among them guilt, loss, helplessness and fear of violation, a number of the women went on to illustrate how the trauma induced by sexualized violence can be made tolerable through storytelling. This was also an important element in the training course as well, where it served either to promote or reinforce positive developments. Indeed, in this regard we cannot overstate how much we enjoyed the resounding vitality and friendliness of the women, and the warmth they showed us.

Finally, the project also confirmed in our minds the importance of difference to feminist theory and practice. That is to say, feminism can only gain by recognizing and celebrating the widely variable cultural contexts from which women emerge. We believe the training course gained by doing so, and we hope that our Bosnian partners share this belief as well.

REFERENCES

Benjamin, J. (1990). Die fesseln der liebe–The bonds of love. *Psychoanalysis, Feminism and the Problem of Domination*, Frankfurt, Stroemfeld/Roter Stern.

Brückner, M. (1997). *Wege aus der Gewalt an Frauen und Mädchen*, Frankfurt: Fachhochschulverlag.

Graessner, S., Gurris, N., and Pross, C. (1996). Folter. An der Seite der Überlebenden. *Unterstützung und Therapie*. München: A. Beck.

Herman, J.L. (1994). *Die Narben der Gewalt*, Frankfurt/Main: Kindler.

Laub, D. and Weine, S.M. (1994). Psychotherapeutische arbeit mit bosnischen flüchtlingen, In *Psyche*, Stuttgart: Klett-Cotta, Vol. 48, No. 12, p. 1101-1122.

Nadig, M. (1992). Der ethnologische weg der erkenntnis das weibliche subjekt in der feministischen wissenschaft. In Knapp, G. and Wetterer, A. (Eds.) *Traditionen Brüche. Entwicklung feministischer Theorie*, Freiburg: Kore, p. 151-201.

Pendzik, S. (1996). *Gruppenarbeit mit mißhandelten Frauen. A manual*. München: A.G. Spak.

Sander, H. and Johr, B. (Eds.) (1992). *Befreier und Befreite*. München: Krieg, Vergewaltigungen, A. Kinder.

Scheffler, S. and Müchele, A. (1996). Nichts wird wieder so sein, wie es vorher war . . . Ein Multiplikatorinnen-Training für die Arbeit mit Kriegsopfern (vergewaltigten und Flüchtlings-Frauen) in Kroatien. In Lueger-Schuster, B. (Ed.) *Leben im Transit. Über die psychosoziale, Situation von Flüchtlingen und Vertriebenen*. Wien: Wiener Universitaetsverlag, pp. 145-154.

Walker, L.E. (1979). *The Battered Woman*, New York: Harper & Row.

The Burden Left My Heart: Psycho-Social Services Among Refugee Women in Zenica and Tuzla, Bosnia-Herzegovina During the War

Berit Schei
Solveig Dahl

SUMMARY. This paper presents psychosocial services for displaced women living in the war zones. Two study groups were formed from two cities in Croatia, Zenica and Tuzla. The services were designed to ameliorate distress and improve psychosocial functioning. A questionnaire-based evaluation indicated that highly distressed women derived greater benefit from group psychotherapy (Tuzla) than did the group

Berit Schei, MD, PhD, currently holds the Atkinson Chair in Women's Health Research at The Centre for Research in Women's Health, Toronto, Canada. Solveig Dahl, MD, PhD, is at the Psychosocial Center for Refugees, Department of Psychiatry, Faculty of Medicine, The University of Oslo, Oslo, Norway.

The authors wish to acknowledge the following:
1. The women who shared with us their experiences under these difficult circumstances, both by completing the questionnaire and talking to us in person. May their stories and courage live in our hearts as constant inspiration for our endeavors to create a better future.
2. The local staff for their initiatives, inspiring comments and practical support.
3. The Norwegian coordinators and the NPA staff in Norway, and particularly Liv Bremer, who chaired the program "Women: The Hidden Victims of War."
4. The Council of Mental Health in Norway.

Address correspondence to: Berit Schei, 790 Bay Street, Room 749, Toronto, Canada (e-mail: berit.schei@utoronto.ca).

[Haworth co-indexing entry note]: "The Burden Left My Heart: Psycho-Social Services Among Refugee Women in Zenica and Tuzla, Bosnia-Herzegovina During the War." Schei, Berit and Solveig Dahl. Co-published simultaneously in *Women & Therapy* (The Haworth Press, Inc.) Vol. 22, No. 1, 1999, pp. 139-151; and: *Assault on the Soul: Women in the Former Yugoslavia* (ed: Sara Sharratt and Ellyn Kaschak) The Haworth Press, Inc., 1999, pp. 139-151. Single or multiple copies of this article are available for a fee from The Haworth Document Delivery Service [1-800-342-9678, 9:00 a.m. - 5:00 p.m. (EST). E-mail address: getinfo@haworthpressinc.com].

who participated in occupational activities (Zenica). *[Article copies available for a fee from The Haworth Document Delivery Service: 1-800-342-9678. E-mail address: getinfo@haworthpressinc.com]*

KEYWORDS. PTSD, psychosocial, trauma, war trauma

The war in Bosnia-Herzegovina started in April 1992 and brought great suffering and hardship to the non-combatant population. Not only were deliberate military attacks upon civilians and civilian areas common, but so were arbitrary arrests, arson, murder, torture, detention, executions, rape and sexual assaults, forcible removal, displacement and deportation.

According to the United Nations High Commission for Refugees (1994), roughly half the country's inhabitants were driven from their homes. Although many sought refuge outside of Bosnia-Herzegovina, the majority were displaced within the former republic.

WOMEN: THE HIDDEN VICTIMS OF WAR

Reports of rape being used as a weapon of war began to circulate in the Western media towards the end of 1992. This information was confirmed by several international missions to the region, including Amnesty International, Helsinki Watch, the World Council of Churches, the European Communities, as well as UNHCR.

In Norway, as in many other countries, news of such victimization aroused an immediate response on the part of women, with the shelter movement in particular putting the issue at the top of its agenda. Meanwhile, Norwegian People's Aid (NPA), a large non-governmental organization that had been among the first to respond to the tragedy in Bosnia-Herzegovina by setting up refugee camps, launched a fund-raising drive called "Women: The Hidden Victims of War." Having already raised two million dollars by the Spring of 1993, the urgent question became one of how best to direct the funds so as to maximize their impact upon refugee women trapped inside the war zone.

PREPARATION: DIALOGUE AND COOPERATION

In order to address this question, NPA retained the services of one of the authors (SD), who is a psychiatrist with long experience in setting up services for rape victims in Norway. Her first task was to assess the situation and advise NPA on what it could do in this field.

During an initial visit to the Former Yugoslavia in 1993, it was impossible to enter Bosnia-Herzegovina due to the fighting. Thus, she used her trip to study the type of projects being set up in Croatia. Community-based women's organizations had set up a variety of services for women, with mental health professionals going into the camps to work with women on a volunteer basis. Among those working in the health field, gynecologists were the most likely to encounter raped women; psychiatrists would only meet those who came to them with severe trauma. Discussion with various groups indicated repeatedly that care for raped women should be made an integral part of all health interventions.

Zenica

In June, SD visited Zenica, a city in Central Bosnia that was under the control of the Bosnian government. With a pre-war population of 120,000, the city had also become home to an additional 40,000 refugees, of whom the majority were women and children. Most were accommodated by their relatives and friends, while the remainder lived in a number of sites, including schools, sports centers, cinemas and public buildings. Living conditions were extremely poor. Refugees had to contend with shortages of food and water, along with frequent power outages. Moreover, their movement was restricted both by the war and the breakdown in infrastructure.

Many of the refugee women were overwhelmed by feelings of helplessness, and had lost interest in life and their children. Since the schools were not in operation, the children were left either to roam the streets with little supervision or to fall into a passive, depressed state. Although various types of services had previously been established for the women and their children, dialogue with stakeholders made it quite clear that there was a continuing need for a range of psychological services.

NPA's psychosocial center for displaced women and their families in Zenica was officially opened in September 1993. Personnel included a Norwegian coordinator, a local coordinator and a professional staff of one psychologist, three social workers, two pre-school teachers, two teachers and one interpreter. In addition, six individuals were hired to provide support services, including cooking and cleaning. Half of the latter contingent were displaced people themselves. The aim of the service was to improve the psychosocial functioning of displaced women by giving them an opportunity to overcome problems of passivity and helplessness, and to identify victims of severe traumatization who were in need of additional psychological intervention, either as individuals or families. The program's agenda was set by staff members and open to change based on feedback from participants. The women engaged in group-based occupational activities, structured group conversations, educational and recreational activities, as well as being given the chance to receive individual or family counseling.

All women and children living in the refugee centers were invited to participate. The response was overwhelming and, in order to provide services to as many individuals as possible, two shifts were created, with participants only allowed to come in every second day. By December 1993, there were approximately 400 women and 250 children in regular attendance at Center activities.

Handicrafts were chosen as one of the activities because many participants wanted this, and it was a pastime that traditionally brought women together. Women were invited to take part in knitting, sewing, spinning and embroidery. Products were either sold in a shop created for this purpose (in the process providing individuals with a source of income), or made for use by family members. Emphasis was also placed upon cultural and educational activities, with courses offered in the English language, music, dancing and singing. Generally, women would also bring their children, who were divided into pre-school and school-age groups. With the educational system in disarray, many children had not attended classes since the beginning of the war.

The various groups were seen as ways for the women to engage in meaningful activities and reawaken their interest in life. The development of a social network was also facilitated by the presence of a social worker, who participated in structured group conversations. While there were no formal psychotherapeutic group activities, the psychologist or social worker routinely met with the women so that they could talk about issues of concern. The focus was on expressing feelings and coping with the present situation. Individual counseling was offered by both the social workers and the psychologist, who also acted in a supervisory capacity. Training in counseling was also provided to those who would be working with the women.

By inviting all female refugees to attend, the aim was to offer a large group of women psychosocial support, and to provide individual and family counseling to those who were in greatest need. The service was also grounded in the assumption that social support is essential for those coping with many types of traumatic experience. Lack of support is often a contributing factor to mental health problems among victims of sexual violence. Many women might choose not to disclose their experience, and a broad-based approach affords women with different traumatic experiences a chance to benefit from the service while giving individuals who have been raped the opportunity to disclose and receive targeted psychological treatment.

The program was expanded in 1994. When it was observed that there were groups of women who wanted to become involved, yet were unable to visit the Center itself, a mobile unit was established, consisting of a number of local professionals who visited refugee centers, where they offered counseling and other services. Also, whenever possible, they arranged for the women to meet together in groups, thereby making it more likely that individuals would receive referrals if they were in need of medical treatment.

Tuzla

Tuzla is an industrial city in northern Bosnia with a population, including outlying areas, of approximately 600,000. During the war, hundreds of thousands of people sought refuge here. As in Zenica, these individuals were accommodated in private homes and in various public buildings. Also like Zenica, NPA had a long-standing presence in the city, where it was involved in building housing for the refugees. In Autumn 1993 the war was in its full intensity. Poverty and blockade meant that the basic preconditions for survival were not being met. Hunger was rampant.

The situation in Tuzla differed from that in Zenica in that the Danish Refugee Council (DRC) had already embarked upon a psychosocial program focusing on the educational and recreational needs of displaced women. However, as UNICEF staff had pointed out, there was an ongoing need for psychological services. NPA decided to respond to this challenge by initiating a project that would complement the interventions of DRC. The aim of NPA's project in Tuzla was to deliver a range of psychological services to support and treat women who had been exposed to war trauma and were at risk of developing serious mental health problems as a result. Furthermore, NPA also sought to build local capacity by offering training to local professionals in the mental health field.

Headed by psychiatrist Dr. Irfanka Pasagic, a group of local professionals had initiated an outreach program in the Fall of 1993 meant to serve the needs of women living in some of the local refugee centers. Their work was undertaken in extremely difficult conditions, without any outside funding. NPA's arrival meant that they could benefit from professional support while at the same time being assured of sustained financing. Drawing upon the expertise of these individuals, NPA's Psychological Center came to employ two coordinators (one Bosnian, the other Norwegian), one project assistant, four part-time professionals and 21 therapists employed on an hourly basis, responsible for one to four group sessions each. Together with UNICEF, NPA developed training and education programs for those who would be employed at the Center, which were to be delivered by outside professionals.

The Center opened in June 1994 and was located in an existing home for women and children. Given that a number of other projects were being delivered in the same building, including a DRC-run activity center and an education program operated by Gemainshaft für Frieden and Hilfe (GFH), it was hoped that inter-organizational cooperation would be facilitated, as would be refugee women's access to a range of services.

Women were either referred to the Center by a health professional or approached project staff themselves. Personnel visited refugee centers in order to describe the project and identify potential participants. An interview guide was developed to assist in the assessment of the women. Individuals who might benefit from the program were interviewed by a staff member and the most distressed were advised to join a psychotherapeutic group. The latter were generally made up of eight to ten women, with their activities guided by a strategy that was at once self-reflective and sensitive to the local environment. It was for this reason that women from similar educational and class backgrounds were placed in the same group, as were sexually traumatized young women. In all other cases, the groups were heterogeneous in composition.

Conditions under which the psychotherapeutic work evolved were extremely difficult. Most of the refugee women were from rural areas with little formal schooling, and many were widows or single mothers. Most suffered from multiple forms of traumatization, such as daily artillery shelling.

The first sessions were used to introduce participants to one another and lay the groundwork for subsequent interventions. Once mutual trust was established, the therapist could then move forward to the next stage, where women were invited to describe their histories. In order to work through the participants' traumatic experiences, a psychoeducational model was applied. In this model, women were shown how to recognize their psychological reactions and understand them, along with the relationship between their experiences and their present emotional state. Anxiety reduction strategies were also addressed. As the trauma became more integrated into the women's life histories, the therapist moved to the last stage, when women were encouraged to face the realities before them and make choices based on this awareness.

The groups met once a week, over a period that ranged from three to four months. The short duration was primarily due to a lack of resources. As more funding became available, the sessions were extended to six months, with staff taking steps to ensure that there was continuing social support for the women after the completion of the psychotherapeutic process. Moreover, therapists also encouraged participants to create self-help groups, with which they would subsequently meet on a monthly basis in order to discuss ongoing problems and concerns.

EVALUATING NPA'S SERVICES IN ZENICA AND TUZLA

Background

The development of NPA's projects in Bosnia-Herzegovina was shaped by local conditions and circumstances; the needs of the refugee women trapped in the war zone; and the heroic efforts of local professionals, many of whom were themselves displaced within the former republic. As the services evolved, we (i.e., both the local and Norwegian professional staff) felt the need to document our activities in a systematic fashion, and determine whether or not we had succeeded in meeting project objectives. Thus, the authors of this paper, along with Atifa Mutpcic, a psychologist, carried out an evaluation of NPA's work in Zenica and Tuzla, drawing upon funding provided by Norway's Council of Mental Health.

THE EVALUATION STUDY IN ZENICA

After the Center had opened its doors in Zenica, there was a discernible change in the attitudes and outlook of refugee women and children. That is to say, they began increasingly to share in the enthusiastic, caring atmosphere generated by the project and the organized activities. As one woman put it, "It makes me feel like I'm worth something." However, despite these impressions, we wanted to address a number of specific questions concerning women's use of the Center and the degree to which they benefited from it. In particular, we asked ourselves:

Were traumatized women able to attend the Center?
Were post-traumatic stress symptoms common among the women?
Was there any relationship between the severity of the trauma and the likelihood that women would suffer from post-traumatic stress?
Was there a discernible difference in women's evaluation depending upon whether or not they suffered from post-traumatic stress symptoms?

Having developed a questionnaire with the assistance of the Center's interpreter, a small pilot test was conducted with four women. It included questions on socio-demographic characteristics, types of traumatic experiences and post-traumatic symptoms. Additionally, women were asked to describe the kinds of activities in which they were involved and how these had affected their psychological well-being. Drawing upon a typology of traumatic events, participants' responses were then grouped according to the severity of trauma. In other studies of human rights violations during wartime, it was generally found that women who had been detained were most likely to have been sexually abused.

Hence, Group 1 consisted of women who reported being incarcerated in a concentration camp, detained with other women, and/or been witnesses or victims of rape. Group 2 was comprised of women who had either witnessed or been victims of interpersonal violence. Group 3 included individuals who had been placed in situations where they felt their lives were in danger. Group 4 was made up of women who indicated that family members had been killed or were missing. Finally, Group 5 consisted of women who had been separated from their families and/or their homes had been destroyed.

The Post-Traumatic Symptoms Scale (PTSS-10) was used to assess the degree to which women suffered from such symptoms during the seven days prior to the study. This is not so much a diagnostic tool, but rather a simple screening test. However, Weisæth (1989) argues that a positive response for six or more symptoms might be taken as indicative of a clinical diagnosis of PTSD. Accordingly, we chose six symptoms as our cut-off point in identifying post-traumatic symptoms cases (PTS-C).

All women present at the Center during the morning shifts of June 13, 14 and 15, 1994 were asked to fill out a questionnaire. Due to a shortage of paper products, only 239 forms were available. These were numbered and given to the women as they arrived. The women were asked to complete the form and leave it in a box. Those who did not wish to participate were asked to leave the questionnaire blank, though they were still encouraged to provide background information. Moreover, we endeavored to ensure that the women were given a measure of privacy by asking half of the women to go into one room and half into another. Staff members were on hand to assist participants if asked to do so. Of the 239 questionnaires distributed, 209 were completed. Results were analyzed with SPSS. We conducted an initial assessment of the data, which was then presented to the Center's staff as a basis for discussion and interpretation (November 17-26th, 1994). Personal interviews were also conducted with three women who visited the Center, as well as three staff-members. Finally, we invited women served by the mobile unit to fill out the questionnaire, with 69 agreeing to do so.

RESULTS OF THE EVALUATION STUDY IN ZENICA

The women who participated in the study ranged in age from 15 to 70 years (mean 35), and had been displaced anywhere from two to 32 months. Of the 119 married women, 31% were separated from their husbands due to the war. Roughly 23% of the participants had children who were less than 13 years of age. While a high proportion of the women had suffered severe trauma (see Table 1), none reported being raped. In total, 111 participants (53%) could be classified as a PTS-C. Incidence of distress was highest (71%) among those in Group 1 (see Table 2). Moreover, it was also found that multi-traumatized women were more likely to suffer from post-traumatic symptoms, as were those with children and/or an absent husband.

When asked to evaluate the Center's activities, women without severe PTS symptoms (91%) were significantly more likely (91%) than those who were

TABLE 1. War Traumas Among Bosnian Refugee Women Involved in the Norwegian People's Aid Centre in Zenica and Attending or Having Attended Group Psychotherapy in Tuzla

Type of traumatic event:	ZENICA		TUZLA			
	# of women	%	# of women	%	# of women	%
Concentration camp	23	11	8	12	11	7
Detained	54	26	26	38	24	15
Raped	0	0	0	0	10	6
Witnessed rape	4	2	1	1	3	2
Experienced violence	29	14	6	9	23	15
Witnessed killing	46	22	20	29	27	17
Witnessed violence	45	22	16	23	31	20
Threats to life	176	84	66	96	134	85
Family member(s) killed	60	29	34	49	95	60
Family member(s) missing	50	24	17	25	69	44
Separated from fam. mem.	138	66	49	71	130	82
House/flat destroyed	155	74	58	84	143	90

TABLE 2. Posttraumatic Stress

Traumatic Background:	ZENICA		TUZLA			
			Centre Population		Attending Groups	
	N	PTS %	N	PTS %	N	PTS %
Detained	55	71	26	69	36	81
Violence exposed	44	50	12	75	28	82
Life otherwise endangered	82	51	29	65	75	62
Severe loss	11	27	0	0	14	71
Loss	17	29	2	50	4	50
Total	209	53	69	68	157	71

PTS-C (82%) to rate "being with other women" as very helpful. Moreover, differences were also identified in women's evaluation of their emotional problems. Among those with few symptoms, 93% stated that they felt "somewhat or much better" after having taken part in Center activities, as compared to 88% among women who suffered from six or more symptoms. However, it should be noted that the incidence of PTS-C was significantly higher among women who never visited the Center (68% as compared to

53% for women who took part in Center activities on a regular basis). While acknowledging that one must be careful in making comparisons between the two groups, there was nothing in the women's profiles that could explain this discrepancy, leading us to conclude that it was likely due to the role of Center activities in diminishing PTS symptoms.

Many traumatized women came to the Center and post-traumatic stress symptoms were common. Although the war took its toll on everyone, individuals who had undergone severely traumatic experiences were among the most likely to suffer from PSTD. Moreover, this group of women appeared to derive less benefit from Center activities than others who were less distressed.

THE EVALUATION STUDY IN TUZLA

As was made clear above, the approach taken in Tuzla was somewhat different from Zenica, in that the project was designed specifically to identify women who were highly distressed, and hence in greatest need of therapy. Moreover, by the time evaluation had begun in Tuzla, several groups had already completed the program and others were starting. The specific questions were:

> How might one characterize the traumatic background of women who are attending or have attended group therapy?
> How did participants evaluate the group treatment?
> Might one identify any differences in symptom level between those who had completed the program and those who were just starting?

The Zenica questionnaire was used as a guide for developing the one in Tuzla, with the only major alteration being the replacement of the word "rape" with "sexual abuse." This change was made at the behest of local staff. Moreover, an instrument was added for evaluating therapeutic success that was based upon Yalom's model: 1995. Twelve statements (see Table 3) were listed, with women asked to identify the one that they agreed with most (ranging from "did not help me at all" to "helped me very much").

Collecting Information

During two weeks in May 1995, women attending the psychotherapeutic groups were asked to participate in the study by completing a questionnaire. The procedure was similar to that used in Zenica, with personnel available for assistance should the need arise. Women who had already completed the

TABLE 3. Evaluation of Group Therapy in Tuzla. Number and % Reporting "helped me a lot"/"helped me very much"

	PTS-Cases n = 111 (%)	PTS-Cases n = 57 (%)
Belonging to a group of people who understood and accepted me	94 (85)	36 (77)
Learning I am not the only one with my type of problem***	105 (95)	33 (70)
Feeling more trustful of group and of other people**	101 (91)	34 (72)
Therapists and group provided me with something to do	101 (91)	30 (81)
Getting things off my chest	81 (73)	29 (62)
Learning how to express my feelings	85 (77)	31 (66)
Trying to be like someone in the group who was better adjusted than me	88 (79)	35 (75)
The group was something like my family***	106 (96)	35 (75)
Seeing and knowing others had solved problems similar to mine	96 (87)	37 (79)
Recognizing that life is at times unfair and unjust	80 (72)	29 (61)
Learning that I must take responsibility for the way I live my life no matter how much guidance and support I get from others**	97 (87)	32 (68)
Helping other group members has made me more satisfied**	103 (93)	35 (75)

** p < 0.01, ***p < 0.001

program were recruited by means of the self-help groups in which they were involved.

RESULTS OF THE EVALUATION STUDY IN TUZLA

Of the 172 questionnaires that were returned, 14 were incomplete. The women had been displaced for periods of time ranging from three months to more than three years. The majority (75%) had children under 13 years of age, and most were separated from their husbands (67%). Not only were many of the participants characterized by severely traumatic backgrounds (23% were in Group 1), but most were PTS-C (70% or 111 women). When comparing the incidence of PTS symptoms among those who had completed group therapy (N = 82) and those who had not (N = 76), no significant difference was observed. However, the groups did differ in other characteristics related to the risk of becoming PTS-C. In particular, among those with children, the level of PTS-C was considerably lower for those who had completed the therapy program (69%) than those who had not (81% were PTS-C). Again, while acknowledging the difficulties inherent in assessing whether or not this is a valid comparison, one might nonetheless suggest that the therapy had helped to reduce the level of distress within this particular subpopulation. Further credence is lent to this conclusion by the fact that the women's subjective evaluation of the therapy points in the same direction. Here, participants with children who were identified as PTS-C were among the most likely to state that the group therapy had helped them a lot or very much (see Table 3).

Although the proportion of participants who indicated that they had been severely traumatized was similar in both Zenica and Tuzla, the level of PTS-C was higher among the latter group. Of course, this is only to be expected given the criteria for taking part in the Tuzla program. Despite the fact that almost all of the women stated that the group therapy was helpful, a higher proportion of participants who were PTS-C reported that specific aspects of the program helped them "a lot" or "very much." As well, women with children who had completed the program were generally found to have fewer symptoms than those who were still in therapy, thereby underscoring the latter's effectiveness. In the words of one of the women, "I feel more relaxed and I can sleep now."

CONCLUSION

Displaced women living in a war zone constitute a high-risk group for traumatization and mental health problems. Moreover, in the context of the Former Yugoslavia in particular, there was wide recognition of the need to empower and support women who were victims of the conflict. As one might imagine, this was largely the product of sustained media attention on the issue of rape as a weapon of war, which served in turn to awaken the international community to the fact that the traumatization of women is closely associated with the destruction of families, social networks and societies.

In this paper, the authors have described two psychosocial projects focused upon the needs of displaced women living in war zones, as well as discussing the results of a questionnaire-based evaluation of the same. Of course, given the degree of difference between the target populations of the two projects (the Tuzla project was aimed specifically at women in need of therapy, whereas the Zenica Center was not), one must be extremely cautious in comparing results. Still, the findings do suggest that highly distressed women derived greater benefit from group psychotherapy (as was offered to them in Tuzla) than they did from the occupational activities organized by the Zenica Center. Those planning future interventions in war conditions may very well wish to take these findings into account.

REFERENCES

Dahl, B. and Schei, B. (Eds). (1996). The burden left my heart. Experiences from a group psychotherapy project among displaced women in a war zone. Oslo, Norwegian People's Aid, 1996.

UNHCR. Information notes on the former Yugoslavia. No 1(1995). Zagreb: UNHCR office of the special envoy for the former Yugoslavia, external relation unit.

Weisæth, L. (1989). The stressor and the post-traumatic stress syndrome after an industrial disaster. *Acta Psychiatry Scand* (Suppl 355) pp. 25-37.

Yalom, I. D. (1995). *Theory and practice of group psychotherapy*, 4th edition, pp. 74-78. Basic Books. New York.

Sympathy for the Devil:
Thinking About Victims and Perpetrators After Working in Serbia

Anja Meulenbelt

SUMMARY. This article describes the personal and professional experiences of the author while working as a mental health trainer in Serbia. In addition, various approaches to victims and perpetrators are reconsidered, along with the ethical implications of this work. The relationship between working with violence in a war zone and in a peaceful society is also explored. *[Article copies available for a fee from The Haworth Document Delivery Service: 1-800-342-9678. E-mail address: getinfo@haworthpressinc. com]*

Anja Meulenbelt has written many articles and several books on gender, sexuality, and other related subjects, combining psychology and sociology, and is also known for her novels. Her first book, *The Shame Is Over,* has become a feminist classic in Europe and was translated into 11 languages. Her latest book, *Chodorow and Beyond,* is about the dynamics in relationships between women and men, and between women. She is also the editor of a series of books called *Gender, Psychology and Mental Health Care* and is a writer and trainer for the Dutch organization, Admira.

The author is grateful to Sandra Visser for allowing her to use this title. It is from an old Rolling Stones song, but she has used it to refer to working with offenders. The author thanks Admira, the organization in Utrecht, that sent her and Gerda Aarnik to Serbia. She thanks them for their support and for this opportunity. Gerda Aarnik, the other trainer, is a friend and colleague and has been the author's main mentor in this work on violence.

Address correspondence to: Anja Meulenbelt, Tichelstraat 26hs, 1015 KT, Amsterdam, The Netherlands.

[Haworth co-indexing entry note]: "Sympathy for the Devil: Thinking About Victims and Perpetrators After Working in Serbia." Meulenbelt, Anja. Co-published simultaneously in *Women & Therapy* (The Haworth Press, Inc.) Vol. 22, No. 1, 1999, pp. 153-160; and: *Assault on the Soul: Women in the Former Yugoslavia* (ed: Sara Sharratt and Ellyn Kaschak) The Haworth Press, Inc., 1999, pp. 153-160. Single or multiple copies of this article are available for a fee from The Haworth Document Delivery Service [1-800-342-9678, 9:00 a.m. - 5:00 p.m. (EST). E-mail address: getinfo@haworthpressinc.com].

KEYWORDS. Serbia, trauma, systemic approaches, feminist therapy, oppression, violence

Dusica doesn't want to eat rice anymore, ever again. During the worst year of the war, it was the only food she could get. Rice and flour. A friend from The Netherlands brought her a package of yeast so she could bake bread. A little embarrassed, she accepted it. Now in 1997, we are here and there is enough food again, but not much money with which to buy it. Dusica, who is a psychiatrist, earns about a hundred dollars a month. She does not complain. There has been no fighting in Serbia itself. No houses have been destroyed. There is water and electricity. But among the problems is a seemingly endless stream of ethnic Serbian refugees from Vukovar, Sarajevo, Mostar, and Krajina. They are farmers who have lost everything, old people who have been uprooted once before in the Second World War, "incomplete" families, usually missing a father, and some people who have professional training, but who do not get jobs.

Many live in crowded apartments with relatives. Those without relatives live in camps. I have visited a camp, one close to Smederevo, called Male Krsna. It is not the worst. There is simple food for everyone every day. The heaters work. Sometimes they get new shoes or sweaters. They have been living here for five years, five to six people in every room, in bunk beds, their few belongings kept in cartons. They have hung pictures of where they come from on the wall, pictures of the famous bridge of Mostar that doesn't exist anymore. They are ethnic Serbs who are not accepted by the Serbian population because they speak with funny accents and want to share in the scarce food, jobs and housing. But they can't go back. They have no idea what the future will bring or how long they will have to stay in the camp.

At the Institute for Mental Health in Belgrade, many of the patients are heavily traumatized. They are women who still wait for a husband who is probably dead. They are girls who have been raped in the war. They are children who have witnessed their mother being raped or their father being clubbed to death. They are young men, teenagers, who have been soldiers. Many families have been torn apart because the ethnic dividing line ran right through mixed marriages and children with a mixed heritage. There is a story about a Serbian girl who fled and asked for shelter at the house of an uncle. He didn't open the door because he was a Croat. Nobody knows what happened to the girl afterwards.

For us, the trainers from Admira, who are invited to give a course on sexual and domestic violence for the therapists from the Institute of Mental Health, it is not a surprise that violence within the family in any form, including sexual abuse of children and battering and abuse of women, has increased in the aftermath of the war. We have also worked in South Africa,

Albania and Palestine. We know that, in times of political turmoil, and especially after the worst seems to be over, violence in the family and between partners tends to increase.

We don't expect this first training in Belgrade to be an easy job. On the first evening, at an informal gathering, we see all the signs of vicarious traumatization, therapists and psychiatrists who are tired, overworked and burned out, who feel isolated, defeated and even cynical. It is a universal story that it is difficult to keep faith in humanity after being faced with so much senseless violence, so much cruelty. This first evening we long for South Africa, where life is also hard, but where we felt a sense of solidarity, togetherness that seems to be absent here.

When we start working we meet different layers of resistance. The first is the professional attitude of psychiatrists who are not used to sharing problems openly and showing their vulnerability to colleagues. The second is that we are women, feminists no less, who are not even trained psychiatrists. Who are we to tell them what to do? The third is that this is Serbia, an ex-communist country that has engendered a psychology of mutual distrust and fear of betrayal. We are representatives of the West, who has accused Serbia of being the main aggressor in the war in Yugoslavia and guilty of the worst war crimes, including the systematic rape of Bosnian and Croat women. They are furious about the international sanctions against Serbia which make it seem that they are the only perpetrators in this war. In *War and Sanctions*, edited by the Institute of Mental Health (Kalicanin, P., Lecic-Tosevski, D., Bukelic, J. and Ispanovic-Radojkovic, V., Eds., 1994), a comparison is made between their camps and Auschwitz. The Serbs were victims in the Second World War. They feel that they are being victimized again by this international condemnation. To me, their attitude bears a great similarity to that of the rapist who is not able to see himself as an offender, but feels that the whole world is one big conspiracy against him.

So we are tested. Do we really want to work with them? Will we listen to them without judgment? Can we be trusted? It is much the same way that a client tests a therapist. It lasts for a day before the first real problems are presented. In the first getting acquainted session, even asking someone's age seems too private, but the urge to talk about the difficulties they face in their work is stronger than their reluctance. "What do you do" asks one psychiatrist who has had classical psychoanalytical training, "when a man comes in who has lost his house, half his family, has no work and no money, who is desperate? Do I treat him for neuroses?" "What do you do" asks another, "when you see a young woman who wants a referral to a plastic surgeon to get rid of the scars on her face? She was mauled by a soldier with a knife, while she was forced to watch her mother being raped. Her father is missing. She wants to go abroad, but wants to get rid of the scars first because every time she looks in the mirror she is reminded of what happened. I asked her, 'Don't you want to talk about the scars that are inside you?' She said 'No', and left. What did I do wrong?"

"My most difficult patient was a woman who traveled many miles to see me once a week. She was mixed Serb and Croat. Her husband was a Serb. She was raped by a group of Muslim soldiers, who forced her to fellate them. The first person she told, a mental health care worker, said she must have done it willingly. She had not told her husband because she feared that he would think the same thing and cast her out. She couldn't go back to her Croatian family because she had been married to a Serb. She came to my office several times, but after the first time she didn't say anything. She just sat there. I waited. After a few times, she didn't come back anymore. I don't know why."

"Maybe because you are a man," someone said. "Maybe because you are a Serb," someone else said. "Maybe because you should have shown more commitment and not waited passively, like we have learned, for her to start talking." Nothing in their training has prepared them for these kinds of problems.

Milan is a man who treats many women who were sexually abused. When we ask about his motives, he says that he thinks about his wife and daughters. It could have happened to them. Then he tells us the story of his most difficult patient–not a woman, but a man. He has sleeping disturbances, flashbacks, difficulties in concentrating, the classical symptoms of Post-Traumatic Stress Disorder. What happened? The patient's daughter turned sixteen. At that moment, he realized with shock that the girl he had participated in gangraping as a soldier had also been sixteen. He had kept her passport. "I listened to him," says Milan, "but I was paralyzed. I couldn't say anything. I didn't know what to do. After that first time, he didn't come back. Was there anything I could have done? What do you think I should have done?" he asks us, women, feminists from another country.

Victims and perpetrators. It would be so easy if we could divide the human race neatly into bad guys and good guys, into innocent victims and evil offenders. Black is o.k.; white is wrong. Women are victims; men are oppressors. A man in Soweto is the victim of apartheid, but what do we do when he sexually abuses children? Jews have been an extremely persecuted people, so we support Israel. But what do we do with the Israeli occupation of Palestinian land? Do we deny it or do we judge even more severely because they, especially they, should know better than to oppress others? "The Jews have learned nothing from the war," I overhear somebody saying. Were the death camps meant for education? The victim can become an offender; it happens. The mother, who, abused herself, mistreats her children; it can happen. The kid from the ghetto who beats up gay men; the shopkeeper who, while trying to survive in a poor neighborhood, becomes racist; the Palestinian man who has been tortured in an Israeli prison who stabs his pregnant wife with a knife because he has been told she has been unfaithful: true stories. Has the rapist chosen to become a rapist? No. Does that make him less responsible for his acts? No again.

When I return from Serbia, I am faced with two different attitudes. The first is, "All those Yugoslavians are equally bad. That's how people are. It will never change. There will always be war somewhere." The other is even more cynical. "Why do you bother? Let them kill each other." The language of powerlessness and resignation, dissociation and indifference. Why should we care? Nothing we do will change anything anyway. Born of the same sense of powerlessness, the simple accusing of one party, the creation of black and white images of who is the real enemy.

Milan is a man. He is ashamed of his own gender, of what men are capable of doing to women. It is very important to him to show that he is a different sort of man, to dissociate himself from perpetrators. He asks for a lot of our attention. He wants us, foreign women, to acknowledge that he is a good man. Like there were good Germans during the war. It is one of his motivations to work with women, with victims of sexual violence. If he doesn't watch out he will turn into one of those knights in shining armor, a man who needs to rescue poor girls to be able to feel better about himself. A newer and softer sort of abuse of women, although it is well meant. "What would you have done with that man if he hadn't been your patient?" I ask Milan. "I would have hanged him by the balls in the middle of the city so everybody could have seen what he had done," Milan says heatedly. "But he was my patient, so I said nothing." "You don't think that he could see by your face what you were thinking?" "Maybe, I don't know. Well, probably. Yes, but what would you have done if you had been in my place?"

What I would have done? What can I do now? My own reaction to this question surprises me. A few years ago I would not even have been able to think these words. As a survivor of violence myself, as a feminist and as one of the women who was part of the Women's Mental Health Care Movement from the beginning, I saw myself on the side of female victims, and that did not leave me much space or even willingness to think about men, to think about offenders. It was us against them. What I would have done, had that man been my patient, was to praise him for the courage he had to admit that he had committed a serious crime. Is that not the biggest problem in working with offenders, their unwillingness to see themselves as responsible for their deeds? This man, in his despair, had already made that first step. It means that part of him, the part that wants to be a caring father of a sixteen-year-old daughter, has not yet been destroyed. Just praising him for his courage would not have been enough. I would have also let him know that what he did was absolutely unacceptable. Did he have guilt feelings? He had reasons for them that I would not want to take away. Maybe, if I had been able to adopt this dual attitude of acceptance and nonacceptance, and if he had stayed and worked through this painful material, there might have come a time when he could have been able to ask for forgiveness sincerely. Maybe then he could have done something to make amends–not to the girl that he raped; that would have been using her again, but at least to the community that she came from. He might have been an example to other men. Maybe he should have to stand trial. Punishment is not our job as therapists and we should leave it to the judges and the police. Yet we also know that punishment alone seldom changes an offender for the better.

Working with offenders asks something different from us than does working with victims and survivors. I am not saying that working with victims and survivors of domestic violence and sexual abuse is easy, but at least we know where we stand: on their side. In working with offenders, there is an inherent complexity. If we offer only understanding and acceptance, they will have no reason to change. If we offer only rejection and judgment, they will have no reason to change. In The Netherlands for a long time, we could afford the "luxury" of working only with victims and survivors. Or so we thought. We were blind to the fact that caring for the victims did not change the offenders, and so, did not change the extent of violence against women. We could only help individual women after the battering or abuse had already occurred. Working in countries where people have not had the opportunity to build a separate women's mental health system or where women, for various reasons (no job, no money, no welfare system, losing their children, being separated from their whole network of kinship), could not leave their violent husbands made me more aware of different therapeutic options than trying to separate victims from offenders. I became more interested in couples treatment when possible, systemic thinking combined with feminism, and with building a working relationship with men who work with perpetrators. I also became aware of my own fear of working with offenders, a fear that I seemed to share with many women, that trying to understand what makes a man into an offender would mean forgiving, forgetting and acceptance, just as many battered and abused women have tolerated their own abuse because they understood the hurt little boy, the vulnerable man hidden inside their persecutor. It was a fear that too much understanding would take away our strength and weaken our commitment.

Virginia Goldner (1997) gave words to this confusion by stating that violence is never acceptable, but can be understandable, and that forgiving is up to the victim. Rather than an either/or approach, it is an and/and one. Sharon Lamb (1996) cleared up another misunderstanding for me. My feeling once was that understanding offenders would put the blame back on victims. Lamb says that this is not a zero sum game. It should be feasible for us to look at the way a victim has colluded in making her own victimization possible, for instance, by giving priority to keeping a marriage intact to her own safety, without taking any responsibility from the offender. It should also be possible to understand the dynamics in relationships, for instance, that many men resort to violence, not when they feel powerful, but when they feel powerless vis-à-vis their wives, without blaming the woman for his anger and without forgetting that he is still the one who has raised his fist against her.

Once I thought systemic thinking and feminist therapy were mutually exclusive. I saw too many examples of hidden victim blaming in a too-orthodox concept that within relationships or families everyone is equally responsible for whatever problems there may be. Yet I also saw the shortcomings of a too-orthodox feminist viewpoint that could see women only as passive victims, men as offenders without any explanation of how they became that way. It is women like Virginia Goldner, among others, who have inspired me to a synthesis: feminist systemic thinking, including contradictions and creative tensions, a fierce combination of commitment to combat oppression, inside and outside of personal relationships (when we really think systemically the world is bigger than just the family), and a deep compassion not only for victims, but also for victims-turned-oppressor.

Working in Serbia has been a rich and challenging experience. It has made me aware of a complexity around the issue of violence that I had not realized as long as I stayed in a relatively peaceful and prosperous country. It gave me more insight into the mechanisms that combine war and oppression, violence in intimate relationships, trauma and gender. It is no coincidence, I think now, that no matter how big the cultural differences in countries like Gaza, Serbia, Albania and South Africa, there are similarities in the rise of violence just at the moment that people expect life to become less difficult. It has a lot to do with the aftermath of severe traumatization. It always has to do with gender. It is the men who have lost many of their traditional ways of proving themselves to be masculine, when they can no longer be providers, and have not been able to protect their families from poverty and the consequences of war, occupation, racial oppression and decline of state systems, who run the risk of becoming more violent in their relationships, while the women, who have somehow survived extremely difficult times without doubting their worth as mothers and wives, endure.

When dealing with violence within families and relations we are not only talking about methods of treatment and intervention, but also about ethics, about finding a way to stop the cycle of violence, about a balance between help and justice, about seeing an offender who has once been a victim himself, perhaps at the hard hands of his father, of the fear of showing weakness or not wanting to join in games and jokes that were denigrating to women, of the pressure of his internalized myths about masculinity. In the case of the Serbian man who raped a sixteen-year-old Muslim girl, the fear of what his fellow soldiers would do to him if he refused to join them. Something happened to this man that made it possible for him to see the body of a sixteen-year-old girl as enemy territory that needed to be destroyed. We have to be able to see the human part in somebody who behaves in an inhuman way, to fight the illness, not the patient, as a Chinese proverb says. I am sure that years ago, if I were faced with Milan's patient, I could not have kept the contempt and revulsion from showing in my face just as it showed in his. I probably would have found it easier to kill than to understand. I probably would have chosen to have nothing to do with the case, to avoid my own contradictory feelings.

When we said goodbye, after that first training in Serbia (there were many to follow), we were tired and happy. So were the participants. Dusica had tears in her eyes when she embraced us and so did I. We promised to come back. At that moment, I realized that our discussion about victims and perpetrators had been a metaphor for the war we had only talked about indirectly. What we said about offenders, we said, between the lines, about Serbia. Working as therapists and trainers in countries with such a complicated political situation does not allow us to divide problems into neat categories of work with battered women, with abused children, with family therapy, but forces us to see the connections between political systems and personal suffering, challenges our way of thinking about women and men, about victims and offenders. It challenges not only our thinking about methods, but also about ethics. That, in itself, is our reward.

REFERENCES

Goldner, V. (1997). De genderdialoog. (The Gender Dialogue) Anja Meulenbelt (Ed.). Uitgeverij Van Gennep.

Kalicanin, P., Lecic-Tosevski, D., Bukelic, J. and Ispanovic-Radojkovic, V. (Eds) (1994). *The stresses of war and sanctions.* Belgrade: Institute for Mental Health.

Lamb, S. (1996). *The trouble with blame: Victims, perpetrators and responsibility.* Cambridge: Harvard University Press.

Some Pitfalls for Effective Caregiving in a War Region

Edita Ostodic

SUMMARY. This article presents an overview of issues and concerns which can negatively impact the effectiveness of caregiving in a war zone by traumatization of caregivers, conflicting agendas and prejudice of foreign mental health organizers and trainers. *[Article copies available for a fee from The Haworth Document Delivery Service: 1-800-342-9678. E-mail address: getinfo@haworthpressinc.com]*

KEYWORDS. Caregivers, war zone, war victims, trauma

From the perspective of a mental health professional, I would like to share my experiences of organizing psychosocial programs and trauma recovery training in a war region. I would also like to stress some of the pitfalls of effective caregiving arising from the psychological state of both local and foreign caregivers/professionals working in such an environment.

The central assumption of this paper is that the professionals working in a war region are more or less traumatized by the war. Being part of a traumatized community as well as mental health professionals, local caregivers suffer both primary and secondary trauma. Playing the role of mental health caregiver, frequently approached by friends, relatives and team members who would like to discuss their own mental health problems, they feel re-

---

Edita Ostodic is affiliated with Medica in Zenica, Bosnia-Herzegovina.

Address correspondence to: Edita Ostodic, WTC Medica, Mokosnice 10, 72000 Zenica, Bosnia-Herzegovina.

[Haworth co-indexing entry note]: "Some Pitfalls for Effective Caregiving in a War Region." Ostodic, Edita. Co-published simultaneously in *Women & Therapy* (The Haworth Press, Inc.) Vol. 22, No. 1, 1999, pp. 161-165; and: *Assault on the Soul: Women in the Former Yugoslavia* (ed: Sara Sharratt and Ellyn Kaschak) The Haworth Press, Inc., 1999, pp. 161-165. Single or multiple copies of this article are available for a fee from The Haworth Document Delivery Service [1-800-342-9678, 9:00 a.m. - 5:00 p.m. (EST). E-mail address: getinfo@haworthpressinc.com].

sponsible and somehow obliged to demonstrate their psychological fitness to help. In trying to overcome their own problems with a range of coping styles, they often suppress or deny signs of their own traumatization. A sense of their professional dignity often persuades them not to show, or even accept the idea of, their own traumatization. Even when local professionals do not obviously suffer from traumatic signs and symptoms, they may be characterized by invisible forms of traumatization that are capable of influencing relationships and communication with foreign caregivers, undermining the effectiveness of caregiving in mental health projects. I would like to touch upon several signs that are not easily visible or recognizable, particularly in comparison with the symptoms of heavily traumatized people in a war region. These include the following:

> Feelings of shame and helplessness. They suffer from a lack of hygiene, clothes and food and are unable to change their material status.

> Mistrust: expressed in relation to the real motives of foreign caregivers in offering help, the goodwill of colleagues, or the stories of clients.

> Increased vulnerability directly related to decreased self-esteem and confidence.

Foreign caregivers are also involved in organizing mental health projects and training in war regions. In all too many cases, they bring with them attitudes and motivations which prove detrimental to the cause of effective caregiving. These might include (inter alia): different motivations for coming to the war region; they expect acknowledgment and appreciation for helping people in need, while seeking to acquire experience (or wages) without adequate commitment to the human beings who are suffering; prejudice concerning the country and the people who live there; superficial statements and generalizations about the beliefs, lifestyle and culture of the people with whom they work; a more or less colonial outlook, given concrete form in such statements as: "They are basically different from us"; "They don't have the needs we have"; "They are not as skilled as we are"; "I know better anyway"; and so on.

The following model illustrates, in concise form, the relationship dynamics that might develop between foreign and local caregivers. Of course, my purpose here is not so much to develop a universal model, but rather to provide a means of sharing experiences for consideration.

1. Feelings of shame and helplessness which, from a foreigner's perspective, offer evidence that appears to validate their colonial way of thinking about local professionals.
2. In turn, this colonial way of thinking exacerbates local professionals' feelings of shame and helplessness. In order to cope with these feel-

ings, they try to present a better picture of themselves and conceal what they feel they lack, whether material possessions or professional competency. Alternatively, they overcompensate with pride or even by putting down the foreigners, saying, for example, that "They could never cope with such a situation, we are better, we are special . . . "

3. Different types of motivation among foreign professionals foster mistrust on the part of local caregivers, who are often left wondering, "What hidden interest do they have in doing that?" or "Do they use us and our situation for their own ends?"

4. Increased mistrust by locals, again from a foreigner's perspective, supplies evidence to justify prejudices already held about local people: "They are different. We cannot understand each other"; or "It is in their culture to be suspicious."

5. Prejudices and colonial ways of thinking serve to heighten local professionals' sense of vulnerability, manifested in statements like "They don't see us as human beings"; and "They have no confidence in our professional abilities."

In this way, communication between local and foreign caregivers who work together on projects becomes saturated with mutual hurt, sapping the energy and morale of both groups in the process.

I worked in a project that was developed and supported by feminist groups from Germany and around the world. Endeavoring to put into practice principles derived from feminist theory, we always sought to ensure that there was an open door for discussing power issues and problems that might arise within the organization. However, power issues themselves determined who appeared in that open doorway.

An analogy could be made here to the kind of interactions that manifest themselves within trauma work between therapist and client as a result of an unbalanced power dynamic. A traumatized local professional, engaging in transference, might expect some kind of omnipotent rescuer and idealize the foreign caregiver/professional. However, this is inevitably followed by disappointment and fury when the reality fails to live up to such unrealistic expectations. The foreign caregiver (engaging in countertransference), faced with so much pain and need, might feel obliged to deal with more problems than is really feasible, thereby building unrealistic expectations among beneficiaries, and ultimately provoking negative reactions. In turn, this leads to feelings of disappointment and resentment towards those with whom s/he is working. Of course, the negative impact of unconscious attitudes and untreated traumatic signs is multi-faceted. In the first instance, this may be seen in foreign caregivers' sense that they are being neglected or have only gained superficial acceptance, leading to resentment and disappointment. In this way, they lose an opportunity to use the crisis situation for learning, development and growth. Meanwhile, local professionals may find themselves caught between identification with their community on the one hand, and their role as mental health professionals on the other. Not allowing themselves to express their real emotions and vulnerability so as to remain professional, they may very well develop problems of dissociation, and have to invest more and more energy into trying to compensate for this gap between their two roles. However, having done so, they run the risk of burning out that much faster.

As for the project's client population, they receive precisely what they do not need or want: false care, overprotection, neglect, misuse, creation of unrealistic expectations and a tendency to become stuck in the role of victims. Needless to say, this process serves to undermine the effectiveness of local professionals, who lose their capacity to meet the real emotional needs of beneficiaries. They may also offer clients inappropriate coping techniques for their trauma symptoms, or discourage them from expressing their authentic emotions.

Along somewhat different lines, foreign caregivers, because of their prejudices and colonial attitudes, may offer false support or not meet the real needs of beneficiaries. Their unacknowledged personal motivations might lead them to build unrealistic expectations among beneficiaries, offering overprotection instead of support and strength. Meanwhile, the temptation of professional self-promotion may cause them to misuse the traumatic stories of beneficiaries.

What can be done to avoid these pitfalls in similar future war situations? There is a need for individuals to assess carefully the roles and goals of all parties, and to sensitize themselves to power issues inherent in the relationship between local and foreign care-providers. Thus, counseling of foreign caregivers/professionals should be provided, and include issues related to their own motivations, expectations, prejudices and colonial attitudes. It is also important that all parties develop a basic knowledge of transference and countertransference issues involved in working with traumatized people, as well as a thorough understanding of trauma issues more generally, including symptoms, relationship dynamics and forms of communication that might be indicative of traumatization in local people and team members.

Training for local mental health professionals should offer them a chance to get in touch with signs of their own trauma. It should provide a space and an opportunity for vocalizing their owns fears and concerns. While such an approach would not necessarily entail therapy, it would provide professionals with an awareness of and sensitivity towards their own emotional problems. At the same time, it would create an opening within which local professionals could receive acknowledgment and acceptance from foreign colleagues and others.

It would be possible to combine this approach with theoretical issues associated with trauma, legitimating caregivers' traumatization without damaging their professional dignity, and encourage them to accept themselves and their vulnerability. Needless to say, it could also serve as an important means of preventing burnout among local mental health professionals.

If these requirements are to be met, the training should be regular, organized as early as possible, and involve stable groups. It should be a combination of self-experience and educational interventions. Exercises and workshops used during the training would also provide professionals with a tool they could subsequently use in their own work with clients.

Index

=MODERN=
IRISH SOCIETY

NORTHERN IRELAND

THE BACKGROUND
TO THE CONFLICT

Edited by
John Darby

APPLETREE PRESS

SYRACUSE
UNIVERSITY PRESS

Published by
The Appletree Press Ltd
19-21 Alfred Street
Belfast BT2 8DL

A catalogue record for this book
is available from the British Library

ISBN 0 86281 521 5

Cover illustration:
Over the Queen's Bridge
by Rita Duffy

9 8 7 6 5

Contents

Contributors

John Darby is a lecturer in Social Administration at the New University of Ulster. Publications include *Conflict in Northern Ireland* (Gill and Macmillan, 1976) and *Violence and the Social Services in Northern Ireland* (with Arthur Williamson, Heinemann, 1978).

Hastings S. C. Donnan is a lecturer in Social Anthropology at Queen's University, and his research interests are in North Pakistan and Northern Ireland.

Paddy Hillyard is lecturer in Social Policy at the University of Bristol. Co-author of *Law and State: The Case of Northern Ireland* (Martin Robertson, 1975) and *Ten Years On in Northern Ireland: The Legal Control of Political Violence* (Cobden Trust, 1980).

Ian McAllister is researching electoral behaviour at the Australian National University, Canberra. Published work includes *The Northern Ireland Social Democratic and Labour Party* (Macmillan, 1977) and *United Kingdom Facts* (with Richard Rose, Macmillan, 1982).

W. Graham McFarlane is a lecturer in Social Anthropology at Queen's University, Belfast. He has carried out research in Northern Ireland and Shetland.

Dominic Murray is a lecturer in Education at University College, Cork, and has written widely on the ramifications of segregated educational structures in Northern Ireland.

Michael Poole is a lecturer in Geography at the New University of Ulster, and his interests are in social and quantitive geography, especially segregation measurement.

Bill Rolston lectures in Sociology at the Ulster Polytechnic. His publications include *Northern Ireland: Between Civil Rights and Civil War* (with Liam O'Dowd and Mike Tomlinson, CSE Books, 1980).

John Simpson is a Senior Lecturer at Queen's University, Belfast. He worked with Professor T. Wilson in the drafting of the Northern Ireland Economic Development Programme in 1963–64, and is the author of many papers on the Northern Ireland economy.

Barry White has been commenting on Northern Ireland politics since the early 1960s as political correspondent, columnist and chief leader writer of the *Belfast Telegraph*. He won the prize for Northern Ireland feature writer of the year in 1980.

Introduction

The most recent bibliography on the Northern Irish conflict contains more than 3,000 references, almost all published since the eruption of community violence in the late 1960s. Their variety is intriguing and bewildering: political scientists, psychologists, historians, demographers and social scientists of all descriptions suspiciously rub shoulders, and occasionally commit the cardinal academic sin of invading each other's territory; polemicists and propagandists of every shade in the Irish political spectrum—orange, green, red and, since the arrival of the British army in 1969, khaki—vie with each other in broadsheets, pamphlets, newspapers and manifestos; to add spice to the stew, more than one hundred novels have been located in the back streets, bogs and beds of Northern Ireland, as if there were not enough fantasy already. The first problem for any new book, therefore, is to justify an addition to the list.

To start by clearing the ground, this book is not an attempt to present another definitive analysis of the Northern Irish conflict. On the contrary, the aim is to provide a more realistic understanding of the variety and complexities of the issues and relationships within the province, avoiding a single diagnosis and solution. For writers outside Northern Ireland in particular, the main interest in the conflict is the apparent starkness and intransigence of its divisions. On closer examination it might be argued more convincingly that the real contribution of the Northern Irish conflict to a better appreciation of community violence lies in the understandings and accomodations which add subtlety to the relationships between Catholics and Protestants in Northern Ireland.

This, of course, is not enough. Every book is based on certain presumptions, sometimes explicit, sometimes disguised and sometimes unknown even to the author. They are important because they exclude certain concerns from the book, and impose limits on its intentions. Why is the issue defined as Northern Irish, rather than Irish, problem? Why are the chapters organised as they are? What are the political and ideological assumptions which underpin it? In the case of a book which contains nine papers by different authors, similar types of questions might be posed for each chapter and can only be answered within that context. However, even before any of the nine pens touched paper, the conception of the book, and the invitations to contribute papers to it, reflected explicit premises. Two were particularly important in directing the aims of the book and shaping its form, and require a brief justification. One is the decision to confine the papers to an internal study of Northern Ireland, and the other concerns the effects of the current violence.

One hundred years ago the issues which provoked political dissention in Ireland were the questions of Irish self-determination and Anglo–Irish relations; Ulster was an irritating subplot to more historic developments. In 1921, however, the island was partitioned. Since then, sixty years of separate institutions have formalised the differences between the two parts of Ireland, and concentrated the constitutional issue within the six counties of Northern Ireland.

For Protestants the reluctant acceptance of the new constitutional arrangements in 1921 had hardened by the 1980s into a fierce loyalty to Northern Ireland. Catholics were more ambivalent; while most aspired towards some association with the rest of the island, many saw an accomodation with Protestants within Northern Ireland as a greater priority. Even the most nationally-minded were affected by sixty years of living within the institutions and rivalries of the province, and even the form of their opposition accorded a level of *de facto* acceptance to the unit, and ambivalence towards the south. The Irish question of 1883 had become the Northern Ireland problem of 1983. For many in Northern Ireland, the issue of Anglo–Irish conflict had been overtaken by the question of Protestant–Catholic relations within Northern Ireland.

The theme of this book is an examination of these relations. The omission of papers on the external dimensions of the conflict arises from this, and is deliberate. To consider properly the roles of Britain, the Irish Republic and the United States would have required a different type of book, and distracted from the primary emphasis of this one. This is not to suggest that the broader setting is unimportant. On the contrary, the presence of the British army since 1969, and the operation of Direct Rule from Westminster since 1974, are only two of the more obvious illustrations of how central are external elements in the origins and nature of the issue. They are clearly essential subjects for study. Indeed the conflict is often discussed exclusively at this level, as if the only important parties in effectively reducing violence are outside the province, despite the fact that their initiatives have been frustrated so often by their failure to find internal acceptance. Local factors are likely to be primary determinants of the duration and violence of the conflict, and they provide the deliberately limited subject of this book.

The second premise is that the violence since 1969—Northern Ireland's longest sustained period of civil disorder—has affected the nature of the conflict and of group relationships. In some respects this is a truism; the abolition of Stormont and the subsequent introduction of Direct Rule from Westminster, and the coincidence of an economic depression and a terrorist campaign aimed at the collapse of the province's economic structure, inevitably altered some of the issues in dispute. Most of all, it seems likely that more than 2,000 deaths, including a number directly resulting from violence between Catholics and Protestants, could not but have affected relationships between the two communities.

A picture of polarised violence, however, while seductive, is very misleading. In fact the level varies greatly from time to time, and between different parts of the province, so that visitors are often confused by the apparent co-existence of violence and normality. One of the themes which recurs in a number of the papers in this book is the constraints and limitations to which both the conflict and violence are subject. These help to maintain a level of accomodation and adjustment in social relationships, which contrasts with the intransigence at political level. They also suggest that the search for non-existent stroke-of-the-pen solutions might fruitfully be abandoned in favour of more modest, and more realistic, strategies, such as those suggested by Arthur Koestler:

> What we need is an active fraternity of pessimists. They will not aim at immediate radical solutions, because they know that these cannot be achieved in the hollow of the historical wave; they will not brandish the surgeon's knife at the social body, because they know that their own instruments are polluted. They will watch with open eyes and without sectarian blinkers for the first sign of the new horizontal movement; when it comes they will assist its birth; but if it does not come in their lifetime, they will not despair. And meantime their chief aim will be to create oases in the interregnum desert.

No attempt has been made to establish a single ideological or theoretical basis for the papers in the book and the views expressed in them reflect a broad range of opinions. They do, however, have two important characteristics in common: all the authors have spent a substantial part of their working lives in Northern Ireland, and most were born and grew up in the province. More important, each has made an important recent contribution, through research or writing, and is well equipped to set his own research and analysis within the broader context of knowledge in his own field. The marriage of general surveys and individual expertise was one of the central objectives in the book.

The chapters themselves are designed to introduce readers to an appreciation of the major themes in the conflict. While the book deals with the origins of the grievances in the years before 1969, there is a progression through the chapters towards an emphasis on subsequent developments.

Chapter 1 sets out to provide an historical backcloth to the main themes developed in the book; in a sense it is a history of community relations in the province before 1969.

The next five chapters examine specific aspects of Northern Ireland's social structure which have particular relevance to the conflict. As already indicated, this decision to concentrate on formal and informal relationships within the context of Northern Ireland did not result from ignorance of broader contexts—particularly the Irish and British dimensions—but rather from a desire to emphasise elements of the conflict which are sometimes neglected. One of the most basic of these elements is law and order, the subject of Chapter 2 by Paddy Hillyard; the issues of policing, extraordinary legislation and internment all underlined fundamentally different views about the legitimacy of the state within the community. The reasons for the failure to construct a workable political system is the subject of Chapter 3 by Ian McAllister. John Simpson's survey of the complex relationship between community conflict and the economy in Chapter 4 is the first analysis of the issue by an economist. Chapter 5 by Hastings Donnan and Graham McFarlane provides the most comprehensive examination of informal social organisation within the province. Finally the relationship between Northern Ireland's segregated education system and the broader community conflict, often regarded by observers as the aspect of the conflict most amenable to change, is assessed by Dominic Murray in Chapter 6.

The fundamental importance of demography in determining the nature and forms of conflict has taken on an added dimension as violence spread during the 1970s. Chapter 7 by Michael Poole, on violence and demography, carries on the examination of aspects of the conflict in chapters 2 to 5, and also leads on to the two chapters dealing specifically with the violence itself. These are Chapters 8 and 9, which examine more closely the influence of the violence during the 1970s and 1980s on the underlying conflict. In chapter 8 Barry White describes the patterns of violence in the province since the late 1960s. The political changes which took place during the same period are evaluated by Bill Rolston in Chapter 9.

For those who intend to carry out research themselves, whether for undergraduate dissertations or major projects, Chapter 10 provides a preliminary guide to the more important sources of primary data, statistics and centres of study.

In content and style the book sets out to introduce readers who are unfamiliar with the conflict to some understanding of its origins and development, and the issues which characterise it. Readers wishing to pursue more detailed study on particular aspects of the conflict will find references in each chapter to the most useful secondary publications and more substantial research in the field. There is, also, an extensive, but selective, bibliography. The intention, therefore, is to provide the opportunity for further study at a number of different levels.

My principal thanks are due to the contributors who, without exception, responded to the irksome editorial need for internal consistency; to Tom Hadden and Bill Rolston, my colleagues on the Appletree Social Studies editorial group; and to Douglas Marshall of Appletree Press for his support and encouragement. Grateful acknowledgment is made to Gill and Macmillan, Ltd., for permission to use material from *Conflict in Northern Ireland* (1976), which forms the basis for Chapter 1 of this book.

John Darby
New University of Ulster
1983

1

The Historical Background

John Darby

W. C. Sellar and R. J. Yeatman in their comic history of Britain, *1066 and all that*, decided to include only two dates in the book, because all others were 'not memorable'. They would have had much greater difficulty writing an equivalent volume on Irish history. 1170, 1641, 1690, 1798, 1912, 1916, 1921, 1969—all these dates are fixed like beacons in the folklore and mythology of Irishmen. They trip off the tongue during ordinary conversation like the latest football scores in other environments, and are recorded for posterity on gable walls all over Northern Ireland.

To some extent this chapter is a history of the above, and other, dates. It is not intended as a pocket history of Northern Ireland, and anyone who wishes a more comprehensive account of the history of Ulster or Ireland will have no difficulty in finding suitable books (see for example Beckett 1966, Lyons 1971 and Hepburn 1980). The intention here is to construct a short introduction for readers unfamiliar with the general sweep of Irish history before 1969, when the latest period of serious violence started. Since the book is concerned mainly with the interactions between the inhabitants of the state of Northern Ireland and their relations with their immediate neighbours, this chapter attempts to isolate some of the historical events and developments which illumine or at least are germane to this theme. In a sense, it is a history of community relations in the province.

Nevertheless Ulster* has a history of separateness which is not explainable in purely regional terms. Before the plantation of the early

* The term 'Ulster' is popularly used in Ireland to describe two different areas. The first is the nine counties of the traditional province—Antrim, Down, Armagh, Derry, Tyrone, Fermanagh, Donegal, Monaghan and Cavan. The other area is the administrative and political unit which since 1921 has formed the state of Northern Ireland: it comprises the first six counties in the list above. In this book the term 'Northern Ireland' will be preferred when describing the latter area.

seventeenth century it was, apart from a few precarious coastal fortresses, the most Gaelic part of the country, and had successfully resisted Engligh colonial ambitions. Nor were the relationships between its chiefs and those in the rest of Ireland particularly close, except when they faced each other across interminable battlefields. Links with Scotland, however, were close; western Scotland and eastern Ulster exchanged immigrants long before the middle ages.

It would be a mistake to regard pre-Plantation Ulster as a cohesive unit. Like the rest of Ireland it was dominated by a number of territorially jealous chiefs, and internal wars and vendettas were not uncommon. But the dominance of the O'Donnells in Donegal, the MacDonnells in Antrim and particularly the O'Neills in the centre of the province did produce some stability; it also produced military cohesion against Elizabeth I's armies and, for a time, success. It took nine years and a blockade of the province to bring the Ulster chiefs to their knees.

It was this very intransigence that accounted for the comprehensive nature of the Plantation of Ulster in 1609. There had been earlier attempts at colonising parts of Ireland during the sixteenth century, but they had usually consisted of little more than the confiscation of land and the grafting on of a new aristocracy. This also happened in Ulster. The leaders of the Ulster families were forced to flee to Europe and their lands were confiscated. By 1703, less than a century later, only 14 per cent of the land in Ireland remained in the hands of the Catholic Irish, and in Ulster the figure was 5 per cent. But these figures are not a real measure of the changes introduced within the Plantation of Ulster. What made it unique in Irish plantations was the comprehensive attempt made to attract, not only British gentry, but colonists of all classes, and the fact that the colonists were Protestant and represented a culture alien to Ulster. This policy of comprehensive colonisation was a result of the advice of the Solicitor General to James I, and was an attempt to replace one entire community with another. The Catholic Irish remained, of course, but in conditions which emphasised their suppression. They were relegated to a state below servility, because the Planters were not allowed to employ the native Irish as servants in the new towns which they built. The towns themselves were unashamedly fortresses against the armed resentment of the Irish. Outside the town they were banished from the land they had owned and worked, and were confined to the boggy and mountainous regions. The reality differed from the intention, however.

There were simply not enough settlers to achieve comprehensive control, and Irish servants were quietly admitted to the towns.

The sum of the Plantation then was the introduction of a foreign community, which spoke differently, worshipped apart, and represented an alien culture and way of life. It had close commercial, cultural and political ties with Britain. The more efficient methods of the new farmers, and the greater availability of capital which allowed the start of cottage industries, served to create further economic differences between Ulster and the rest of Ireland, and between Catholic and Protestant within Ulster. The deep resentment of the native Irish towards the planters, and the distrustful siege mentality of the planters towards the Irish, is the root of the Ulster problem.

The next two centuries supplied a lot of the dates and other trappings essential to the conflict. The Rising of 1641 against the Planters provided a Protestant massacre, and the Cromwellian conquest in the 1650s a Catholic one. Most important of all was the battle of the Boyne in 1690, sanctified on a hundred gable walls and Orange banners as the victory of the 'Prods' over the 'Mikes'. Historians keep trying to debunk these myths, but historical scholarship has never had much effect on a folklore socialised into generations of Ulster people.

The aftermath of William of Orange's victory at the Boyne was much more important than the campaign itself. It was a mark of the sustained hostility between Planter and Gael that the Penal laws, often included in the catalogue of England's evils in Ireland, were enacted by Irishmen through the Irish parliament in Dublin. The laws were of vital importance in broadening the differences between the Irish establishment and its opponents. Having established an exclusively Protestant legislature in 1692, a comprehensive series of coercive acts against Catholics were implemented during the 1690s and after: they were excluded from the armed forces, the judiciary and the legal profession as well as from parliament; they were forbidden to carry arms or to own a horse worth more than £5; all their bishops and regular clergy were banished in 1697, although secular clergy could remain under licence; Catholics were forbidden to hold long leases on land or to buy land from a Protestant, and were forced to divide their property equally among their children in their wills, unless the eldest conformed to the Anglican faith; they were prohibited from conducting schools, or from sending their children to be educated abroad. Some of these laws, and notably those affecting property, were rigidly enforced, while others were unenforceable. Their main effects were to entrench the divide between Catholics and Protestants, to strengthen Irish Catholicism by adding a political component to it, and to drive underground some aspects of the Catholic Gaelic culture, notably education and public worship.

During the second half of the eighteenth century relations between the religious communities in Ireland were in a situation of considerable flux. Acting as a counterbalance to tendencies dividing Catholics and Protestants, the coerced and the coercors, was the rivalry between Presbyterians and members of the Church of Ireland. The fact that there were also penal laws against the Presbyterians which excluded them from a share of political power—although certainly not as severe or comprehensive as those against Catholics—created a Catholic-Presbyterian relationship which was in some ways closer than that between the Protestant sects. This was particularly true in Ulster, and some of its fruits have persuaded some historians that this was an age of tolerance. Most of the Penal laws were repealed by the 1790s; a convention of the Irish Volunteers—an exclusively Protestant body aimed at creating greater Irish independence from Britain—met at Dungannon in 1782 and passed a resolution 'that as men and as Irishmen, as Christians and as Protestants, we rejoice in the relaxation of the Penal laws against our Roman Catholic fellow-subjects' (Beckett 1966, 222). Belfast Volunteers, Protestant to a man, formed a guard of honour for Father Hugh O'Donnell as the first Catholic Church in Belfast, St Mary's in Chapel Lane, was opened, and Protestants contributed £84 towards the cost of its building. The early success of the Society of United Irishmen in attracting both Presbyterians and Catholics into a revolutionary republican movement during the 1790s appeared to indicate a new Irish cohesion which disregarded religious denominationalism and was determined to establish an independent republic of Ireland. The abortive 1798 rebellion, best known for the Catholic rising in Wexford, also included risings in Antrim and Down; in the resulting judicial investigations thirty Presbyterian clergymen were accused of participation, three of them were hanged, seven imprisoned, four exiled or transported and at least five fled the country (Boyd 1969, 2).

Such a benign interpretation of the late eighteenth century ignores equally powerful evidence pointing towards the existence of strong community divisions. Secret organisations like the Defenders, the Peep o' Day Boys and the Steelboys, strongly sectarian and determined to ensure that tenancies were prevented from passing into the hands of the other religion, waged persistent and occasionally bloody skirmishes with each other in the country areas. Indeed it was one of these skirmishes in Armagh which led to the formation of the Orange Order, an organisation which stressed the common interests of all Protestants and effectively challenged the Presbyterian-Catholic alliance in the United Irishmen. Inside Belfast the tolerance towards Catholics was not unrelated to their numbers in the city. In 1707 George McCartney, the Sovereign of Belfast, reported to his superiors that 'thank God we are not under any great fears here, for... we have not among us above seven papists' (Beckett and Glasscock 1967, 47). The industrial expansion of the city towards the beginning of the nineteenth century attracted very large numbers of Catholics to the city. Between 1800 and 1830 the proportion of Catholics in Belfast rose from 10 per cent to 30 per cent and the first signs of serious urban conflict occurred as a result of competition for jobs and for houses. The same period saw considerable changes within the Presbyterian church. The liberals within the church came under increasing challenge from hardline opinion which was represented by Henry Cooke and closely linked with the Orange Order. The dispute was along both theological and political lines, and resulted in a complete victory for Cooke and his supporters. The liberals under Henry Montgomery broke away and formed the Non-subscribing Presbyterian Church. The community divisions in Ulster began to assume a form similar to that well-known today.

The first serious communal riots in Belfast took place on July 12, 1835, and a woman was killed. An English witness to the riot, John Barrow, contrasted Belfast with the industrial cities in Britain where such disturbances were frequent. 'In Belfast, where everyone is too much engaged in his own business, and where neither religion nor politics have interfered to disturb the harmony of society, it could not fail to create a great and uneasy sensation.' (Barrow 1836, 36). It was a sensation which Belfast citizens were to experience frequently ever since. Andrew Boyd mentioned eight other years 'of the most serious rioting' during the rest of the nineteenth century, and indeed few years passed without some disturbances (see Boyd 1969). The main effect of these riots was to ensure that the expanding population of the city was separated into sectarian areas, and to fortify the communal differences between Catholics and Protestants.

The nineteenth century also witnessed the growth of conscious separatism between Ulster and the rest of Ireland. The effects of the industrial revolution in Ireland were confined almost entirely to the northern part of the country, strapping even closer its industrial and commercial dependency on Britain. The greater prosperity of the north, its economic structure, even its physical appearance, increased its alienation from the rest of Ireland. The potato famine of the 1840s, undoubtedly the most far-reaching event in nineteenth-century Ireland, had much more severe consequences in the south than in the north and had profound effects on political, economic and social developments there which were less dramatic in Ulster. Economic differences found a political voice when the campaign for the repeal of the act of Union with Britain caused a petition to be organised as early as 1834 against repeal or, if a Dublin parliament was restored, in favour of a separate legislature in Ulster. In 1841 Daniel O'Connell, the champion of repeal, visited Belfast. His coach had to avoid an ambush, the meeting hall was stoned, and his entourage was protected by a strong police force on its way southwards.

It was the Home Rule campaign in the 1880s which was to give Protestant Ulster its organised basis and its tradition. As late as the general election of 1885, 17 out of 33 Ulster seats were carried by the Home Rule party. The next two decades transformed this picture and stiffened Ulster's resistance to Home Rule. The resistance was strengthened by the growing identification between Ulster unionism and the Conservative party in Britain. The basis of the new Conservative policy was an identification with Protestant fears, and particularly with the province of Ulster. If the motive was frank political opportunism from the Conservatives, the Ulster Unionists were glad of such powerful support. Nevertheless, although this support was important, it was events inside Ulster which gave the anti-Home Rule campaign its real power. Amidst the outbursts against Home Rule by churchmen, Unionists, MPs and Conservative politicians, it was the Orange Order which emerged to provide the leadership and organisation to maintain the union. The Order's fortunes during the eighteenth century had been chequered; outlawed and abused on many occasions, it had nevertheless survived. The anti-Home Rule campaign served to transform the Order from a disreputable to a respectable body. For its part the Order supplied the ready-made framework of an effective organisation for growing Protestant dissatisfaction, especially in Ulster. By 1905 it had played a major role in uniting disparate unionist voices within the Ulster Unionist Council—the coalition from which the Unionist party was to emerge.

The Home Rule campaign against which this unionist reorganisation was aimed was not confined to parliamentary strategies. The Irish parliamentary party which attempted to achieve Home Rule by legislative action, was at times complemented and at times rivalled by revolutionaries of both the physical force and the cultural variety. The Irish revolutionary tradition, represented by the Fenians from the 1850s, and later by the Irish Republican Brotherhood, the IRA and others, loomed over the parliamentary campaign. It was strategically useful to Charles Stewart Parnell, the Irish Nationalist leader, as evidence of what would happen if Home Rule were rejected—but it became a serious and in the end a more powerful rival to the parliamentary party as public impatience grew. The formation of the Gaelic Athletic Association to encourage Irish sports, and the Gaelic League to encourage interest in Irish language and literature, reflected a growing nationalism which was more closely tuned to the revolutionary than the parliamentary tradition. These developments were adopted with enthusiasm by nationalists in the north of Ireland, just as the organisation of the anti-Home Rule campaign included branches all over the country. But as the crisis came to a head between 1906 and 1914, the quarrel was regarded in increasingly general geographical terms as one between the northern and southern parts of the country. Lip-service was paid to the existence of minorities within the enemy camps, but their causes did not receive really serious attention until the 1920s when their minority conditions had been confirmed within separate states.

The decade between 1912 and 1922 was a momentous one for Ireland. Civil conflict between north and south, where private armies were openly drilling, was averted by the outbreak of the First World War; the Easter 1916 rising in Dublin and the subsequent guerrilla campaign shifted the spotlight southward; the signing in 1921 of a treaty between the British government and Sinn Fein, the political wing of the Irish Republican Army, established a state from which Northern Ireland opted out. These events and the first years of both new states were accompanied by civil disorder. Belfast experienced a guerrilla campaign and sectarian conflicts. The new state was created in the midst of the troubles and divisions which were to characterise its history.

As J. C. Beckett has pointed out, it is not correct to regard the establishment of Northern Ireland as a response to the current European demand for self-expression. 'The six north–eastern counties of Ireland were grouped together and given a parliament and government of their own, not because anyone in the area wanted (let alone demanded) such an arrangement, but because the British government thought that this was the only possible way of reconciling the rival aspirations of the two Irish parties.' (Beckett 1972, 11). Indeed it was intended as part of a wider settlement which never materialised. The Government of Ireland act (1920) proposed two states in Ireland, one for the six counties and the other for the remainder of Ireland. Each was to have its own parliament to deal with domestic matters; each was to have representatives at Westminster; and a Council of Ireland was to deal with matters of common interest. In fact the terms only came into operation in Northern Ireland, and the Council of Ireland never met. Having fought against Home Rule for almost a century Unionists were, in the words of Rev. J. B. Armour, 'compelled to take a form of Home Rule that the devil himself could never have imagined'. (Lyons 1972, 682).

The size of the new state was a case in point. The county boundaries had never been intended as anything more than local administrative limits, and fairly arbitrary ones at that. Now some of them became international frontiers. As to why six counties had been selected rather than four or nine or any other number, the reasons were unashamedly straightforward. The traditional nine counties of Ulster held 900,000 Protestants, most of whom supported the British connection, and 700,000 Catholics, most of whom wanted to end it. However, in the six counties which were later to become Northern Ireland, the religious breakdown was 820,000 Protestants and 430,000 Catholics. In 1920 C. C. Craig, brother of James Craig, the first Prime Minister of Northern Ireland, expressed the case frankly in the House of Commons: 'If we had a nine-county parliament, with sixty-four members, the Unionist majority would be about three or four: but in a six-county parliament, with fifty-two members, the Unionist majority would be about ten.' (Shearman 1971, 16). It was this more than any other consideration which persuaded the Unionists to accept the six-county area.

The two most pervasive problems of the new state of Northern Ireland were the continuing polarisation of the nationalist and unionist communities which occasionally flared into violence, and relations with its two closest neighbours, Great Britain and the southern part of Ireland. Both of these problems were closely related to economic circumstances. The troubles of the 1930s were triggered off by the depression and, indeed, accusations of economic discrimination were among the most bitter reasons for discontent by the Northern minority. And the relationships with southern Ireland and Britain became increasingly dependent on economic ties and divisions.

Northern Ireland: Internal Matters

The new state was born amid bloodshed and communal disorder. In 1922, 232 people were killed in the violence in Northern Ireland, and almost 1,000 wounded. The nationalist minority refused to recognise the new state; the twelve anti-partitionist MPs refused to attend parliament; Catholic teachers shunned the educational system, submitting pupils for examinations in Dublin and even refusing salaries. At the very time when the institutions of the new state were being established, a considerable minority of its citizens were refusing to participate on committees or to perform any action which might lend support to its authority.

As time passed, and the state remained, most nationalists decided on a reluctant acceptance of the need to come to some accommodation, at least in the short term. In some cases they found that the institutions which had been established and those which were still being set up were so arranged as to effectively exclude them from positions of power. Partly as a result of Catholic unwillingness to participate in a state whose existence they opposed, and partly as a result of bias by the establishment against a section of the community which it considered as traitorous, many of the institutions were heavily biased in favour of Unionists. The local government franchise, for example, which remained unreformed until 1969, reflected property rather than population, excluding non-ratepayers and awarding many people with more than one property extra votes. Housing allocation and the gerrymandering of constituency boundaries were actively used in some cases, notably Derry city, to maintain Unionist majorities. In the membership of the police force and the Ulster Special Constabulary, formed to help combat the IRA threat in 1921, a combination of nationalist unwillingness and Unionist distrust created forces which were to become largely Protestant. As late as 1961 only 12 per cent of the Royal Ulster Constabulary was Catholic, and the 'B' Specials were exclusively Protestant. Education too was an area where Catholics felt bitterly that the system established by the Education Act (NI) of 1930 was one which had been tailored by Protestant pressure, producing a state education system which was in fact Protestant, and forcing Catholic schools to find 50 per cent of the cost of education. In the administration of justice Catholics have long alleged that the Special Powers Act, which placed considerable powers in the hands of the Minister of Home Affairs and which, although emergency legislation, operated permanently within Northern Ireland, was designed exclusively against the nationalist minority. Further allegations have been made, and vindicated by the Cameron Report in 1969, about discrimination against Catholics in public employment. The most serious general allegation in this field was that the government operated a policy of deliberate discrimination against part of the province—counties Derry and Fermanagh in particular—creating conditions which encouraged emigration to counter the higher Catholic birth rate in these areas. Disputes about the extent of institutional discrimination, and about the reasons for it, have always been particularly bitter, but one point is clear. Far from resolving intercommunal suspicion and fear, the establishment of the state actually served to render them more precise.

Beckett's judgement that 'between the early 1920s and the late 1960s Ireland enjoyed a longer period of freedom from major internal disturbance than it had known since the first half of the eighteenth century' (Beckett 1972, 14) holds less validity if confined to the Northern state. The years which followed immediately upon the establishment of the state were among the most violent in the history of Ulster, although they were clearly related to political opposition to the new state. The familiar relationship between economic recession and inter-communal strife was bloodily revived in the depression of the 1930s. The dependency of Northern Ireland on exports made her particularly vulnerable to world trends. The linen industry was severely restricted; in 1933 no ships were launched from Belfast shipyards for the first time in over 100 years. Between 1930 and 1939 the unemployment rates in the province never fell below 25 per cent. The bitter competition for too few jobs inevitably took a sectarian turn, which was exacerbated by worsening relations between the United Kingdom and the Irish Free State. The Ulster Protestant League was formed in 1931 and encouraged Protestants to employ other Protestants exclusively, a sentiment endorsed by Basil Brooke, the Minister of Agriculture and future Prime Minister. Whether this was a concerted policy or, as Hugh Shearman claims, merely caused by 'the nervous and vituperative atmosphere of the early 1930s' (Shearman 1971, 174) made little difference to those who were jobless.

Certainly the early 1930s were nervous and vituperative years. Widespread riots in 1931, some of which involved the IRA, resulted in between 60 and 70 people being injured. 1932 saw riots in Belfast, Larne, Portadown and Ballymena. In 1935 the troubles reached their peak. Twelve people were killed and six hundred wounded. Incidents like the 1932 Shankill riots in support of the Falls hunger marchers who had been baton charged by the police disturbed the pattern but did not alter it. The frequency of sectarian violence gradually faded as the employment situation improved, but few believed that it had retreated far below the surface.

The comparative peacefulness, by Northern Ireland standards, of the next twenty years set the scene for the important changes which appeared to be taking place in the 1950s and 1960s. This period of communal peace, or rather of absence of overt conflict, coincided with a growing and deliberate emphasis on economic expansion for the province. In the first place, the war years brought unprecedented prosperity to Northern Ireland. Her shipbuilding, engineering and aircraft production boomed; agricultural production shot up; and the economic expectations of the people rose accordingly. The post-war years consequently saw determined attempts on the part of the Northern Ireland government to attract foreign capital and industry, and its success was considerable. As a result of various incentive schemes 150 new factories, supplying 55,000 new jobs, were established. The new industries, many of which were branches of international combines, offered hopes to Catholics, especially from the middle and lower managerial classes who had formerly found promotion prospects restricted, although recent research suggests that the newcomers often came to adopt local practices (O'Dowd 1980, 66).

An improvement in the prospects and conditions of the minority was also evident in other spheres. The post-war legislation which greatly broadened the social benefits of the welfare state particulary benefited the poorer classes in society, and in Northern Ireland this included a disproportionate number of Catholics. The 1947 Education act opened doors of educational opportunity by introducing free secondary education, and the remarkable rise in the number of Catholics attending university was one measure of its effectiveness. Although the extent of these changes is often debated, there is no doubt that the 1950s saw a growing tendency for Catholics to see their future in terms of a Northern Ireland context rather than in an all-Ireland state. The most dramatic pointer to this change was the failure of the IRA offensive of 1956–62. Its defeat owed more to apathy than to the efficiency of law enforcement machinery, and this was recognised by the IRA in its statement formally ending the campaign. The decision taken by the IRA shortly afterwards to abandon military methods and concentrate on socialist objectives by political means seemed to promise that the 1960s would be free of republican violence. This coincided with a Social Studies conference at Garron Tower in 1958, where G. B. Newe called for greater participation by Catholics in Northern Ireland affairs and Terence O'Neill, the future Prime Minister, appeared to indicate that they would be welcomed. In 1959 there were other signs of a possible erosion of traditional attitudes. The republican party, Sinn Fein, lost its two seats at Westminister, their percentage of the votes plummeting from 26 to 14. Just as dramatic was the attempt by some leading Unionists to suggest that Catholics might be permitted to join the party. The attempt was thwarted by the obduracy of the Orange Order, but that it had been made at all was seen as a sign of changing times.

So the 1960s started as the decade of hope. The retirement in 1963 of the Prime Minister, Lord Brookeborough, who was to many Catholics the personification of right-wing Unionist opinion, and his replacement by Terence O'Neill, appeared to be another victory for moderation. The policies of the new premier encouraged this view. In 1964 he declared, 'my principal aims are to make Northern Ireland prosperous and to build bridges between the two traditions.' (O'Neill 1969, 23). The same year saw an important step in facilitating both aims. The southern connections of the Irish Congress of Trade Unions, to which most Northern workers were affiliated, had ensured its non-recognition by the Brookeborough administration. In 1964 a compromise was reached whereby the Congress was recognised by Stormont in return for greater independence being granted to its Northern Ireland Committee. But the most dramatic gestures towards reconciliation were the exchange visits between Captain O'Neill and the southern premier, Mr Lemass, in 1965. As a direct result of this visit the Nationalist party in Northern Ireland agreed to become the official opposition party in Stormont.

Such developments persuaded many contemporaries and not a few later observers to regard the 1960s as an age of tolerance reminiscent of the 1780s and 1790s. Like the earlier epoch, however, there were many warning signals, remembered in retrospect but underrated in the exuberant optimism of the 1960s, that basic attitudes had not altered significantly. Moderate values in Ulster have their mythology, just as extremist values; and, like all mythologies, they ignore those pointers which challenged the popular view of the tolerant sixties. The traditional Ulster values, which would have been threatened by reconciliation, may have been in temporary hiding, but they soon emerged with banners flying. Indeed the flying of a banner and an attempt to remove it—in this case a tricolour in the Divis Street headquarters of Liam McMillan, the Republican candidate for West Belfast—provoked a riot in 1964, when liberal mythology had republicanism at its lowest ebb.

A man who played a leading role in demanding the removal of the flag was to provide leadership to those Unionists and Protestants who opposed the current doctrines of political reconciliation and religious ecumenism. The attitudes expressed by Ian Paisley, head of the Free Presbyterian Church and the Protestant Unionist Party, had roots which stretched far into history. But the classic duel between liberal and right-wing Presbyterianism fought between Cooke and Montgomery in the 1820s was repeated when the Presbyterian General Assembly was picketed and attacked by Paisley in 1966. In the same year the murder of a Catholic in the Malvern Arms public house, and the apprehension of the murderers, revealed the existence of the UVF (Ulster Volunteer Force) which saw itself as the loyalist equivalent of the IRA. The presures for change in Northern Ireland society had produced defenders of the status quo.

The changes which they were resisting seemed less substantial to some Catholics. Indeed the failure of the O'Neill administration to translate its intentions into practice caused considerable frustration and resentment. A series of measures—notably the closure of the main rail link to Derry, the decision to establish a new university at Coleraine instead of in Derry where a University college was already operating, and the establishment of a new growth centre at Craigavon— were seen by both Catholics and Protestants in the west of the province, and especially in Derry city, as blatant discrimination against the disadvantaged west. In March 1967 the Republican Clubs, which represented an attempt by Republicans to find a legitimate method of political expression, were declared illegal by the government, a move which seemed narrow and repressive to many people who did not share republican views. As late as 1969, the failure of a Catholic to secure the Unionist nomination as a parliamentary candidate led to his resignation from the party. Louis Boyle, in his resignation statement, declared:

> One of my main hopes and guiding aims as a member of the party,
> has been to work towards a newly structured Unionist Party in
> which Protestants and Catholics could play a part as equal partners
> in pursuing a common political end. Now I know this is not
> possible... The Unionist Party arose out of, and is still essentially
> based on a sectarian foundation, and only a reconstitution of the
> party away from its sectarian foundation could make Catholic mem-
> bership a real possibility. (Boyle 1969).

Other Catholics too had decided that reform would not come
without pressure, believing that, whether Captain O'Neill wanted
reform or not, the conservatism of his party would sabotage any
changes. Housing allocation provided the issue for this pressure, and
the success of the Civil Rights campaign in America suggested non-
violent protest as the means. The Campaign for Social Justice in
Northern Ireland, formed in Dungannon in 1964, developed through
Housing Action committees in many parts of the province. In 1967 the
broader-based Northern Ireland Civil Rights Association (NICRA)
was formed. Its campaign, followed with increasing interest by international news media, was to make the Northern Ireland problem an
international issue, and ushered in the most dynamic years in the
history of Northern Ireland.

One of the most remarkable aspects of the Civil Rights campaigns of
1968 was their success in forcing through some reforms. After two
marches, to Dungannon in August and to Derry in October, the
O'Neill administration agreed to replace Derry City Council with a
Development Commission, to establish an Ombudsman and to
abolish the unfair company vote. Certainly complaints remained,
notably about the Special Powers act and remaining inequalities in the
franchise (one man, one vote), but promises were given that the
schemes for allocating publicly-owned houses would be clarified and
the Special Powers act reviewed. These successes ultimately split the
Civil Rights movement. Those, like the members of the People's
Democracy (PD) who were moving towards a more radical position,
believed that it would be foolish to abandon a successful campaign
before it had achieved all its objects. Others felt that both the reforms
and the dismissal from office in December of William Craig, the
Minister of Home Affairs, demonstrated the government's good
intentions, and that a suspension on marches should be agreed to
enable the passing of further reforms. The decision by the People's

Democracy unilaterally to march from Belfast to Derry in January 1969, and the violent opposition to the marchers at Burntollet Bridge, destroyed any hopes of non-violent protest. Many Protestants and liberal Catholics who had participated in the early campaigns now drifted out. The campaign became more radical. Nineteen sixty-nine was one of the seminal years in Irish history.

It was the events during the summer of that year which set the province on a new and violent course. Community tensions had been increased by the events of 1968, and the months leading up to the traditional celebrations were marked by riots in Strabane, Derry and Belfast. On 12 August the Protestant Apprentice Boys of Derry held their march and were attacked. The violence of the police reaction in the Catholic Bogside produced two important responses. The Prime Minister of the Irish Republic, Jack Lynch, made his famous 'we will not stand by' speech, the strong language of which it is now clear was intended to compensate for his inability to do anything else; and the violence spread to Belfast. In August the Catholic Lower Falls area was invaded by a hostile mob, seven people were killed, more than 3,000 lost their homes. On August 14 the British government sent the army into Derry, and on the next day to Belfast. Ironically its initial function was the protection of Catholic families. More important, however, it restored the ultimate republican symbol of oppression—British troops on Irish soil. By January 1970 the Provisional IRA had been formed, and the stage was set for the violence of the 1970s.

Any attempt to assess the internal performance of the Northern Ireland state between the early 1920s and the late 1960s must consider its record in economic matters. After an abysmal inter-war record in housing and employment, considerable advances were made after the Second World War—changes which altered the economic and social structure of the province. When it comes to measuring attitudes, the most significant development had been on the Unionist side. The downright opposition to or reluctant acceptance of the new state in 1920 had been converted to a pride and loyalty towards its institutions. The steadfast prime loyalty to Great Britain was both fortified and challenged by this more local pride. But no significant improvement had been made in the age-old community problem within Northern Ireland. The very processes and institutions which had created fierce loyalties among Protestants had deterred Catholics from accepting the state as their own. The apparent willingness of Catholics to accept the status quo in the post-war years was always conditional. For a genuine transition towards full participation in the new state Catholics demanded a number of institutional and social changes. The failure of the government to produce these changes made pressure inevitable. The pressure was applied seriously from 1969.

Northern Ireland: External Relations

Her relationships with the southern part of the country and with Britain provide Northern Ireland with the issue which determined prime political loyalties. In simple terms this issue has been whether the Northern Ireland area should be included within the United Kingdom or within an all-Ireland state. The state of diplomatic relations between southern Ireland and Britain to some extent was reflected in the relationship between the two communities inside Northern Ireland, as were the interactions between the two parts of Ireland.

The relationship between the Northern Ireland and British legislatures was not defined in any great detail by the Government of Ireland act (1920). Nevertheless some indisputable guidelines were laid down. One of these was the superiority of the Westminster parliament to which Northern Ireland sent twelve representatives. The subservience of the Northern Ireland parliament precluded it from some areas of government, notably foreign affairs and defence, which remained the responsibility of Westminster. This meant that all dealings between the northern and southern parts of Ireland were outside the jurisdiction of Northern Ireland's legislature.

During the first decade after the treaty, both Irish governments were more preoccupied with internal affairs to court conflict between each other; Britain was determined to remain, as far as was possible, outside Irish affairs. The attitude of the Cosgrave administration, which remained in power in Dublin from 1922 until 1932, was relatively benign. In 1925 an agreement was signed by Great Britain and both Irish administrations which formally acknowledged the existing partition of the island.

Governments are transitory things, and the history of Ireland from the 1920s was to demonstrate that fluctuations in North–South relations depended more on governmental changes south of the border than on those in Northern Ireland. The coming to power of de Valera and the Fianna Fail party in 1932 had an immediate effect on these relations. Their aggressive policy of separatist nationalism immediately affected the Irish Free State's relations with Britain. De

Valera's decision in 1932 to end the annuities which had been repaid to the British government since it had financed land purchase schemes for Irish tenants, produced retaliatory British tariffs on Irish cattle and finally led to the raising of general tariff walls between the two countries. The new Irish constitution of 1937 introduced a distinctly Catholic and Irish flavour, recognising the 'special position of the Holy Catholic Apostolic and Roman Church as the guardian of the faith professed by the great majority of the citizens.' Northern Ireland was directly affected by these new policies. In 1933 de Valera marked the new Northern policy by standing as an abstentionist for a seat in South Down. More important, Article 2 of the 1937 constitution stated unequivocally, 'The national territory consists of the whole island of Ireland, its islands and its territorial seas.' The trade war between Eire and Great Britain ended with the trade agreement of 1938. But the challenge against partition was not so readily dropped.

Paralleling the deterioration of relations between Northern Ireland and the Irish Free State during the 1930s was a less spectacular but critical tightening of the bonds between Northern Ireland and the rest of the United Kingdom. This development particularly applied to the economic lnks between the two areas. Originally it was thought that taxes levied in Northern Ireland would adequately cover its expenditure, and even leave a surplus for an imperial contribution which was determined at £6.7 million for 1922–23. With the rise of United Kingdom social expenditure and a decline in Northern Ireland's industrial expansion, it soon became clear that such hopes were illusory. Although a token Imperial contribution was main- tained—descending to £10,000 p.a. during some of the depression years—a situation was rapidly reached where the rest of the United Kingdom was subsidising Northern Ireland's social benefits. The British Chancellor of the Exchequer recognised and supported this situation in 1938. The Simon declaration of that year not only ack- nowledged Northern Ireland's entitlement to similar social standards as Great Britain, but that the Westminster exchequer must supply the necessary funds for this if a deficit occurred in Northern Ireland. This principle of parity was naturally welcomed in Northern Ireland. Its short-term effect was to further widen the standards of social services north and south of the border; it was some time before it became clear that such financial concessions might imply conditions and obligations from Westminster which had been avoided in the early years of the new state. The increase in Britain's financial involvement in Northern

Ireland following the Second World War—the establishment of the welfare state—led to the first British insistence that Stormont was obliged to adopt British standards in legislation. The Education Act (NI) in 1947 and the increase in family allowances in 1956 were two examples of British intervention to prevent the possibility of social services funds being distributed in a discriminatory fashion.

The immediate post-war years also saw statements in both Southern Ireland and Great Britain about the position of Northern Ireland. Ironically enough, the declaration of an Irish Republic and its withdrawal from the British Commonwealth was carried, not by Fianna Fail which had lost office in 1948, but by a coalition government under John Costello. Sheehy may exaggerate when he claimed that these actions 'set the seal on Irish disunity' (Sheehy 1955, 66) but they certainly aroused fervour among Northern Ireland unionists. The 1949 general election there, known as the Union Jack election, was fought largely on the issue of the union, thought by some to be in danger from a Labour government in Britain. In 1949 the Ireland act was designed to dispel such fears:

> It is hereby declared that Northern Ireland remains part of His Majesty's dominions and of the United Kingdom, and it is hereby affirmed that in no event will Northern Ireland or any part thereof cease to be part of His Majesty's dominions and of the United Kingdom without the consent of the parliament of Northern Ireland.

This strong British guarantee, and the severing of the Commonwealth relationship between Southern Ireland and Great Britain, might have been expected to inflame passions between the two parts of Ireland and within Northern Ireland itself. There were indeed communal stresses in the North following the election, and the Republic launched an international anti-partition campaign. But by the early fifties matters returned to normal, and a period of comparative stability returned for almost two decades. Britain had Conservative governments between 1951 and 1964. Never keen to enter the murky waters of Irish politics and diplomacy unless dragged in, they confined their interest to the economic field. Today Britain takes almost 70 per cent of the Republic's exports, and supplies more than half her imports; and this relationship is reflected in emigration patterns from the Republic. Before 1936 well over half of Ireland's emigrants went to the United States; after that date, Great Britain became the main destination. The economic dependency on Britain was conspicuous enough for Boserup to claim that, in economic terms, the union between the Republic of Ireland and the United Kingdom was being restored. Nor was this all. The Republic of Ireland, quite apart from her relations with Britain, developed a much more outward-looking foreign policy from the 1950s, becoming actively involved in the United Nations movement, and eventually joining the European Economic Community in 1973.

It was in this new context of internationalism that the first few cautious steps of North–South co-operation began. Significantly, they were largely confined to economic interests which affected both areas. Thus in 1952 agreement was reached that both governments should take over the Foyle fisheries. This was followed by joint involvement in draining the Erne basin and in a hydro-electric development there. Between 1953 and 1958 the Great Northern Railway, which included the Belfast–Dublin line, was operated jointly by the two governments and has since been operated jointly.

The meeting which took place in 1965 between the Northern and Southern premiers, Terence O'Neill and Sean Lemass, was a logical extension of these developments, but its symbolism was not lost in both parts of the island. They seemed to many to represent the new Ireland which had at last shaken off the past, men interested in prosperity rather than politics, in opportunities for co-operation instead of excuses for conflict. The effect inside Northern Ireland was considerable. The Nationalist party agreed to become the official opposition at Stormont and the Catholic hierarchy appointed a chaplain to parliament. 'Twin towns' were established across the border, their citizens exchanging visits and experiences. Relations between north and south, and between both of them and Britain, had never been closer, and the prospects of a period of community harmony seemed good. They were to be destroyed by a mixture of majority tardiness and minority impatience. The events following from the Civil Rights campaign were to alter radically both internal relations inside Northern Ireland, and Northern Ireland's relations with her immediate neighbours.

2

Law and Order

Paddy Hillyard

The principal aim of this chapter is to describe the different strategies which the authorities have used to deal with political violence in Northern Ireland over the last twelve years. The analysis will attempt to draw out some of the more important features which have tended to be overlooked in those accounts which have been more concerned to highlight the sectarian aspects of the strategies. The principal conclusion of the analysis is that the form of the repressive strategy adopted during the last six years, far from being exceptional and a product of the unique circumstances of the political violence in Northern Ireland is, on the contrary, the form which many modern capitalist states are evolving.

No understanding of the various strategies adopted over the last twelve years is possible without a discussion of law and order in the period from the setting up of the regional government and parliament in the six counties by the Government of Ireland Act (1920).

1920–1969: Special Powers Extraordinary

By mid-summer 1920 the British government had to contend with two law and order problems in the six counties. Both were to remain a feature until the present day. On the one hand, it had to deal with attacks by the IRA and on the other it had to cope with the sectarian attacks, which were mainly carried out on Catholics. It had two forces at its disposal: the Royal Irish Constabulary (RIC), which was controlled by a divisional commissioner outside Belfast and a city commissioner within the city; and various military units stationed in the North. (see Buckland 1979, 179–205). At the time the British government was hard-pressed in the south and west and no more troops could be sent north. Indeed, there was in fact pressure for troops from the north to be sent south (Farrell 1980, 126). In October 1920, the

British government announced the establishment of the Ulster Special Constabulary (USC). (For full details of the creation of the USC see Farrell 1980, 125–137). It was based upon the UVF—a totally Protestant paramilitary force—which had been reorganised a few months earlier with the tacit approval of the British government. Hence, the USC was from the outset exclusively Protestant. It was divided into three classes. Class 'A' was for those willing to do full-time duty and be posted anywhere within Northern Ireland; Class 'B' was for those willing to do part-time duty in their own locality; and Class 'C' was for those willing to go on reserve and who could be called upon in an emergency. This last class was vaguely defined and became little more than a device to give gun licences to loyalists and refuse them to Catholics. (Farrell 1979, 127). By August 1922 there were 7,000 'A' Specials, 20,000 'B' Specials and 17,000 in a re-constituted 'C' Class. There were also 1,200 full-time members of the newly formed Royal Ulster Constabulary (RUC) which had replaced the RIC in May of the same year.

The Specials played the central role in the establishment of the authority of the new government in Northern Ireland. From the outset their activities were controversial. They were undisciplined and partisan and were regarded by Catholics with a bitterness exceeding that which the Black and Tans inspired in the South.

Their sectarian conduct, as Farrell (1979, 184) points out, contributed to the peculiarly intense hatred with which the RUC has been regarded ever since by the Catholic population in the North. Not only were the two forces linked together in the public mind, but also half the initial recruits for the RUC came from the 'A' Specials.

While Farrell emphasises the role of the British government in the creation of the USC, Bew, Gibbon and Patterson (1979, 57–74) draw attention to the changes which were taking place within the Protestant class bloc. They argue that, in order to challenge republicanism independently of the British, the Unionist leadership had to give up some of its power to the Orange section of the Protestant working class. The form of the Unionist state apparatus can therefore be seen as a product of the class relations within the Unionist bloc coupled with British approval and support. In other words, they argue that the form of the Unionist state apparatus was not exclusively a product of external politics.

Another central element of the Unionist repressive state apparatus was the Civil Authorities (Special Powers) Act. This was passed in

1922 and gave the Minister of Home Affairs power 'to take all such steps... as may be necessary for preserving peace and maintaining order'. It conferred wide powers of arrest, questioning, search, detention and internment on the police and other agents of the Ministry of Home Affairs. It constituted an effective abrogation of the rule of law in the sense that the forces of law and order had the power to arrest and detain anyone they pleased without having to give any justification and without fear of being called to account in respect of any decisions later shown to be unjustified. Northern Ireland from the outset was therefore a state with extraordinary powers.

The Civil Authorities (Special Powers) Act was renewed annually until 1928 when it was extended for five years. At the end of 1933 it was made permanent. It was extensively criticised in the late thirties by NCCL (1935).

The law and order strategy of successive Unionist governments was unequivocal. A constant watch was maintained on Catholic communities and, whenever the state appeared to be under threat—for example, during the IRA campaigns of 1921–22, 1938–39 and 1956–62—the government introduced internment under the Civil Authorities (Special Powers) Act. It was also used on other occasions, as for instance when Republican politicians were interned for a week during a Royal visit in 1951. The main point to emphasise about internment was its wholly executive nature. The formal power provided for in the Civil Authorities (Special Powers) Act permitted the arrest and detention of anyone who was acting, had acted or was about to act 'in a manner prejudicial to the preservation of the peace and maintenance of order'. The responsibility for making the internment order after arrest lay with the Minister who was also personally responsible for ordering the release of internees. While there was provision for the appointment of an advisory committee to review the cases, the Minister was not bound to accept the recommendations. Internment was therefore a wholly executive measure. Its use highlighted the executive's direct involvement in suppressing political opposition. It was not surprising that the Cameron Commission found that its presence on the Statute book, and the continuance in force of regulations made under it, had caused widespread resentment among Catholics (Cameron 1969, 62–63). It had after all been used almost exclusively against them to suppress all political opposition to the Northern Ireland regime.

As well as the lack of confidence in the forces of law and order and the festering grievance of the Civil Authorities (Special Powers) Act, Catholics also had little confidence in the courts in Northern Ireland. This stemmed principally from the composition of both the judiciary and juries. The Northern Ireland judiciary throughout its history had been mainly composed of people who had been openly associated with the Unionist party. Of the twenty high court judges appointed since 1922, fifteen had been openly associated with the Unionist party and fourteen of the county court appointments had similar associations. Residents magistrates had also been drawn from the same source. While it does not follow that the decisions of judges and magistrates would be partisan, the composition of both the magistracy and the judiciary did little to inspire the confidence of Catholics in the administration of justice.

The composition of juries further exacerbated the problem of confidence in the administration of justice. Partly as a result of property qualification and partly as a result of the rules concerning the right to stand by or challenge jurors, the composition of juries was mainly Protestant. The qualification for jury service was based upon the ownership of property and as Catholics owned less property, this ensured that the majority on the jury list were Protestants. At this stage, the prosecution was entitled to stand by any number of jurors and the defence might challenge up to twelve without giving any reason, and might object to others for good cause. The end result was that most juries, particularly in Belfast, were Protestant. The risk of bias against Catholics was therefore always present.

It can be seen from this brief analysis of the law and order strategy adopted by successive Unionist governments that it was highly repressive, sectarian and centralised. Moreover, throughout the period, no attempt was made to disguise the political nature of the struggle nor of the response. It was successful in so far as it maintained the regime in power for fifty years. But from the outset it continually alienated the minority community from both the law and the state.

1969–1971: Reform and Repression

The response of the British government, after deploying troops in Northern Ireland in August 1969, was to pressurize the government at Stormont to introduce a series of reforms which, in essence, were aimed to establish a series of institutions to guarantee equality of treatment and freedom from discrimination for the Catholic community.

The principal reforms in the area of policing followed closely the recommendations of the Hunt Committee (1969). The object of the reform was to neutralise the political control of the police and to establish a wholly civilian and non-armed police force. Consequently, the 'B' Specials were disbanded and a new force, the Ulster Defence Regiment, was established under the control of the British Army. In addition, the RUC was disarmed and made accountable to a Police Authority. The continuing violence, however, soon led to the rearming of the police.

The Hunt Committee also recommended the introduction of an independent prosecutor on the Scottish model. But the Unionist government delayed in the implementation of this reform by establishing a committee to consider the proposals (MacDermott Working Party 1971). It was not until after Direct Rule in 1972 that a new office of a Director of Public Prosecutions was set up with full responsibility for the selection and prosecution of all serious criminal charges.

At the same time as the police was being reformed the Unionist government brought in tougher legislation under the Criminal Justice (Temporary Provision) Act (1970) to deal with rioters (Boyle 1970). The Act provided a six months minimum mandatory gaol sentence for anyone convicted of 'riotous behaviour', 'disorderly behaviour' or 'behaviour likely to cause a breach of the peace'. The new law immediately gave rise to numerous allegations of the partisan way in which the legislation was being enforced.

Outside the area of the administration of justice, other reforms were taking place. The discriminatory practices of local government were dealt with by extending local government franchise but at the same time denuding local authorities of considerable powers. A new centralised housing authority was established and administrative units were set up to manage education, planning and health and social services. (For full details see O'Dowd, Rolston and Tomlinson 1980; and Birrell and Murie 1980.)

While all these legislative changes were taking place, the situation on the streets was deteriorating. The relations between the army and the Catholic community were rapidly declining as the army took a tougher line against rioters. In 1970, a routine house search precipitated a large scale riot and the army introduced a curfew (O'Fearghael 1970). The conflict was slowly escalating into a guerrilla war between the army and the IRA.

In summary, in this period the strategy of the British government was not to define the problem in terms of law and order but to deal with it at a number of different levels. On the one hand, there was a very real attempt to correct the arbitrary and inequitable administration of criminal laws and to establish institutions which would deal with the widespread problem of discrimination. Liberal notions such as the separation of powers, the rule of law, the impartiality and objectivity of judges, and democratic institutions to check the exercise of power were mobilised in support of the reforms but no attempt was made to ensure that the notions were realised in practice. The creation of new institutions and the dispersal of power has meant that the various bodies, which are relatively autonomous, have established their own modus operandi; they have structured their own targets and objectives. The dominant feature has been their tendency to reconstitute practical and legal problems as technical matters. On the other hand, the increasing violence on the streets, coupled with the demands of the Protestant community for tougher measures, led to the development of a more coercive strategy to deal with the problem of violence.

1971–1975: Internment and Military Security

The strategy in this period was dominated by the use of internment and the development by the army either through encouragement or by default of its own military security policy. This involved the introduction of a series of techniques which have been used in colonial emergencies in the past and developed by Brigadier Kitson (1971). The combined aim of these techniques was to collect as much information on the IRA in particular and the Catholic community in general. I will deal with each component in turn.

Internment and Detention

Internment was introduced with the agreement of the British government on the 9th August, 1971. The army and police arrested 342 men on the initial sweep. Within six months 2,357 persons had been arrested and 1,600 released after interrogation. The introduction, impact and subsequent use of internment has been extensively documented and the details need not concern us here (see, for example, McGuffin 1973; Faul and Murray 1974). The main point to emphasise is that its use provided an example of unfettered ministerial discretion and highlighted the political nature of the struggle. The state's involvement in suppressing political opposition was clear and unequivocal.

After internment, the level of violence increased rapidly. Many Catholics holding public appointments withdrew from these offices and a rent and rates strike was begun. In January 1972 the army killed 13 civilians during a Civil Rights march in Derry. An official inquiry by the Lord Chief Justice only inflamed the situation as his report exonerated those responsible. (Widgery Tribunal 1972; for critical commentaries see Dash 1972; McMahon 1974).

After Direct Rule was imposed in March 1972, a slight shift took place in the internment strategy. Following the breakdown of discussions between the IRA and the government, a new system of detention without trial was introduced. The principal development was to replace the executive authority of the Minister under the Special Powers Act by a new system of judicial determination. All cases now came before an independent judicial Commissioner (see Boyle, Hadden and Hillyard 1975, 58–77). The aim was to distance the executive from the day-to-day administration of the emergency powers in an attempt to depoliticise the nature of the response in order to gain the confidence of the minority community in the system. It represented the beginning of a strategy which was to find its ultimate and most sustained and strongest expression in the criminalisation policies which were introduced in 1975. The operation of these new procedures received widespread criticisms (see, for example, Faul & Murray 1973). The whole system of detention appeared to be dominated by the policies of the security forces and the quasi-judicial hearings were farcical. The new scheme did little to gain the confidence of Catholics. When the government began detaining Protestants in February 1973 the opposition to detention became more widespread.

The last point to note about detention is that those who were detained were not treated like other convicted persons. They were placed in compounds and accommodated in huts rather than cells and were permitted considerable autonomy within the compounds. They were also granted the same rights as prisoners on remand. This meant that they could wear their own clothes and have more visits, letters and parcels than convicted persons. Similar rights were also extended in June 1972 to those who had been convicted in the courts and who claimed to have been politically motivated. These concessions amounted to what was called 'Special Status Category'.

Further changes were made to the detention procedures after the review of measures to deal with terrorism by a committee chaired by Lord Gardiner (1975). These changes were incorporated in the

Northern Ireland (Emergency Provisions) Act of 1975 and involved a slight move back towards a system of executive detention. But they were of little importance as the use of detention without trial was suspended in February 1975 and a totally new strategy for dealing with those involved in political violence was introduced. During the period in which internment and detention had been in operation a total of 2,158 orders were issued.

Diplock Commission

At this point it is useful to consider the Diplock Commission (1972) because it strongly influenced the way in which the police and army operated in this period. It was also responsible for the form of the strategy adopted in the period 1975 onwards, which will be dealt with later.

The first point concerns the composition of the Commission. The members of the Commission were Lord Diplock, Lord Rupert Cross, Sir Kenneth Younger, a former Intelligence Corps Major, and George Woodcock, a former General Secretary of the TUC. The late Lord Cross was a Professor of Criminal Law and had been a member of the Criminal Law Revision Committee which recommended the abolition of the right to silence (1972).

The second point concerns the type of evidence the Commission collected. The Commission did not go to Northern Ireland. Only Lord Diplock visited the Province and then only on two occasions. The bulk of the evidence was oral and was taken from people with responsibility for the administration of justice in Northern Ireland, and from representatives of the Civil and Armed Services.

The third and most important point is that the report was produced for the authorities responsible for law and order and not for the people of Northern Ireland as a whole. The underlying problem of the political struggle between opposing groups of very different aspirations was totally ignored and the sole focus was upon the maintenance of public order. In this context, civil rights in general and the rights of suspects in particular, appear as exceptional, anachronistic and even subversive. Long-established common law principles were reconstituted as 'technical rules'. For example, the principle concerning the admissability of statements, which is fundamental in an adversary system of criminal justice, was described in a number of places as a 'technical rule'. Burton and Carlin (1979, 83–84) appear to make a similar point, regrettably in jargon-ladened and absurdly complex language, when they describe the Diplock report in the following way:

> Its intra-discursive logic is as incoherent as its epistemological justi-
> fication. Though argued in terms of essentialised justice, relocated
> within legal evolution, the changes in the technical guarantees of
> objectivity remain but a part of the syntagmatic strategy which
> orders the paradigms of the common law mode towards a unity of
> its discursive object: the discursive appropriation of an official word
> whose otherness is beyond recognition.

Most of the Commission's recommendations were included in the
Northern Ireland (Emergency Provisions) Act which came into force
in August 1973. The army was provided with the power to stop and
detain a suspect for up to four hours, and both the army and police
were also given the further power to stop and question any person as
to his or her identity and knowledge of terrorist incidents. In addition,
the police were given the power to arrest any one they suspected of
being a terrorist and detain them for up to 72 hours. No grounds of
reasonableness were required. This particular provision, it should be
noted, was introduced to enable the administrative procedures
required by the Detention of Terrorist Order to be carried out. The
Act also provided extensive powers of search. Finally, the Act
abolished juries and introduced far-reaching changes in the rules of
evidence.

The Northern Ireland (Emergency Provisions) Act, like the Special
Powers Act, constituted an effective abrogation of the rule of law.

Military Security

The Act provided ample opportunities for the army to extend its
military security policy, which it had been developing throughout 1970.
This involved among other things the creation and maintenance of as
complete a dossier as was practicable on all inhabitants in Republican
areas. The military strategists referred to this as 'contact information'
(Kitson 1971, 96). The principal methods involved interrogation in
depth, frequent arrest for screening, regular house searches and head
counts.

Internment provided the first opportunity for interrogation in depth
to be used by the army. A group of internees were selected and
interrogated in depth using a selection of techniques based upon the
psychology of sensory deprivation. (see for details McGuffin 1974;
Amnesty International 1973; Faul and Murray 1972). The impact and

effect of these techniques were considerable (Shallice 1973). While subsequently there was a committee of enquiry set up under the chairpersonship of Sir Edmund Compton to consider the allegations of torture and brutality during interrogation, the principal issue as to whom authorised the techniques was never investigated (Compton 1971). As it was, the Compton Committee produced a most unsatisfactory conclusion that while the techniques used did constitute physical ill-treatment they did not amount to brutality. A further enquiry was later established under the chairpersonship of Lord Parker to consider whether interrogation in depth should be permitted to be continued (Parker 1972).

In the meantime, the Irish Republic filed an application before the European Commission of Human Rights (1976). The case eventually went to the European Court where it was held that the techniques, contrary to the findings of the Commission, did not constitute a practice of torture but of inhuman and degrading treatment. The British government undertook that the techniques would never be reintroduced. The government subsequently paid out £188,250 in damages to the persons involved.

The other methods of army intelligence gathering included the use of foot patrols to build up a detailed picture of the area and its inhabitants, house searches, and frequent arrests for questioning. While these methods were used extensively under the Special Powers Act, their use was increased after the introduction of the recommendations of the Diplock Commission in the Northern Ireland (Emergency Provisions) Act.

No figures are available on the number of people stopped and questioned on the street. Nor are any figures available on the number of persons arrested and detained up to four hours. But it is known that these methods were used very widely. On occasions large scale arrest operations were initiated and people arrested at random for apparently no other reason other than to collect more information on the local community (Boyle, Hadden and Hillyard 1975, 41–53).

Figures are, however, available for the number of house searches and these provide some indication of the extent of the army's intelligence gathering operations and how they expanded over the period after the introduction of the Northern Ireland (Emergency Provisions) Act. In 1971, there were 17,262 house searches. By 1973, this had risen to 75,000, one fifth of all houses in Northern Ireland.

Many of the intelligence gathering activities carried out by the army were of dubious legality. It is very doubtful whether large scale house searches or the extensive screening was justified under the Act.

In 1974, the powers of arrest and detention were extended still further under the Prevention of Terrorism Act. This was introduced for the whole of the United Kingdom in the wake of the Birmingham bombings. It provided the power of arrest upon reasonable suspicion and forty-eight hours detention in the first instance, which could be extended by up to a further five days by the Secretary of State. In practice, this was another form of executive detention, admittedly for only a three day period. (For a detailed analysis of its operation see Scorer and Hewitt 1981.)

As the conflict between the army and the IRA intensified the army resorted to a variety of other techniques in order to attempt to defeat the IRA. There is considerable evidence to suggest that the army used agents provocateurs, a variety of undercover techniques and assassination squads (Lindsay 1980; Brady et al. 1977; Geraghty 1977). In addition, it developed new technologies. These included new methods of crowd control, new surveillance apparatus and the computerisation of all its intelligence information (see Ackroyd et al. 1977; Wright 1977; Wright 1978).

The RUC during this period took a subordinate role. It was largely excluded from policing the main Catholic areas. There was thus a very clear difference in the deployment patterns of the security forces with the police mainly controlling Protestant areas where they used an approach closer to traditional police approach and the army operating principally in Republican areas where it used the methods described above. This differential deployment served only to alienate further the Catholic community.

One response of the RUC to the crisis of confidence within the Catholic community was to concentrate on developing community relations work. A community relations branch was established in October 1970 and the Chief Inspector in charge of the branch was despatched to London to study the methods used by the Metropolitan Police in both youth and community relations. The branch worked mainly with young people organising discos, rambles, adventure holidays and football matches. In addition, the RUC has made strenuous efforts to establish working relationships with all the local politicians.

From a broader perspective, it can be seen that the strategy in this period had three dominant features. In the first place, the strategy openly acknowledged the political dimensions of the struggle. Detainees were treated like 'prisoners of war' and the politics of those convicted in the courts was recognised in the granting of 'special status category'. Secondly, the strategy gave the army considerable autonomy. There was little attempt to control its operations and practices, many of which were of dubious legality. The third feature of the strategy was the extensive use which was made of judges. They were not only used to provide a veneer of detention, but were also used to chair enquiries. Up to the end of 1975 seven enquiries had been chaired by judges. These were of two types. On the one hand, there were those which investigated some controversial incident or event, such as a Bloody Sunday. On the other, there were those which reviewed the appropriateness of particular policies, for example the Diplock Commission's review of the 'legal procedures to deal with terrorist activities'. The role of judges in part stemmed from the nature of the investigations, but it also reflected the extent to which the authorities hoped to diffuse a difficult political situation or to distance themselves from recommendations which were likely to be controversial. As Harvey (1981, 6) has pointed out:

> The fiction of the doctrine of the constitutional separation of power has never been more clearly exposed than by these attempts to assure the public that British judges can provide solutions to the political problems of Northern Ireland.

1975–1982: Reconstituting the Problem of Political Violence

Following the Labour Government's victory in 1974, it began to reconsider the strategy of dealing with violence in Northern Ireland. It subsequently initiated a totally different strategy. The central aim was to deny totally the political dimensions of the conflict and to reconstitute the problem in terms of law and order. To this end, the Government initiated three related policies. First, it began to restore full responsibility for law and order to the RUC. This policy has since been described as Ulsterisation. Second, it stopped the use of internment in February 1975 and began to rely upon the courts as the sole method of dealing with those suspected of violence. Third, it announced that special status category would be withdrawn for any prisoner sentenced for crimes commited after March 1st, 1976. The latter two policies have been widely referred to as a policy of criminalisation.

Ulsterisation

The first indication of the Ulsterisation policy came in April 1974 when the new Secretary of State for Northern Ireland, Merlyn Rees, announced that he intended to restore 'the full responsibility of law and order to the police'. Later in the year he announced a five-point plan for the further extension of policing. The plan consisted of setting up a series of new local police centres in selected communities to act as focal points for policing. They were to be mainly staffed by RUC reserves working in their own areas.

The impact of the policy of Ulsterisation can be best illustrated by considering the numbers in the security forces. In 1973, there were 31,000 security personnel of whom 14,500 were in the UDR, RUC and RUC Reserve. In 1980, the total numbers were roughly similar, but the numbers in the UDR, RUC and RUC Reserve had expanded to 19,500. As the vast majority of personnel in these forces are Protestant, one effect of the policy of Ulsterisation has been to replace British security personnel by Ulster Protestants. The policy of Ulsterisation has also been characterised by an expansion in the weaponry for the force. The RUC is now armed with pistols and sterling sub-machine guns, M1 carbines and SLRs. In this respect, the RUC has therefore returned to being a military force rather than a civilian force which the Hunt Committee had recommended.

Perhaps the most important development since the start of the Ulsterisation policy has been the strengthening of the intelligence capacity of the RUC. This has taken a number of different forms: an expansion in the number of confidential telephones, the use of police informers and various surveillance techniques and the use of arrest and detention powers to interrogate at length all those whom the police consider may provide them with information. The use of these powers for interrogation has been a major feature of the strategy and it appears that the widespread screening and trawling which the army carried out in the previous period is now being carried out by the RUC.

The police, as has been noted, have very extensive powers of arrest and detention under the Northern Ireland (Emergency Provisions) Act and the Prevention of Terrorism Act. In addition, they have ordinary powers of arrest under the criminal law. The most frequently used power is Section 11 of the Northern Ireland (Emergency Provisions) Act which allows the police to arrest anyone they suspect of being a terrorist. The use of this power is not surprising as this power is broadest in scope in terms of the degree of suspicion required and allows detention for a longer period than all the other provisions except the seven day power under the Prevention of Terrorism Act. The almost exclusive use of Section 11 rather than ordinary powers of arrest illustrates very clearly the way in which emergency powers become the norm. More importantly, the effect of mainly using this particular power has been to shift the basis of arrest from suspicion of a particular act to suspicion of the status of the individual (Hillyard and Boyle 1982, 8).

No figures are regulary published for the number of arrests and pro-secutions under the Northern Ireland (Emergency Provisions) Act in contrast to the practice for arrests under the Prevention of Terrorism Act. However, two sets of arrest figures have been published which illustrate not only the extent to which arrest and detention powers are used only for intelligence gathering, but also how the practice is on the increase.

The Bennett Committee (1979, 141) noted that 2,970 persons were arrested under the Northern Ireland (Emergency Provisions) Act and Prevention of Terrorism Act and detained for more than four hours between the 1st September and 31st August, 1978. But only 35 per cent were subsequently charged with an offence. In other words, over 1,900 people were arrested, interrogated and subsequently released.

The other set of arrest figures was published in reply to a parlia-mentary question in Hansard on the 7th December. These figures show that between 1st January and 30th October 1980, 3,868 persons were arrested under the Northern Ireland (Emergency Provisions) Act and Prevention of Terrorism Act and detained for more than four hours. Yet only 11 per cent were charged. When the actual number of persons arrested, interrogated and released are compared and adjusted so that the figures refer to periods of the same length, they show that the number of persons involved has more than doubled from 1,900 in 1978 to 4,131 in 1980.

Even those who were subsequently charged are often extensively questioned about 'other matters' not associated with the offence in question. In the most recent survey of the Diplock Courts it was found that in over 80 per cent of all cases the suspect made a confession within the first six hours of detention. Yet the vast majority of these people were interrogated for substantial periods after the confession (Walsh 1982, 7).

The evidence is therefore unequivocal. The powers of arrest and interrogation are being primarily used by the police to collect information on individuals and communities rather than to charge and prosecute. Policing in Northern Ireland has therefore moved from a retro-active form, where those suspected of illegal activities are arrested and processed through the courts on evidence obtained after the event, to a pre-emptive form, where large sections of those communities which are perceived as being a distinct threat to the existing *status quo* are regularly and systematically monitored and surveilled.

Monitoring and surveillance of problem groups is being extended in other directions. In January 1979, a committee was set up under the chairpersonship of Sir Harold Black to review legislation and services relating to the care and treatment of children and young persons. It recommended a comprehensive and integrated approach to provide help for children emphasising the important roles of the family, school and community (Black Review 1976). More specifically, it proposed a dual system of coordinating teams in schools and at district level. The school-based care teams are to be made up of the appropriate counsellor, the education welfare officer, the educational psychologist, the social worker familiar with the catchment area, as well as representatives from the police and probation service. At the district level, it was suggested that representatives of statutory agencies concerned with the interests of children should meet together to discuss the best policies to deal with identified problems. In December 1979, the government endorsed the strategy proposed by the report and accepted its recommendations in principle. The government is at present consulting the various interests concerned.

The report appears to be remarkably progressive. It begins with an analysis of the social and economic problems of Northern Ireland. Throughout, it emphasises that the needs of children are paramount. Furthermore, it argues that it is imperative to avoid as far as possible segregating children from their families, schools and communities or labelling them as deviant, abnormal, troublesome or delinquent. The Report, however, is totally uncritical of its own assumptions. In particular, it assumes that the task of identifying children in need is unproblematic and that professionals and parents will agree. But how many working-class parents in West or East Belfast, would view 'the lack of attainment at school, apathy, persistent behaviour, truancy, or involvement in delinquent or criminal activity' as 'the outward manifestation of complex, personal or family problems' (Black Review 1979, 6) rather than the result of their children's position in the broader cultural and political environment in which they are brought up?

If the strategy of a coordinated approach through school-based and district care teams is implemented in full, it will extend the monitoring and surveillance of particular populations. It is clear from the Report that this is the principal aim of the approach. It states (Black Review 1979, 9):

> There should be a free exchange of information among the agencies involved in the multi-disciplinary team. Problems manifesting themselves in the school, in the home or in the community, whether they first come to the attention of the education authorities, the social services or the police should be referred to the School-based Care Team for discussion and consideration of what help, if any, each of the agencies might provide for the child and his family to help solve the problem.

The more efficient control of particular populations has been attempted at other levels. There is now some evidence to suggest that both the RUC and the Army are playing a significant role in the physical planning of Belfast. An article in the *Guardian* of the 13th March, 1982 claimed that the Belfast Development Office, to which the Housing Executive forwards all its proposed building plans for clearance, has representatives from the security forces. It was also suggested that the security forces has interfered with a number of planning decisions: they had insisted that a group of houses were removed from a planned development in the Ardoyne; asked for reinforced pavements in the new Poleglass estate to bear the weight of armoured vehicles; and recommended high 'security walls' in new developments in the Lower Falls and at Roden Street in West Belfast (see also Alcorn 1982).

Other sources have argued that the involvement of the security forces has been more extensive. It is claimed that new housing estates have been built with only two entrances and that factories, warehousing and motorways have been deliberately constructed to form barriers. The aim of these developments, it is suggested, is to prevent residents in Catholic areas from moving from one part of the city to another through safe areas and to force people out on to the main roads, which are more easily policed. If all these developments have occurred then the authorities would appear to be making strenuous attempts to confine the problem of violence within particular areas. In other words, they seem to be deliberately creating ghettos in which dissident populations may be easily contained.

The role of the army in the period from 1975 has changed considerably. Its method of intelligence gathering has altered substantially with the rise of the RUC's work in this respect. There has been a very sharp decline in the number of houses searched by the army and the large-scale screening operations have been curtailed. However, there is evidence to suggest that the army still carries out undercover and substantial surveillance operations. In addition, they are responsible for all the bomb disposal work.

The strategy of Ulsterisation has not been without its problems. The army has resented the curtailment of its operations and has developed its own strategies on occasions to deal with those involved in political violence. In a series of incidents, a number of alleged terrorists have been shot dead. While the strains between the RUC and the army have been in existence for a long time, they appear to have deteriorated since the RUC took the dominant role. In August 1979 following the assassination of Lord Mountbatten and the killing of eighteen soldiers at Warrenpoint, the Prime Minister visited Ulster and was told that the strategy of Ulsterisation had failed and that the army should once again take the dominant role. A few weeks later Sir Morris Oldfield was appointed as Security Coordinator. The appointment clearly was an attempt to deal with the differences of approach between the two forces.

The Diplock Court Process

The strategy of relying upon the courts was made possible by the radical modifications in the ordinary criminal process which the Diplock Commission recommended in 1972 and which were enacted in the Emergency Provisions (Northern Ireland) Act 1973. These changes, however, did not become significant until the courts were relied upon as a sole method of dealing with those involved in political violence from the end 1975 onwards.

It was abundantly clear from the Diplock Commission's report that interrogation was considered to be an essential element for the successful prosecution and conviction of those involved. The Commission was critical of what it described as 'technical rules and practice' concerning the admissibility of statements. It drew attention to the 'considerable rigidity' with which the judges rules had been interpreted in Northern Ireland. It noted a decision of the Court of Appeal in which it had been ruled that the mere creation by the authorities of any 'set-up which makes it more likely that those who did not wish to speak will eventually do so' renders any confession involuntary and inadmissible. It clearly disagreed with judgments such as these and it pointed out (Diplock Commission 1972, 30):

> The whole technique of skilled interrogation is to build up an atmosphere in which the initial desire to remain silent is replaced by an urge to confide in the questioner.

It recommended that all statements in breach of the common law should be admitted provided that they could not be shown to have been produced by subjecting the accused to torture or to inhuman or degrading treatment. The recommendation was enacted in the Emergency Provisions (Northern Ireland) Act 1973. The provision not only eliminated any retrospective control over the way interrogation was conducted but also legalised, in combination with the power to detain a person up to 72 hours under the Emergency Provisions Act or seven days under the Prevention of Terrorism Act, prolonged interrogation.

The Commission however was not only responsible for legalising prolonged interrogation. In not supporting the Court of Appeal position concerning 'set-ups' which were designed to make it 'more likely that those who did not wish to speak will eventually do so', it gave the green light to the authorities to create special interrogation centres. Two were built, one at Castlereagh and the other at Gough Barracks and were designed to create the most conducive environment for the interrogation process. Castlereagh was opened in early 1977 and Gough later in the same year.

The subsequent history of these centres is now well-known (Taylor 1980). From early 1977 the number of complaints against the police in respect of ill-treatment during interrogation began to increase. The Association of Forensic Medical Officers made representations to the Police Authority as early as April 1977. In November 1977 Amnesty International carried out an investigation and called for a public enquiry into the allegations (Amnesty 1978). The Government, shortly after receiving Amnesty International's report, established the Bennett Committee not however to investigate the allegations themselves but to consider police interrogation procedures. Notwithstanding their restrictive terms of reference the Committee (1979, 136) however did conclude that:

> Our own examination of medical evidence reveals cases in which injuries, whatever their precise cause, were not self-inflicted and were sustained in police custody.

Apart from the evidence of ill-treatment, the other aspect of the interrogation process which gave rise to concern during this period, and subsequently, has been the extent to which the outcome of the trial was in fact determined in the police interrogation centres. In an analysis of all cases dealt with in the Diplock Courts between January and April 1979, it was found that 86 per cent of all defendants had made a confession (Boyle, Hadden and Hillyard 1980, 44). Of these, 56 per cent of prosecutions relied solely upon evidence of admission, and in another 30 per cent this was supplemented by additional forensic or identification evidence which pointed to the guilt of the accused, although this additional evidence would often not have been sufficient to justify a conviction on its own. In a more recent study, a very similar pattern has been found (Walsh 1982). What these figures show is the extent to which the forum for determining guilt or innocence is only very occasionally the courtroom.

The Bennett Committee made a large number of recommendations to prevent abuse of the suspect during interrogation. The most important of which was perhaps the recommendation that all interviews should be monitored by members of the uniformed branch on close-circuit televisions. Most of the Bennett Committee's proposals have now been implemented. It should be emphasised, however, that all the recommendations were designed to prevent physical abuse during interrogation. The safeguards do little to curtail the extreme psychological pressures which are at the heart of the interrogation process.

Since the introduction of the Bennett Committee's suggestions there have been far fewer complaints against the police in respect of ill-treatment during interrogation. It is however hard to ascertain whether this is simply due to Bennett. The underlying assumption was that the pressure to break rules and physically assault suspects stems from the individual policemen themselves. It was assumed that they are either over-zealous or in some circumstances deviant. A similar assumption can be found in the deliberations of the Royal Commission on Criminal Procedure (Hillyard 1981, 86–87). It is a highly questionable assumption, however. There is a considerable body of evidence which suggests that the pressure on the police to break the rules does not stem from the personality characteristics of the policeman but is located within the organisation of policing. The pressures generating physical assaults during questioning tend to be developed in response to the perceived seriousness of the problem and often decisions concerning particular responses are taken at a very high level. Taylor's analysis provides some support for this view. In a chart noting the number of complaints it is clear that there was a tendency for complaints to increase when political pressure was exerted on the police to produce results, such as when there was some public outrage, for example, at the La Mon bombings. When there was public concern about police behaviour, complaints tended to decrease (Taylor 1980, 323).

It is more likely that the introduction of new policies following the appointment of Jack Hermon as the new Chief Constable from the 1st January, 1980 may have been more influential in changing the practices at Castlereagh and Gough than any of the Bennett recommendations. It is certainly known that Hermon was opposed to a policy which relied on confessions to defeat the IRA.

Apart from the centrality of confessions to the effectiveness of the Diplock Courts, there are a number of other important features of the whole process. To begin with, the Diplock system is now handling a large proportion of offences which do not appear to be connected with Loyalist or Republican paramilitary activity or with sectarianism. It is estimated that 40 per cent of all cases processed through the Diplock Courts have nothing to do with the troubles (Walsh 1982, 2). In other words, a system which was widely regarded as a temporary measure to deal with the particular problems of political violence is now becoming the normal process for all offences.

A second feature of the Diplock Court system is the extent to which judges appear to have become case-hardened (Boyle, Hadden and Hillyard 1980, 60–62). Since the introduction of juryless trials, the acquittal rate has been declining. There are a number of possible explanations for this. One widely stated explanation is that the prosecuting authorities are now taking greater care in the selection and preparation of cases. But when the trends for jury trials, for which the same prosecuting authorities have responsibility, are considered, no similar decline in the acquittal rate is observable. On the contrary, jury acquittals have been increasing. These very different trends provide strong support that the declining acquittal rate is principally a result of judges becoming case-hardened.

A third feature of the Diplock Court system is the extent of bargaining. This may occur in connection with either the charges, where the defence enters into negotiations to secure the withdrawal of the more serious charge or charges, or the plea, where the defendant pleads guilty to lesser charges in the expectation of a lower sentence in return for the subsequent saving of time and costs. No research has been carried out to ascertain the extent of plea bargaining, but two separate groups of researchers (Boyle, Hadden and Hillyard 1980, 71–74 and Harvey 1981, 32–33) both note that those involved in the trial process have confirmed that it takes place. Boyle, Hadden and Hillyard (1980, 72) in their study of the cases which were dealt with in the Diplock Courts between January and April 1979 found specific evidence of charge bargaining. In about 20 per cent of all cases the prosecution withdrew or substituted a number of charges which were already on the indictment sheet and in which the defence pleaded to the remaining or substituted charge.

Charge and plea bargaining are, of course, features of other criminal justice systems. What is important about the phenomenon of bargaining in Northern Ireland is that the pressure to bargain is likely to be much more intensive than in other systems. The number and seriousness of cases in Northern Ireland are of a different magnitude and this will tend to place certain organisational demands upon the prosecuting and court authorities to encourage bargaining. In addition, the Bar in Northern Ireland is very small. The importance of this has been well expressed by Harvey (1981, 32):

> Defence lawyers, both solicitors and barristers, are under their own professional, institutional and financial pressures to co-operate with the prosecuting authorities and avoid judicial disapproval. The smaller the bar the greater the presure on its members to avoid a reputation for contesting cases with little likely chance of success.

The study of the Diplock courts in 1979 could not establish that any specific sentence had been reduced as a result of bargaining (Boyle, Hadden and Hillyard 1980, 73). But what did emerge from the data was that the severity of sentences were imposed on defendants refusing to recognise the court while the lowest sentences were imposed on those who pleaded guilty at the very start. In between were sentences on those who pleaded not guilty and seriously contested the case against them. The evidence suggests that the differential in terms of length and severity of sentences as between Loyalist and Republican defendants is not to be explained, as is often suggested (Workers Research Unit 1982) in terms of simple religious or political bias, but rather in terms of the defendant's choice whether to co-operate or not to co-operate with the system. This important point emphasises the need to consider decision making in this or any other criminal process not as a series of sequential phases which can be dealt with in isolation but rather a process involving a complex series of interacting stages in which decisions taken cumulatively contribute to outcomes. Thus, the much discussed argument of whether judge or jury is superior for normal offences should not be conducted without emphasising that decisions as to guilt or innocence are in fact an outcome of this complex bureaucratic process where the principles of criminal law and its procedures interact with the demands of the administration. The context in which judge or jury operates is much more important than whether the final decisions are left to judge or jury or solely to a judge.

The fourth feature of the Diplock Court system which needs to be mentioned is that a higher standard of proof appears to be required in the case of charges laid against the security forces than against civilians. The Bennett Committee (1979, 82) notes that, between 1972 and the end of 1978, 19 officers were prosecuted for alleged offences against prisoners in custody or during the course of interrogation. Of these, only two were convicted but the convictions were set aside on appeal. Another case was *nolle prosequi* and the rest were acquitted. The 1979 study of cases dealt with in the Diplock Courts between January and April 1979 found an acquittal rate of 100 per cent for members of the security forces (Boyle, Hadden and Hillyard, 1980, 79).

Special Category Status

The other strand in the Labour Government's criminalisation policy was to phase out special category status. This, as has been noted above, was granted in 1972 to members of paramilitary organisations who had been convicted in the courts and who had claimed to have been politically motivated. The Gardiner Committee had considered that its introduction had been 'a serious mistake' and argued that it should be abolished (1975, 34). One argument was that the compound system in which the special category prisoners were held made it more likely that prisoners would emerge with an increased commitment to terrorism. The other argument was that it could see no justification in granting privleges 'to a large number of criminals convicted of very serious crimes, in many cases, murder, merely because they claimed political motivation' (Gardiner 1975, 34). The Government concurred with these arguments and announced that no prisoner sentenced for crimes committed after 1st March 1976 could be granted special status category. In March 1980 it announced that this would apply to any prisoner charged after 1st April, 1980 for crimes wherever committed. In practice, this meant that all those convicted would be put into a conventional cellular prison and denied the special privileges which had been granted in 1972. To accommodate the prisoners the government built 800 cells in the form of an H, hence the H-Block protest, at the cost of £19,000 per cell.

There have been many previous struggles in British prisons over special or political status (see Radzinowicz and Hood 1979). But the decision to phase out special category status in Northern Ireland was to lead to the longest ever collective struggle over this issue. (For a detailed account see Coogan 1980). The protest started in September 1976, when Kieran Nugent was sentenced to the new cellular prison at the Maze. He refused to wear the prison clothes issued to him. The authorities reacted with considerable severity. He was kept in solitary confinement, denied exercise and all 'privileges', visits, letters, parcels. In addition, he lost a day's remission for every day of his protest. He was soon joined by other prisoners. The Blanket Protest, as it became known, as the prisoners had only blankets to wear, had begun. The protest soon escalated. In early 1978, after what appeared to be considerable intransigence by the authorities combined with a desire to make life as uncomfortable as possible for the prisoners, the prisoners extended the protest by smearing their cells with their own excreta. In 1980 the women in Armagh prison joined the dirty protest (see McCafferty 1981). On October 10th, 1980 it was announced that prisoners were starting a hunger strike on October 27th, four and a half years after the initial protest had begun.

Hunger strikes have a long tradition in Irish history. They had been used in previous prison struggles and under early Irish Brehon law of the sixth and eighth centuries an offended person fasted on the doorstep of an offender to embarrass them into resolving the dispute. On October 27th, seven men went on hunger strike. This strike was called off on December 18th mainly because one of the seven was about to die and there was, at that time, a widely held view in the prison that the British Government would make a number of important concessions. When the concessions were revealed, they failed to meet the prisoners' expectations. It was their understanding that they were to receive their own clothes and then be issued with civilian prison clothing. The British Government statement, however, issued on the 19th December announcing the concessions, reversed the sequence. Civilian prison clothing had to be accepted before the prisoners could be moved to clean cells (For full details see Browne 1981).

Inevitably, another hunger strike was organised but on this occasion it was decided that volunteers should begin their fasts at intervals. Sands was the first volunteer and began his hunger strike on 1st March, 1981. He died on the 5th May. Nine others died before the hunger strike was ended on the 5th October, 1981, after the Government made a number of concessions. Prisoners were granted the right to wear their own clothes, and new facilities to improve association between prisoners were promised. In addition, a proportion of the loss of remission arising out of the protest was to be restored. In terms of penal reform, these concessions were trivial, but in the face of the Government's intransigence over the five and a half years of prison protest, they were considerable.

Throughout the length of the protest numerous attempts were made by various individuals and organisations to seek a solution to the problems. In 1978, a number of protesting prisoners initiated procedures before the European Commission of Human Rights. They claimed that the regime under which they lived amounted to inhuman and degrading treatment and punishment in breach of Article 3 of the Convention. They also claimed that their right to freedom of conscience and belief under Article 9 of the Convention was denied to them because the prison authorities sought to apply to them the normal prison regimes. The British Government's case was that the conditions were essentially self-inflicted and that the Convention afforded no preferential status for certain categories of prisoners.

In June 1980, the European Commission declared that the major part of the case was inadmissible. It concurred with the British Government's view that these conditions were self-inflicted. It also agreed that the right to preferential status for certain category of prisoners was not guaranteed by the Convention. The Commission, however, was critical of the authorities (1980, 86):

> The Commission must express its concern at the inflexible approach of the state authorities which has been concerned more to punish offenders against prison discipline than to explore ways of resolving such a serious deadlock. Furthermore, the Commission is of the view that for humanitarian reasons, efforts should have been made by the authorities to ensure that the applicants could avail of certain facilities such as taking regular exercise in the open air and with some form of clothing (other than prison clothing) and making greater use of the prison amenities under similar conditions.

The decision, however, did nothing to end the protest. As the confrontation between the authorities and the protesting prisoners intensified, Provisional Sinn Fein began a political campaign in support of the prisoners' claim to political status. An H-Block information centre was established to supply local and foreign journalists with information. The authorities on their part increased their efforts to emphasise the criminality of the activities of the IRA. They issued numerous press releases as well as glossy brochures entitled 'H-Blocks: The Reality', 'Day to Day Life in Northern Ireland Prisons', and 'H-Blocks: What the Papers Say'. In August 1981, they began to issue 'fact files' on each of the hunger strikers. These included a brief description of the activities leading to conviction and a montage of selected newspaper reports on the case.

All these activities emphasised the extent to which the authorities were prepared to go to maintain its policy of criminalisation. They were largely successful in convincing the British media of its case as almost without exception all newspapers and the media accepted the government's position. (see Hillyard 1982; Elliott 1977; Schlesinger 1978; *Information on Ireland* 1979).

The policy of eliminating special category status, however, was fraught with contradiction. To begin with, those involved in political violence are dealt with in a very different way from the ordinary person who gets involved in crime. They are arrested under emergency powers and convicted in radically modified courts. Secondly, the motivations for their activities are very different from those of 'ordinary' criminals. They carry out their activities for deliberate political purposes. They do not regard themselves as 'ordinary' criminals, nor are they seen as such by the communities from which they are drawn. Neither does the law under which they are convicted define them as 'ordinary' criminals. Most were arrested under suspicion of being a 'terrorist'. 'Terrorism' is defined as 'the use of violence for political ends'. As Tomlinson points out, 'they are considered as political in the courtroom but criminal for the purposes of punishment' (O'Dowd, Rolston and Tomlinson 1980, 193).

Third, the abolition of special status category created the anomalous situation in which hundreds of prisoners who had committed similar offences, but at different times, were serving their sentences with special status category in compounds in the very same prison.

Fourth, the penological justifications for the elimination of special status category, namely that the compound system made it more likely that prisoners would 'emerge with an increased commitment to terrorism', was not supported by any empirical evidence. All the evidence which now exists tends to support the opposite conclusion. The 1979 Diplock Court study found that only 11 per cent of all those who came before the courts had previous convictions for scheduled offences (Boyle, Hadden and Hillyard 1980, 22). In other words, very few people who had been released from the Maze were subsequently reconvicted. Further support for the view that the compound system does not encourage 'terrorism' is presented in the only sociological study of the Maze, carried out by Crawford (1979). He found that of a cohort of prisoners leaving the compound between 1976 and 1979 only 12 per cent had been reconvicted for either political or non-political offences (Crawford 1979, 101).

Fifth, the claim that the prison system in Northern Ireland is the best in the world is only part of the truth. Certainly the facilities are better than most but the regime within the prisons, particularly the Maze, is repressive.

When the first hunger strike began, it received widespread support. There were huge demonstrations in Belfast and Dublin. In the north there were 1,205 demonstrations requiring two and a half million hours of police duty. The total cost of policing these parades and the ensuing order was over £12 million (RUC 1982, xii). During the period a hundred thousand rounds of rubber bullets were fired, sixteen thousand in one month alone. The hunger strikes and the authorities response did more to unite Catholic opinion than any other single event since internment in 1971 or Bloody Sunday in 1972.

One very significant feature of the rioting and marches which took place during this time was the extent to which they were confined to the Catholic areas and away from the centres of Belfast and other towns. Any attempt to march to the Belfast city centre was strenuously resisted. The Troubles and the protests have now become ghettorised. The barriers across certain roads and the huge security gates on the roads leading out of the city centre to the Catholic areas are physical reminders of the extent to which this process has taken place. It shows how possible it is for the authorities to confine the problem of street violence to specific areas while life goes on 'normally' elsewhere.

The struggle which developed out of the authorities attempt to deny the political nature of the conflict in order to curtail support for the paramilitaries had considerable unintended consequences. Ironically the policy had the effect of depoliticising the IRA campaign to the extent that it pushed the central aim of the IRA's struggle, its object of achieving Irish unity, into the background. But in its place it provided a powerful humanitarian issue around which to mobilise support. The H-Block issue to the Catholic community was yet another example of a long line of injustices which had been inflicted upon them by Unionist and British administrations.

Conclusions

From a broader perspective a number of the more important characteristics of the repressive response of the state to the conflict in Northern Ireland may be stressed. The first point to note is the extent to which the emergency laws have now become normalised. The emergency legislation is regularly reviewed, the Northern Ireland (Emergency Provisions) Act every six months and the Prevention of Terrorism Act every twelve months, with little or no opposition usually in a sparsely attended House of Commons. This is a product of parliamentary procedures, political compromise as well as government pressures to accept emergency powers as the norm (Smith 1982). It is also a product of the decline of general power of parliament to which I will return. The normalisation, however, goes further than the constant renewal of the emergency legislation, it also involves the extension of use of the emergency powers in circumstances for which they were never intended, such as their use for the arrest and trial of offences which have nothing whatsoever to do with the emergency.

The second feature has been the scant respect paid to the rule of law in all the strategies. During internment and the military security policy no attempt was made to observe the rule of law. Internment and, to only a slightly lesser extent, detention were executive responses and the army practices of screening and trawling were of dubious legality. More recent security policies have been little better. Notwithstanding Merlyn Rees' statements in 1976 when he emphasised that they conformed to the rule of law, the extensive abuse by the police of arrest and detention powers and the modifications in the rules of evidence provide ample evidence of the extent of legal arbitrariness. The dominant form of policing in Northern Ireland is not an arrest followed by a charge and prosecution for a specific offence known in law, but regular questioning on the streets or in custody of all those perceived as potentially subversive to the existence of the present constitutional arrangements.

This represents a fundamental shift within the criminal justice system from policing offences to policing people; a shift from crime to status. On the one hand it opens up the relationship between the citizen and the state, which had been abstracted in the apparently neutral and objective concept of an offence. On the other hand, it reintroduces the possibility of policing classes of people through the criminal law rather than, as under the Unionist strategy, special powers.

The third feature has been the increased bureaucratisation of the response. Instead of a relatively informal system of the administration of the criminal law, there are a number of separate and relatively autonomous agencies with responsibilities for different aspects of the process. The setting up of the Director of Public Prosecutions in 1972 represented the beginning of the bureaucratisation.

The fourth feature has been the decline in the power of the legislature in the development of law and order policies. The policies are increasingly being developed by the executive in conjunction with the higher echelons of the police and the army. They are frequently helped in this task by judges who redefine traditional problems in technical and operational terms. All the recent policing policies, for example, as has been shown, have been developed through internal reviews. The public are never consulted and members of Parliament are simply presented with the formulated policies. They have little or no impact on them.

The fifth feature has been the mobilisation and routine employment of other state agencies in the exercise of informal control. Planners and social workers and other professionals are slowly being drawn into the general task of controlling particular sections of the population.

These changes in the strategies of control have run alongside broader economic and social developments in Northern Ireland. Economic intervention has taken place on a vast scale to aid both productive capital and also projects such as the Local Enterprise Development Unit. One feature of this intervention has been the extent to which it has been antinomian in the sense that the intervention has not been guided by rational-legal norms, the rule of law, but by its effects upon capital accumulation. These developments have paralleled the disrespect for the rule of law which has been a feature of the security strategies. Linked to these new forms of economic intervention has been the reorganisation of local government. The creation of a centralised Housing Authority and new administrative units to manage health and social services, education and planning has consolidated executive control of these services, led to the decline in formal representative democracy, which has, of course, also occurred at the higher level since direct rule, and an increased bureaucratic domination over civil society.

There is now much empirical data to suggest that the form of the state's repressive apparatus in Northern Ireland is not unique and that many modern capitalist states are evolving repressive apparatus with very similar characteristics. In the rest of the United Kingdom, while neither the army nor a paramilitary police patrol the streets, the movement towards the new form of a repressive apparatus is unmistakable. Over recent years in Britain, there has been an enormous growth in the technology of control and the military capabilities of the police have been greatly expanded. Moreover, there have been moves to reform the criminal justice system along similar lines as the changes introduced into Northern Ireland in the early seventies. Trial by jury has been constantly questioned in recent years and the Royal Commission on Criminal Procedure's recommendations in relation to police powers and rules of evidence were very similar to those of the Diplock Commission (see Hillyard 1980). Other state agencies are being mobilised to exercise greater informal control. And as in Northern Ireland all these developments are taking place not in Parliament but in the offices of those responsible for law and order.

Similar developments are taking place elsewhere. Poulantzas (1978, 203–204) has argued:

> In western capitalist societies, the State is undergoing considerable modification. A new form of State is currently being imposed—we would have to be blind not to notice (and passion always blinds, even if it springs from the noblest motives). For want of a better term, I shall refer to this state form as *authoritarian statism*. This will perhaps indicate the general direction of change: namely, intensified state control over every sphere of socio-economic life *combined with* radical decline of the institutions of political democracy and with draconian and multiform curtailment of so-called 'formal' liberties, whose reality is being discovered now that they are going overboard.

While the political struggle in Northern Ireland is obviously unique, the form in which the state, in general, and the repressive apparatus, in particular, has developed in recent years, follows closely transformations elsewhere. The principal difference is that the Northern Ireland state appears to have the unenviable honour of having its repressive apparatus transformed somewhat sooner than some other modern capitalist states.

3

Political Parties: Traditional and Modern

Ian McAllister

Despite Northern Ireland being constitutionally a subordinate part of the United Kingdom, it sustains a party system that differs in most important respects from the parent state—notably in the number of parties that are active, in the political cleavage that divides them, and in the political system within which they operate. In contrast to the British two-party system, Northern Ireland has a multi-party system, with the number of parties prepared to contest elections fluctuating constantly. The political cleavage that divides the parties is the constitutional future of the Province, underpinned by religion, whereas in Britain the cleavage is socio-economic. As a result, electoral outcomes are largely pre-determined and there is consequently no alternation of parties in office. As McCracken notes, 'there is no floating vote on the constitutional issue' (quoted in Darby 1976, 80). Finally, Northern Ireland has had a history of possessing a devolved legislature and government, with control over a wide range of important functions; Britain has a centralised government, with only limited administrative devolution to Scotland and Wales.[1]

Three themes run through party development in Northern Ireland and help to account for its unique evolution within the United Kingdom. Firstly, there is the *numerical balance between the two communities*, with Protestants constituting two-thirds of the population, Catholics one-third. Thus, so long as religion remains the basis of partisanship and a model of government used that confers power on the majority, the Protestant community are guaranteed political power *sine die*, while the Catholics are consigned to permanent political opposition. Historically, therefore, the Ulster Unionists, as the party political representative of the Protestants, have had every incentive to engage in electoral competition, to maintain an effective political organisation, and to ensure the loyalty of a mass party membership. By contrast, without the prospect of political power, the Nationalists, representing the Catholics, had no incentive to maintain the basic functions of a political party, and as a result failed to contest constituencies that did not have a secure Catholic majority.

Secondly, the *main parties are confessional* in so far as they strive for religious exclusiveness and class inclusiveness. Thus the Unionist and Nationalist parties had everything to gain from exacerbating the religious cleavage to ensure the maximum support for their community, while concomitantly muting intra-communal differences, such as class. Consequently, both parties emphasised the single issue of union with Britain versus the reunification of Ireland to the exclusion of other, often pressing, socio-economic issues.

The final theme which helps to account for the evolution of the party system is the element of *parochialism in politics.* Northern Ireland's political culture emphasises ascription, local attachment, and a form of clientelist politics common in many rural countries, including the Irish Republic and many Mediterranean countries. The style of politics that has evolved looks to the power of personality and politicians perform a brokerage role by mediating between the constituent and the government (see Sacks 1977; Bax 1976). Politicians therefore rely on their personal charisma rather than on a party label for election, and internal party disputes are swiftly settled by a resignation, rather than by utilising internal party channels to argue their case.

This chapter seeks to explain the unique development of the Northern Ireland party system from the rest of the United Kingdom through these three themes. It also groups the party system into three conceptually clear tendencies—Unionism and Loyalism, Bi-Confessionalism, and Anti-Partition. Each tendency has demonstrated a remarkable stability over a long period in the votes it wins, whatever the different party labels that are used to define them.[2] The Unionist and Loyalist tendency has encompassed the major Protestant party, the Ulster Unionist Party, and its splinter parties. The Bi-Confessional tendency was filled, before 1969, by the Liberal and Labour parties, but since 1970 has become synonymous with the Alliance Party. The Nationalist Party, the traditional vehicle for Catholic aspirations, was the largest component of the Anti-Partition tendency prior to 1969. It gradually became moribund after 1969, and was replaced by the Social Democratic and Labour Party (SDLP). Traditional nationalist and republican groups have periodically mounted an electoral challenge to the SDLP, but have normally been unsuccessful.

Since the start of the Troubles in 1969, academic writing in Ulster has represented a growth area. A bibliography published in 1980 listed no less than 780 academic works, not all of enduring quality, dealing with Northern Ireland politics (Pollock and McAllister 1980). The best background histories of Northern Ireland politics are to be found in Buckland (1980) and Farrell (1976), the latter having well-researched sections on pre-1969 Catholic politics. The operation and subsequent development of the Northern Ireland political system is outlined with perception by Arthur (1980). Rose (1971) provides an important analysis, based on a 1968 opinion survey, of political attitudes in the Province, and a subsequent work (Rose 1976) concentrates on events between 1969 and 1976. Bew *et al.* (1979) give a well argued Marxist account of the development of the Northern Ireland state. On Unionist politics, Harbinson (1973) gives an account of the party's organisation and development, while Buckland (1972) presents a thorough and highly readable exposition of its origins. On the politics of the Catholic community, Rumpf and Hepburn (1977) give a valuable summary of Nationalist politics before 1969, and McAllister (1977) describes the emergence and development of the SDLP.

Unionism and Loyalism

Throughout the half century between the founding of the Northern Ireland state in 1920 and the outbreak of the Troubles in 1969, the Ulster Unionist Party won a majority of both votes and seats in every election to the Stormont parliament. As Table 1 illustrates, the number of Unionist and Loyalist MPs never fell below 34 in a chamber of 52 members; over the 1921 to 1969 period as a whole, it averaged 38 MPs. The numbers of Nationalist and Republican MPs, by contrast, fluctuated from a low of 6 in 1969 to a peak of 12 in 1921 and 1925. This peak reflects the fact that these elections were conducted under proportional representation, and with its abolition in 1929 and replacement by the simple plurality method, it became harder for minority parties to secure representation relative to their strength in votes.

Because the Ulster Unionist's permanent electoral majority guaranteed it perpetual political power under a Westminster model of government, internal unity was obviously crucial for party survival. Notwithstanding its overall majority across the Province, the Unionists successively attempted to retain control of local government in areas where they constituted a narrow or even a clear minority. This they did through the manipulation of electoral boundaries and a

Table 3:1

ELECTORAL SUPPORT AND PARTY REPRESENTATION IN THE
NORTHERN IRELAND HOUSE OF COMMONS, 1921–69

Election Year	Unionist and Loyalist		NILP		Nationalist and Republican		Other		Total	
	MPs	% Vote	MPs	% Vote	MPs	% Vote	MPs	% Vote	MPs	% Vote
1921	40	66.9	0	—	12	32.3	0	0.8	52	100
1925	36	64.0	3	4.7	12	29.1	1	2.2	52	100
1929	40	64.9	1	8.0	11	13.0	0	14.1	52	100
1933	39	64.5	2	8.6	11	26.9	0	—	52	100
1938	42	85.6	1	5.7	8	4.9	1	3.8	52	100
1945	35	55.4	2	18.6	10	9.2	5	16.8	52	100
1949	39	63.3	0	7.2	9	27.2	4	2.3	52	100
1953	39	60.3	0	12.1	9	15.5	4	12.1	52	100
1958	37	52.6	4	16.0	8	17.5	3	13.9	52	100
1962	34	48.6	4	26.0	9	15.4	4	10.0	52	100
1965	36	59.1	2	20.4	9	8.4	4	12.1	52	100
1969	39	67.4	2	8.1	6	7.6	5	16.9	52	100
Mean 1921–69	38	62.7	2	11.3	10	15.0	3	8.8		

Source: Adapted from Elliott (1973, 96).

restricted franchise which tended to disproportionately reduce the number of Catholic voters (Cameron Report 1969, Ch. 12). The imperative of maintaining political control in as many areas as possible meant that the party organisation which evolved formed an important cross-local framework, interlocking with and complementing other organisations dealing with the security and survival of the Protestant community, notably the 'B' Specials (part-time paramilitary police) (see Hezlet 1972; Farrell 1978) and the Orange Order.

Historically, the Orange Order has been an important institutional factor in the political mobilisation of Ulster Protestants. It emerged in the late eighteenth century as the latest in a tradition of sectarian secret societies which had terrorised the countryside since the early seventeenth century (see Williams 1972). It was relatively unimportant politically until 1885, when it was used as a base for organising Protestant opposition to the first Home Rule Bill (Savage 1961). With the emergence of the Ulster Unionist Party and the formation of the Northern Ireland state in 1920, it provided an ideological framework for justifying opposition to Irish nationalism and Catholicism, and for maintaining Protestant political unity. During the period of the Stormont system of government, the Order also played a latent political role by ensuring that the Unionist Party did not implement any policies it felt were not consonant with Protestant dogma (see Roberts 1971;

Bonnet 1972). Rose (1971, 257) found that 32 per cent of Protestant male respondents in his 1968 survey were Orangemen, giving the organisation a very substantial membership of around 90,000 across Northern Ireland.

Despite the potential divisions caused by drawing support from all social classes, political divisions in the Ulster Unionist Party, prior to 1969, were relatively rare. Overall, Unionists of various backgrounds and persuasions were united on the single issue of maintaining the constitutional link between Northern Ireland and Britain, but on little else. In sum, they represented 'an unhappy and unholy alliance of people thrown together by what they were fundamentally opposed to rather than by any positive or co-operative principles' (Arthur 1980, 65). What challenges were made to the authority of the parent party usually concerned individual issues, and came from working class organisations which combined a strong class identity with traditional unionism. The precursor of this tradition was the Belfast Protestant Association, founded in 1901 to oppose official Unionists on the grounds that they treated the working class simply as voting fodder (Boyle 1962). This tradition of popular Protestant radicalism was carried through after 1920 in the Independent Unionists, who ranged from groups concerned with furthering temperance to blatant anti-Catholicism and the 'view that politicians should be vigilant in defending the socialising institutions and practices of Protestant society' (quoted in de Paor 1970, 114). Less manifest were intra-Unionist dissidents: Whyte's study of the issues Unionist backbenchers voted against during the Stormont government indicated that most opposition came from the right, but that there was a strain of economic populism which criticised government bureaucracy and inadequacy in meeting the needs of the socially disadvantaged (Whyte 1972).

This mild pattern of Protestant dissent to the Unionist Party was overturned by the violence of 1969. Historically, Protestants have seen the Ulster Unionist Party as one guarantee of their political security in times of crisis—the concept of the 'public band' (Miller 1978)—but the Ulster Unionist Party's failure to halt the violence precipitated vocal opposition to its policies both from inside and outside the party. Two groups emerged from within the Unionist Party itself. Firstly, there were the majority of Unionists who remained party members but were committed to policies that were often at odds with the leadership. Secondly, those dissidents who demanded more stringent security measures and better constitutional guarantees grouped themselves as a pressure group within the party in 1972, leaving to form their own party, the Vanguard Unionist Progressive Party, in 1973. A third group wholly external to the Unionist Party were the Protestant Unionists (called the Democratic Unionist Party after 1971 to underline their populist roots) who established themselves as a vociferous opponent of official Unionism in the Independent Unionist tradition.

The breakup of the Ulster Unionist Party was crystallised in the 1969 Stormont general election, in the then prime minister Terence O'Neill's own phrase, 'the crossroads election' (see O'Neill 1969, 140). Fractionalisation within the party over the question of O'Neill's leadership was extreme: 29 constituency associations favoured O'Neill, while 15 opposed him. In addition, 15 unofficial pro-O'Neill candidates were nominated. The election result failed to silence Unionist opposition to O'Neill and forced his resignation as premier in April 1969, thereby enabling most of the anti-O'Neill Unionists to return to the party. However, opposition to the prevailing constitutional and security policies of the Unionist government continued. In February 1972 many of these dissidents helped to form Ulster Vanguard, an umbrella pressure group within the Ulster Unionist Party; in March 1973 Vanguard became a political party, approximately half its 10,000 membership opting to leave the parent party. The party's main platform was the need for stronger security measures against terrorism, and to that end it was less discriminating in including leaders of paramilitary groups within its ranks.[3]

Vanguard, under the leadership of a former Unionist Home Affairs minister, William Craig, followed a distinctive, if erratic, course for four years. Craig expressed a strand in Unionism which saw the Province more as an independent state than as a subordinate regime, and saw the Stormont parliament as not only an expression of identity, but also as a safeguard of Protestant security. This apparent militancy evaporated during the 1975–76 Constitutional Convention, when Craig advocated voluntary coalition with the main Catholic opposition party, the SDLP, in order to persuade the British government to return a devolved parliament to the Province. This *volte-face* split the party, and a year later Craig announced that he and the rest of his supporters were returning to the Official Unionist Party.

The alternative tradition of dissent to the Ulster Unionist Party— Independent Unionists—also became electorally important from 1969. This tradition has been channelled through the Rev. Ian Paisley since 1969, whose personal appeal represents a cross-fertilisation of fundamental biblical Protestantism and economic populism. Paisley's Democratic Unionist Party has consistently emphasised the mainstream unionist values of loyalty to Britain, stronger security against terrorism, and opposition to a Catholic presence in government. The DUP has consolidated a secure electoral position within the Protestant community as the major alternative to the Ulster Unionists—after 1977 reunited with its erstwhile Vanguard competitors. The DUP thus articulates the views of a significant Protestant minority who start from a fundamentalist religious standpoint in opposing social and political change—whether it be constitutional links with the Irish Republic or the legalisation of homosexuality.

The paucity of Protestant dissent to the pre-1969 political hegemony of the Ulster Unionist Party illustrates how well the balance of forces that helped to ensure its unity worked. Unionists could point to the negative uncompromising stance of the Nationalist Party, coupled with periodic physical threats to the integrity of Northern Ireland from the IRA. In return for loyalty, they could hand out patronage at the local level in the form of government employment, and also provide a ladder for the politically ambitious. To Unionists, the attitude of the British government and politicians appeared unsympathetic, a feeling which dated from the founding of the state in 1920, and which further served to isolate Protestants (Buckland 1975, 219–222). Finally, the Unionist leadership was able to manipulate natural Protestant deference and realign the Protestant electorate along the constitutional-religious cleavage when it seemed as if its salience was declining—most notably, during the outdoor relief riots in 1932 (Bew and Norton 1979). This balance enabled the party to accommodate a remarkable diversity of support encompassing almost the entire spectrum of normal political views.

After 1969 this fragile balance of forces altered, and the Unionist Party began to fragment. Through the SDLP, Catholics became more conciliatory and prepared to participate in normal political activity, although the IRA threat continued. The ability to deliver patronage declined after the 1969–70 local government reforms and vanished totally after the imposition of direct rule in 1972, while the authority of the two Unionist prime ministers to succeed O'Neill—James Chichester-Clark and Brian Faulkner—was constantly eroded by divisions within the Unionist Party. Perhaps most importantly, the British government gradually increased its responsibility for Northern Ireland, culminating in the imposition of direct rule from London, which made the Unionists merely one of a number of competitors seeking to influence British policy.

Bi-Confessional Parties

Although groups which have sought support from both religious communities have had relatively little electoral success compared to the confessional groupings, bi-confessional parties have regularly won around one-tenth of the vote in Provincial elections. Prior to 1969 the main bi-confessional party was the Northern Ireland Labour Party (NILP). The party initially emerged from the trade union base which was a by-product of the growth of ship-building in Belfast in the late nineteenth century. Formally, the labour movement opted in 1923 not to take a stand on the constitutional question (previously it had been in favour of home rule) and a precarious balance was maintained on the issue until 1949. In April 1949 a special NILP conference decided 'to maintain unbroken the connection between Great Britain and Northern Ireland as part of the Commonwealth...' (Harbinson 1966, 232), a decision which precipitated the departure of many Catholic members who formed other republican and socialist political groups.

The split had one immediate benefit. Freed from its constitutional ambivalence, the NILP was able to make a direct appeal to the Protestant working class. The strategy was to emphasise two aspects. Firstly, the party underlined its constitutionality through the policy of preserving the British link, which acted as a safeguard for Protestants. Secondly, the party promoted its qualities as an effective opposition, ready to criticise the Unionist Party on economic grounds and undertake the role of Her Majesty's Loyal Opposition, a role the Nationalists were understandably loath to fulfil. Overall, the intention was to gain a secure power base within the Protestant community before crossing the religious divide to actively recruit Catholic support (Graham 1973).

In the late 1950s and 1960s, it seemed as if this strategy might have a chance of success. In the 1958 Stormont general election, the party won 4 of the 52 seats, all of which were retained in the succeeding 1962 election; between the two elections the party's share of the poll correspondingly rose from 16.0 per cent to 26.0 per cent. However, the fragility of the party's support was demonstrated by the loss of 2 of the 4 seats in the 1965 general election. At the same time, traditional religious attitudes began to reassert themselves within the party, initially over the sabbatarian issue, later in response to the reassertion of sectarian attitudes in the Protestant working class. Socially, these incidents illustrated how much the party owed its limited gains 'to evangelical Protestant influences rather than orthodox socialist ones' (Rumpf and Hepburn 1978, 206). Politically, it demonstrated that the party could not compete with the Unionist Party on economic issues when the constitutional question appeared to be at stake (see Rutan 1967).

The deepening post-1969 conflict, coupled with the formation of a competitor for the moderate vote, the Alliance Party, hastened the NILP's decline. Up until 1973 the party endeavoured to maintain a conciliatory position in the face of increasing religious militancy within its potential political base, the Protestant working class. The May 1974 Ulster Workers' Council strike, which brought down the power-sharing Executive, marked a turning point. The strike highlighted the impotence of the official trade union movement, to which the NILP is linked, when matched against loyalist working class leaders. The strike suggested that the party's only hope in retaining support lay in promoting loyalism at the expense of bi-confessionalism. As a result, the NILP's manifesto for the 1975 Convention election opposed both institutionalised power-sharing and any form of association with the Irish Republic. This provoked dissent from many of the remaining Catholic members, some of whom left the party.

The NILP's pro-union stance after 1949, coupled with the Nationalist Party's post-war withdrawal from contesting Belfast constituencies, created a vacuum which was filled by a number of schismatic anti-partitionist labour groups competing for the Catholic vote. All contained elements what had split from the NILP, but saw themselves sustaining the labour tradition within a nationalist or republican framework; none succeeded in gaining any significant electoral support. Some NILP dissidents persuaded the Dublin-based Irish Labour Party to organise in Northern Ireland, and it elected one MP (Jack Beattie) to Westminster in 1951, but fell apart shortly after due to personality clashes. One of the Irish Labour organisers, Frank Hanna, left and formed Independent Labour in 1958, a highly clericalised group that had some success in Belfast Catholic areas. Another Irish Labour member, Gerry Fitt, helped form the Republican Labour Party in 1962, with Harry Diamond. Fitt had been elected to Stormont in 1962 and was subsequently elected to Westminster in 1966. In 1970 he left the Republican Labour Party to become a founder member and first leader of the SDLP.

Although almost all of the factions splitting from the NILP after

1949 have been anti-partitionist, for the obvious reason that pro-union elements have been happily accommodated within the NILP, one Unionist Labour group is worthy of note. The Commonwealth Labour Party was formed by Harry Midgley in December 1942 to protest against the NILP's then ambivalent stance on the constitutional question. The party was committed to maintaining the British link and to mildly social democratic policies. In 1943 Midgley became the first non-Unionist cabinet minister as Minister for Public Security. In 1947, without consulting his party colleagues, Midgley decided to join the Unionist Party because, he declared, there was now 'no room for divisions among those ... who are anxious to preserve the constitutional life and spiritual life of our people' (Farrell 1976, 192). As a result Commonwealth Labour disintegrated.

Since 1969 the Alliance Party has dominated the bi-confessional tendency. The fragmentation of the Unionist Party in the February 1969 Stormont election, plus the intervention of independent pro-O'Neill candidates, provided the political base for the Alliance's formation. The party was formed in April 1970 from O'Neill supporters, Northern Ireland Liberals, and unaligned elements who had been active in the New Ulster Movement, a pressure group formed in 1969 specifically to mobilise support for O'Neill and his policies. The Alliance Party immediately established itself as a deviant within the Northern Ireland party system. The failure of labour bi-confessional groups to replace religion with class values had shown that there was little future in trying to emphasise a cleavage not coterminous with, or closely adjacent to, the religious divide. By contrast, Alliance placed its central appeal firmly on religion, so far as the issue became uniting Catholics and Protestants within a common political framework.

That Alliance has succeeded in achieving its fundamental aim of uniting Protestants and Catholics in a bi-confessional framework has been demonstrated by a survey of Alliance activists (McAllister and Wilson 1978). For Protestants the party offers a strong constitutional stand on retaining the British link; for Catholics, the party emphasises anti-discrimination issues and social reform. To some extent, Alliance represents the 'extreme' point to which individuals of each community will move, rather than an actual bridge for individuals to cross the sectarian divide (Laver 1976, 23). Survey evidence has however suggested that, rather than uniting the two religious communities simply on the religious dimension, the membership has a homogeneity of opinions on a wide range of social, economic and political issues (McAllister and Wilson 1978).

Tactically, Alliance's conciliatory appeal has led it to support power-sharing, and the party leader, Oliver Napier, held a portfolio in the ill-fated 1974 power-sharing Executive. Generally, the party has endorsed the SDLP's demand for power-sharing, an association which was strengthened during the 1975–76 Constitutional Convention when both opposed the Loyalist Coalition's demand for a return to majority rule. This close liaison effectively ceased in the late 1970s with the SDLP shift towards a stronger nationalist stance. The party's overall influence has been limited by its weak electoral support, and in particular by its singular failure to penetrate either the Belfast working class areas or the rural areas west of the River Bann, where religious tensions are highest. Alliance's appeal finds its strongest response in the middle and upper socio-economic groups, making its support disproportionately concentrated in the prosperous conurbations surrounding Belfast.

Nationalism and Republicanism

By virtue of their numerical minority, the Catholic community in Northern Ireland has never had the opportunity to win political power, so long as the principle of majority rule pertains, and consequently party unity has never been imperative. Two broad groups have vied for Catholic support between 1921 and 1969: constitutional nationalists and physical force republicans. While constitutional Nationalists have exclusively oriented their activities towards electoral competition, physical force republicans have used every means at their disposal, from electoral activity through to civil disobedience and armed assaults on the state.[4]

Since 1921 constitutional nationalism has been the dominant political strain within the Catholic community. Because of the electoral thresholds set for candidates in Stormont elections (for example, candidates had to declare their intention to take their seats if elected), republicans have tended to focus their electoral excursions on Westminster elections where no such thresholds apply, leaving Provincial elections free to constitutional nationalists, unhindered by the threat of competing Catholic candidates splitting their community's vote. This informal division of electoral activity was one mutually agreed between the two groups, at least at the level of an unspoken understanding (see Coogan 1966, 309). The Northern Ireland Nationalist Party was in fact the surviving Ulster remnant of the Irish Parliamentary Party, under Redmond, which had been crushed by Sinn Fein in the

1918 Westminster election. Catholic adherence to the Nationalist Party was cemented after 1922 by the Ancient Order of Hibernians, the Catholic equivalent of the Orange Order, which was headed by the Nationalist Party's first leader, Joe Devlin. Although organised throughout Ireland, the Order was strongest in Ulster and boasted the highest membership in the rural west.[5]

The use of the title 'Nationalist Party' demands two caveats. Firstly, the title was a broad one encompassing most of the groups which espoused Irish unity to be achieved by constitutional means. Formally, the Nationalist Party utilised the title except for two periods: between 1928 and the mid-1930s it was known as the National League of the North, which was linked to a similar neo-Redmondite group in the south; in 1945, it was known as the Anti-Partition League, a body which gradually disappeared in the mid-1950s. Secondly, the Nationalist Party was not a political party in the generally accepted sense of the term. It has no formal organisation or structure (annual conferences were not held until 1965) and no formal statement of policy was ever issued until November 1964. In effect, the party operated only at the parliamentary level and consisted of 'a loose alliance of local notables' (Rose 1971, 221). The most sophisticated organisation it ever developed was that of Catholic registration committees, a form of political organisation common in societies on the threshold of universal suffrage.

Because of the Nationalists' lack of organisation, and because of the close identification with the Catholic community, clerical influence in nationalist politics was strong. Nationalist candidates were frequently selected by meetings chaired by Catholic priests, and until the 1950s, nomination papers for Nationalist candidates were often signed by a priest: in the 1924 Westminster general election, for example, 8 of the 12 Nationalist candidates were proposed by priests (Farrell 1976, 103; see also Fahy 1971). Overall, this clerical influence tended to equate 'Catholicism with hostility to the state (and) detracted from the effectiveness of opposition criticism of the government even on issues which had no bearing on the constitutional question' (McCracken 1967, 154). Although committed to constitutional politics, the Nationalists frequently employed parliamentary abstentionism as a political tactic. They abstained from 1921 until 1925, and after an unproductive return, from 1934 until the late 1940s. Abstention highlighted the Catholic community's political dilemma: to contest elections and voice grievances in parliament could gain minor concessions, but doing so would effectively consolidate the legitimacy of a state they were pledged to oppose.

Throughout the 1950s and 1960s the Nationalist Party became increasingly anachronistic. Its electoral base was entirely rural; it emphasised the reunification of Ireland to the exclusion of all socio-economic issues; and it was periodically abstentionist, thereby robbing Catholics of what limited representation they might already have. Attempts by such groups as National Unity and the National Democratic Party to force reform on the Nationalists failed dismally (see McAllister 1975b). In the event the party was completely by-passed by another form of political expression, the Northern Ireland Civil Rights Association (NICRA), which began to mobilise mass support on the streets behind limited aims after 1968. NICRA won such concessions from the Unionist government that they were, in sum, 'greater than Catholics had won in 47 years of parliamentary opposition' (Rose 1970, 124). The Nationalist Party rapidly declined and was replaced in 1970 as the political mouthpiece of the Catholic community by the SDLP.

Although filling the place of the Nationalist Party as the major anti-partitionist group representing the Catholic community, the apparent continuity belied three fundamental differences between the SDLP and the Nationalists. Firstly, while the Nationalists refused to recognise the state and were abstentionist, the SDLP accepted that there would be no change in the Province's constitutional position without the consent of a majority. Since a permanent majority has always existed to retain the British link, in practice the SDLP thus accepted the constitutional status quo—a hitherto unprecedented position for a Catholic party in Northern Ireland. More significantly, it enabled the SDLP to participate in the institutions of the state, something the Nationalists were committed never to do. Secondly, the SDLP created political organisation with branches, constituency machinery, an executive and an annual delegate conference. Thirdly, it adopted a coherent set of socio-economic policies in a wide variety of areas.

The SDLP's experience in the Northern Ireland party system has been unique. In its short history it has occupied a variety of party political positions. For example, in 1970 and 1971 it acted as a constitutional opposition in the classic British context, waiting to win an electoral majority and hence accede to political power; in 1971 and 1972 it was an anti-system opposition, employing parliamentary abstentionism and civil disobedience to bring down the regime; and in early 1974 it participated in a power-sharing government, contributing 6 ministers to a total administration of 15. Throughout, the party has remained the sole electoral representative of the Catholic community; in both the 1973 Assembly and 1975 Convention elections, no other party or individual basing its support on the Catholic community succeeded in gaining election. This apparent Catholic unanimity can be traced to two factors. Firstly, there has been undoubted Catholic support for the aim of power-sharing between the two communities at the executive level of government. As power sharing requires Catholic participation in government, it gives them an incentive to engage in constructive political activity. Secondly, the party's political organisation has absorbed dissatisfaction into various forums within the structure and preserved party unity at times when the pressures to fragment have seemed irresistible—notably after the fall of the power-sharing Executive in May 1974 and the failure of the Constitutional Convention to find an agreed settlement in March 1976.

Despite the apparent resilience afforded the SDLP by these two factors, the party has been subjected to acute strain in recent years. Of the original six founding MPs, two have resigned, including the party leader for nine years, Gerry Fitt. A majority in the party refused to participate in the 1979 devolution talks organised by the then Conservative Northern Ireland Secretary, Humphrey Atkins. Fitt argued that participation was imperative to maintain the party's credibility within the Catholic community, and resigned to protest when the decision went against him. A more serious challenge to the party was the 1981 hunger strike by imprisoned Republicans. Ten prisoners died during the protest, radicalising popular Catholic opinion towards the IRA. One of the IRA hunger strikers, Bobby Sands, won a Westminster by-election for Fermanagh and South Tyrone in March 1981, shortly before his death. The SDLP had failed to fight the seat both against Sands, and in August 1981 against his Republican successor, Owen Carron. By twice failing to oppose militant Republicanism through the ballot box, the party forfeited much credibility among moderate Catholics, while gaining no corresponding support from more extreme Catholics.

Republican politics (as opposed to Republican military activity) has been consistently cast into a secondary role by the dominance of constitutional nationalism, both before and after the radical disjuncture of 1969. Typically, Ulster Catholics have been distrustful of physical force republicans, feeling that they do not understand their vulnerable position vis-a-vis the majority Protestant community. Political activists have therefore gravitated towards constitutional nationalism, leaving the republican movement the preserve of a small core of dedicated militarists. Republicans have, however, had infrequent electoral success. In the 1921 Stormont election, Republicans won more votes than Nationalists; in 1955 they had two candidates elected, both serving terms of imprisonment for terrorist offences; and, as already noted, in April 1981 a jailed IRA hunger striker, Bobby Sands, was elected at a by-election, and subsequently died of his hunger strike while still technically an MP.

After the failure of the 1956 to 1962 IRA border campaign, the republican movement took on a political aspect and emphasised housing, welfare and employment issues over the perennial partition question. However the movement's inability to protect Belfast Catholics from attack in the 1969 civil disturbances split the organisation in two. One group, the Republican Clubs (linked with the Official IRA) have enthusiastically contested elections on a Marxist platform; the other group, Provisional Sinn Féin (linked with the Provisional IRA) have based their appeal on a rudimentary combination of Catholic conservatism and orthodox physical force republicanism, and equally enthusiastically urged abstention in elections. Neither group has secured sufficient support within the Catholic community to enable it to mount a potential electoral challenge to the SDLP.

Traditionalism and Modernity in the Northern Ireland Party System

The Northern Ireland party system contains elements of both traditionalism and modernity. It is *traditional* by virtue of the permanent majority–minority balance between the two communities, because of the confessional nature of the parties, and because of the parochial and personalistic nature of the political culture. It is *modern* in so far as the political parties organise themselves around elections, operate relatively sophisticated machinery, and resemble parties that can be found in other advanced Western European democracies. The history of Northern Ireland parties can be viewed as a balance between these two themes: each party contains elements of both, to a greater or lesser degree, and each sustains a constant conflict between them.

Up until the 1960s, the party system was essentially dominated by traditionalism. There was little challenge to the accepted *status quo*, the parties maintained their confessional bases, and there was no attempt to introduce anything other than strictly constitutional issues into political debate. The limited attempts of the labour movement to raise such issues in the 1920s, and the dramatic but brief unity between working-class Catholics and Protestants in Belfast over outdoor relief in 1932 did not disturb this pattern (Bew and Norton 1979). Traditionalism first seriously came under attack when Terence O'Neill became prime minister in 1963. O'Neill's long term objective was to undermine the political and social basis of these traditional attitudes, and force through modernisation in the Province.

O'Neill's strategy was to achieve reform in three key areas which would eventually challenge the nature of the political system. Firstly, he sought to change the party system to resemble British two-party competition, with two parties competing for votes on socio-economic platforms. The initial stage was to get the Nationalists to participate constructively in the institutions of the state. This step was tentatively accomplished in 1966 when the Nationalists agreed to become the Official Opposition in the Stormont parliament, although they withdrew from the position in 1968. Secondly, O'Neill sought to undermine the confessional basis of the political parties. In the Ulster Unionist Party, his attempts to gain formal acceptance for Catholic membership were thwarted. Thirdly, by attracting industry and commerce and thereby stimulating affluence, he hoped to erode the parochial rural attitudes which suffused political debate.

In the relative economic prosperity of the mid 1960s, it appeared as if these policies might have some chance of success. However, O'Neill's central dilemma was that he was moving too slowly for most Catholics, who were seeking an end to discrimination and looking for upward social mobility in the growing economy, while many Protestants viewed reform as marking an end to their traditional supremacy. His problem was his inability to win sufficient Catholic backing to balance defections from the intransigent Unionists who were distrustful of his conciliatory approach. The paradox of O'Neillism was that its 'moderation lay in avoiding bigotry. It did not extend so far as to endorse change sufficient to dispel the Catholic sense of grievance' (Rose 1972, 124). In the event, O'Neill's attempt at modernisation failed and Catholics turned to the civil rights movement for remedial action on their grievances.

The civil rights movement represented another potentially modernising influence. NICRA presented the Unionist regime with a novel threat. Previous threats had invariably been violent, ephemeral and universally ineffective: faced with the threat of physical force, the government could easily retaliate in kind. But non-violent street protest presented a novel challenge, since it could neither be ignored, nor broken by undue force. The Unionist response was initially to concede some of NICRA's demands, while the popular Catholic response was a strong endorsement of street protest as a legitimate political tactic. While the civil rights movement achieved most of its short-term demands, its long term impact on Northern Ireland has been profound. Its reformist demands engendered a violent loyalist response, which in turn stimulated the growth of the Provisional IRA, initially as a Catholic defence organisation. It also had the effect of tipping the party system, particularly on the Catholic side, into turmoil. The extent of the changes wrought by post-1969 events can be illustrated by the fact that only two of the parties active today—the Ulster Unionists and the NILP—existed before 1970, and both have been subjected to frequent schisms (Rose 1976, 33).

Post-1969 Ulster has been dominated by two themes: firstly, the gradual withdrawal of powers from local elected representatives by the British government, and secondly, the emerging of extra-constitutional groups willing to use violence as a political means. The initial withdrawal of powers took place in local government and involved the transfer of housing, planning, and certain other contentious powers to a central authority. The process continued with the abolition of the Stormont parliament in 1972; the legislative assembly that was intended to replace it boasted considerably less powers than its predecessor, most notably it did not have control over security and the administration of justice. The result of this process has been to reduce the importance of political activity and hence of the parties themselves, and simultaneously shift the focus to Westminster, which to most Ulster people still remains a remote and unsympathetic forum.

The growth of extra-constitutional groups willing to use violence has further reduced the saliency of political activity. Agreements reached between elected politicians can have little legitimacy when they can be wrecked by non-elected gunmen. There is an ambivalence to the use of physical force in politics which transcends religious affiliation and party label. Each community expresses its fear of the other by the maintenance of an armed faction, which gains latent support as the last guarantor of the community's safety in the event of a disaster. The IRA has filled this role for Catholics; Protestants traditionally looked towards the 'B' special paramilitary police as their guarantor until their disbandment in 1969, after which time more traditional armed groups such as the Ulster Volunteer Force became active.

After more than a decade of civil disturbance and violence, Northern Ireland politics still displays the conflict between traditionalism and modernity. The political parties still personify the constitutional conflict over the Province's future, and the British government, by virtue of its role as the main arbiter in the conflict, still withholds political power from elected politicians in the absence of inter-communal agreement. The various attempts to impose modernisation through political elites—from O'Neill's reforms in the 1960s, to the imposition of the 1974 power-sharing Executive—have largely failed because the social and political attitudes within the two communities were unresponsive to change. Any hope of future progress must come from a change in these attitudes, and from no other source.

Notes

1. For introductions to the Northern Ireland party system, see Arthur (1980, 52–65), Darby (1976, Ch. 4) and McAllister and Nelson (1979). On the relationship between the Northern Ireland and British States, see Rose (1982).
2. For example, in the 1973 Assembly election, the three tendencies—Unionism and Loyalism, Bi-Confessionalism and Anti-Partitionism—received 61.9 per cent, 11.8 per cent and 25.3 per cent of the first preference vote, respectively. In the 1975 Convention election, each received 62.5 per cent, 11.2 per cent and 26.2 per cent of the first preference vote, respectively. See McAllister (1975a, Table V.1).
3. For example, at least three of Vanguard's 1973 Assembly candidates had connections with paramilitary organisations: Tommy Herron and Glen Barr were associated with the Ulster Defence Association; George Green with the Ulster Special Constabulary Association.
4. There is no separate history of the Nationalist Party, but the best accounts are to be found in Rumpf and Hepburn (1977) and Farrell (1976). The best account of republicanism and the IRA is Bowyer Bell (1972). On the SDLP, see McAllister (1977).
5. For example, in 1892 the AOH had just over 1,000 members in County Armagh, but only 70 in County Down. See Foy (1976, 18–19).

4

Economic Development: Cause or Effect in the Northern Irish Conflict

John Simpson

Northern Ireland has an unenviable record as the least affluent region of the United Kingdom and one of the least prosperous areas within the European Economic Community. Within the EEC, Northern Ireland is one of five areas qualifying, because of the scale of the local problems, for various forms of priority treatment from, for example, the European Regional Development Fund. However, as later evidence will show, the regional economy has, in some ways, shown significant improvements in the past two decades.

Economic issues are not new to any discussion about Northern Ireland. Professor Lyons summarised the position when he argued:

> The history of Northern Ireland has been dominated by three principal problems which have changed extraordinarily little throughout the entire period of its existence. These are, first, the problem of the triangular relationship with the rest of the United Kingdom and the rest of Ireland; second, the problem of the deep and continuing internal division of the population between, in the main Unionists and Protestants on the one hand, and Nationalists and Catholics on the other; finally the problem not only of developing a viable economy in such a small area, but of securing for the people public services and standards of welfare comparable with those in Britain. (Lyons 1972, 695)

After more than a decade of physical violence, any assessment is complicated by the undoubted consequences of this violence on the economy. It is perhaps helpful, for analytical purposes, to examine the state of the economy, and its underlying characteristics, as it was revealed in the 1950s and 1960s and then to make some tentative suggestions on the changes during the violent decade of the 1970s.

Naturally, any examination of the Northern Ireland economy must

79

acknowledge that the state of the economy may have contributed to the emergence of community disorder. The discussion cannot prove any causal relationships. Indeed from the evidence, since the assessment is subjective, different observers would, and do, draw different conclusions. Anticipating the discussion which follows, this writer would not subscribe to the view that the state of the economy was the *main* factor in explaining the emergence and continuation of violence. However, in an explanation of the development of the economy in the 1970s, there can be little doubt that political instability and continuing disorder have had a major effect of the economy. Since the divisions, based on differences in the cultural and political identities in the island of Ireland, have been of sufficient strength and duration, it is at least credible to argue that relative economic disadvantage within Northern Ireland, if it is accepted that it existed, was not a *necessary* element in an explanation of the causation of violence.

An assessment of the state of the Northern Ireland economy can be attempted in different ways. The absolute scale of the economic problems has been well documented in the several official reports on the economy such as those by Isles and Cuthbert (1955), Wilson (1965) and Quigley (1976). The discussion which follows sets out, first, to examine the performance of the Province as a region of the United Kingdom where the main comparisons are made with the United Kingdom as a whole, and areas such as Scotland and Wales; in this first part of the discussion, comparisons with the Republic of Ireland are omitted in order to emphasise how Northern Ireland compared with other United Kingdom regions. Later, however, because of the obvious relevance of North–South comparisons, the discussion focuses on how the two parts of the island have been faring. Towards the end of the chapter, the examination turns to factors internal to Northern Ireland. Has the distribution of economic change within Northern Ireland been such as to illustrate any unnatural bias in the results in recent years?

Each of these elements is analysed with incomplete data. In fact, sometimes, for the best of reasons, data on the contentious issues are not available. How can an observer quantify whether a 'fair' proportion of new jobs or government investment was attracted to, or allocated for, areas of high unemployment? For this chapter reliance has had to be placed on the information which is available. It is, therefore, in some cases not as adequate or directly relevant as might be wished.

Northern Ireland: as a region of the United Kingdom

The long standing evidence is that Northern Ireland has experienced higher unemployment and lower average incomes than the average for the rest of the United Kingdom. Such a situation certainly predates the second world war and probably dates back earlier than the creation of a devolved administration in Northern Ireland in 1920. Statistical comparisons on a pre-1939 basis are not available in the forms which are now current, but the basic indicators of unemployment and incomes confirm these statements. In 1922, on the basis of the unemployment insurance scheme then in operation, Northern Ireland experienced an unemployment rate of 22.9 per cent compared with a United Kingdom average of 14.3 per cent. In the years up to 1937, the absolute difference in annual unemployment percentages fluctuated but at no time was it less than 3.4 per cent (1927) and at one time (1925) it widened to 12.9 per cent. In 1938 the difference increased again to 13.3 per cent. (British Labour Statistics, 1886–1968, table 160)

Comparisons of relative income levels, pre-1939, are even more primitive. Using some early estimates of personal income, prepared by Isles and Cuthbert (1957, 457), and comparing these with early estimates for the United Kingdom, it seems that in 1938 personal income per head of the population was about 55 per cent of the United Kingdom average. By 1950, Northern Ireland incomes, per head of the population, had improved, mainly because of the impact of war on relative pay levels, to some 68 per cent of the United Kingdom average. These differences, which are discussed further below, stemmed in part from lower average earnings in similar occupations, but more significantly were also caused by differences in the sectoral structure of the economy and differences in the proportion of the population in the labour force. Greater proportionate dependance on textiles and agriculture, as well as a higher proportion of dependents in the population would both have contributed to such a difference.

Unemployment is the most conspicuous sign of the economic problems faced in Northern Ireland. Even in the post-1945 era of full employment in the United Kingdom, the levels of unemployment remained high in Northern Ireland. Only rarely, and for short periods, has unemployment fallen below 6 per cent of the insured employees, whilst a figure of less than 2 per cent was commonplace for the United Kingdom in the 1950s and 1960s.

Although unemployment in the period from 1945 to the early 1970s was, in absolute terms much lower than the general earlier experience of the 1920s and 1930s, there are two ways in which the relative position can be argued to have worsened. First, by comparison with the improved position in the United Kingdom as a whole, Northern Ireland's relative position was worse. Second, in a comparison with the experience in Scotland and Wales, which are used here to make an illustrative inter-regional comparison with other less prosperous regions, Northern Ireland fared badly. This is illustrated in table 4:1, which shows, for each area, the distribution of unemployment in these regions of the United Kingdom. If a region had an unemployment experience the same as that for the whole country, the ratio would be equal to 1.0; a ratio of 2.0 therefore means that unemployment was twice as high as the national ratio. Table 1 brings out clearly that pre-1939, unemployment in these regions, although high in percentage terms, was usually less than double the national average. In the 1950s and 1960s, Scotland and Wales did not experience the same relative deterioration as Northern Ireland. In other words, full employment in the United Kingdom was shared more adequately in Scotland and Wales than in Northern Ireland. Only with rising national unemployment in the late 1970s has Northern Ireland's relative experience seemed better!

Table 4:1

UNEMPLOYMENT AS A PROPORTION OF THE
CIVIL LABOUR FORCE
(expressed as a multiple of the average U.K. ratio)

	N. Ireland	Scotland	Wales
1923	1.3	1.5	0.6
1929	1.2	1.2	2.0
1935	1.4	1.5	2.1
1938	2.1	1.4	2.0
1947	3.9	2.0	3.2
1950	3.4	2.1	2.2
1955	5.3	2.1	1.4
1960	3.6	2.2	1.4
1965	3.7	2.0	1.6
1970	2.5	1.6	1.3
1975	1.9	1.3	1.3
1980	1.9	1.4	1.3

Source: Derived by the author from British Labour Statistics, 1886–1968 and later editions of the Department of Employment Gazette.

Unemployment in the 1950s and early 1960s remained a serious problem and was more noteworthy because of the relative improvement in the position in other regions of the United Kingdom. The easy explanation offered for this situation was to point to the importance of three sectors in the regional economy, all of which were contracting in employment terms throughout the United Kingdom. Agriculture, shipbuilding and textiles, in the early 1950s, accounted for over 35 per cent of the labour force, three times higher than the national average. Consequently, with a higher dependence on industries where employment was contracting, maintaining or increasing total employment was necessarily a continuing process of seeking expansion in other sectors. Because of the technical changes in production methods and the relative increase in the availability of competitive imports, the fall in employment in these sectors was unavoidable. For the Northern Ireland economy the absence of adequate alternative expansion, in a period of national full employment, was a feature of greater concern.

Attempts to encourage the expansion of manufacturing industry developed in Northern Ireland in the 1930s and increased rapidly in the 1950s. However, the government policies, which were gradually increased in scope and scale during the 50s, 60s and 70s have not been such as to have the effect of reducing unemployment to acceptable or desirable levels. The analysis which lay behind the efforts to expand the manufacturing sector as the means of securing wider economic development was unexceptional. Similar analytical conclusions formed the basis of Development Area policy in Great Britain, were a prominent part of the Irish programmes for economic expansion and were reflected in other countries in western Europe.

Government policies and/or inducements do not necessarily make a dramatic change in the pattern of location decisions for new industrial projects. Basic economic factors such as distance, material availability and costs, energy costs and labour costs are often influenced only marginally by government actions. Isles and Cuthbert (1957) summed up the position by saying:

> Because of Northern Ireland's geographical situation and its lack of raw materials, together with its smallness as a market for most goods, industry encounters transport and other situation costs which ... are a strong deterrent to the expansion of economic activity.
>
> ... the ratio of pay demanded by the workers and the ratio of profit on capital and enterprise required by investors and entrepreneurs, tend to approximate to those obtainable elsewhere in the

United Kingdom. In consequence, the amount of new investment undertaken in Northern Ireland . . . always tends to fall short of the amount required to yield enough jobs . . . Unemployment is therefore not merely a passing phase but a chronic tendency.   (p. 346)

If industry is normally to expand fast enough to keep the unemployment rate down to about the same average level in Great Britain, costs of producton must somehow be lowered enough to offset the retarding effects of the higher costs due to the natural handicaps . . . there would appear to be some scope for action . . . if (workers) were able and willing to reduce labour costs, per unit of output, so as to offset part of the higher costs arising from the disadvantages of location.   (p. 347)

Central to the assessment of the 1950s and 1960s is some evidence on the effectiveness of Northern Ireland in securing, or failing to secure, adequate industrial expansion and some conclusion on the factors affecting profitability, particularly labour costs, as outlined by Isles and Cuthbert. This should include the efforts by the Northern Ireland Government to stimulate expansion both by direct financial incentives to industrial projects and by indirect measures to improve the quality of manpower available (and incidentally help to ensure more efficient production, with lower labour costs per unit) and the wider infrastructure.

Industrial Employment

The basic strategy adopted by successive Government policies in Northern Ireland implicitly argued that if the industrial structure could be changed by attracting new modern industry to replace the sectors where employment was contracting, this new industry, after overcoming the initial disadvantages during a start-up period, might be able to operate on a continuing viable basis. Government direct assistance, as in other regions, has been (and is) heavily weighted to reduce the setting up costs: advance factories are available with an initial rent free period of tenancy, as are percentage grants on fixed capital costs and grants based on employment numbers in the early years. Without going into detail, (interested readers should consult the Wilson Report (1965), the Development Programme (1970) and the Quigley Report (1976)), the evidence is that Northern Ireland has had a scale of financial inducements somewhat higher than the other United Kingdom Development Areas since, at least, the mid 1950s, and in the past 25 years these inducements have, generally, been increased.

In view of the policies adopted and the expenditure incurred in their implementation, the evidence in terms of manufacturing output and employment is, at first sight, not very encouraging. Over the past 25 years manufacturing employment has, with fluctuations, tended to fall. Between 1956 and 1979 the number employed in manufacturing in Northern Ireland fell from 185,000 to 140,000, a decline of 24 per cent; the decline in the United Kingdom as a whole for the same period was 19 per cent. Only for the period 1961–1970 did manufacturing employment in Northern Ireland increase relative to the United Kingdom position.

Output levels from manufacturing industry compared somewhat more favourably: Output in Northern Ireland, from 1956 to 1979, increased by 96 per cent whereas in the United Kingdom the comparable increase was of 65 per cent. The decade of the 1970s is not adequately reflected in this comparison. Production peaked in 1973 in both areas and the subsequent contraction has been larger in Northern Ireland, down 9 per cent, than in the United Kingdom which experienced a fall of 4 per cent.

The period when output grew more quickly than that in the United Kingdom did not commence until the early 1960s and ended in 1971.

The overall picture is, therefore, one of decreasing industrial employment, increasing output and therefore increasing output per person employed. The evidence is consistent with a gradual improvement in Northern Ireland's relative position in the 1960s, after a fairly static period in the 1950s, followed by a significant deterioration in the 1970s. From this evidence alone, however, it would be simplistic, and possibly incorrect, to conclude that, because the experience of the 1960s showed that progress was being made and that this ended in the early 1970s, the later deterioration can solely be attributed to the impact of local disorder. The post 1973 international oil price rise and the emergence of unemployment more generally in Western Europe gives at least a *prima facie* argument that other factors may have played a part, even if a small one, in this reversal.

The gradual relative improvement in the 1960s can also be documented with reference to the figures published by the Department of Commerce on new projects announced as intending to provide extra industrial employment. From the limited official evidence available, the years when industrial expansion was most rapid (measured by the number and prospective size of the projects announced by the Department of Commerce) continued from the mid-1960s to the early 1970s.

Isles and Cuthbert quoted (p. 390) figures for the late 1940s and early 1950s of announcements of about 2,000 prospective new industrial jobs per annum. The figures from the mid 1960's rose to an average of 7,000 jobs per annum and this improvement was maintained into the early 1970s. However, by 1974 a distinct fall was in evidence and the low point was reached with only 3,000 jobs promoted in 1976. Some recovery took place in the later years of the 1970s.

Two cautionary points should be made on these figures. First, these are project announcements. There is always some shortfall in the numbers of jobs actually created. Many projects do not meet the optimistic targets set at the date of their launch. Second, allowing for the gradual process of industrial change, inevitable in any setting, it must be emphasised that the *net* change in total industrial employment would be much lower and in some years it has even been negative.

The gross and net characteristics are illustrated in the table below.

Table 4:2

MANUFACTURING EMPLOYMENT ('000s)

	Total	Assisted projects	Remainder	New jobs announced	Change in No. of jobs in assisted projects
1960	181	34	147		5(4) year totals
1965	174	49	125	N.A.	15 (1960–65)
1970	177	67	110	32	18 (1965–70)
1975	156	70	86	31	3 (1970–75)
1979	140	64	76	19	—6 (1975–79)

Sources: Department of Manpower Services Gazettes, Department of Commerce Facts and Figures.

The picture is, therefore, one of:

(1) an overall decline in industrial employment.

(2) an improvement, relative to the overall United Kingdom average in the 1960s.

(3) a major contraction in employment in the 'non-assisted' firms.

For Northern Ireland, the inflow of new industrial employment has been inadequate to offset the contraction in existing firms. This contraction, as evidenced earlier, has to a significant extent been a reflection of the existing structure of industry with its particular dependence on textiles and shipbuilding. (A more detailed examination is to be found in Appendix 3 of the Northern Ireland Development Programme, 1970.) However, the amount of 'new' industrial employment, although inadequate to offest this contraction, was not small by the evidence of the success or otherwise of other United Kingdom regions.

One of the earliest attempts to assess how different regions fared in the search for new industrial projects was undertaken by R. S. Howard of the then Board of Trade (1968). This quantified the number of jobs promoted in regions by firms which moved into those regions in the period 1945–1965. As a percentage of 1966 employment, Northern Ireland's new employment, at 21 per cent of the jobs existing in 1966, was better than any other region, except Wales where the comparable figure was 29 per cent. Scotland's figure was much lower, at 14 per cent of the total industrial jobs.

In a more refined analysis of the period 1952–1965, Howard (1968) shows that Northern Ireland's experience was even more marked. Northern Ireland had a higher ratio of new jobs to existing employment than any other United Kingdom region. The results were some 50 per cent better than those for Scotland, the next highest region. The same analysis (Howard, 1968, 11) shows that the ratio of job losses to existing employment in industry was also much higher in Northern Ireland (−13 per cent in 13 years) than elsewhere. The region with the nearest comparable figure was the North West of England (−8 per cent).

Not only did Northern Ireland do, relatively, better than other regions in the attraction of new employment, but the evidence (Howard, 1968, Appendix B–E) is that the situation improved in the 1960s. The proportion of the new jobs in the United Kingdom coming to Northern Ireland compared to the Scottish record was as follows (per cent):

	N.I.	Scotland
1945–1951	3.8	13.0
1952–1959	2.6	7.3
1960–1965	8.0	15.4
1945–1965	4.6	11.9
% of U.K. industrial employment in 1966	2.1	8.2

More recent evidence, on a different basis, comes from the work of Moore and Rhodes and was summarised by Marquand (1980, 47). Moore and Rhodes have estimated how much employment, in industry, has been created by regional policy, in the period 1960–1976. Until 1971 Northern Ireland was estimated to have, relatively, done much better than Scotland or the North of England and the nearest comparable result was that for Wales. Again the evidence confirms that the mid 1960s were the best period.

Table 4:3

EMPLOYMENT EFFECTS OF REGIONAL
POLICY 1960–1976 ('000s)

	N.I.	Scotland	Wales
1960–1963	10	13	10
1963–1967	16	28	22
1967–1971	14	16	30
1960–1971	40	57	62
1971–1976	0	19	14

Source: Marquand (1980) p. 47
Note: Employment in Scotland is some 4 times
that in Northern Ireland; in Wales it is nearly
double.

The above table also includes the dramatic conclusion that the efforts to attract new industry to Northern Ireland produced little or no result in the early 1970s. (i.e. although some new projects were announced, these did not reflect a positive gain solely attributed to regional policy). A more recent study (Pounce, 1981) of industrial movement confirms that in the period 1972–75, the amount of employment promised in new projects fell dramatically when compared with other United Kingdom regions.

The argument in this section can now be put into perspective: The worst feature for the region was that in spite of efforts to expand the industrial sector, employment contracted. However, this contraction would have been considerably higher without the gross inflow of a large number of new plants. The records suggest that Northern Ireland's rate of employment turnover (job gains and job losses) was much higher than in any other United Kingdom region. In the years prior to 1971, and particularly during the 1960s, the rate of job promotion in Northern Ireland was better than in any other region. The evidence suggests that although Northern Ireland was the most successful region in attracting new industrial employment, the *net* result, in employment terms, was slightly worse than the United Kingdom average which, in itself, was poor by comparison with some other European economies. Overall, this result was disappointing and inadequate to meet the needs of the region. The only short period when significant net gains were recorded was from 1963 to 1970 approximately.

Industrial Investment

The loss of employment in textiles and shipbuilding was a major factor in offsetting the employment growth from new industrial projects. It was, however, given the *national* position of these industries in the faces of international trading changes, not surprising. The critical factor for Northern Ireland was the scale of new industrial investment and its determinants. Northern Ireland, as a United Kingdom region, did well, but not well enough. Since the 1950s and 1960s were a period of national full employment, why did Northern Ireland not attract a larger fraction of the new investment? The deflection of an extra 2 per cent of the national industrial investment total (about a 40 per cent increase in the amount which located in Northern Ireland) would have made the position radically different.

The first point of interest is whether Northern Ireland was sufficiently attractive as a location. Its disadvantages in terms of geography and domestic market size were and are constraints. Industry will not locate new projects in Northern Ireland if they would be conspicuously more profitable elsewhere. Yet there is no easy way of assessing, and no satisfactory way to make general statements about, the viability of plants in the province.

In any scrutiny of the factors affecting relative viability compared to another region the main elements are probably transport costs (on materials and final products), fuel costs, wage levels (*not* simply *rates*), efficiency in use of labour, and capital costs.

As Isles and Cuthbert (1957, 346) make clear, these must combine to give a rate of return which is preferably better than, or as good as, alternative locations. Using the only information available on profits (the figures on gross profits before depreciation in the regional GDP estimates for the early 1970s), it is of interest that gross profits in manufacturing were estimated at between 2 per cent and 2.2 per cent of the UK total. Since employment was, at the same time, about 2.1 per cent of the United Kingdom total, this is not inconsistent with the hypothesis that the average rate of return on capital invested for the new projects in Northern Ireland was not much in Northern Ireland's favour. Admittedly, this is not a very firm piece of evidence.

Transport costs are, in any average comparison, a disadvantage to location in Northern Ireland. Capital costs, because of government grants on capital spending are an advantage. Fuel costs, until 1974, were a relative advantage which, with oil price increases, swung to disadvantage and by 1981 had become more nearly equalised by government subsidies; some regions, notably Scotland, still have a small advantage. The major cost element, as elsewhere, is the labour cost per unit of output. A 20 per cent extra transport cost is often less than the equivalent of a 1 per cent extra element in labour costs.

For continuing viability, industry locating in Northern Ireland probably examines how its labour efficiency and costs compare with elsewhere. Government incentives and inducements, mainly paid at the time of establishment, would be less effective if labour efficiency and costs compared adversely.

For this reason, comparison of labour costs and costs per unit may give an interesting indication of how Northern Ireland's relative viability has been changing. The simple presumption that wage costs are and were relatively low in Northern Ireland, and that this is evidence in favour of location in Northern Ireland, is not justified.

Average hourly earnings (*not* rates) for adult males in industry were, in 1960 (the earliest comparison readily available) 83 per cent of the United Kingdom average. However, on an industry by industry basis, and for occupations within industries, such a figure is misleading. The greater part of this difference is explained by differences in the structure of industry in Northern Ireland. Isles and Cuthbert (1957, 230) even in the early 1950s emphasised that many national wage agreements, or their equivalent, produced near parity of rates particularly for skilled occupations.

From 1960 to 1980 the average hourly earnings 'difference' had narrowed from the 83 per cent in 1960, to 89 per cent in 1970 and 94 per cent in 1980. This narrowing of the gap reflects both the changing structure and the further reduction in any remaining occupational differences between Northern Ireland and the rest of the United Kingdom. A similar trend can also be observed in, for example, Scotland.

The earlier evidence was that Northern Ireland's ability to attract new industrial investment was most effective in the early 1960s. With hindsight this may be explained in terms of:

(1) full employment elsewhere in the United Kingdom.

(2) some difference in earnings levels or labour costs.

(3) government inducements.

(4) lower energy prices (as a mainly oil-dependent region).

By the mid 1970s, factors (1) and (4) had been reversed. Government inducements (3) had, however, been increased. Average earnings (2) have tended to catch up, but this is partly a feature of structural change.

If it is assumed that Northern Ireland had a wage cost per unit of industrial output which was slightly below the United Kingdom average in 1956 and that the increase in average earnings was not affected by structural components (which is unfavourable to the comparison), then in the period up to 1973 the relative position improved slightly.

INCREASE IN WAGE COSTS PER UNIT OF OUTPUT

	U.K.	*N.I.*
1956–1973	+88%	+69%
1973–1979	+134%	+148%

Source: Author's calculations from indices of production, employment and earnings.

The relative position deteriorated slightly in the mid 1970s. Although Northern Ireland's relative competitive position, in terms of earnings, marginally improved within the United Kingdom, it is also relevant to note that allowing for exchange rate changes, the relative comparison with continental labour markets improved more dramatically. Germany is the extreme example.

INCREASE IN WAGE COSTS PER UNIT OF OUTPUT

	Northern Ireland	*Germany (in sterling equivalent)*
1956–1973	+69%	+186%
1973–1979	+148%	+100%

Source: as above

The major change in the 1970s is therefore *not* between Northern Ireland and the United Kingdom, but between the United Kingdom and other countries. Exchange rate changes have not compensated for the faster domestic inflation and therefore the position of all regions in the United Kingdom in trying to attract external investment was, in the late 1970s, despite the advantages which EEC membership might have added much less favourable. On top of this, Northern Ireland had its own local difficulties as an unquantifiable disadvantage.

Consequently, the main factors, (not necessarily mutually exclusive) which eroded the net advantages of the mid 1960s were:

(a) the rise in national unemployment.

(b) the rise in energy prices after 1973.

(c) the rise in U.K. costs relative to other countries.

(d) the deterrent effect of the local disorder.

The Role of Government Spending

The earlier discussion suggested that it is possible to show, with justification, both that Northern Ireland, pre-1970, was perhaps the most successful region of the United Kingdom in attracting additional industrial investment and that the overall result was a relative *net* reduction in industrial employment greater than that for the United Kingdom.

Analysing the role of government produces another apparent contradiction. During the whole period of devolved government in Northern Ireland, but especially in the years after 1945, government spending was justified by the principle of 'parity' with Great Britain, and balancing the Budget of the Stormont government was often argued to be more a presentation issue than a sharp practical problem. The Treasury effectively ensured that agreed spending, based on parity principles and making up 'leeway', could be financed. This led to an appreciation, still accepted in 1981 and reinforced because of the impact and cost of the local disorder, that Northern Ireland's living standards were greatly increased by the scale of the net inflow of Exchequer funds. Reviewing the evidence now available, it seems that this conclusion needs to be presented more carefully.

Two contrasting statements illustrate the different interpretations of the issue. First, it is indisputable that Northern Ireland, as a relatively unprosperous region, has received a net inflow of government funds, over and above its own tax payments. This has obviously added to the total of personal incomes in the province. Second, and more surprisingly, the scale of government financial transfers to Northern Ireland has, by specified standards, not always reflected what might be considered the degree of fiscal redistribution justified by objective or comparative criteria. If the latter point is confirmed, it is an important restraint on any argument that Northern Ireland's violence should not be explained, even partially, by suggestions of unfavourable treatment in terms of government spending. If government spending, pre-1968, was in some sense below parity, then the question of any causation through regional disadvantage is at least relevant if not necessarily proven.

The statistical evidence on this problem is readily assembled (see Simpson, 1981). The accounts of the Northern Ireland Government, until 1972, and the Direct Rule administration since then, are published and presented to Parliament. There is no dispute that during the 1950s and 1960s government spending was (if public corporations and nationalised industries are excluded) higher in Northern Ireland, on a per capita basis, than the national average. In the late 1960s, before the impact of extra spending because of the civil disorder, Northern Ireland was spending 15 per cent more on a per capita basis (Simpson, 1981, Table 2). Since then the relative figures have increased and increased by more than the amount linked to directly offsetting the cost of violence. In 1978–1979, the ratio was over 50 per cent higher per capita than in the United Kingdom as a whole.

There are, however, at least two other possible approaches to this issue. The first asks not whether Northern Ireland government spending is comparatively higher or lower than in Great Britain, but whether, if such expenditure is measured in relation to some criteria of need, Northern Ireland compares as favourably. This question is conceptually of relevance but, in practice, harder to quantify. The United Kingdom Treasury has, however, for the six main social functions of government (including housing, education, health, social services, transport and roads, environmental services, and law and order) attempted such an exercise (H.M. Treasury, 1979). This study concluded that, in 1976–1977, in Northern Ireland, public sector spending was, relative to England, slightly higher than indicated by need (5 percentage points), but for earlier years the position was less favourable. Need was assessed at 131 per cent of the level in England; the actual figure was 136 per cent.

Table 4:4

PUBLIC SECTOR SPENDING
(In each year England = 100)

	N.I.	Scotland	Wales
1959–1960	88	105	95
1962–1963	92	118	99
1965–1966	97	111	94
1968–1969	103	134	101
1971–1972	111	125	104
1974–1975	112	118	97
1976–1977	136	123	101
1977–1978	141	128	100

Source: Treasury: Needs Assessment Study (1979) Table 2

A second approach is to compare the additional Exchequer transfers to Northern Ireland to the transfers in Great Britain to local authorities through the Rate Support Grant and to ask, if Northern Ireland were to receive a separate Rate Support Grant for the local government type services in the province, how would this compare with the total recorded financial transfers. (Such an approach is not fully justified since it presumes that Northern Ireland's taxable capacity is so low that the whole Rate Support Grant would be an extra flow of funds. However the over-statement may not be too misleading!) Estimating a hypothetical Rate Support Grant on a crude proportion of that paid in Great Britain gives a somewhat unexpected result.

Before 1973, Northern Ireland, by this standard, was not particularly favoured. Since then, local disorder and, it must be emphasised, a rapid relative expansion in public sector spending in many other areas (see Simpson, 1981) has produced a much more favourable result. The difference between a hypothetical Rate Support Grant and the actual financial transfers was almost non-existent before 1971. Since then subventions to Northern Ireland have risen, above the Rate Support Grant, to meet some 20 per cent of public sector spending.

Public sector finances in Northern Ireland have, over the years from the mid 1920s, been supplemented by transfers from the United Kingdom Exchequer. By the 1960s these were the equivalent of some 16 per cent of total public sector spending; this is the basis of the argument that Northern Ireland was treated favourably. However, the degree of social and economic need in Northern Ireland, stemming from higher unemployment, a greater proportion of family dependants, a poorer stock of social capital in housing and health, and lower living standards, was such that the scale of government financial transfers was, until the early 1970s, below the level which might have applied if Northern Ireland had 'enjoyed' the scale of spending justified by need. This is a significant conclusion, both in terms of the remedial action taken in the early 1970s to expand public sector spending and in terms of the continuing major social problem in the housing sector where, it is argued, the current (1980–1981) spending programmes may still be inadequate on a comparative basis.

Comparisons within the United Kingdom

Despite the efforts made to improve Northern Ireland's relative position in the United Kingdom, unemployment and emigration remained at higher levels than would be indicative of economic prosperity.

More reassuring evidence is given by the basic indicators of living standards. Whether measured by Gross Domestic Product or personal income levels, the evidence is that in the past twenty years the difference in standards between Northern Ireland and the United Kingdom, as a whole, has narrowed. Indeed on the less elaborate evidence, for example, from Isles and Cuthbert, this process has gone on since, at least, 1939. The following crude comparisons, with dates chosen because of the limitations of comparable statistical evidence, illustrate the change since 1961.

Table 4:5

INDICATORS OF LIVING STANDARDS

(as % of U.K. average)

| | Gross domestic product per head | | Personal income per head |
	Northern Ireland	Scotland	Northern Ireland
1961	61	87	71
1978	77	97	80
Gain	+16	+10	+9

Sources: Derived from National Income Blue Book, Regional Trends, Scottish Abstract of Statistics and Wilson Report

No single indicator gives a 'best' indication of relative prosperity. To illustrate both the range of possible answers, and the differences which they bring out, the following comparisons of Northern Ireland with the United Kingdom, for 1978, are relevant:

Table 4:6

COMPARATIVE INDICATORS

1978	*% of U.K.*
Gross domestic product per head	77
G.D.P. per person in labour force	86
G.D.P. per person at work	91
Personal income per head	80
Personal income per person in labour force	91
Personal income per person at work	96
Personal disposable income per head	82
P.D.I. per household	90
P.D.I. per person in labour force	93

P.D.I. per person at work   98
Consumers expenditure per head   88
C.E. per household   96
C.E. per person in labour force   100

(*Source:* Regional Trends, 1981. Adapted by the author)

The political reader now has evidence either of a 23 per cent gap or a parity of spending, depending on motivation, interpretation and purpose. For those who are unemployed or who have involuntarily emigrated such comparisons may, very reasonably, seem somewhat academic!

Northern Ireland and the Republic of Ireland: economic comparisons*

The preceeding sections were deliberately constructed with no reference to the Republic of Ireland. The intention was to try to assess the Northern Ireland economy in a United Kingdom context only. Of course, this was incomplete if only because one of the hypotheses for debate by all political groups in Northern Ireland is that Northern Ireland has, or has not, done better as a region of the United Kingdom than it might have done if it had been part of an enlarged Irish state. Not many political parties would suggest that their views on the unification of the island of Ireland or the retention of Northern Ireland as part of the United Kingdom are based solely, or even mainly, on the economic issues. Nevertheless, attempts have been made to use the economy as a supportive issue for the different viewpoints.

The arguments, in terms of the comparative performance of the two economies, Northern Ireland and the Republic of Ireland, do not readily lend themselves to one particular political viewpoint. Some of the quantifiable indicators can be presented and are listed here in two obvious contrasting groups.

Table 4:7
NORTH–SOUTH COMPARISONS, 1978

	N.I.	R. of I.	Relative N.I. position
Gross domestic product per head	£1,949	£1,744	+12%
G.D.P. per employed person	£5,316	£5,186	+2%
Personal income per head	£2,034	£1,837	+11%
Personal disposable income per head	£1,647	£1,471	+12%
P.D.I. per employed person	£4,493	£4,329	+4%

* The statistical sources in this section are, for Northern Ireland, as indicated earlier, and, for the Republic of Ireland, are drawn from the parallel official publications.

(1) Northern Ireland, on average, enjoys a higher standard of living than the Republic of Ireland and has done so continuously since the two units were created, although this did not occur *because* the island was divided. For 1978, the comparisons are illustrated in table 4:7.

(2) Although unemployment in Northern Ireland has been high, the position has, until recent years (which may be partly a reflection of the local problems), tended to be slightly lower than that in the Republic of Ireland. The published unemployment rates differ conceptually, in a manner which understates the position in the Republic relative to that in Northern Ireland, but still confirms this point.

Table 4:8
UNEMPLOYMENT RATES (%)
(annual average)

	N.I.	*R. of I.*
1951	6.1	7.3
1956	6.4	7.7
1961	7.5	5.7
1966	6.1	6.1
1971	7.9	7.2
1975	7.9	12.2
1979	11.3	9.3

(3) Emigration rates, pre 1971, were much higher for the Republic of Ireland than from Northern Ireland. In the period 1937–61, emigration rates from the Republic were almost double those from Northern Ireland. In the 1960s, both areas experienced similar emigration rates (see table 4:13, below).

Figures for the 1970s will be, when published, very different, showing a higher emigration rate from Northern Ireland and a net immigration flow into the Republic of Ireland.

(4) Living standards have, since the late 1950s or early 1960s been rising faster in the Republic of Ireland than in Northern Ireland.

Table 4:9
LIVING STANDARDS COMPARED

Gross domestic product per head (as % of U.K.)	*Northern Ireland*	*Republic of Ireland*
1961	61	40
1978	77	69
Gain	+16	+29

Personal income per head
    (as % of U.K.)

1961	71	50
1978	80	71
Gain	+9	+21

(5) The growth of employment in the Republic of Ireland has, when the contraction in agricultural employment is taken into account, been better than that in Northern Ireland. This has been most conspicuous in the industrial sector. Employment in manufacturing has tended to decrease in Northern Ireland; in the Republic of Ireland there has been a general increase.

Table 4:10
EMPLOYMENT IN MANUFACTURING
('000s)

	N.I.	R. of I.
1956	185	167
1961	171	180
1966	179	197
1971	172	214
1976	147	219
1979	140	239

(6) The number of new industrial jobs promoted in the Republic of Ireland has increased both in absolute terms, and in comparison with the achievements in Northern Ireland.

Table 4:11
NEW JOBS PROMOTED

	N.I.	R. of I.
1966–1970	32,000	44,000
1971–1975	36,000	78,000
1976–1980	30,000	142,000

Sources: I.D.A. reports, Department of Commerce Facts & Figures
Note: I.D.A. 1966–70 = April 1966 to March 1971; N.I. includes Local Enterprise Development Unit.

The statistical comparisons, if they are to be summarised, present a picture of the economy of the Republic of Ireland expanding more quickly than that in Northern Ireland. The process of 'catching up' has been accelerated in the 1970s and, to a significant degree, can be attributed to the effect of the civil disorder in Northern Ireland. However, it would be misleading not to acknowledge that the evidence of a faster growth rate and a 'catching up' process pre-dates the emergence of the civil problems in Northern Ireland.

The faster expansion in the Republic of Ireland, pre-1970, was not particularly to be credited to a difference in the ability to attract investment. The experience of the 1960s was that, proportionately, Northern Ireland did rather better in securing new projects, but that this was counterbalanced by the contraction in the older industries. This 'declining sector' problem was less significant in the Republic of Ireland because, before 1960, it had a much smaller industrial sector than Northern Ireland.

In the 1970s the major difference has been the continued industrial expansion in the Republic of Ireland, contrasting with Northern Ireland's relative contraction. A further major difference has been the increased scale of the support for public sector spending in Northern Ireland which is not paralleled in the Republic. The net result has been that employment in both areas has expanded in similar proportion in the 1970s but in very different sectors of the economies.

Comparing the factors which contribute to the generation of economic expansion, the net gains for the Republic of Ireland in the past twenty years can possibly be traced to:

(a) the combination of full employment elsewhere and relatively cheaper labour supplies in the Republic attracting industry, together with a generous incentive package;

(b) the opening up, with guaranteed prices, both of the British and, later, EEC markets to Irish agricultural produce;

(c) the advantages, financial and economic, of EEC membership;

(d) the absence of the same dependence as Northern Ireland on textiles and heavy engineering industries where employment was contracting;

(e) the achievement, and retention of, a reputation for political stability.

Various points can be developed from these arguments. First, argument (a) is not so relevant in the early 1980s and is further weakened by the faster growth in wage costs per unit of output in the Republic of Ireland than elsewhere in Europe. Second, relative to Northern Ireland, arguments (b) and (c) are not now areas of significant advantage particularly if U.K. Exchequer transfers to Northern Ireland are taken into account. Argument (d) is still in the Republic's favour and argument (e) is certainly to Northern Ireland's disadvantage. Other factors in Northern Ireland's favour are, despite the earlier unfavourable comparison with Great Britain, the better provision of physical infrastructure and social facilities in Northern Ireland. It is not immediately obvious that, so long as both the United Kingdom and the Republic of Ireland remain members of the EEC, any of the direct *economic* factors would be moved in Northern Ireland's favour by changing its political relationship to take it out of the United Kingdom. Nor is it obvious how such a change would be arranged without prejudicing the large scale United Kingdom government financial transfers which are currently made to Northern Ireland. The major caveat to this conclusion is that the attainment of political stability is probably the most important factor in generating economic progress in Northern Ireland and this may have implications involving some elements of political change.

Variations within Northern Ireland: the issue of discrimination

There is, however, one further and important hypothesis which, even if the earlier arguments gave no part of an explanation of the tension in Northern Ireland (which is a more extreme statement than this writer would feel to be justified) would, on its own, link the civil disorder with economic factors. This is the suggestion that, *either* because of the scale of the regional problems *or* in spite of the scale of the problems, the distribution of the costs and benefits of the unemployment, new jobs and government spending, etc., falls unfairly within Northern Ireland. As a shorthand, with its admitted failings, this will be discussed in terms of whether the Roman Catholic community, either by the result of the interplay of market forces or by the result of deliberate acts of commission or omission, has done less well than the Protestant community.

This discussion is, if anything, even more difficult than the issues raised in earlier sections. In common with some of the earlier discussions, perceptions of reality or causation are often as strong, or stronger, factors than the reality itself in an analytical discussion. A *belief* that something is true can be an explanation of causation even if it is *not* true or cannot be shown to be true or false. The section is also made more difficult because certain evidence is simply not available. For example, the average incomes of Roman Catholics, or Protestants, is simply not recorded because the economic statisticians do not ask questions on earnings by religion and would not be encouraged or permitted to try.

In basic terms, there is no disagreement that unemployment and emigration have been higher in the Roman Catholic community than the Protestant. The problem of interpretation is one of what conclusions should be drawn from these facts. For some, these facts alone will be sufficient evidence. However, the geographical and structural factors determining the areas and occupations in which the communities are to be found may be an important determinant in any economic factors explaining the situation.

From the 1971 Census the Fair Employment Agency (1979, 8) has estimated the unemployment rates for Roman Catholics and Protestants and these are shown in table 4:12.

Table 4:12
UNEMPLOYMENT AND RELIGION, 1971 (%)

	Males and females	Males only
All Northern Ireland	8.5	10.4
Roman Catholics	13.9	17.3
Protestants	5.6	6.6

The Fair Employment Agency also presented evidence to show that unemployment (apart from within the inner Belfast area) tended to be higher the further the area was from Belfast, for both groups. In every District Council area, however, male unemployment for Roman Catholics was higher than for Protestants. This ratio, which on a Province-wide basis was 2.5 to 1, varied, between areas from the highest in Armagh (3.5 to 1), Castlereagh, Londonderry and Craigavon, to the lowest in Moyle (1.4 to 1), Ballymena, Coleraine and Newry.

Normal location theory would suggest that unemployment would be higher in the more rural areas of the Province and this, on a simple demographic relationship, would mean higher unemployment rates for Roman Catholics who are much more likely to reside in, what the Fair Employment Agency define as, peripheral areas (1979, 12). However, this is not adequate as more than part of this explanation.

The different unemployment ratios, by area, are not very consistent with an explanation which relies heavily on a pattern of deliberate discrimination in favour of one or the other community in some areas and not in others, although this does not rule this out as some part of the explanation.

One piece of evidence which seems to explain more of the difference in unemployment experience is the pattern of certain occupations being more heavily frequented by one group than the other. Whatever the historical explanation, Roman Catholics are more likely to be found in the occupations which have experienced the highest rates of seasonal and long term unemployment (Fair Employment Agency, 1978). For example 52 per cent of the Roman Catholic work force in 1971 was in the group classified as semi-skilled and unskilled, whilst the Protestant proportion was 40 per cent (Fair Employment Agency, 1979). This fact alone would explain a major part of the difference in unemployment rates, although the consequential question on the origins of this occupational structure then becomes relevant.

Emigration rates have also been higher in the Roman Catholic community. The evidence is summarised in the following table.

Table 4:13
NET EMIGRATION RATES FROM NORTHERN IRELAND
(Rate per 1000 per annum)

	Roman Catholics	Non-R.C.	Both Groups	R. of I.
1937–1951	6.5	2.3	3.7	6.9
1951–1961	10.8	4.6	6.7	13.8
1961–1971	6.9	2.8	4.3	4.8

Source: 1937–61 Barritt and Carter (1962), 1961–71 Author's calculation

The emigration ratios are consistent with an explanation that higher unemployment and emigration have been strongly correlated. One feature with possible relevance to the comparison with the Republic of Ireland is that in 1961–1971 the rate of Roman Catholic emigration from Northern Ireland became *higher* than the emigration rate in the Republic. In the earlier periods, emigration was higher from the Republic than even that experienced by Roman Catholics in Northern Ireland.

Given this demographic data which, whatever its causes, gives some insight into suggestions of 'unfairness', the question of economic policy is whether this situation was adequately assessed in the formulation and execution of government policies in the period under review.

As has been outlined earlier, the main thrust of government policy in attempting to generate economic development has been the expansion of industrial investment. This has been executed through a series of inducements and incentives to firms locating in the province, usually privately owned, from within or without the United Kingdom, supplemented by indirect policies of manpower training and infrastructure provision. Both in relation to infrastructure planning and industrial location there have, over the years, been allegations of inadequate recognition of the needs of the less prosperous parts of the province. Such complaints have focused on 'West of the Bann' or particular areas such as Londonderry, Strabane and Newry. Londonderry was a special focus for complaint when, in the late 1960s, it suffered a series of major economic setbacks. The then largest single male employing industrial firm (B.S.R.) closed completely in acrimonious circumstances; the rail link through Omagh to Belfast was closed; the New University was located at Coleraine and the decision to put extra resources into the development of Craigavon was seen as a diversion from the needs of the North–West of the Province.

Although government spending decisions may not be explicable in terms of 'pleasing all of the people all of the time' the underlying criticism was that government policy did not ensure an adequate, or fair, distribution of resources. This charge was particularly levelled at industrial projects. Successive governments relied on the strength of market forces to defend their position.

As far back as 1957, Isles and Cuthbert argued that

> Owing to the ...relationship between industrial density and distance from Belfast, this means also that most areas in which a large proportion of the insured workers are engaged in manufacturing are fairly near to Belfast, and most of those which have a small proportion in manufacturing industries are situated in outlying parts of the province (p. 112)

Their evidence was that over 80 per cent of industrial employment was within 30 miles of Belfast and, by implication, that, given the characteristics of this area of $1\frac{1}{2}$m. people, this was not surprising.

The criticism of the past thirty years is that the areas of high unemployment in 1950 are the same areas that experience high unemployment in 1980. The defence of the situation is, first, that unemployment in total is still too high and that changes in its distribution (if they had occurred) would only have been a shifting of the problem. More positively, government would point to:

(a) the development of the growth centre strategy in the 1960s which resulted in New Towns legislation being used in Craigavon, Antrim–Ballymena, and Londonderry;

(b) the attempts to restrain the growth of Belfast in the 1960s;

   (c) the co-ordination of infrastructure planning, manpower training and advance factory building to make various centres more likely to attract industry;

   (d) the expansion of transport facilities through Larne and Warrenpoint;

   (e) even during the disorder of the past decade, the efforts to ensure that physical development strategies evolve for the period to the end of the century (Regional Strategy, 1975–1995, published in 1975);

   (f) the introduction of a differential in the scale of financial inducements to firms which locate in the areas of worst unemployment; usually a 5 per cent extra grant on capital spending (on top of the existing regional grants of some 40 per cent),

. . . and would add that a decade of disorder and the external image created by political uncertainty can be as powerful a disincentive as all the above positive efforts.

An analysis of the number of new projects by the district of location shows the spread of the new projects established since 1945. Employment figures are not available, to give a better indication of the employment impact, but the evidence is some indication of the combined effect of market forces and government policy.

New industrial projects have, in number, if not in employment terms, been widely spread throughout the province. Indeed a calculation shows that there is a close comparison of percentages unemployed in sub-regions and the number of new industrial projects.

Greater Belfast	37% of projects;	43% of unemployed in 1981
'East of the Bann'	66% of projects;	68% of unemployed
Londonderry	9% of projects;	10% of unemployed
Newry	9% of projects;	5% of unemployed
'West of the Bann'	33% of projects;	32% of unemployed

(For these purposes Newry and Armagh have been classified as West of the Bann)

Since the larger projects, in employment terms, may have tended to locate nearer to Belfast, this comparison is probably biased against the areas away from Belfast.

Another characteristic of the process of change is that the ratio of closures to new projects varies significantly. The worst records for closure rates (excluding Moyle) are in:

Newry	61%
Banbridge	57%
Ballymoney	55%
Belfast City	51%
Armagh	50%
Castlereagh	50%
Carrickfergus	50%
Londonderry	46%
Down	44%
Omagh	44%

against an overall average of 38%.

Another method of assessing the results is to examine the changes, if any, in the distribution of unemployment. This is done in table 4:14, which examines the position in 1955, 1961, 1968, and 1975. These dates have the common characteristics that the overall unemployment rate was at a similar level in each of these years, so that any changes would not be expected to reflect differences in the distribution of unemployment in periods of, for example, recession. 1981 has been added to show both the latest figures and to indicate whether the present recession has changed the picture, which it has.

Table 4:14

PROPORTION OF UNEMPLOYMENT IN DIFFERENT TRAVEL-TO-WORK AREAS

	June in each year				
	1955	1961	1968	1975	1981
Belfast	39	43	40	36	43
Ballymena	5	5	3	7	9
Downpatrick	5	5	4	3	4
Craigavon	8	6	6	6	5
Coleraine	7	5	6	6	5
Above areas	64	64	59	58	68
Londonderry	13	13	13	12	10
Strabane	5	4	5	5	3
Strabane	5	4	5	5	3
Omagh	2	2	3	3	3
Enniskillen	3	3	5	5	4
Dungannon and Cookstown	5	3	5	6	5
Armagh	4	4	3	3	2
Newry	4	7	7	8	5
Above areas	36	36	41	42	32
TOTAL	100	100	100	100	100

Source: Department of Manpower Services Statistics, adapted by author.

The location of new industrial projects is, however, only a part of the explanation of unemployment differences. No figures are available to show, for example, the spread of direct government spending throughout the Province. Areas of high unemployment almost always create a natural and understandable pressure for a reallocation of government spending in their favour.

A major part of the debate on allegations of discrimination in employment opportunities inevitably focuses on the unemployment problem in the city of Belfast. The 1971 Census of Population shows that unemployment was higher in Roman Catholic areas of the city than in Protestant areas.

During the 1960s, government would probably have argued that within a modern urban area, differences in unemployment could not be the basis of policies which were specific to particular suburbs. There was, in all the Government planning documents, an implicit assumption that Belfast could be treated as a single travel to work area. West Belfast was part of the city, with major social problems, but its economic welfare was treated as dependent on the overall welfare of the city as a whole.

This argument, which was not accepted by politicians representing the Roman Catholic areas of West Belfast, has been less defensible in the 1970s. Prior to the 1970s, the argument was vulnerable to the criticism that several major industries in the Belfast area had employment structures which reduced the opportunities for Roman Catholics. The law has since been altered to make deliberate discrimination illegal. Less amenable to legal action is the effect of the decade of violence on the preparedness of people to seek employment freely throughout the city. Violence, fear, and social tensions have themselves had a differential effect on the labour market.

The 1971 Census shows that unemployment is directly correlated with the social status of people in particular suburbs. This correlation is probably stronger than any other explanation of why employment rates vary. However, unpublished research into the Census results shows that when religion is added, unemployment experience for Roman Catholics, even when socio-economic status is taken into account, is, in the North and West of Belfast, about 50 per cent worse than in non-Roman Catholic areas. It is not yet possible to be sure of the basis for this difference. Contributory factors would include lack of preparedness to travel to some places to work, the historical consequences of discrimination, and demographic factors. It is a difference which is not easily reduced by explicit government policies.

The basic figures show a trend for unemployment in the period of relative success (the 1960s) to be alleviated proportionately more in the Belfast region. (In 1981, this has been sharply reversed.) The areas which did worst were Enniskillen and Omagh, but not, as might have been expected, Londonderry. In so far as a correlation between *worsening* unemployment and the emergence of civil disorder is being investigated, then this evidence is not particularly supportive of the thesis since the initial disorders were associated with Londonderry and Belfast. However, this is not to ignore the fact that the main sources of community tension and disorder have been in areas of *continuing* high unemployment.

Violence and the economy: the 1970s

The earlier discussion has continually emphasised the theme that, in the 1970s, economic analysis has been severely complicated by the interaction of local violence and disorder on the economy. The cost in terms of human suffering is, of course, unquantifiable and more important than the economic consequences in terms of finance.

The direct financial cost of more than a decade of violence can be presented in terms of Exchequer spending. Extra internal government spending for compensation and law and order, excluding the army, in 1979 probably was about £200m. Other government spending by 1979, in total, was some £350m. higher than it would have been by the (admittedly too low) standards of the late 1960s. In this sense government spending is now some 25% higher than by the relative U.K. standards of the 1960s.

Government revenue is down because of the tax loss from the loss of employment that might otherwise have existed. This, however, is a speculative area.

Among the other costs of the decade are the jobs lost, the investment deterred and the people who involuntarily emigrated from the Province. If Northern Ireland had managed to continue to increase industrial production at three-quarters of the rate in the Republic of Ireland, as was the position in the 1960s, then, at the end of the decade of the 1970s, production would have been 39 per cent higher. This is the equivalent of over 50,000 jobs. Even if this is an optimistic overstatement, as it seems, a loss of over 30,000/35,000 industrial jobs is a conservative estimate.

To estimate what might have been is always hazardous. However, even allowing for the 'ill-wind' effects of increased government spending, it would be hard *not* to conclude that the regional economic problems have been increased sharply in the past decade after an earlier period when there were some small but significant improvements.

An Overview

In the late 1960s, the position of the Northern Ireland economy seemed to be improving and, for a brief period, it seemed as if real long term gains were being realized. In the main autonomous sectors of the economy, reassuring trends or features could be cited.

In agriculture, the United Kingdom post-1945 price support system had generally given Northern Ireland farmers a satisfactory set of income guarantees and discussion of changes in the support system, partly in anticipation of EEC membership, was not seen as a major threat.

In industry, the rate of inward investment was meeting the targets set in the Wilson report (1965) and seemed to be capable of offsetting the loss of employment in existing firms.

The Government had devised financial arrangements to increase the financial transfers from Westminster (the new Health Services Agreement and the Social Services Agreement, 1971) and the level of public sector spending per capita was well above the United Kingdom average.

The effects of this buoyancy were, of course, transmitted to the other, induced, sectors of the economy.

This is the structure of the argument that emphasized that Northern Ireland had 'never had it so good' (to abuse the Macmillan description of the late 1950s). However, the problems were far from being removed.

Agricultural employment, but not output, continued to contract. Industrial employment did not expand as rapidly as needed or hoped. Government spending was low when assessed by comparison with relative needs, or certain other regions.

Developments in the 1970s have, with some exceptions, tended to erode the gains of the 1960s. Agricultural incomes, at the end of the decade have fallen sharply, and this is attributed to the problems of financing the agricultural policy of the EEC. Industrial investment has fallen sharply; it would have been deterred by the local disorder, but wider economic forces would also have produced adverse consequences, although on their own these would presumably not have been so severe. The increase in Government spending programmes in the 1970s has, in fact, been the major offset to a sharp contraction in the regional economy. This increase was on a scale which may have increased total employment (and incomes) by some 7–10 per cent in the decade. Even the restraints on public sector spending in 1980 and 1981 were small by comparison.

There is no doubt that Northern Ireland is still the least prosperous region of the United Kingdom. That fact alone may be relevant in an assessment of the origins of social tensions and violence, but has it been less prosperous because of neglect by government or because of defective government policies?

Earlier sections have shown how the Northern Ireland economy could be described as having had to 'run hard to stand still'. Industrial development was not large enough to offset the loss of industrial jobs. Government spending increased and was higher per head than in Great Britain, but was, until the early 1970s below the level assessed on the basis of 'need'. Although unemployment and emigration have remained at relatively high levels, the objective indicators of living standards showed a marked relative and absolute improvement.

The improvement in the performance of the economy of the Republic of Ireland was, even before 1970, more marked than in Northern Ireland. In the 1970s, the Republic has been catching up somewhat faster.

This evidence, if the arguments are accepted, does not *prove* the hypothesis that economic progress in Northern Ireland was significantly deterred because of factors inherent in the political structure of two separate units. There has been some political support for the suggestion that Northern Ireland would have benefited economically by being linked to the faster growing economy of the Republic. This argument, on the evidence cited earlier, is unproven unless it is presumed that the existence of 'one' economy might have somehow created conditions which would have avoided the indirect effects of violence on the economy. Put in a quasi-political style, what were the *economic* gains to commend a change (a) when both were members of the EEC and (b) when the main economic benefit of the existing framework was and is the continuing large scale government financial transfers to Northern Ireland from the United Kingdom Exchequer which would be difficult to sustain in an all-Ireland setting.

5

Informal Social Organisation
Hastings Donnan and
Graham McFarlane

Any assessment of the current state of Northern Irish society must deal with the relevance of being a Protestant and being a Catholic in the mundane areas of everyday life. While it is true that dramatic events can lay bare the dominant characteristics of a society, it is also true that any understanding of a society's make-up cannot be achieved without paying detailed attention to those aspects of life which appear trivial when set against the big issues of the day. Only too often a focus on the dramatic blinds the observer to the complexity to be found in a society's fabric.

This paper deals with the sociological and social anthropological literature which has focused its attention on the informal social relations which exist between Catholics and Protestants. The literature with which we will be concerned is all based on some kind of research using fieldwork, i.e. the active participation of the researcher in the day to day life of the people whose activities are being investigated. We will not discuss that research which uses the more depersonalised attitude surveys and questionnaires, even though this means that we will have to disregard the literature which looks specifically at Catholic and Protestant *attitudes* (the best of these are probably O'Donnell 1977 and Rose 1971). We believe that attitude surveys in general provide little more than a partial and sometimes distorted view of day to day life: in day to day life attitudes are fluid, and responsive to the exigencies of the situation. Consequently, attitudes and actions are not in any simple relationship with one another: not only do they interact but they often seem to be in apparent contradiction to one another. It is for these reasons, and not because of some simple professional preference or bias, that we consider the battery of techniques used most consistently (but not exclusively) by social anthropologists to be the most suitable for research on the social interaction between groups (cf. Harris 1982). These methods comprise, briefly, a blend of formal and informal interviews supported by, and dependent upon, lengthy periods of intensive involvement with a limited number of people (this latter aspect is vaguely described as 'participant observation'). All the literature with which we will be dealing is based on research using these approaches to varying degrees.

We will start by providing a brief overview of this literature, then go on to review in some detail what we know (or think we know) about the relevance of the Catholic-Protestant division in various areas of social life.

Informal Social Organisation in Northern Ireland: An Overview of the Literature

Although a somewhat impressionistic analysis of Catholic and Protestant relations was undertaken by a team led by Mogey in the 1940s (Mogey 1947; 1948), and although Barritt and Carter have provided a brief overview of social life in Northern Ireland (see Barritt and Carter 1972, chapt. 4), Rosemary Harris' research around the border town of 'Ballybeg'* in the early 1950s constitutes the most sensitive early attempt to get behind the public attitudes of Protestants and to a lesser extent Catholics. This research was the basis for her M.A. thesis (Harris 1954), but it was substantially reworked for her paper on political leadership in the area (Harris, 1961) and for her justly acclaimed book *Prejudice and Tolerance in Ulster* (Harris 1972). Since Harris' work has had great importance for later research, in that many of her themes are echoed there, it is worthwhile to spend some time looking at it in detail.

Harris sets about making explicit the attitudes of local Protestants towards Catholics and then tries to deal with what looks like a paradox: those Protestants with the strongest anti-Catholic attitudes were at the same time those who interacted most tolerantly with their Catholic neighbours. Harris' explanation of this apparent paradox has two parts. Firstly, the generally negative attitudes towards Catholics were intensified by the distrust the less prosperous Protestants felt towards the Protestant elite (both in the local and national context). The fear was of being 'sold out' to the Republic of Ireland, and it was this fear

---

*'Ballybeg' is a pseudonym for the place in which Harris carried out her research. We have put all such pseudonyms within inverted commas the first time they appear in the text but thereafter have not distinguished them. Concealing the identity of the area studied has long-been a commonplace anthropological practice.

which motivated the poorer Protestants' appeal to Protestant solidarity in their dealings with the elite in the local Orange Lodge (the only arena they had for interaction with them). Secondly, their behaviour towards their Catholic neighbours was guided by conflicting values relating to the proper behaviour between neighbours of whatever religion: the Catholic and Protestant identities were underplayed. These values were part of what Harris calls the 'common culture' which seemed to derive not only from being neighbours but also from sharing a similar class, or position on the economic ladder. Harris argues that the conflict built into the basic dichotomy between Catholic and Protestant was restrained by cross-cutting personal relationships and the norms which pertain to them. In short, Harris shows the amount of common ground which existed between members of each religious category at given socio-economic levels. The religious dichotomy did, however, remain basic, as evidenced especially by the limited number of marriages and hence kinship ties across the boundary.

Harris followed up her suggestion, that the lack of kinship ties across the boundary maintains social distance, with historical work which seems to show that where kinship networks did cross the boundary in Rathlin Island, they actually encouraged mixed marriages, and hence the creation of more kinship and affinal ties across the boundary (Harris 1979). Ultimately, she argues, such marriages across the boundary were engendered by a shared culture which itself had been generated out of mutual opposition towards the landlord class.

Harris has since returned to the paradoxes of Northern Irish life in a recent comparison between community relations in Ballybeg and 'Patricksville' in southern Eire (Harris 1979; Bax 1976). On the surface, according to Harris, political attitudes in Patricksville in the 1960s seemed to exhibit a kind of consensus, while on the surface in the 1950s Ballybeg political life showed signs of considerable disunity, to say the least. On the other hand, actual day to day life in Patricksville seemed to be replete with obvious tensions, clashes of interest and, indeed, violence; while among the population of Ballybeg there was a playing down of blatant hostility.

Other work mirrors much of what is to be found in Harris' material. The forces which operate, not only to divide, but also to integrate Northern Irish society are summarised by Leyton, in a paper written around the same time as Harris' *Prejudice and Tolerance in Ulster,* but based mostly on research in two communities in South Down in the 1960s (Leyton 1974a). Leyton has also elegantly demonstrated the importance of class, or one's relative position in economic hierarchies, for the understanding of patterns of inheritance (Leyton 1970a; 1970b; 1975) and for the understanding of attitudes towards, and interaction with, kin and friends in the Protestant village of 'Aughnaboy' (Leyton 1974b; 1975). Leyton has also looked at how disputes are channelled and contained in this Protestant village: here he argues that the shared values and the balance of power which were created by the community served to counterbalance the negative forces which operated within it (Leyton 1966). Similar mechanisms containing open hostility seem to be at work in the 'Upper Tullagh' (Buckley 1982). Extending Harris' remarks on the language of debate in the Ballybeg Orange Lodge, McFarlane's work in a predominantly Protestant north Down village shows how notions about Catholic, Protestant, and class identities and values functioned as part of the rhetoric used to wage the trivial and not so trivial disputes which are probably the stuff of everyday life in any community in Northern Ireland (and elsewhere). McFarlane has also taken up Harris' interest in mixed marriages, attempting to un-ravel the significant factors which people take into account when evaluating such marriages (McFarlane 1979). In an effort to get behind public responses to mixed marriages, Monaghan (1980) has attempted to detail the ways in which a small number of middle class couples coped with their stigmatised position. Bell has taken up Harris' interest in co-operation between farmers in a comparative study across Northern Ireland (Bell 1978). Finally, Blacking, Holy and Stuchlik's work in four rural communities (in north and south Down, Fermanagh and Antrim) returns to one of the central questions of Harris, though from a slightly different methodological angle (see Blacking *et al* 1978, and McFarlane 1980 for a brief summary). Unlike Harris, they do not attempt to account for the religious divide, but like Harris they do try to show exactly where, when and how the division was made relevant or irrelevant in the 'private' and 'public' domains of community life. Their findings seem to be very similar to Harris', so they add a 1970s dimension to her research.

Thus, Harris' work does seem to be a kind of touchstone for research into the informal social organisation in Northern Ireland. It is certainly the major text which has to be taken into account for any new research in this area. However, in setting the pace it has also been partly responsible for directing research on social organisation into small scale rural networks, probably because the very sensitivity of the approach precludes its application to large populations. No once can deny the usefulness of Boal's extensive and innovative analyses of territoriality and population movement in Belfast (see Boal 1969; 1970; 1971; 1972; Poole and Boal 1973), nor the value of Kirk's work on religious segregation in Lurgan (Kirk 1967), but urban research into Catholic and Protestant relations has, until recent years, been based on questionnaires or indirect social indicators rather than 'on the ground' reportage. It has missed out on the qualitative element. It is only recently that anthropological type research has been carried out in such areas. The most important recent text is based on research carried out in 'Anro', a Catholic enclave in West Belfast, over a period of eight months, between 1972 and 1973 (Burton 1978). Burton's work is another milestone, not only for its focus on an urban area but also because his book is the first to look at a completely Catholic community. Burton attempts to uncover the dynamic and fluid relationship which existed between the Provisional IRA and the embattled community, a community with a Catholic view built up around the three features of community solidarity, sectarianism and Republicanism. Most important for a consideration of Catholic-Protestant relations is Burton's analysis of sectarianism, According to Burton, the dimension of sectarianism is both demonstrated by, and is sustained to uncover or 'tell' the religious affiliations of new acquaintances prior to social interaction (see Burton 1978, chapt. 2; 1979). This practice is also discussed in Harris 1972, 148). Other enthnographic work which is now beginning to bear fruit has been carried out by Nelson on the world view of a group of Protestant activists in Belfast (see Nelson 1975; 1976a; 1980); by Jenkins who has researched into the problems confronted by Protestant youngsters entering employment in Belfast (see Jenkins 1978; 1981a; 1981b); and by Taylor who has looked at the interaction between religious and political ideas among Free Presbyterians (Taylor 1979; 1980; 1981). New research is being carried out by Blacking on Catholic and Protestant relations in Larne.

Informal Social Organisation in Northern Ireland: Detailed Research Findings

This section deals with the detailed findings of the research work which has been carried out on social relations between Catholics and Protestants. To provide some order in our presentation of these findings, we have used a range of easily identifiable areas of everyday life as a framework, assessing the relevance of the Catholic and Protestant division in each area. We have also made a broad categorization of these areas into two domains: public and private. We will turn to the private domain first.

The Private Domain

Economic Co-operation

One of the most important gauges of the social relevance of the Catholic and Protestant identities in everyday life is the extent to which they co-operate with one another. Co-operation may be of two types: primary co-operation for gaining a livelihood, and secondary co-operation like babysitting, lending ladders, etc. Most social anthropologists have concentrated on the first of these, and all the detailed investigation has been carried out in rural areas.

Harris (1972: especially chapt. 5), puts her emphasis on the different co-operation practices to be found among the Catholic and Protestant hill farmers and more prosperous (and mostly Protestant) infield farmers in Ballybeg in the 1950s. In the infield, co-operation was a matter of contributing labour: depending upon who was available, kin, friends or in-laws would form work teams (or 'swop') with one another. One of the consequences of this class difference in co-operation practices was the fact that some of this neighbourly co-operation went on between Catholic and Protestant; the fact that one did not have machinery nor kin or neighbours who were co-religionists tended to encourage 'swopping' labour across the divide. On the other hand, because most infield farmers were Protestant, co-operation between Catholics and Protestants there was limited; and when it existed, it had an element of imbalance in it, since machine owners (usually Protestant) expected labour from non-owners (usually Catholic) in return for the use of their machinery.

Harris does not assess the relative stress placed on different types of social relationship in co-operation practices in Ballybeg, although neighbourhood proximity did seem to have a primary role. Co-operation depended on some degree of geographical proximity: where kin were also neighbours, that was even better but if neighbours were mostly Catholic, that was not insurmountable. At first glance Leyton's work on Aughnaboy seems to contradict Harris' emphasis on neighbourhood. Leyton wanted to assess the role of kinship in the economic affairs in Protestant Aughnaboy. Despite the fact everyone in the village agreed (though for different reasons) that relatives and economic affairs ideally do not go together (cf. Bell 1978, 49), there were some differences in co-operation practices within the population. Leyton identifies two broad economic levels which he refers to as the working masses and the elite, each of which exhibited different attitudes towards such co-operation. The working masses needed kinsmen for information about jobs, and occasionally for obtaining jobs, while some of the elites in the area saw kin as an encumbrance to their social and economic mobility. The masses actively manipulated kinship relations, while the elites tried to prevent their kinsmen manipulating them. Those among the masses who had no kin in the area made up for this deficiency by making use of friends or, if they had married into the village, in-laws and other affines.

The difference between the Aughnaboy masses' emphasis on kinship and affinity for economic co-operation and the general emphasis on neighbourhood proximity in the Ballybeg area is probably a result of the different economic bases in the two areas (cf. Leyton 1977). In the hills around Ballybeg, co-operation was more direct and materialistic and it was rooted in space: in Aughnaboy, co-operation between kin was more a matter of exchange of indirect services and spatial factors counted for less. The two patterns have obviously different consequences for Catholic and Protestant co-operation. The importance of kinship and affinity for economics for the masses in Aughnaboy, together with the fact that kin and affines tend to be co-religionists, seemed to preclude any co-operation across the religious divide; in Ballybeg, as we have seen, the demands of proximity in farming allowed it to some extent. Buckley's conclusions from his work among the farmers of Upper Tullagh seem to be anomalous here (Buckley 1982). To Buckley, economic co-operation between Catholic and Protestant farmers is not a simple product of the economic necessity of co-operation with those living nearby; it is rather a matter of conscious design. Buckley argues that since any close relationship can be disrupted and contaminated by economic considerations, there are obvious dangers in co-operating with such people. Arguments with one person can lead to the severing of many ties. According to Buckley, the farmers in the Upper Tullagh therefore tended to cut their losses, and they chose to co-operate with those with whom any disruption of relations would have the least social costs, i.e. with neighbours of the opposite religion.

Although the argument is intriguing, the evidence advanced to support it is unconvincing. Moreover, can it be argued that people choose to co-operate with one another simply with an eye to the consequences of a disruption in that relationship, or do they mix these considerations with an awareness of the *positive* benefits of co-operation with particular people? For instance, it could be that one avoids co-operation with kinsmen in favour of neighbours, not out of a fear of spoiling good relations with kin, but out of a desire to extend one's sphere of co-operation outside the kinship network. One does not have to continually and deliberately foster good relations with kin (good relations are in a sense assumed), but one does have to invest in relations with neighbours if one wants to have an extensive sphere of co-operation. It is possible that co-operation with neighbours across the religious divide also has practical roots: if a Protestant/Catholic can obtain something from a Catholic/Protestant which he or she cannot obtain from a co-religionist then this will encourage cooperation.

While kinship and neighbourhood have different degrees of importance for primary economic co-operation in different areas and at different times, it can be gleaned from the available evidence that there is a strong tendency for people in local communities to rely chiefly on kin, if kin are available, for most *secondary* favours. This is the conclusion of Blacking *et al* (1978, 23-25) from their work in four villages, of Burton from his work in Anro (1978, chapt. 1), and of McFarlane from his work in a north Down village (1978, 141). Of course, non-kin were often involved in the exchange of such favours as babysitting etc., and people with no kin nearby had to rely on other people. Nevertheless, the emphasis on kinship still stands.

Blacking *et al* have some interesting things to say about the importance of the Catholic and Protestant division in this area. They point out that there were various strategic reasons for such a stress on kinship relations in the four villages they investigated—for instance, safe-guarding reputations, or the fact that direct or immediate returns of favours are not necessary; consequently such co-operation was quantitively less frequent outside the kinship field. Since most kinsfolk were of the same religion, given the small number of mixed marriages, this implies that such co-operation was almost certain to be between co-religionists. But the religious factor cannot then be used to explain such co-operation, since some people did have kin of the opposite religion and they *did* co-operate with each other. According to Blacking *et al*, the religious factor seems to be of only contingent relevance: as a subtle constraint on mutual aid between specific kin who are not co-religionists, and an *additional* constraint among people who are not kin.

Informal Visiting

Perhaps the safest generalisation one can make about social relations in Northern Ireland is that most inter-household and informal visiting goes on between close relatives. This is emphasised by most writers (see Blacking *et al* 1978, 25-26; Boal 1969, 43; Buckley 1982, 124-125; Harris 1972, chapters 5 and 7; Leyton 1974b; 1975, chapters 4 and 5; McFarlane 1978, 199; Harris 1972, 144-146). This is most important for women, and in many rural areas most inter-household visiting goes on between female relatives (Blacking *et al* 1978, 25-26). Given the importance of kinship, it is obvious that there is little to produce a definite pattern of visiting across the religious divide (cf. Harris 1972, 146). Nevertheless, in the case of the exchanging of small favours, with which visiting is closely tied up, it does seem that those who have kin of the opposite religion can justifiably maintain a visiting relation with kinsfolk: however, this is less frequent when kin of the same religion are equally accessible. Of course, visits with non-kin did occur in the areas studied, and not only with co-religionists, but this was most evident and important among those who do not have relations in the vicinity. Blacking *et al* have calculated that of all the visits between unrelated Catholics and Protestants, most were between individuals who had kinship ties to a particular locality and individuals on the other side who lacked such ties. Visiting relations across the divide were also often established between people who both lacked kinship connections in a given locality, especially among incomers to that locality.

It would seem, therefore, that the informal visiting pattern is based on close relations of kinship and friendship, ties which are usually to be found among co-religionists, but which do, of course, occasionally cross over the divide. As in the case of exchange of small favours, in this sphere religion seems to be contingent in two ways: it is a restriction on the relative frequency of visiting between Catholic and Protestant who have accessible kin of the same religion, and it is an additional constraint on the amount of visiting undertaken by non-kin. To counterbalance this emphasis on religion, it is important to point out that differences in the perceived class of individuals can operate in a similar way. Differences in perceived class did seem to limit interaction with secondary kin (cousins, uncles etc.) among the elite of Aughnaboy (Leyton 1975, 44-45), and it operated similarly in the four communities investigated by Blacking *et al* (1978, 25). Further perceived differences in class operated to preclude informal visiting between non-kin.

Personal disputes

Not so much of a systematic nature has been written about involvement in personal disputes, apart from Leyton's paper (1966) on his data from Protestant Aughnaboy, and Blacking *et al* (1978), which includes some material on interpersonal disputes across the religious divide. This area is a crucial one, since disputes are probably the most obvious indication of 'on the ground' social strain. What does this material tell us?

It is probably safe to say that there is a value put on harmony in most communities in Northern Ireland: practically every observer has commented on this. However, this value on harmony is not enough either to contain disputing, nor does it help us to understand the regularities or patterns to be found in disputes. Leyton argues that involvement in disputes among the Protestant villagers in Aughnaboy was determined by the different mixes of costs and benefits built into the relationships between the disputants and others. The weighing up of these costs and benefits account for variation in the intensity and number of disputes between different types of people: among kin, benefits outweigh costs (especially among kin related through women, between whom conflict over property was unlikely), so disputes were on an individual level and were relatively easily settled. With non-kin the potential for social strains outweighs the benefits which are built into such relations, so disputes were more likely. However, these disputes were also kept at an individual level, and were usually easily settled, since if whole families were to be involved, numerous valuable cross-cutting social ties would be disrupted; there was pressure on the disputants either to settle, or to maintain a low key in the dispute. With people who did not have a dense network of kin to support them, these disputes could last longer. Most disputes were between people related by marriage, where costs usually outweigh benefits, and they were at their most severe when, as was usually the case, in-laws lived in different communities. These findings are very similar to those of Blacking *et al* (1978, 27).

Given the logic to be found in this dispute pattern, it would seem likely that disputes which break out between unrelated Catholics and Protestants should be both common and difficult to settle. Moreover, they should escalate into a group confrontation between members of different kinship networks, if not whole religious blocs. In fact, there does not seem to be any evidence that disputes between unrelated Catholics and Protestants are more frequent than they are within each bloc. Nevertheless Blacking *et al* argue that, when such disputes develop, they are not settled quickly. This is logical enough, since there are usually few direct benefits in settling quickly, or in putting pressure on others to do so. This is also because such anti-social behaviour can be easily defended. One can challenge the value placed on harmony and escape sanctions by arguing that one is fighting from a Protestant corner. This is especially the case when the dispute is not about control over people or about breakdown in reciprocity, but about resources like land (cf. Barritt and Carter 1972, 61). However, in no case recorded by Blacking *et al* did disputes escalate into a conflict between Catholics and Protestants as groups; in the four rural communities investigated, the network of supporters of those involved seemed to cross over the religious border.

Life Cycle Events

Buckley has neatly summed up one aspect of Northern Irish social life when he describes it as 'endoritualistic', a piece of anthropological jargon which means that Catholics and Protestants do not participate directly in each others' rituals (cf. Barritt and Carter 1972, chapt. 2 and p. 64; Harris 1972, 132; and Leyton 1974a, 192-193). Here we are concerned with rituals pertaining to the life cycle, baptisms, weddings and funerals, all of which are principally the concern of kin (see Blacking *et al* 1978, 28-29, 31 for detailed data on the parts played by kin in these rituals). However, when it comes to less direct involvement in rituals, this clear boundary around those who should be involved seems to become a little blurred.

In Ballybeg, Aughnaboy and in the four communities investigated by Blacking *et al*, local morality emphasised that community membership entailed an interest or concern for the passage of all co-residents through the life cycle. Harris stresses the obligation felt by all people in the Ballybeg area to show respect at funerals; and she shows how in the hill area at least, it was important to attend *all* neighbours' wedding parties: in the more prosperous infield, invitations to wedding parties were more restricted (Harris 1972, 79-80, 108-110). Leyton refers to the obligation of community members to help bury the dead (Leyton 1975, 11). Blacking *et al* reiterate that it was the obligation of all senior adult males at least to walk behind the coffins of all fellow villagers, but they point out that greatest emphasis was placed on relationships based on kinship, neighbourhood, friendship and affinity. This was symbolised by the fact that only people in these relationships attended pre-funeral wakes and returned to the house for post-funeral snacks and meals. Where such relationships cross the religious divide, the duties built into such relations are played up, and the Catholic and Protestant identities are underplayed.

This section is probably a suitable point to bring up the question of mixed marriages. Although Buckley argues, somewhat controversially, that the conventions prohibiting mixed marriages are decreasing in importance in the Upper Tullagh (Buckley 1982, 127), most of the available evidence suggests that mixed marriages are still the ultimate challenge to the rules defining proper relations between Catholics and Protestants. The material collected by Blacking *et al* in the 1970s does not suggest that attitudes towards or practical responses to such marriages among the population at large were much different from those of the residents of Ballybeg in the 1950s (Blacking *et al* 1978, 29-30). Harris argues that mixed marriages were very rare indeed (Harris 1972, 143-144, 171). Leyton argues that in Protestant Aughnaboy in the 1960s there was a total prohibition on marrying Catholics (Leyton 1975, 57), while elsewhere he refers to the threat of violence from the prospective bride and groom's families, (Leyton 1974a, 191).

While all mixed marriages seem on the face of it to be anathema to the lay population in Northern Ireland, commonsense tells us that this is not all there is to it: it is likely that some mixed marriages are worse than others. McFarlane (1979) has indicated the factors which people seem to use to evaluate different types of marriage. There are different types of mixed marriage in the sense that there are different likely outcomes for the future children of various marriages: these outcomes depend upon the sex of the spouse who is of the other religion and upon which spouse has decided to change religion. Out of this McFarlane has devised a cultural scale dealing with the relative unpopularity of different types of marriages.

The Public Domain

Political Involvement

It almost goes without saying that political support and opinion in Northern Ireland has for the most part been based on the Catholic-Protestant division. Each side has its own political parties and movements. We are not concerned here with the factors lying behind this sectarian division in politics. Our concern is rather with putting politics into its social context (the approach advocated by Harris 1979): to assess what is known about grass roots political activities and what is known about the relations between political groupings and surrounding community structures and attitudes. We will start by looking at what is known about the activities of local branches of official political parties.

Surprisingly not very much has been written on this, and some comments which have been made raise more questions than they answer. A lot of disparate pieces of useful information are hidden behind the statement that in the Aughnaboy area 'virtually all Protestants are members or supporters of the Unionist Party, and virtually all Catholics are members or supporters of the various Catholic parties such as the Nationalists, the Republicans, or Sinn Fein' (Leyton 1974a, 191). Who are members? Who is involved? What are their attitudes? Harris refers to the great deal of distrust felt by the poorer Ballybeg Protestants for the Belfast Unionists (1972, 189-190), but she does not give many details about political activities in the area, either by the poorer hill farmers or by the infield farmers. One would expect that the infield farmer population would have included a few local political activists.

There are only a few suggestive remarks made elsewhere. McFarlane's data (1978) indicates that it was only a small core of middle class Protestants who were members of, and actively participated in, the affairs of the local branch of the Unionist Party in the north Down village in which he did his research. Moreover, the same people are prominent in other organistions. Blacking *et al* also note that in the four communities which they studied, active involvement in both Orange and Green political parties was mostly restricted to the categories of businessmen, professionals (especially teachers), farmers (especially large scale farmers in the Unionist case), retired members of these groups, and spouses of those belonging to these groups. There is obviously a considerable variation in the factors which might be used to account for low levels of direct political involvement: for instance, where a party's seat is considered safe, party supporters may be too complacent to become actively involved, while opponents may see activism as pointless (see McFarlane 1978, 280). However, in general terms it could be argued that the low level of popular involvement has at least something to do with the easily discernible set of popular attitudes towards politics and political activity. Blacking *et al* report (like Harris 1961; 1972, chapt. 11) that those who become involved in political affairs were both distrusted and ridiculed as upstarts.

As far as we can tell, the rural studies focus their attention only on the political parties whose legitimacy is not in question. Burton's analysis of the relationship between the Provisional IRA and the community of Anro presents a picture of the struggle for legitimacy faced by paramilitaries. Burton anchors the ideology of the activists in a divided society, but, more important, he assesses the mainsprings of support for the IRA in its local social milieu of Anro, rather than in any broad commitment to Republicanism or Nationalism. Support was fluid and waxed and waned within the community: it responded to outside forces which affected the community, it responded to the periodic challenges of other parties (for example, the Catholic Church) and it took into account that activists were known 'in the round' as someone's kinsman or neighbour. The debate about the rights and wrongs of IRA activists was contained within Anro: it was seen by the local people as an internal debate and only members of the community had the right to be involved.

Burton's focus on the claims and counterclaims of the various parties to this internal debate demonstrates as neatly as possible the potential of the ethnographic method and the importance of examining the broad social backcloth against which politics is played out. The fact that there was a debate about the legitimacy of the IRA in Anro meant that support could not be attributed to a given section of the population in a simple way. The fluidity of the situation meant that there were shifting allegiances over time, and it meant that support could be given to different arguments even at the same time. Despite what a recent critic has suggested (see Patterson 1979), Burton does not seem to deny that there were other traditions, or other rhetorics, operating in the community: he just suggests that it is superficial to view support as somehow fixed and a limited resource which can be given to only one organisation or movement. Commonsense tells us that support can be given to different organisations, for different purposes. This fluidity of support also seemed to characterise relations between working class Protestant communities in Belfast and Protestant paramilitaries in the early 1970s (cf. Nelson 1976b).

The political importance of the Protestant Orange Order and, to a lesser extent, the Catholic Ancient Order of Hibernians has been stressed by virtually every commentator on Northern Ireland. There is virtually nothing in the literature on the local organisation of the Ancient Order of Hibernians and virtually nothing on the urban Orange Lodges. However, there is some evidence of a distinct pattern in membership in rural Orange Lodges. Blacking *et al* report that overall membership of the lodges in their rural communities amounted to between 30 and 40 per cent of the total adult male Protestant population (Blacking *et al* 1978, 36). In addition, many spouses of Lodge members belonged to ladies' committees (emphasising the Lodges' social role) and many sons belonged to Junior Lodges or bands attached to Lodges, prior to becoming members of the local Lodge. Most members of the rural Lodges belong to the skilled, semi-skilled or unskilled manual occupational categories, while there were very few professionals involved (cf. Barritt and Carter 1972, 62; Buckley 1982, 147-148).

The class composition of at least the rural Lodges is understandable when we consider attitudes towards the Lodges. Harris reports that the Ballybeg Lodges were regarded with disdain by the more prosperous infield farmers in the area (Harris 1972, esp. 191-193), while the Protestants in the less prosperous hill area regarded it as the last bastion of Protestantism. Similar attitudes have been recorded by McFarlane (1978, 225-226).

Voluntary Organisations

The intensification of conflict in urban areas in the early 1970s brought in its wake a proliferation of local community associations, many of which were formed initially to offer protection and to alleviate housing intimidation (see Burton 1978, 29; Darby 1976, 159; Griffiths 1978). With the failure of the authorities to deal satisfactorily with the demands from both communities and with their increasing inability to provide even basic social amenities (such as refuse collection and transport to and from the city centre) in some areas, living conditions could be maintained or improved only when local residents tackled the problems themselves. Consequently, self-help seemed the only solution and many new tenants' associations were founded to operate in this capacity. As the Troubles intensified the role of these associations broadened and in some cases even matured into experiments in self-government (see, for example, Burton's discussion of the Anro Community Council and Relief Committee 1978, 29ff).

In urban areas membership in these associations was almost entirely religiously homogeneous. This seems to have been partly a consequence of the fact that they were formed initially to protect the areas in which they emerged (and like Anro's Relief Committee were therefore sectarian by definition), and partly also the result of residential segregation (cf. Darby 1976, 160). Such segregation, and so such homogeneity of membership, seems likely to continue despite efforts to change it; though the Anro Redevelopment Association itself intended to rehouse the original Protestant inhabitants in dwellings which it had restored within Anro, its attempts have so far been unsuccessful (Burton 1978, 30). The situation with regard to membership in such associations in rural areas is not so clear and the available literature tends to give them scant attention. Exceptions here are the work of Blacking *et al* (1978), and McFarlane (1978). In all four of the communities investigated by Blacking *et al* there were tenants' associations, all of which were established as a result of the centralization of local government functions, especially those concerned with housing and planning. These have marked a change in the traditional leadership pattern described by Harris (1961); the minister, priest, doctor and teacher no longer have a monopoly of influence. However, membership in each was low and, despite the fact that they were *de jure* open to all comers, they were dominated by businessmen, farmers and professionals. It would be extremely difficult to argue that there was any sectarian basis to recruitment into these organisations; membership of the association in the largely Protestant north Down village investigated included middle-class Catholics. (Blacking *et al* 1978, 34). Much more significant was the low level participation by both Catholics and Protestants. Both Blacking *et al* and McFarlane (1978, 231) argue that low participation is a consequence of a general reluctance to set oneself up as a spokesman for the community and to leave oneself open to ridicule if one does not perform well at meetings. This is the 'modesty' syndrome discussed by Harris (1972, chapt. 6). Its consequences are exactly the same as those described by Harris (1961); only those who have little or nothing to lose from criticism, or who are confident enough to be active, take part. As Blacking *et al* point out, the fact that one can be denigrated for participation only dignifies those who are able to participate effectively. These people tend to be in a different league; they are middle-class, and very often middle-class immigrants to local communities.

Information on other kinds of voluntary associations does not seem to have this urban bias, and most writers give at least some attention to membership of organisations like the Women's Institute, Young Farmers' Club, Lions' Club and so on. The avowed aim of many of these associations in both rural and urban areas is to transcend the sectarian divide and most of them actively try to recruit members along nonsectarian lines (Buckley 1982, 150; Darby 1976, 155: Harris 1972, 138).

However, though expressed policies may be consistent it is less easy to generalise about actual membership. Thus while membership in the Women's Institute was predominantly Protestant in Ballybeg in the 1950s (Harris 1972, 138), it was entirely Protestant in Aughnaboy in the 1960s (Leyton 1975, 12), and mixed in 'Kilbeg' in the 1970s (Buckley 1982, 150). Similarly, while membership in Young Farmers' Clubs in some areas might have been drawn from both communities (see Barritt and Carter 1972, 146; Buckley 1982, 150), in Ballybeg it was once again predominantly Protestant (Harris 1972, 138). Certainly in Belfast, and in some provincial towns, membership in voluntary organisations has often reflected the religious divide and, in some places such as Lurgan, parallel associations have existed for both Catholic and Protestant (Darby 1976, 155; Kirk 1967). Perhaps not surprisingly, such religious homogeneity of membership has been particularly characteristic of youth clubs, since many of these are connected to particular church congregations (cf. Barritt and Carter, 1972, 146; Buckley 1982, 145).

While the difficulties of making generalizations are therefore apparent, certain kinds of voluntary association seem to be consistently quoted as examples of organisations which do have cross-cutting membership. Thus Barritt and Carter note that both Catholic and Protestant participate in societies associated with the Arts, in Rotary Clubs, the Round Table and in Business and Professional Women's Clubs (Barritt and Carter 1972, 142, 144); Leyton notes that in Aughnaboy voluntary associations like the 'Perrin' Development Board and the Golf and Country Club did cut across the division (Leyton 1974a, 196); and Buckley comments on the religious mixing characteristic of the Kilbeg Historical Society and Camera Club (Buckley 1982, 150). What is striking about these particular associations and societies, however, is that their membership is drawn primarily from the middle-class. In Belfast and Lurgan, for example, while those associations with a predominantly working-class membership tended to recruit only Catholic or Protestant, those associations with middle-class membership were frequently mixed (Darby 1976, 156; Starling 1970); thus in Lurgan links were fostered among the professional classes of both communities in the town's art club, film society and local history society (Kirk 1967). Membership of similar associations in Kilbeg was also drawn from the farming, business and professional classes (Buckley 1982, 150). Indeed, in certain areas it appears to have been only the wealthy who were considered to make suitable members of some associations, and low economic position was often the reason for the reluctance of both poorer Protestants and poorer Catholics to join local associations (see Harris 1972, 138).

The danger here, therefore, is in making generalizations about the nature of Protestant-Catholic interrelations within voluntary associations which are valid only for people in certain socio-economic positions. While working-class Protestants and Catholics may have their separate associations this does not seem to be so true of middle-class Protestants and Catholics. Before we make generalizations about voluntary associations, we must first consider what kind of association we are talking about, and specify the class position of those involved.

Recreation and Leisure

Many writers have noted that, in general terms at least, there exist in Northern Ireland sports which are distinctively 'Protestant' and sports which are distinctively 'Catholic' (see for example, Barritt and Carter 1972, 148-151; Blacking *et al* 1978, 37; Darby 1976, 152-153; Harris 1972, 134; Leyton 1974a, 191 and 1975, 12). Interest in a particular sport frequently derives from schooldays, though Darby has warned us against overemphasising the dichotomy in sport at school level (Darby 1978, 218-219). In many areas, however, Protestants do learn to play soccer, rugby, hockey and cricket at school, while Catholics learn to play Gaelic football, hurling and camogie. The political associations of these sports are historically based: while rugby and cricket are often associated with the rich and the Protestant 'Ascendancy', the Gaelic games are encouraged and promoted by the Gaelic Athletic Association founded in 1884, which now, as then, has close links with political and cultural nationalism. Any possibility of participation in both has been effectively precluded by a ban imposed by the Gaelic Athletic Association on playing or watching certain non-Gaelic 'foreign' games, until the ban was removed in 1971.

In some cases spectators have also tended to be recruited along sectarian lines (see Boal 1969, 38; Darby 1976, 153). Until it was disbanded in 1951, Catholic soccer fans supported Belfast Celtic while Linfield received the encouragement of a predominantly Protestant following. However, rugby internationals, which are held in Dublin and which are organised on an all-Ireland basis, have tended to attract both a Protestant and Catholic following from north and south of the border. Though not all sports are organised on an all-Ireland basis, occasionally the organisation of international teams and matches gives rise to disagreements over the correct protocol (see Darby 1976, 154, for some examples of this).

Even though boxing, soccer, athletics and darts are among a number of sports played by members of both religions, obviously this does not always mean that both sets of players and spectators will meet on and off the field of play. Frequently sporting activities revolve around the church and teams formed on this basis will more than likely be involved in different church leagues. Furthermore, the venue for sporting activities may not always be considered equally suitable by both sides. For example, the bowling club in Kilbeg met in the Orange Hall (Buckley 1982, 148).

However, it is not always clear when support and interest in a particular sport is based purely on sectarian grounds and when it is the result of differences in social class. Though few Catholics play rugby or cricket it is also true to say that so do few working-class Protestants (cf. Darby 1976, 153), and cricket in particular seems to have a predominantly middle-class following among members of both communities (Barritt and Carter 1972, 150). Golf also seems to be played by the more wealthy and, when Barritt and Carter note that the golf course is often cited as 'a prime example of a place where Protestant and Catholic meet in friendship', it may only be the middle-class who are able to meet in such circumstances (*Ibid,* 151; see also Harris 1972, 134).

Despite the separation of Catholic and Protestant sports, a separation apparently almost so complete in some areas that no one sports club could unite Ballybeg even in the event of a match with outsiders (Harris 1972, 9), common residence does seem to promote a certain degree of interest in the fortunes of *any* teams representing a given community (see also Blacking *et al* 1978, 37). Here there seems to be a rural-urban difference. For example, while most Belfast Protestants are apparently ill-informed about what goes on in Gaelic football, there seems to be more Protestant interest in the success of a local club in rural areas (Barritt and Carter 1972, 150). However, partly because the games are played on Sunday, and partly because of their symbolic significance, this interest does not seem to extend to active participation as either player or spectator (cf. Darby 1976, 152; Harris 1972, 135). Thus Harris notes that in Ballybeg attendance at Gaelic matches was 'almost as much a purely Catholic activity as was attendance at Mass' (1972, 135). Nevertheless, though Protestants may not turn up to watch a Gaelic match, many do take an interest in the result, this tendency having been noted in several rural areas (Buckley 1982, 166; Harris 1972, 135).

Perhaps the most important meeting place everywhere in Northern

Ireland during leisure hours is the public house. While in general terms it may be true that Protestant and Catholic each prefer to drink in the establishment of a co-religionist, it is difficult to assess from the existing evidence exactly to what extent this is actually the case. Certainly it seems to vary with time and place. The Republican associations of the drinking clubs which replaced the burnt-out pubs of the predominantly Catholic Anro district of Belfast in the seventies and eighties ensured that their clienteles were exclusively Catholic (Burton 1978, 12-13). A consequence of the increase in open conflict during this period was that it was no longer safe for the Anro residents to patronise the facilities in the neighbouring Protestant areas, and by the same token of course, Protestants were excluded from Anro. On the other hand, in Tyrone in the early fifties, though the town of Ballybeg could boast two pubs one of which was Protestant-owned and the other Catholic-owned, patrons of each were not segregated on the basis of religion. While 'in general, groups of men composed of Catholics only went to the Catholic pub, and Protestant groups to the Protestant pub' it was by no means uncommon that groups of mixed religion would drink in either pub (Harris 1972, 141). Particularly on occasions such as Fair Days, either bar would be used by traders of both religions to conclude a sale. The more contemporary situation in Upper Tullagh seems to be similar. Here the groups which drank together were based on ties of kinship, neighbourhood, work, leisure or co-membership of voluntary associations (Buckley 1982, 155). Similarly for the four communities in north Down, south Down, Fermanagh and Antrim studied in the mid-1970s (Blacking *et al* 1978, 32). It would be difficult to argue that Catholics and Protestants in mixed rural areas deliberately select co-religionists as drinking companions. It would seem that drinking groups are recruited not in terms of religion *per se,* but rather in terms of other relationships which may cross the divide even if to a limited extent. To conclude that the situation is clearly one where Protestant and Catholics drink exclusively in their own bars, therefore, would be a misleading over-generalization.

Since they are much more anonymous, it is difficult to make reasonable generalizations about the degree of segregation to be found in cinemas and dance halls. Nevertheless, the main factors which seem to determine the religious composition of participants are the loyalties of the organiser and the venue of the event. Where such activities are organised as private enterprises it would seem that some mixing is inevitable, and Barritt and Carter note that the youth at least have an opportunity to meet in commercial dance halls (Barritt and Carter 1972, 146). However, in many rural areas in the past, such amenities were unorganised on a commercial basis, and those that existed tended to be organised by bodies with religious or political associations and centred in their halls. With only one television and no cinema in Ballybeg in the early fifties, for example, the screening of a film every Sunday in the Catholic parochial hall assumed some significance. Nevertheless, because Sunday was considered to be an unsuitable day to pursue such pastimes, and because of the location, few Protestants attended, while those who did attend were severely criticised by other Protestants (Harris 1972, 135). Elsewhere Protestant attendance at Catholic dances was similarly frowned upon, and for similar reasons (see Barritt and Carter 1972, 64). Even more recently, in many smaller towns it would seem that the church and associated political bodies occupy a central position in the organisation of social activities, particularly those that concern the young (see for example, Buckley 1982, 145 and Kirk 1967). In Aughnaboy, for example, the adolescent's '"courting" begins and continues at dances held throughout the Perrin region, Protestants dancing to Scots music in Orange Halls and Catholics dancing to Irish Show Bands in Hibernian Halls and Catholic auditoriums' (Leyton 1974a, 191; see also Leyton 1975, 12). Here, apparently, one of the main reasons for church involvement in the organisation of social activities was to encourage contacts among those of the same faith, and at the same time to reduce the opportunities for contact between boys and girls of the opposite religion. These contacts would have opened up the possibility of permanent relationships of mixed marriages (cf. Darby 1976, 152; Harris 1972, 136).

As in the case of sporting activities, class differences again seem to affect the religious composition of those attending a dance. However, this is only hinted at in the available literature. Thus Harris notes that the more middle-class Catholics and Protestants both went only to expensive formal dances held at the Hospital or Golf Club in a neighbouring town; and even though both communities here attended the same dance, they usually went as paired couples or in organised parties, so that there was not the same opportunity for mixing as at the local dances (Harris 1972, 136).

Shopping and Other Services

There is a certain amount of evidence to suggest that in a number of areas Catholics and Protestants patronise only those services owned or controlled by co-religionists. This practice tends to result in a duplication of certain facilities and ensures that no one owner will manage to acquire a monopoly in a single trade. Thus Harris notes that the pattern of sectarian loyalties in Ballybeg was largely responsible for limiting competition between shops, with the result that though the town was small, it was able to support a relatively large number of businesses. Indeed, in some places the moral responsibility to support one's own side seems to be so strong that for the Protestant owner to attract Catholic customers, or vice-versa, he must first offer considerable advantages over his rivals (Harris 1972, 6; see also Leyton 1975). Except in certain circumstances it is unacceptable to patronise the business of the other side. Thus, for example, only when the interests of the person providing the service are felt to be inherently incompatible with one's own interests, as when Ballybeg farmers traded with cattle and sheep dealers, or when none of one's co-religionists provide a particular service, can one seek the service of a member of the opposite religion without embarrassment (cf. Harris 1972, 139, 142). Yet other situations may give rise to a conflict of loyalties as when a co-religionist newly provides a service previously provided only by someone of the other religion. This seems to have been the case when the Protestant doctor, who for years had been the only doctor in Ballybeg, was joined by a Catholic counterpart; many Catholics felt it was their duty to transfer allegiance, though apparently only against their better judgement (*Ibid,* 142). Such conflict of loyalties seems less often to be an issue in areas like the largely Protestant Aughnaboy, where there were high expectations that members of each religion would support their own side (Leyton 1974a, 193; 1975, 12).

However, it should be emphasised that, even in areas dominated by a single religion, the tendency to patronise co-religionists is not always clearly defined but can vary from time to time. This seems to be true even of the religiously homogeneous districts in Belfast and Londonderry. While in the early sixties it was noted that 'Catholics now shop in the Protestant area of the Shankill Road, because it is known to be a good shopping centre' (Barritt and Carter 1972, 76), by the late sixties this pattern was less obvious; and factors like geographical proximity to shops were often less inducement to do business there than was the religion of the owner (Boal 1969, 41). While it does seem that Catholic and Protestant often do patronise only their co-religionists, it would again be misleading to obscure the variations which can and do occur.

Annual Festivities and Other Occasional Events

It is well known that every year each of the two religious communities in Northern Ireland hold their own separate, special commemorative events. While the Protestants commemorate the Battle of the Boyne and the Derry Apprentice Boys, Catholics celebrate the Easter Rising and certain feast days such as the Feast of the Assumption and Lady Day. This seemed to be as true for urban Anro as it was for the rural Aughnaboy (Burton 1978, 14; Leyton, 1974a, 192). Both sets of celebrations are accompanied by street processions, bands and bunting. Participants in either set of events belong exclusively to one religion or the other to such an extent that participation in the Twelfth of July celebrations, for example, can be taken as an indicator of Protestant territoriality in urban Belfast (cf. Boal 1969, 34). Catholic solidarity is similarly reaffirmed in their celebrations; thus Burton notes that 'internal coalescence . . . (is) . . . vividly portrayed within Anro during its ceremonies and celebrations' (Burton 1978, 16). However, there is some indication of a slightly ambivalent attitude towards the celebrations of the other side, and they are not always and not everywhere as mutually exclusive as they might at first seem. For example, while some Kilbeg Catholics expressed resentment at the march on the Twelfth of July, and while no bunting or flags were displayed in this largely Catholic village on this date, other Catholic villagers supported and even helped to organise a concert to raise money to pay for instruments for the accordian band which lead the parades on this day (Buckley 1982, 148-149). Elsewhere Catholics have made similar contributions to support local bands (McFarlane 1978, 253).

Some annual village festivals do not seem to be of sectarian interest and are not organised along sectarian lines, but are held solely with the intention of bringing the whole community together. The annual festival in Kilbeg seems to be of this type. For a week during the summer months the Festival Committee, headed by a working-class Catholic and including both Catholic and Protestant members, arranged a variety of outdoor events and activities which not only attracted tourists to the area but also drew together the local residents. This is an event, it is argued, at which 'religion and politics are absent' (Buckley 1982, 153). Fair Day in Ballybeg seemed to be another occasional event at which sectarian loyalties were superseded; on this occasion economic interests usually took precedence. Indeed , Harris notes that the question of moving the Fair to a new site was the only important issue over which sides were taken on an entirely non-sectarian basis (Harris 1972, 3).

Several authors have remarked that both Catholic and Protestant support each others' occasional fund-raising activities, fetes and bazaars (Barritt and Carter 1972, 63; Blacking *et al* 1978, 38; Buckley 1982, 149; Harris 1972, 137). This seems to be particularly true of small country towns and villages where perhaps, Barritt and Carter suggest, there are few alternative attractions (Barritt and Carter 1972, 63). However, residents of Ballybeg apparently made a distinction between different kinds of fund-raising events, and they did not lend support indiscriminately to all events arranged by the other side. Thus, while they considered it neighbourly to support the other side's collections for religious causes, they believed it to be entirely inappropriate to support the fund-raising efforts of their political organisations (Harris 1972, 137; see also Blacking *et al* 1978, 39). Nevertheless, actual attendance at a sale or fete even for religious causes was a different matter and such attendance was almost entirely restricted to members of one religion or the other. In Ballybeg fund-raising was never undertaken for charities of a non-sectarian or non-political nature (Harris 1972, 136).

Conclusions

On the basis of the evidence presented above there are some deceptively simple generalizations which can be made about the day to day relevance of being a Catholic or a Protestant in Northern Ireland.

First, it would seem that the degree of everyday segregation seems to be more acute in working-class urban areas than in the small towns and villages of the countryside. Recent conflict at territorial boundaries and population movements seem to have re-emphasised working-class residential segregation in urban areas. Consequently, they have reinforced the tendency for community life in these areas to be centred in single religion enclaves. In rural areas and villages, geographical proximity has given rise to a *modus vivendi* which has found expression in a value on community harmony and in the underplaying of Catholic and Protestant relations in middle class suburbs.

Second, within the mixed areas studied in detail (unfortunately almost entirely in rural areas) the relevance of the religious division varies to a certain extent according to the areas of life being investigated. There is a logical system to be found however. It would seem that in most areas segregation in the *private* domain does not derive simply from a desire to maintain close relations with co-religionists: in most rural areas the religious divide seems to be underplayed (at least explicitly in attitudes). Actual segregation derives much more from the fact that people emphasise the importance of kinship and to a lesser extent neighbourhood relations for ordering everyday contact and co-operation. In the *public* domain, on the other hand, segregation seems to be an aim: the concerns here are the political and economic well-being of one side or the other. Mixed marriages seem to be a link between the two domains. They are seen as political actions as much as matters of personal or family concern: as such they are viewed with antagonism by both sides. Consequently, few marriages are contracted across the divide. This feeds back into the private domain: the lack of mixed marriages means that family ties, so important for everyday life in rural areas, do not cross the divide.

This is what the available literature seems to tell us. However, we have suggested that these generalizations are deceptive; as our review shows, there seem to be some contradictory findings even within the body of literature discussed. Moreover, these generalizations are probably open to objections not only from professional social scientists but also from all the casual observers who seem to be the bane of those who do research in Northern Ireland. For instance, everyone can give examples of occasions when rural areas seemed as sharply divided as any urban areas (as we write, this seems to be the case in some border communities). Furthermore, people can point out that not every area in working-class Belfast is riven by sectarianism.

Given the co-existence of different views on Northern Irish society the relations to such local level research can be envisaged. First, it can be argued that the small community or network of people whose affairs are investigated is not representative of Northern Irish society, or even representative of urban or rural Northern Ireland. It is doubtful whether this can be resolved completely satisfactorily, because it is doubtful whether there is such a thing as a representative community. The nearest thing to a solution is to add more studies of local areas or of different sectors of the population (the middle class is virtually unresearched, for example) to add more evidence for any generalization. We should emphasise again that this work could not be done in pursuit of the truth or the final word on Northern Irish society: there is no magical number of studies which would provide the truth. All we can ask for is more research. But how should this be carried out?

This brings us to the second line of objection to a given set of observations: they might derive from inappropriate methods. We pointed out in our introduction that we were not going to discuss research which used questionnaire surveys because they are too unreliable. However, even in the research carried out by more personalised methods, there are certain to be differences in emphasis. It is perfectly reasonable to conjecture that the tolerance and harmony to be found in many reports is simply a product of using interviews more than any other research tool. Everyone in Northern Ireland knows that few people are willing to be frank and open about their strong opposition to the other side, especially to seemingly educated researchers. The solution here is probably to carry out more research using the more informal methods *and* to be more explicit about the methods which are used.

A third objection to pieces of research on relations between Catholics and Protestants derives from the fact that they are often carried out in communities without an eye to events which are taking place outside the community. One could argue that apparent harmony in local relations can give way to apparent conflict in response to events in Northern Ireland. Hence a study carried out in one community in one year might give rise to different results from a study done the next year in the same community. Is there a solution to this? It might be possible to do research *in* a community, but to focus on the community's reaction to events *outside* the community. It might even be possible for researchers to extract such material from their existing data.

This problem of the interaction between the local community and events outside it brings us full circle. We noted in our introduction that dramatic events and the big issues of the day can do two things: they can lay bare the true fabric of society or they can cover up and blind us to the true fabric of society. Opting for one of these alternatives is a product not only of observation but also of the set of assumptions (or ideology) of the researchers. Any piece of research on Catholic and Protestant relations in Northern Ireland can be challenged in terms of two sets of assumptions. One set, usually held by sociologists, is that Northern Ireland has a core problem which hides beneath a veneer of superficial good relations. This core problem erupts at certain times and in certain places, and subsides beneath the veneer at others. The other set of assumptions, seemingly shared by most social anthropologists, is that Northern Irish society has a reasonable balance at its core, which is only temporarily disrupted by dramatic events. As assumptions these can obviously not be proven or disproven, though further detailed research on informal social relations might suggest which is the more likely.

6

Schools and Conflict

Dominic Murray

In order to more readily appreciate any relationship which may exist between educational segregation and broader community divisions in Northern Ireland, it is essential first to consider the conception and historical development of the separate systems of schooling.

The Development of a Segregated System

In 1921, the original Government of Northern Ireland *inherited* a segregated system of schooling. The National (primary) system of education, established in 1831, had continued to provide the only education experienced by the vast majority of children in Ireland until the formation of Northern Ireland as a separate political entity. Although originally conceived as a non-donominational system, it rapidly evolved into segregated schooling, usually under the management of the local parish priest or minister.

Secondary education in 1921 was provided in the main for Catholic pupils within the religious school which came into being during the nineteenth century as a result of the Catholic Relief Act of 1782. Protestant secondary education was provided almost exclusively by the Anglican Diocesan schools, Royal schools, or the Presbyterian established academic institutions. There were few free scholars in the secondary sector as a whole. Thus it catered mainly for the children of middle class Catholics and Protestants.

This then was the segregated nature of educational provision at the onset of the State of Northern Ireland in June 1921.

One of the major problems experienced by Northern Ireland's new Minister of Education was the refusal of a large number of Catholic schools, both primary and secondary, to recognise his authority. In border areas some continued to claim, and receive, salaries from the Government in Dublin. Their position collapsed in 1922 when the

Southern authorities, prompted it would seem more by pragmatism than by patriotism, announced the cessation of such payments.

The reticence of clergy and teachers to accept the authority of the Northern Ireland Ministry of Education had a significant effect on the educational interests of Roman Catholics in general. Akenson (1973) claimed that

At the very moment when the Ulster Government was establishing the new educational system, the Church's already weak bargaining position was being destroyed by the non-co-operation policy.

As a consequence, no Catholic clerical representatives were included in the educational policy committees which had been set up. Nonetheless, despite the abstentionist position of Catholics, the initial machinations of the Ministry of Education under the able leadership of Lord Londonderry, was characterised more by fairness than chagrin. Inevitably, however, the resulting educational structures catered for Protestant rather than Catholic concerns.

The Lynn Committee (1921) commissioned by Londonderry, recommended *inter alia* that schools which were handed over to the Ministry should receive 100 per cent grants for both capital expenditure and maintenance. Such schools were termed Controlled schools.

Those schools whose managers wished to remain entirely independent were to receive only grants for heating and cleaning. These were called Voluntary Schools.

It was also suggested that in Controlled schools the Bible should be taught without note or comment. Londonderry baulked at this latter suggestion since he perceived it to be an implicit endowment of Protestantism in Controlled schools. However, an amendment to the original (1923) Act, introduced by the then Prime Minister Sir James Craig, reinstated Lynn's suggestion.

It would seem that requiring Bible instruction, while prohibiting comment, did in fact reflect the teaching of Protestantism, since the Catholic Church insists on interpretation in the light of Church teaching. It was this amendment which sowed the seeds of the perception of Roman Catholics in Northern Ireland that Controlled schools are *de facto* Protestant institutions. This view still prevails today.

The 1930 Education Act made concessions to both Protestant and Catholic concerns. To the former it increased guarantees about the selection of teachers, i.e. only Protestant teachers would be appointed to Controlled schools. The latter were more or less appeased by the raising of grants to Voluntary schools (50 per cent of capital expenditure, 50 per cent towards maintenance). These grants to Voluntary schools were increased in The White Paper of 1944 to 65 per cent for capital expenditure and 65 per cent for maintenance. By 1947 almost all Protestant schools had transferred control to the Ministry to become known as Controlled and, more recently, State schools.

Catholic schools remained 'voluntarily' aloof until an Amendment Act (1967) produced increased incentives for them to concede one third of the seats on their management committees to public representatives. In return, 80 per cent grants were offered towards capital expenditure together with 100 per cent grants for maintenance. The less suspicious Catholic managers soon acquiesced and by the late 1970s almost all Catholic schools had accepted the new '4 and 2' or Maintained status.

The present situation is that State (formerly Controlled) schools are perceived by Catholics as being Protestant while Maintained schools are seen by all as being Roman Catholic institutions. One must ask, however, how much quantative or objective evidence exists to support these generally held perceptions.

Research on Segregation

Surprisingly, in the light of the perennial debate on the deleterious social effects of segregation, little research has been carried out into the segregated nature of schools in Northern Ireland. Akenson (1973) commences his bibliography,

> The most striking thing about the historiography of Northern Ireland is how little historical writing of any real quality there is . . . there is as yet no satisfactory general history of Northern Ireland since 1920.

Akenson was especially concerned with the dearth of writing on education in the Province. In fact a good deal of historical research has been carried out on the Northern Irish educational system (Dent 1965; McElligott 1969; Musson 1955; Robinson 1967; Spence 1959). However, little has been made available in the form of published works. In fact most early available material seems to have been preoccupied with global structures and political influences on schooling in Northern Ireland. Akenson for example has written an illuminative account of education in Northern Ireland between 1920 and 1950. His book is essential reading for anyone with an interest in educational structures in the Province especially during the formative years of the State itself. Campbell's (1964) slim volume is perhaps the best existing exposition of the Roman Catholic viewpoint on education with Cardinal Conway's (1971) pamphlet also of interest in this context.

Barritt & Carter's (1972) fine sociological survey of Northern Ireland seemed, for the first time, to direct attention not only to the segregated nature of structures in the Province, but also to its ramifications. This shift in emphasis can be argued to have engendered a novel approach to research in education and especially its effects upon children attending religiously (and therefore culturally) segregated schools.

Typical of this new approach was the work of Robinson (1971) and Russell (1972). The former, a case study carried out in Derry in 1969 demonstrated interesting differences in perception between Catholic and Protestant school children. 62 per cent of Catholic children named either Bishop Farren or John Hume as Derry's most important citizen while 70.9 per cent of the Protestant children named Northern Ireland's Prime Minister or the Lord Mayor of the city. When asked to name the capital city of the country in which Derry was situated, more than half the Catholic pupils named Dublin while more than two-thirds of the Protestant children cited Belfast. While it would be erroneous to attempt to attribute such variance to school experience alone, Robinson concludes that the schools seem to do little to moderate them.

Russell's (1972) research demonstrated a greater liklihood for Catholic children to exhibit negative attitudes towards Government, although it is again difficult to determine the extent to which schools can be deemed responsible for the formation of such attitudes.

Research which has been carried out on the effect of schooling on children's attitudes and cultural identity in Northern Ireland has tended to concentrate on the curricular areas of religious instruction and history teaching. Greer (1972) in a study of Protestant sixth form boys describes a notable gap in most religious instruction courses. He claims that while Hinduism, Buddhism and other religions are studied in both types of school, 'little reference is made to the problem of comparative religion which lies at the root of so many social problems in Ireland, the Protestant-Roman Catholic division'.

This selective approach also applied to history teaching. In describing history teaching in Northern Irish State schools, Magee (1970) pointed out that, 'Irish history was taught only where it impinged in a significant way on the history of Great Britain'. Hadkins (1971) describes the deliberate use of emotionalism in some Nationalist text-books. Darby (1974) has voiced the concern that bias in presenting (especially) history to school children may help to propagate two hostile cultural traditions. (For a fuller account of curricular practices within segregated schools see Darby (1972)).

All of these studies provide information about the effects upon children of school curricula and materials. Little evidence exists, however, which provides insight into the extent to which the overall process of, or experience within, segregated schools may contribute to the attitude formation of children. For this type of information we have had to rely on autobiographical or semi-fictionalised accounts. Devlin (1969) for example, describes the secondary school which she attended as, 'a militantly Republican school'. The Principal is portrayed as a women to whom everything English was bad and who, 'although she did not hate Protestants (unlike the English whom she did hate), believed they could not be tolerated because they were not Irish'. *No Surrender* is an appealing, auto-biographical account of experiences of growing up in a Protestant district and attending a Protestant school (Harbinson 1960).

In this context, one research project is worthy of a more comprehensive description. *Schools Apart?* (Darby *et al* 1977) attempted to blend quantative evidence about segregated schools with more illuminative data obtained within them. The underlying objective of the project was to attempt to, 'fill the gap between the wide general interest in the subject of integrated schooling in Northern Ireland and the shortage of information about segregated schools'.

Segregation and its Effects

It must be said that the bulk of public debate on the subject of integration seems to be carried on without any apparent appreciation of either the nature or magnitude of segregation in schooling. This has tended to sterilise such debate. In order to ensure that future discussions are more fruitful, three vital aspects must therefore be addressed.

1. The actual extent of segregation in Northern Irish schools.

2. The degree of difference between the two types of school.

3. The possible relationship between educational segregation and broader community divisions.

1. How extensive is segregation?

Barritt & Carter (1962) claim that as far as can be discovered at least 98 per cent (and probably more) of all Catholic primary school children attend Catholic schools. Data obtained in the *Schools Apart* project infer that 95 per cent of State schools have less than 5 per cent Roman Catholic enrolment and over 98 per cent of Catholic schools have less than 5 per cent Protestant children attending them.

The *Schools Apart* data demonstrated a similar polarisation in the employment of teachers. Of the 1,521 secondary teachers studied in the survey, only 29 were employed in schools where the predominant religious affiliation was different from their own. Of 480 Grammar school teachers studied, only 9 were thus employed. Polarisation is even more extreme at primary level where only 3 teachers (out of 750 surveyed) were employed in schools of a different religion from their own.

Apart from the confessional preponderance among pupils and teachers, there is also historical evidence to demonstrate that schools in Northern Ireland can be described with accuracy as either Protestant or Catholic. In the latter case the schools are self-avowedly Catholic and acclaim rather than resent the title. In the former the claim is often made that State schools are open to all and therefore should not be described in religious terms. Nonetheless, State schools have always been perceived as Protestant establishements.

In September 1981 the *Sunday News* published official documents from the PRONI (Public Record Office of Northern Ireland) which had become available under the fifty year rule. Some of these demonstrate clearly the official perception of State schools prevailing at the time. For example, Dr. Hugh Morrison, a member of Parliament for Queen's University, referring to the possibility of regional educational committees being established in 1923 and their possible influence on schools, claimed that, 'in some areas where Catholics were in the majority, they would have the power to appoint teachers to Protestant (sic) schools . . . This is a situation which the Protestant Church will not submit to'. Dr. Morrison was in fact referring to State schools. Another member of Parliament, Joseph Morgan, was even more outspoken in a Government debate in 1946: he asked, 'Is it too much to ask that a Protestant Government elected by a Protestant people, should maintain that we should have Protestant teachers for Protestant children?'

It is also noteworthy that the passing of the 1930 Education Act (N.I.) was acclaimed by the joint education committees of the main

Protestant bodies as the conception of a state system of education which would, 'maintain the Protestant nature of the State'.

More recent events suggest that the general perception of State schools being Protestant establishments is no less strong. In August 1981 a petition was prepared for submission to the Minister responsible for education, Lord Elton, asking that the Western Education and Library Board should restrict its representation on management committees of State schools to non-Roman Catholic members because, 'in the vast majority of cases, pupils at State schools are Protestant'. This petition was organised by parents of Protestant children and members of management committees of State schools in the area.

There is also evidence of at least tacit acceptance by official bodies of a denominational school system on religious lines. Few people in Northern Ireland would deny that some schools are overtly Catholic. It is not surprising therefore that statutory bodies deal directly with the Roman Catholic Church when a new Maintained (Catholic) school is being built. What is significant is that when a new Controlled school— a State school entirely financed by public funds—has been built, the main Protestant Churches are asked to contribute nominees to its management committee, but the Roman Catholic Church is not. It is of course, possible that the Roman Catholic clergy would not wish to be consulted. That they are not, however, demonstrates an acceptance that State schools are *de facto* Protestant schools and are acknowledged as such by statutory bodies.

2. *How different are the two systems?*

Implicit in the arguments of both sides in the debate about segregated schooling is the belief that there is a real difference in the experience undergone by Catholic and Protestant children within their denominational schools. The Roman Catholic case for retaining their schools rests on a conviction that they provide a religio-moral ethos which is integral to Catholic education. Those opposed to segregation usually base their case on the belief that separate schools encourage a divisiveness by propagating different and perhaps hostile cultural heritages. Both of these stances are premised on the conviction that schools attended by Protestant and Roman Catholic children are significantly different kinds of institutions.

The differences between the two systems of schooling are often overstated and overemphasised. Obviously no two schools, whether they be Catholic or Protestant, will ever be identical. Each will have its own unique character constructed by a myriad of interrelating influences. One should therefore evaluate any differences existing between the two sets of schools in the context of the many similarities in their day-to-day procedures.

It is fair to say that in the majority of schools, the single most significant factor affecting curricular procedures is the existence of external examinations. The transfer assessment at primary level, and G.C.E. and C.S.E. at secondary level, are all common to Catholic and Protestant schools.

Again, although Gaelic games are played exclusively in Catholic schools, there is in fact a wide variety of sports which are equally popular in both sets of schools. These include athletics, soccer, netball basketball and hockey.

At a curricular level, the *Schools Apart* project recorded a high degree of commonality of practice across a broad range of activities:

> In both (types of) schools the educational qualifications of staff were roughly similar; the work profiles of principals were almost indistinguishable; most classroom procedures are common to both systems—they stream pupils to similar extents and are equally likely to practise some form of integration within the curriculum.

In addition, the authors claim the possibility of an acceptance by both school systems of a shared heritage. This conclusion is based on the wide use by both types of school of broadcasts and project materials which deal with value-laden areas such as religion and history. They went on to argue:

> The popularity of such venues within Northern Ireland as The Ulster Folk Museum, The Ulster Museum and The Ulster Transport Museum is of a sufficiently high level in all schools to suggest the existence of a shared Ulster culture.

It must be questioned whether participants in such activities perceive them in terms of culture or heritage or simply as outings away from the school. Therefore, the claim that they represent some form of shared heritage may have been overstated. Nonetheless, it must be emphasised that there are many more similarities of practice within Protestant and Catholic schools than there are differences between them. Why then does the conviction, that a high correlation exists between segregated schools and community conflict, continue to flourish?

3. *Is there a relationship between educational segregation and broader community divisions?*

The high degree of polarisation of both staff and pupils in State and Maintained schools inevitably results in State schools being perceived as Protestant institutions and Maintained schools as Roman Catholic establishments. However, if religion is the sole criterion used to demonstrate the divisive potential of Northern Irish schools, then how much more pernicious must be the separate churches themselves? If community division is seen exclusively in religious terms, then the various churches must be seen as the most divisive structures in society. Nevertheless, when churches are referred to in debates about community conflict in the Province, the approach is invariably to ask why they are not doing more to stop it rather than in terms of how the separate churches may have caused the conflict. On the other hand, debates about segregated schools carried on in this same context inevitably stress their actual contribution to the perpetuation of violence and conflict. It would seem therefore that churches are accorded with less positive influence with regard to community conflict than are schools. One must ask therfore what are the aspects of schools which identify them as being the principal villains of the peace.

In order to answer this question with any degree of confidence, much information is required about the actual day-to-day practices within segregated schools. In this sensitive area, qualitative rather than quantative data is essential. In view of the widespread general interest in segregated schooling and its ramifications, it is quite amazing that so little qualitative information is available. In fact no research has attempted to isolate the specific influence of the school.

In a realisation of this dearth of information, Murray (1982) attempted to study the relationship between segregated schooling and community conflict. His objective was to investigate the claim that schools attended by Roman Catholic and Protestant children are significantly different types of institutions with real differences in experience being provided within them. His participant approach, entailing one year being spent in two primary schools (one Catholic, the other Protestant) reveals interesting insights into these segregated schools. The findings suggest that at a curricular level the schools were almost indistinguishable, the one significant exception being the content of, and approach to, religious instruction. In the Protestant school this was rigidly curtailed to the 'non-secular day' i.e. between 9.00 a.m. and 9.45 a.m. In the Catholic school however, at certain times of the year, religion and religious instruction took precedence over all other subjects. For example, the class being prepared for First Communion had, on occasion, two thirds of the day allotted to this preparation. School Mass, daily prayers, receiving the Sacraments and attending other religious celebrations all took up a significant amount of the school day.

It is difficult to relate such disparate emphasis on religion in the schools to broader community divisions in Northern Ireland. Different religious groupings proliferate in the Province, and will continue to do so irrespective of whether schools are segregated or not. No one would deny the right or desirability of such pluralism. It would seem therefore that we must consider other factors in an effort to identify specific relationships between separate schooling and community division. Murray has identified the concepts of culture and identity as being of most significance in this respect, claiming that schools, and individuals within them, can be distinguished to some extent by the dominant cultural ideology to which they subscribe. This culture of the school is constructed by such factors as history, tradition, pupil background and recreation.

Any cultural analysis of Northern Ireland must take into account the peculiar position which schools occupy in the Province, where religion, politics and culture are inextricably enmeshed. Most Protestants subscribe to a Unionist/British political ideological position and maintain their own cultural traditions, attitudes and values which are largely a function of an English or Scottish identity. Most Catholics, on the other hand, aspire, to varying degrees, towards a Nationalist ideal and possess a set of values and traditions emanating from and identifying with an Irish heritage.

Since it has been demonstrated previously that segregated schools in Northern Ireland can validly be described as either Catholic or Protestant, it is not unreasonable therefore to expect that each type of school will reflect the cultural aspirations of each religious group as a whole. However the problem with segregated schools, with regard to community divisions, lies not predominately in the fact that they reflect different cultures but rather in the meanings which are attributed by observers to the overt demonstrations of such cultural affiliation. Controlled schools in The North-Eastern Library Board area are required to fly the Union Jack daily outside. Individuals within these schools may see this as a natural manifestation for a State school. The response among Catholics however may be somewhat different. Murray cites a general reaction from staff in an adjoining Catholic school:

They fly the flag down there to show that they are more British than the British themselves. It's also to let us know that they are the lords and masters and that we (Catholics) should be continually aware of it.

Again, quite naturally, symbols abound in Catholic schools which emphasise their Catholicity (statues, Papal flags, crucifixes etc.). It might be difficult to imagine how these might cause offence. Indeed they can justifiably be seen as a *sine qua non* of Catholic education which has always posited salvation higher than education. However, this observation too can be transferred into a rather different reality, as it was by a Protestant teacher:

We play St. Judes often in games and visit their school regularly. I never fail to be impressed by the plethora of religious pictures and icons staring at you around every corner. It's hard to escape the view that a special show is being put on for our benefit . . . This doesn't just apply to St. Judes of course, but they must know that these are the very things that we object to, yet still they are flaunted everywhere.

These two examples give insight into the gulf which exists between intention and perception in Northern Ireland. The two dominant cultures are so mutually antipathetic that any demonstration of one is perceived as an assault on the other. There is no doubt that the two separate systems of schooling do reflect the two dominant cultures in the Province. Murray has demonstrated this with regard to textbooks, library materials, ritual, symbols and general ethos. But is this necessarily an undesirable aspect of schooling? Can pluralism be undesirable in any society?

Hitherto the tendency has been to accept tacitly the undesirable effect of segregated structures, and debate has proceeded at this axiomatic level. However, such structural approaches have contributed little with regard to ameliorating divisions in society. Perhaps a phenomenological analysis is more likely to prove fruitful in this context.

Segregated schooling exists uncontentiously in other countries yet fails to do so in Northern Ireland. This may suggest that the problem lies not within segregated education but rather in the perceptions of the society in which it is operating. It could well be that the actual existence of segregation has less influence on community divisions than have the meanings which are attributed to it by members of that community.

Thus there may well be some kind of self fulfilling prophecy in operation—schools are perceived as divisive and hence become so in their consequences.

Structuralists would argue of course that if segregated schools are abolished and an integrated system (whatever the phrase is taken to mean) is introduced, then these societal perceptions will disappear. This argument is only tenable however if segregated schools can be demonstrated to be *intrinsically* divisive. This has yet to be shown. Indeed, in countries other than Northern Ireland, it seems not to be the case.

It would seem essential that social attitudes are tackled before social structures. However, Lagan College, the first officially integrated school in Northern Ireland, seems to have been founded on an opposite rationale. While its efforts can, and should be accorded both respect and applause, it can only have an effect on the relatively few children who attend it. Added to this is the possibility that only the converted will 'hear the sermon'. In other words it is likely that only those individuals who are already sympathetic to the concept of integration will support such an integrated structure. Thus when structural change precedes attitudinal change, it is probable that any impact will be restricted to within that structure only.

This analysis has been confined to the possible connection between segregated schooling and community conflict. It would seem however that a stronger argument can be made against segregated schools which is based on the harmful educational and cultural consequences of such structures. In the first place, most educationalists would agree that schools should present as broad a range of experiences as possible to children attending them. With two groups of children attending their own exclusive schools, such experience is necessarily curtailed. At a cultural level, segregation entails that both Catholic and Protestant children are denied a knowledge of elements of history, tradition and culture which should be common to them both.

Another aspect of segregated schooling more likely to contribute to community division than either culture or religion is the concept of identity, i.e. the extent to which individuals within separate schools accept, or identify with political or institutional bodies outside the schools. Russell's (1972) survey of children in Northern Ireland has suggested that Roman Catholic children are more likely to demonstrate negative attitudes towards the Northern Ireland Government. Robinson (1971) suggests that Protestant and Catholic children held very different views of the society in which they both lived.

The Schools Cultural Studies Project (1982) attempted to introduce into Northern Irish schools a programme which encouraged children to clarify their values, and especially cultural values. The experience of the project was that it was much more readily accepted in Catholic than in Protestant schools. A conclusion of the project team was:

> Any attempt to introduce an innovation which requires participants to question previously sacrosanct societal values will be likely to evoke different responses from the two existing educational systems. On the one hand, Catholic schools which may have no great empathy with such values may find it expedient to embrace such an innovation. On the other hand, staffs in State (Protestant) schools may see any such assault on the *status quo* as a positive threat to their position and as such to be opposed, or at least ignored.

Murray, in his study of two schools, also commented on this aspect of segregated education:

> It appeared that the Protestant school identified much more closely with the policy-making and administrative sections of the educational system. These were deemed to be natural and effective support structures which, through dissemination of information and close contact, moulded a kind of solidarity among all State schools. There seemed to be a sense of belonging to, and identity with, an extended educational family.

The Catholic school on the other hand, only contacted administrative bodies on occasions of dire necessity, 'Otherwise', as one teacher put it, 'they would be crawling all over us'. In fact one senior Library Board official claimed that his office received ten times as many enquiries of a relatively trivial nature from Protestant schools than from Catholic schools.

The disparity of approach to educational bodies between the two schools may well reflect the historical lack of empathy of Catholics with broader political structures in Northern Ireland. In this sense, educational policy-making may be being equated with a political power base to which Catholics have never subscribed. Whatever the reasons, the fact that such a disparity of practice prevailed in the schools is of significance with regard to community divisions. Of even more import is the possibility that other structures of society exist to which Catholics in general, and Catholic schools in particular, attribute similar negative responses.

A cameo from the Catholic school in which Murray researched suggested that this kind of negative attitude was not confined to educational bodies. It was noted that pupils in the Protestant school paid much more frequent visits to community organisations such as the fire station, post office, local Government offices, police station etc. The Catholic teachers agreed that this was probably so, but asked, 'What would be the sense in our kids going there? They will never get a job in any of them'. The inference was that they would be discriminated against because they were Catholics.

It is interesting that the Catholic teachers perceived these visits in vocational, rather than civic terms. If this perception is common to the Catholic sector as a whole, it seems inevitable that the two groups will relate to, and identify with, the ordinary day-to-day structures of their community in entirely different ways. More to the point, it may mean that Catholic teachers were not only curtailing the vocational aspirations of their pupils but also restricting their occupational possibilities. Again, a self-fulfilling prophecy may be operating. If pupils are advised, or given the impression, that they will not get a job in these establishments because of their religion, then it is hardly surprising that they will become underrepresented in these occupational sites.

This rationale therefore may contribute to and perpetuate community differences and divisions. The construction of behaviour based on a perception of division may in fact reify that division.

Conclusion

The religious polarity of both teachers and pupils within segregated schools has no doubt contributed to them being viewed as separate institutions. Unfortunately this separateness in itself has been equated with community division in Northern Ireland.

At the levels of religion and culture, the influence of the school seems to have been grossly exaggerated. Commentators have tended to assume that segregated schools create differences in society rather than reflect them.

The 'identity' aspect of segregation may give more cause for concern. It is possible that certain Catholic schools may see their occupational task as preparing children for what they perceive as a discriminatory society. They can therefore validly be said to perpetuate community division by directing their pupils either towards, or away from, certain sectors of their community. Perhaps this could be rectified by actively fostering increased communication between Catholic schools and statutory bodies. This might be facilitated through an emphasis of their common concern—the successful education of children.

There is evidence (Darby *et al,* 1977) to suggest that, presently, suspicion between the two systems of education in Northern Ireland is contributed to, in no small way, by the stereotypes of the members within them. These stereotypes are spawned largely in a mutual ignorance of each other's schools. It would seem, therefore, that fruitful debate can only take place in the future if it is supported, not only by in-depth studies of the schools themselves, but also an awareness of the perceptions and consciousness of the individuals for whom they exist.

7

The Demography of Violence

Michael Poole

Background

A survey of recent ethnic violence in a sample of nineteen different societies selected from all five continents has not only classified Northern Ireland as a 'high violence' society, but has bracketed it in this category with just four other geographical regions. These four are Zanzibar, Lebanon, Cyprus and Guyana. Clearly, Northern Ireland is by no means unique in suffering this form of violence—in fact, it ranked fourth or fifth in this survey, depending on the specific measure used—but, set in international context, it is one of a small group of societies with a much higher death rate from ethnic violence than any of the others considered (Hewitt 1977).[1]

The special significance, for this chapter, of Hewitt's international survey is the analysis he undertakes of the hypothesis that demographic structure is salient in the explanation of where ethnic violence occurs. The specific aspect of demography explored by Hewitt is the ethnic composition of the population.[2] The demographic situation is, in fact, one of three groups of factors whose possible effect on the incidence of this type of violence is considered by this author. The others are economic and political grievances, and he finds that all three are significant.

This evidence from Hewitt's investigation may be placed alongside the contention of Darby (1976, 26) that, within Northern Ireland, on a 'local level it is often religious segregation, especially in towns, which converts distrust and dislike into violence'. He considers that towns which have religiously integrated housing have escaped the worst 'community violence'. Darby does not support his contention by referring to any quantitative evidence, but it does constitute a plausible hypothesis relating the local demographic situation to the geographical places where violence occurs.

The common tie linking this observation of Darby to the conclusion reached by Hewitt is that there is a relationship between demographic characteristics and the most violent forms of ethnic conflict. The demographic characteristics receiving attention from both authors are concerned, more specifically, with ethnic composition. The principal difference, on the other hand, distinguishing Darby's suggestion from that of Hewitt concerns geographical scale. Hewitt's study-area is the whole world, and the individual places for which he analyses data are separate 'societies', of which Northern Ireland is the only one which has not been, at some stage in the study-period, a sovereign state. For Darby, however, Northern Ireland is the study-area, and the individual places about which observations are made are specific towns.

Indeed, the scale-level difference between the material quoted from these two authors is, in a sense, even greater than this, for, whereas Hewitt is not concerned with the geographical variation in ethnic composition within such a place as Northern Ireland, Darby is concerned with such variation within his towns. This is precisely what is implied by the latter's use of the concept of segregation in housing.

Objective

The idea of geographical scale-level is a sufficiently fundamental one in the context of the argument in this chapter to be used as a basic principle for its organization. We shall consider both the two extremes represented by the material referred to from Hewitt and from Darby and also certain intermediate scale-levels. As in the extracts already taken from these authors, the main element of population structure to be examined in this chapter at the varied range of scale-levels specified is the ethnic composition of the geographical areas in which people live.

This is not, however, a study of ethnic composition in isolation, for such general reviews are available elsewhere (Walsh 1970; Darby 1976, 25–47; Compton 1976; Compton 1982). Instead, an attempt will consistently be made in this chapter to relate this demographic characteristic to ethnic conflict. Such conflict takes many forms, including electoral contests and pressure-group struggles (Osborne 1982; Birrell and Murie 1980, 110–131), but the specific form examined in this chapter is the most violent one already referred to in the work of Hewitt and Darby.

Even this topic of violent conflict can take many forms. Schellenberg (1976, 10–17), for example, studied the statistics on shooting incidents, explosions, injuries and deaths, while Darby and Williamson (1978, 13) mapped the location of the last three of these, along with riots, gun-battles and armed raids. However, in this chapter only one aspect of violent conflict will be considered. This will be deaths directly attributable to the current spate of Troubles since 1969.

The reasons for concentrating on this aspect of violence have been succinctly summarized by Murray (1982, 310) in justifying the use of the data on fatalities, and also explosions, for his own inter-regional analysis: 'They are the incidents that arouse greatest public and political concern, they have the greatest impact on the community and, not least, they are the best documented.' To this set of reasons can be added the fact that most research on the relationship between demography and political violence in Northern Ireland has concentrated on deaths, so the only way of achieving consistency of subject-matter at all geographical scale-levels, without undertaking fresh empirical analysis at virtually every such scale-level, is to follow this other research by focusing on fatalities. Therefore, fresh analysis is restricted to just one of the several scale-levels considered, the inter-urban, and the attempt at an original contribution elsewhere in this chapter takes the form of a hopefully innovative interpretation of the relationship between violence and the demography of ethnicity, especially to take account of the effect of geographical scale-level.

The work of Hewitt and of Darby referred to in this introduction treated violence as a consequence of certain factors—including demographic factors—and this approach, Murray and Boal (1979, 153–154) have suggested, is common to almost all studies of violence. In fact, there is at least one exception to this general rule within the Northern Ireland context, in the set of contributions edited by Darby and Williamson (1978) investigating the effect of violence on the organization of social services in the province. Murray and Boal, in making their point, were especially keen to assert that violence is a factor affecting urban spatial structure, including what is particularly relevant to this chapter, the geography of ethnic composition. Their conclusion that violence, as both cause and consequence, is 'an inseparable component of the urban system', and probably of the rural system, too, is an inescapable one. However, it is one which will be almost ignored in this chapter.

The reason for ignoring that aspect of the relationship between demography and violence dealing with the effect of the latter on the former follows from our decision to limit the form of violence discussed, to deaths. The point is that there is little evidence that this aspect of the violent conflict, despite its seriousness, has had any significant effect on the demography of ethnicity by, for instance, the stimulation of population movement. In this respect, there is a strong contrast between this manifestation of violence and certain other forms, especially intimidation and property damage, which have caused a considerable movement of refugees, especially in Belfast (Poole 1971, 9; Darby and Morris 1974, 16–18). This movement, in turn, has had the effect of intensifying, albeit not on a vast scale, ethnic residential segregation since 1969. For example, 66 per cent of Belfast County Borough's households were located in streets in which they were in at least a 91 per cent ethnic majority in 1969, and this proportion has risen to 76 per cent by 1972 (Boal et al. 1976, 106), shortly after which there was a sharp decline in the numbers rendered homeless by violence (N.I.H.E. 1978, 15).

True, it is impossible to distinguish the separate components of violence and identify the contribution of each to refugee movement. However, there is no suggestion, either in the literature already quoted or in other studies of this type of movement (Black *et al.* 1971; Black 1972; Murray et al. 1975; Murray and Boal 1980), that the actual occurrence of deaths has had much impact on population mobility, whereas many of the other manifestations of violence are accorded a great deal of significance. Therefore, in investigating the relationship between violent death and ethnic demography in this chapter, we shall take what Murray and Boal identified as the most conventional approach, that of dealing with violence, not as a cause, but as a consequence.

A further narrowing of the subject-area is that the frequently-investigated hypothesis that the chronology of violence is a response to changing ethnic composition, such as the initial rapid rise, and subsequent decline, in the Catholic share of Belfast's population in the nineteenth century (Jones 1956, 168–170; Baker 1973) will be omitted. Rather than studying this essentially historical question, this chapter will tackle a problem which has received much less attention in the literature. This is the basically geographical one of understanding the location of violence.

National or International Scale

International Context

We shall begin this initial part of the analysis at the same point at which we began the introduction—at the extreme end of the spectrum of geographical scale-levels where Hewitt analysed international variations in ethnic violence. The specific variables involving demographic characteristics, which Hewitt hypothesized to be related to conflict, were two in number. These were the minority percentage, the term we may use to refer to the size of the minority ethnic group relative to the total population, and the rate at which this percentage is changing through time.

Firstly, he suggests that, the larger the minority percentage, the greater the likelihood of violent conflict, partly because small minorities are too vulnerable to get involved in conflict and partly because large minorities are a threat to the power of the majority in 'winner take all' democratic societies. This threat to majority power is particularly severe if a large minority shows signs of growing into a new majority, and this is the main reason why he suggests that the rate of change in the minority percentage is positively correlated with the level of conflict. In addition, however, any growth in the minority share of the population will create friction, Hewitt proposes, in those societies where the style of democracy practised involves some form of political power-sharing.

Having outlined these hypotheses, Hewitt classified the nineteen societies he examined into three groups according to the level of ethnic violence suffered, and he suggested that all five of the societies he classified as having a high rate of violence have demographic characteristics conducive to conflict. However, such a confident and unequivocal statement seems at odds with the quantitative evidence he presents. Only two of his high-violence societies, Lebanon and Guyana, satisfy his first hypothesis by having a large minority percentage. Northern Ireland occupies an intermediate position, with a minority share of 34 per cent, while the other two, Zanzibar and Cyprus, have much lower figures.

Hewitt's second demographic hypothesis, concerning the growth of the minority percentage, is again confirmed in the case of Lebanon and Guyana, where he states that the minority has now grown into a majority, and is again disconfirmed for Zanzibar and Cyprus, where no such demographic event is possible.[3] Northern Ireland is again intermediate, but, he suggests, it confirms his hypothesis because he maintains that the minority will become a majority within a generation if present trends continue. Thus, he argues, Northern Ireland is like Lebanon and Guyana in that one community is frightened by the population increase of the other.

The evidence for and against the two demographic hypotheses cannot be assessed solely by looking at the high-violence societies. We need to see whether any of the other societies have a demographic situation which would have led us to expect more violence than actually occurred. In fact, there are, as Hewitt acknowledges, deviant cases, such as Fiji and Trinidad, and their existence is an indication that his three groups of factors—economic and political grievances, and demography—are by no means perfect predictors of ethnic violence. In fact, a careful examination of his own evidence suggests that the demographic group is an even worse predictor than he maintains.

There is, however, one other variable he records for his nineteen societies which is a reasonably good predictor and which, though classified by Hewitt as a characteristic of the political situation, could be argued to be demographic. This is the occurrence of a difference between the majority and the minority over the constitutional identity of the state. Such a difference is a feature of no less than four of the five high-violence societies, including Northern Ireland, the only exception being Guyana. Moreover, the only other society amongst the nineteen studied in which there is said to be a conflict over the existence of the state in its present form is Israel, which Hewitt has classified as having only an intermediate level of violence after ignoring Palestinian guerrilla activity because he regards it as international violence, rather than domestic ethnic, a distinction which he concedes may be spurious.

The reason why it may be valid to reinterpret this constitutional difference as a demographic variable is that the redrawing of state boundaries wished for by one of the ethnic groups in each case results from that group identifying ethnically with a larger neighbouring political unit. Thus, to use simply the evidence from Hewitt's own commentary, Greek Cypriots identified with Greece, Northern Ireland Catholics with the Republic of Ireland, and Zanzibar Africans with the former Tanganyika, while Lebanese Muslims have links with Syria and Palestine.

Double Minority: Static View

In the case of Northern Ireland, this identification of one of its ethnic groups with the inhabitants of a larger neighbour has led to the conceptualization of the conflict situation in terms of what has been described as the 'double minority' model. Several recent academic writers have referred approvingly to this model (Stewart 1977, 162–163; Whyte 1978, 276; Douglas and Boal 1982, 3–4), all attributing it to the journalist Jackson. He had written, shortly after the start of the present Troubles, that 'within their own enclave the Protestants of Ulster, one million strong, outnumber their Catholic brethren two to one. But in the wider context of Ireland they themselves are easily outnumbered three to one. The inevitable result has been the disastrous advent of a ruling establishment... acting under the stresses of a beseiged minority'. (Jackson 1971, 4). For most of the Protestant community 'there has only been one issue—the preservation of the border with the Catholic Republic', for this has been viewed as essential to prevent their absorption into a political state in which, inter alia, their minority status would, they fear, deprive them of power. Correspondingly, Jackson suggests, it is the actuality of suffering, for several decades, such a deprivation of power consequent upon minority status which generates 'a burning sense of grievance' amongst the Catholic community of Northern Ireland. This is augmented by their awareness that they are part of the ethnic majority in the island of Ireland, which many see as the legitimate political state to which the region should belong.[4]

The academic writers who have endorsed the double minority model have differed significantly in their treatment of it. Whyte follows Jackson closely in referring both to the minority status of the two communities and to the consequent stress suffered by each, but Stewart places more emphasis on the stress felt by the Protestant community, tracing its historical continuity from 1886 to the present. Douglas and Boal, too, emphasize these Protestant fears, induced by being a minority, and they contrast them with the confidence and resolve given to the Catholic community by its perceived island majority status.

Above all, however, Douglas and Boal complicate the original double minority model by incorporating the United Kingdom dimension. Stewart (1977, 173) had pointed out that, before partition, the Protestant people of north–east Ireland saw themselves as part of the Protestant majority of the United Kingdom, but the implication of the reasoning presented by Douglas and Boal is that it is more relevant to argue that the Northern Ireland Protestant community is not only a minority within Ireland but, even within the United Kingdom, it is, on its own, 'again a minority with ultimate political power beyond its control'. It is, in fact, a mere 1.7 per cent minority at this scale-level (Compton 1978, 81; Paxton 1981, 1288–1366), with a consequent sense of powerlessness, especially since direct rule of Northern Ireland from London was introduced in 1972.

A further result of this minority status within the United Kingdom, stressed by Douglas and Boal, is the way in which it compounds 'the political uncertainty and territorial ambiguity of the Northern Ireland problem'. This is because the Protestant community is fearful not only of the anti-partitionist stance of Irish Catholics but also of the possible unreliability of the British government, despite its repeated pledges that 'in no event will Northern Ireland or any part of it cease to be part of the United Kingdom without the consent of the majority of the people of Northern Ireland' (*The government of Northern Ireland* 1980, 5).

It is curious that Douglas and Boal did not consider Northern Ireland's Catholic community in the context of the United Kingdom. Clearly, it, too, is a minority in an obvious sense: it constitutes a mere 1.0 per cent of the entire sovereign state's population, it is a component of what is a 10 per cent Catholic minority within this state (Compton 1978, 81; Paxton 1981, 1288–1366), and it is part of an approximately 4 per cent minority formed by the 'Irish Catholic community' in the United Kingdom.[5] Yet Northern Ireland Catholics are, in a certain political sense, part of a majority in the United Kingdom, for opinion polls in Great Britain throughout the present period of Troubles have consistently shown that a 60–65 per cent majority of those people with opinions have approved of Irish unification (Rose et al. 1978, 29; *Sunday Times* 21.12.80).

There thus exists a complex mosaic of alternative geographical frameworks for considering which of Northern Ireland's two ethnic groups is a socially and politically meaningful minority. And this mosaic could, in fact, be added to with further geographical frameworks of relevance from within Ireland itself. However, the most critical contemporary frameworks for identifying meaningful minorities are the ones we have discussed—Northern Ireland itself, the island of Ireland, and the United Kingdom.

Double Minority: Dynamic View

There is a further aspect of demography at the provincial scale-level to consider in the context of the double minority model. This is the problem of change over time, which has already been referred to when dealing with Hewitt's analysis of high-violence societies. His specific assertion that the Catholic community will become a majority of Northern Ireland's population within a generation if present trends continue is, at first sight, perhaps surprising in view of the remarkable stability over time in the Catholic share of the province's population.

Thus, from 1901, twenty years before partition, to 1961, this share was consistently recorded at between 33.5 and 35.2 per cent at every single census (Compton 1976, 434–436).

It has long been recognized that a higher Catholic emigration rate has just been sufficient to offset the higher Catholic birth rate and hence achieve this stability (Barritt and Carter 1962, 108; Park 1962–63, 12; Walsh 1970, 22). However, between 1961 and 1971, the differential between the two ethnic migration rates was no longer able to counter the further increased differential in rates of natural increase between the two ethnic groups (Compton 1982, 87–92). Therefore, the Catholic share of the total Northern Ireland population rose to 36.8 per cent in 1971 (Compton 1978, 80–81), and this rise has continued, it is estimated, to about 38 per cent in 1980 (Compton 1981, 3), caused by a continuation of the migration differential's inability to offset the ever-widening differential in natural increase (Compton 1982, 90, 93).

More specifically on the prediction of when the Catholic community might form a majority of the Northern Ireland population, several sets of projections have been made, differing somewhat in the degree of elaborateness and, above all, incorporating more and more up-to-date demographic trends (Walsh 1970, 22–23, 35–36; Compton and Boal 1970, 462–463, 471–475; Compton 1976, 446–447; Compton 1982, 98–99). The most recent of these projections suggests that the earliest possible year by which Catholics could form a majority of the total population of the province is 2020. However, if all the most recent demographic trends continue, which is the scenario referred to by Hewitt, a Catholic majority could not be expected until the middle of the twenty-first century.

In terms of the effect of demography on conflict, however, it is at least arguable that perception is more important than reality—that what people believe about population trends is more significant than the actual trends themselves. In this context, a special feature of the early paper by Compton and Boal (1970, 475–476) was the survey of student opinion, which showed that the average date by which these young people expected Catholics to form a majority of the Northern Ireland population was 1990. This is much sooner than any of the dates given by the projections, and the perceived imminence of this critical event fuels the fears of the current Protestant majority and the hopes of the current Catholic minority within the province (Rose 1971, 364; Cameron 1969, 55, 65).

This anticipation of the future leads Compton and Boal (1970, 455) to refer to 'the paradox of two minorities' in Northern Ireland which 'is explained, on the one hand, by the existence of the current Catholic minority, and, on the other, by a Protestant group, in the majority at present, fearing that in time it will become a minority'. Here yet again, therefore, is the double minority model, but this time solely in the context of the ethnic composition within the political boundaries of Northern Ireland.

Double Majority

We end up, in consequence, with no less than three totally distinct ways in which the Protestant community of Northern Ireland can be conceptualized, and indeed sees itself, as an ethnic minority. It is currently a minority both within the island of Ireland and within the United Kingdom, and it fears future minority status even within Northern Ireland. Moreover, the way in which all three of these minority situations achieve behavioural relevance is by generating apprehension about the future (Poole and Boal 1973, 11). The corollary of this is that there are also three distinct ways in which the Catholic community of Northern Ireland can be perceived as an ethnic majority, and its awareness of this gives it, one may suggest, an otherwise surprising confidence about the future.

Indeed, in the context of trying to understand violent conflict, it may be much more relevant to emphasize a remarkably ignored implication of the double minority model, which is that a society to which this model is applicable is also characterized by having a double majority. The significance of this is that, while minority status may generate conflict because of a sense of grievance and because of apprehension about the future, it may be argued that violence is more likely to be encouraged by the confidence and sense of strength associated with majority status, together with the feeling of moral righteousness resulting from that perceived status. This sense of righteousness, for example, is very apparent in Randolph Churchill's notorious phrase which was so enthusiastically adopted by the Protestant community towards the end of the nineteenth century, 'Ulster will fight, and Ulster will be right' (Buckland 1973, 10). If both ethnic groups have a sense of strength and a sense of moral justification, as in a double majority situation like Northern Ireland, an eventual violent clash may be very hard to avoid.

Whichever aspect of this model, however, double majority or double minority, is stressed, it must be applied in a rather more varied and complex way than any single writer seems to have suggested in the literature reviewed here. Moreover, when this complexity is reasonably fully ex-plored, it appears that not only can both of Hewitt's two demographic hypotheses about the preconditions for violent conflict—concerning the present minority percentage and its rate of growth—be included in the double majority model, but so also, at least in some cases, can another of his hypotheses. This is the very successful proposition that a difference between the minority and the majority over the constitutional identity of the state is conducive to political violence. At the national or provincial scale-level, therefore, the concept of the double majority appears to be a very powerful demographic model for understanding conflict.

Inter-Regional Scale

Simple Hypotheses

Quantitative analysis of the geographical location of political violence at the inter-regional scale-level within Northern Ireland has been under-taken principally by Schellenberg (1977), Mitchell (1979) and Murray (1982). Each of these three authors has produced such analysis at more than one scale-level, and, though they differed in the specific measures of violence used, they all referred to the relationship between violence and the demography of ethnicity. However, the hypotheses proposed for the form of this relationship by Schellenberg and Mitchell were much simpler than those suggested by Murray. It is therefore appropriate to begin by considering the contribution of the first two writers.

Schellenberg's principal analysis was done at a scale-level involving the use of 34 regions consisting of the old County Boroughs of Belfast and Londonderry, together with 32 others formed primarily from the amalgamation of Boroughs and Urban Districts with the adjacent Rural Districts. He used correlation and regression analysis to study the relationship between the death rate and each of eleven other variables. Several of these eleven are demographic, including population size, population change, population density, and the proportion of adult males, but the variable of most interest for this chapter is the Catholic share of the total population. Schellenberg concluded that just two of the total of eleven variables could, between them, explain a very high proportion of the inter-regional variation in deaths. These were population density and the proportion Catholic, both of which were positively correlated with violence. In relation to the proportion Catholic, this positive correlation indicates that, the larger the Catholic share of the population in a region, the higher the death-rate there.

Mitchell's principal reference to the relationship between violence and ethnicity is a statement that the death-rate in areas with Catholic majorities is six times as great as in areas which are over 80 per cent Protestant and is twice as great as in areas with large Catholic minorities (Mitchell 1979, 196). The geographical framework he has used is unfortunately obscure, but the findings are consistent with those of Schellenberg on the positive correlation between violence and the Catholic share of the population.

Ethnic Origin of Violence

Neither Schellenberg nor Mitchell is strongly assertive about the reasons for this correlation. The two writers agree that support for the established regime is lowest in Catholic areas, and both suggest that the main violent challenge to established authority has come from the Catholic community (Schellenberg 1977, 77; Mitchell 1979, 182, 196). Schellenberg adds that it is within areas whose population is predominantly Catholic that such a challenge can most easily be organized, but it could be argued that, analogously to the suggestion of Spilerman (1970, 643–645) in the context of black involvement in United States riots, Catholic-dominated areas simply have more Catholics and thus more people willing to carry out the necessary violence.

The concentration of violence in predominantly Catholic areas can, in fact, be partly explained by making further use of the double majority model, introduced in the earlier discussion at the provincial scale-level. Specifically, this model can help to explain why so much of the violence originates in the Catholic ethnic group. The relevant argument suggests that, of the two groups in a double majority society, only one is likely to be a frustrated majority in the sense of having its wishes in relation to the constitutional identity of the state blocked. This is also likely to be the group which is the most frustrated in the sense of being deprived of political power. In the Northern Ireland context, this frustrated majority is, of course, the Catholic community, and its perceived majority status, especially at the island and United Kingdom scale-levels, is critical in bestowing at least a section of it with the sense both of strength and of moral righteousness to encourage it to indulge in violence to achieve passionately desired political goals which are viewed as otherwise beyond reach. For the frustrated majority, therefore, violence is legitimized.

Empirical evidence for the suggestion that the violence originates primarily in the Catholic community comes mainly from the work of the third writer listed at the start of this section, Murray (1982, 322–325). After classifying the violence into three broad categories, he estimated that, up to 1977, 53 per cent of the deaths had arisen from either the classical guerrilla war or the economic campaign, both of them fought amost exclusively by paramilitary organizations drawn from the Catholic community. The remainder was caused by sectarian conflict, in which most of the killers were Protestant. This last feature has been particularly documented by Schellenberg (1976, 15–16), whose data suggests that about 70 per cent of sectarian killers have been drawn from the Protestant community.

Much interpretation is necessarily involved in such estimates, but these figures are encouragingly consistent with those of McKeown (1977). It thus appears that about two-thirds of all killings have their ethnic origin in the Catholic community, in the sense that they are committed either by Catholics themselves or by security forces involved in a struggle with certain elements of the Catholic community.

In addition, however, the geographical variation in the ethnic origin of the violence is important in trying to understand where the killings actually occur. A re-working of Murray's data shows that, as a result of the heavy concentration in Belfast of deaths arising from sectarian conflict, the proportion of the non-Belfast deaths which have had their origin in the other type of conflict, the Catholic guerrilla and economic campaigns, is much higher than the corresponding figure for the province as a whole: this proportion is, in fact, 67 per cent. In addition, of those sectarian deaths that did occur outside Belfast, the proportion committed by Catholic killers was higher than it was in Belfast. The effect of these two factors produces an estimate that between 75 per cent and 80 per cent of all deaths attributable to the troubles outside the Belfast region have their origin in the Catholic community.

Thus, to a very large extent indeed, it is the Catholic community, rather than the Protestant, which has given rise to these deaths outside Belfast, either directly by committing them or indirectly by indulging in activities which may be said to have provoked killings by the official security forces. In view of this, it is not surprising that there is a positive correlation, as was found by Schellenberg and by Mitchell, between the Catholic share of the population and the total death rate when these two variables are studied at the inter-regional scale-level.

This is because, when Northern Ireland is divided into a large number of regions, the great majority of them outside Belfast, nearly all the inter-regional variation investigated involves regions other than Belfast. And, since killing in these regions has its origin so overwhelmingly in the Catholic community, it follows that most of the inter-regional variation occurring in the death rate is likely to be inter-regional variation in the rate of killings originating directly or indirectly in the Catholic community. In consequence, it is only to be expected that so many of the high-violence regions are regions whose population is very Catholic.

Complex Hypotheses

Murray (1982) began his discussion of the link between violence and ethnic composition by referring to the findings of Schellenberg (1977) which we reviewed earlier. Murray suggested, however, that at the much more detailed scale-level of 332 areas based on the wards of Northern Ireland, at which a large part of his own analysis was conducted, the correlation between ethnicity and violence was not at all strong. This led him to suggest two principal deviations from the tendency for a positive correlation. The first is the existence of many parts of Northern Ireland where Catholics form a majority, yet there is little political violence. This is a point to which Mitchell (1979, 196) had earlier drawn attention as an exception to the general trend he described: Catholic regions in the east of Northern Ireland, he suggested, had low levels of violence.

The second deviation suggested by Murray is, in a sense, more ambiguous. He pointed out that, if Belfast is examined as a single entity, it has a Catholic minority, yet it is a high-violence location. He added, however, that, because of intense ethnic residential segregation in this city, Catholics are a majority in certain areas and, moreover, he claims, these are the most violence-prone parts of it. Therefore, whether Belfast is an exception to the tendency for a correlation between the ethnic composition of a region and its level of violence depends entirely on the scale-level at which the investigation is conducted.

Even more important, however, Murray is here introducing the concept that the amount of violence in a region may be related not just to the over-all ethnic composition of that region, but also to the geographical distribution of ethnic groups within that region. Thus the level of violence in a region may be related to the ethnic composition existing at more than one geographical scale-level. This is a very important point to which we shall return later.

It was in order to allow for his two deviations that Murray proposed that, while a Catholic majority in an area or within easy travelling distance was a necessary condition for violence, it was not a sufficient condition. For there to be much political violence in a region, he suggested that three other conditions must be satisfied, and this inevitably generates a more complex set of hypotheses than those examined by Schellenberg and Mitchell. These three supplementary conditions were the presence of historical precedents, a high level of alienation of Catholics from Protestant society, and an environment providing both targets and security for the perpetrators of violence. Of these three further conditions, the first is not intrinsically demographic, but the other two have explicitly demographic elements which we must consider.

The alienation referred to by Murray has two main components. One is provided by opposition to partition being fostered by proximity to the Border, for, he suggested, Catholics living closest to the Border must be expected to be most aware of being in a majority in the island of Ireland because of their frequent contacts with the Republic of Ireland. The other component of alienation is stimulated by ethnic residential segregation, for, where it occurs, this will inhibit inter-ethnic contact. Thus both components of alienation have clear demographic elements. The last of Murray's necessary conditions, an environment offering both targets and security, has many non-demographic elements, but he suggested that, in towns, the large, dense population and the existence of ethnically segregated neighbourhoods provide a secure base for guerrilla activity.

It can be argued that, enshrined within these four conditions that he states are necessary for political violence to occur, Murray is introducing four refinements, compared with Schellenberg and Mitchell, into the way that he hypothesizes that the demography of ethnicity affects violence in Northern Ireland. Firstly, an assumption was made clearly by Schellenberg, and more ambiguously by Mitchell, that violence is positively correlated with the Catholic share of the population over the entire range of proportions from zero to 100. Murray, however, proposed that the difference between Catholic majority areas and Catholic minority areas is more salient in affecting the location of violence—or, more specifically, of the guerrilla warfare and the economic campaign which originate in the Catholic community. Moreover, this acknowledgment that there is another aspect of violence, the sectarian conflict, leads to a second refinement from Murray. Thus he stated that sectarian conflict is associated with Protestant majority areas, albeit in a complex way: it is greatest where there is a substantial Protestant majority, but not an overwhelming one.

The remaining two refinements introduced by Murray are, in a sense, the opposite of each other. In the first place, he suggested that a high-violence region need not itself have a Catholic majority, as long as it was within easy travelling distance of such a region. Thus, he hypothesized, it is not just the ethnic composition of the specific geographical region where the violence takes place which is relevant, for the ethnic character of adjacent areas can help to generate violence at a particular place. On the other hand, even when we are considering the ethnic structure of the region of the conflict itself, it is not just the over-all ethnic composition which is salient, for the internal geography of this composition within the region being considered may affect its over-all level of violence. This fourth refinement is the same point which was quoted in the introduction to this chapter from the suggestion of Darby, that the amount of violence in a town is influenced by the extent to which its housing is ethnically segregated.

Implications

The implication of these four refinements identified in Murray's work is that the amount and type of violence in a geographical region depends on the nature and identity of the ethnic majority in that region, on the geographical distribution of that majority within the region, and on the nature and identity of the ethnic majority in the wider territory around. The level of violence at any one location is thus dependent on the ethnic composition at a whole series of spatial scale-levels involving that location.

This inference, drawn from the work of Murray, can be used to provide some demographic reinterpretations of his material. Firstly, it can be argued that the relevance of the proximity of the Border for fostering anti-partition feeling, and thus violence, is that the Republic of Ireland is overwhelmingly Catholic, both over-all and even in most of its Border areas (C.S.O. 1977, 10–27). Therefore, regions in Northern Ireland which themselves have a Catholic majority and which are near the Border form part of a wider territory which not only has a Catholic majority over-all but which consists of a series of adjacent regions, each of which individually has a Catholic majority. The relevance of this is that, just as ethnic residential segregation fosters Catholic alienation from the Protestant community by inhibiting inter-ethnic contact, so the location of a region within a wider territory, consisting entirely of adjacent regions with a Catholic majority, will inhibit contact between ethnic groups and lead to alienation.

The second demographic reinterpretation of Murray's contribution is that, when he suggests that proximity to the Republic of Ireland facilitates violence by offering a secure base for guerrilla activity, it is the implication of such proximity for a region's location in a wider territory of adjacent regions, all with a Catholic majority, that is critical. This provides the relatively secure environment for the Catholic guerrilla in Border areas which, as Murray himself says, is ensured by ethnic residential segregation in urban areas.

These two demographic reinterpretations of the significance of the Border in affecting the location of political violence can be used to provide a demographic explanation for the remarkable concentration of such violence into a small part of the province. That such a concentration exists is made clear by Murray's inter-regional analysis, in which he identified three major violence-prone regions—Belfast, Londonderry, and a narrow, discontinuous Border region—with 59, 8 and 16 per cent respectively of deaths attributable to the Troubles in the province. Even taken together, these three regions only occupy 23 per cent of Northern Ireland's land-area, so the remaining 77 per cent of its area has only had 17 per cent of its deaths.[6]

A straightforward demographic explanation of this concentration, based only on the individual ethnic composition of the regions whose violence is being measured, is not very successful, as Murray pointed out in refuting what we have termed the 'simple hypothesis'. For example, the nine District Council Areas in which Catholics form a majority occupy, because of their low population density, no less than 55 per cent of the land-area of Northern Ireland (Compton 1978, 10–12, 80–81; N.I.G.R.O. 1975b, 2–13). This is clearly a much more extensive area than Murray's high-violence regions.

On the other hand, the hypothesis that a region must not only have a Catholic majority itself, but be part of a wider territory of adjacent localities, all with a Catholic majority, before it has much political violence, appears to go a long way towards explaining the concentration of Northern Ireland's violence into such a small portion of its area. This is because, although Catholics are in a local majority, albeit very often a small one, in rather more than half the land-area in the west of the province, as well as in certain scattered pockets in the east, the pattern of dominantly Catholic and dominantly Protestant areas in the west forms such a complex mosaic that few areas of the first type are far from an area of the second (Compton 1976, 434–435; Darby 1976, 32–33; Compton 1978, 81–83). Therefore, òf all the places in Northern Ireland, it is only those areas which have a local Catholic majority and which are close to the Border that satisfy the hypothesis proposed here.

Further support for this hypothesis is provided by the actual location of Murray's (1982, 318–319) high-violence regions. They are all within 30 kilometers of the Border, except for Belfast, and, indeed, all but Belfast and part of a County Tyrone region centred upon Dungannon and Coalisland are within 20 kilometres of the Border.

In this sub-section we have only provided empirical evidence for considering two elements of what we saw as the critical scale-level implications of Murray's complex hypotheses on the relationship between ethnic composition and the level of political violence in a region. These were the nature and identity of the ethnic majority both in that region itself and in the wider territory around. The remaining element of the scale-level implications of Murray's work is the geographical distribution of the ethnic groups within the region whose over-all level of violence is being measured. The principal aspect of this intra-regional distribution is urban residential segregation, and that is why its consideration, in the light of empirical evidence, has been deferred until the next section, dealing with the inter-urban scale-level.

Inter-Urban Scale

Shortage of Information

In addition to proposing hypotheses about the relationship between political violence and ethnic residential segregation, Murray (1982, 328–329) observed that the extent to which individual towns were subject to such violence appeared to be correlated with the intensity of their ethnic residential segregation. This apparent verification of the hypothesis of Darby, referred to in the introduction to this chapter, is not, however, supported by any empirical evidence, even of a non-quantitative nature, except for Belfast. This city, Murray states, exhibits high rates of all three of his categories of political violence because it contains both Catholic and Protestant majority areas. Darby (1976, 26) himself went a little further, for he provided a larger number of specific examples, albeit without numerical evidence, arguing that 'the worst communal violence has been concentrated in urban centres where one polarized religious bloc adjoins its rival—towns like Belfast, Derry, Lurgan and Portadown'.

The omission by these authors of any numerical data to support their contentions about the relationship between violence and urban segregation is hardly surprising in view of the remarkable dearth, until very recently, of quantitative information on ethnic residential segregation in Northern Ireland's towns (Poole 1982, 281–284). A programme of data collection to fill this information void has been reported on at the half-way stage (Poole 1982, 284–293), and this programme is now sufficiently complete to permit the measurement of segregation in 1971 for every town in the province. A section of this data, along with the list of deaths attributable to the Troubles between 1969 and 1981, will now be used in the rest of this section of the chapter to investigate the relationship between the variation of violence between towns and the urban demography of ethnicity (see table 7:3). It is hoped that this analysis will go some way towards meeting the shortage of information currently available on this aspect of the relationship between violence and ethnic demography.

The particular towns considered will be the set of 27 which had a population in excess of 5,000 within their built-up area according to the 1971 census.[7] In recording the violence and the demographic characteristics for each of these towns, it will, in fact, be the limits of the built-up area which will be taken to define the urban boundaries. The particular measure of violence employed will be the number of separate fatal incidents, which will be preferred to the more commonly-used total number of deaths because the former appears to be a better measure of the degree of risk associated with living in a place.

Urban Fatal Incidents

The total of 2,161 deaths, analysed here, between 1969 and 1981 happened in 1,715 separate fatal incidents, according to our classification. Of these, 1,260 (73.5 per cent) were urban in the sense of occurring within one of the 27 towns defined earlier. The rate of fatal incidents, expressed as a frequency per 1,000 people, is 1.29 in urban areas and 0.81 in rural areas. Political violence of this type is thus disproportionately an urban phenomenon, though not overwhelmingly so, when measured in relation to the distribution of population.

The next point to consider is whether all towns are equally prone to violence. Table 1 shows that there is, in fact, a tremendous concentration of urban violence in the two cities of Belfast and Londonderry, with 77.8 and 10.1 per cent respectively. This particular concentration has already been suggested in the work of Murray (1982, 318–319), so what is more interesting is the variation amongst the other towns, from 28 incidents in Lurgan to no incidents at all in as many as four settlements.

Table 7:1

FATAL INCIDENTS (1969–1981) AND POPULATION (1971) IN TOWNS WITH OVER 5,000 PEOPLE

Town	Fatal incidents	Population	Fatal incidents per 1,000 people
Belfast	980	554,450	1.77
Londonderry	127	66,645	1.91
Lurgan	28	27,930	1.00
Portadown	25	22,207	1.13
Armagh	21	13,606	1.54
Newry	20	20,279	0.99
Strabane	14	9,413	1.49
Dungannon	9	8,190	1.10
Bangor	5	35,260	0.14
Carrickfergus	5	16,603	0.30
Lisburn	4	31,836	0.13
Omagh	4	14,594	0.27
Ballymena	3	23,386	0.13
Larne	3	18,482	0.16
Three towns with two incidents	6	32,037	0.19
Six towns with one incident	6	56,382	0.11
Four towns with no incidents	—	23,534	—
TOTAL	1,260	974,834	1.29

Source: Fatal incidents: derived from list supplied by the R.U.C. Press Office. Population: N.I.G.R.O. (1975b, 2–13); Government of Northern Ireland (1971, 12); N.I.G.R.O., Antrim (1973, 3, 10), Armagh (1973, 2), Belfast County Borough (1973, 2), Down (1974, 2–6).

Clearly, Northern Ireland towns do vary enormously in the extent to which they have suffered political violence, but it is equally clear that there is a tendency for the larger towns to have the most incidents. Thus Belfast and Londonderry, at one extreme, are by far the two largest urban settlements in the province, while, at the other, the four towns which have suffered no incidents at all have an average population of less than 6,000. True, there is no simple correlation between violence and population-size, as the relatively small number of fatal incidents in the third and fourth largest towns in the province, Bangor and Lisburn, testifies. However, there is a sufficiently strong correlation to suggest that we shall not get much further in explaining the inter-urban variation in violence without re-expressing the number of fatal incidents as a rate per 1,000 people. When this is done, the differences between towns are reduced very substantially indeed. The range is now from a maximum of 1.91 in Londonderry to a minimum of zero in the four towns already referred to.

Table 7:2 lists the 27 towns in order according to the rate of fatal incidents per 1,000 people. This table shows that, while Belfast and Londonderry are still the top two towns on the criterion of this rate, as they were on the criterion of the absolute number of incidents, there is no longer a marked gap between these two and the rest. In fact, when towns are listed as in Table 7:2, Belfast and Londonderry are merely the top two in a set of eight high-violence towns which do not differ massively from one another in their level of violence according to this measure.

Table 7:2

FATAL INCIDENTS (1969–1981) PER 1,000 PEOPLE IN TOWNS WITH OVER 5,000 PEOPLE IN 1971

Town	Fatal incidents per 1,000 people	Town	Fatal incidents per 1,000 people
Londonderry	1.91	Larne	0.16
Belfast	1.77	Cookstown	0.14
Armagh	1.54	Bangor	0.14
Strabane	1.49	Ballymena	0.13
Portadown	1.13	Lisburn	0.13
Dungannon	1.10	Banbridge	0.13
Lurgan	1.00	Coleraine	0.12
Newry	0.99	Antrim	0.07
Limavady	0.33	Newtownards	0.06
Carrickfergus	0.30	Ballyclare	—
Omagh	0.27	Downpatrick	—
Enniskillen	0.21	Portrush	—
Comber	0.18	Portstewart	—
Ballymoney	0.18		

Sources: See Table 6:1.

What is particularly noticeable from Table 7:2, however, is the large gap between Newry, with the lowest rate of incidents per 1,000 people amongst these eight high-violence towns, and the next town in order of susceptibility to violence according to this index, Limavady. Newry has a rate of 0.99, but that of Limavady is only 0.33. In comparison with the width of this gap, there is very little variation in the rate amongst the nineteen towns below the gap—even less than there was amongst the eight towns above the gap. Therefore, there emerges a clear dichotomy in the list between the eight high-violence towns and the nineteen low-violence towns, and the attempt to relate ethnic composition to violence, which will now be made, will concentrate on discovering the extent to which ethnic variables are correlated with this dichotomy.

Ethnic Demography and Violence: Three Scale-levels

The ethnic aspect of urban demography certainly, on first examination, seems to have a potential explanatory power, for its variation from one town to another is very considerable indeed. For example, the Catholic share of the total urban population varies from the lowest value of 5.1 per cent in Comber to the highest of 83.9 per cent in Newry, with nine of the 27 towns considered having Catholic majorities and the remainder Protestant majorities. Similarly, the dissimilarity index, which measures residential segregation on a scale from zero to 100, representing minimum and maximum segregation respectively, ranges from 19.5 in Antrim to 74.0 in Armagh. In fact, only seven towns have a dissimilarity index above the mid-point of 50 and can thus be thought of as high-segregation towns, while no fewer than twenty lie below this mid-point.

The ethnic variables, whose relationship with urban violence is to be tested, can be divided into three groups according to the geographical scale-level involved. The first is a group of three variables relating to each town taken as a single entity. These are the Catholic percentage share of the population, together with the absolute size of the Catholic community and the absolute size of the Protestant community. The method of analysis used with the variables both in this group and in the later groups was the simple one of identifying the dichotomy in the ethnic variable which best predicted the dichotomy in the rate of violence. For example, for the Catholic share of the whole urban population, the best dichotomy for this purpose was a division into towns over 50 per cent Catholic and towns under 50 per cent Catholic.

Table 7:3 shows how successful this variable was in predicting the dichotomy in the rate of fatal incidents per 1,000 people. There was clearly a positive correlation between the two variables, as indeed there had been between violence and the Catholic share of the population in the inter-regional analysis examined in the last section of this chapter. The level of violence was, in fact, correctly predicted in 22 of the 27 towns considered. Not surprisingly, in view of this positive correlation, the absolute size of the Protestant community was not a good predictor of the level of violence, but Table 7:3 shows that the total number in the Catholic population was an even better predictor than the percentage Catholic share of the population. In only three towns is the level of violence incorrectly predicted by the absolute size of the Catholic community.

Table 7:3

THE ASSOCIATION BETWEEN THE RATE OF FATAL INCIDENTS PER 1,000 PEOPLE AND EACH OF EIGHT ETHNIC VARIABLES FOR THE 27 TOWNS WITH OVER 5,000 PEOPLE IN 1971

Ethnic variable	*Ethnic category*	*Rate of fatal incidents* High	Low	*Incorrectly predicted towns*
Catholic % share of population	Over 50%	6	3	5
	Under 50%	2	16	
Absolute size of Catholic community	Over 6,000	7	2	3
	Under 6,000	1	17	
Absolute size of Protestant community	Over 15,000	3	3	8
	Under 15,000	5	16	
Dissimilarity index	Over 50	6	1	3
	Under 50	2	18	
P* (Catholic)	Over 60	7	3	4
	Under 60	1	16	
Catholic population in areas over 90% Catholic	Over 500	8	1	1
	Under 500	—	18	
Distance from Border	Over 20 km.	3	18	4
	Under 20 km.	5	1	
Catholic % share of D.C.A. population	Over 40%	5	5	8
	Under 40%	3	14	

Sources: Fatal incidents: derived from list supplied by the R.U.C. Press Office. Ethnic variables: unpublished Small Area Statistics of the 1971 Northern Ireland Census of Population; Compton (1978, 80–81); unpublished clergy data on religious affiliation; electoral registers; N.I.G.R.O. (1975a, 34–36).

The second group of ethnic variables involved what, in general terms, we can refer to as the scale-level of the neighbourhood within towns. More specifically, they all involve the ethnic residential segregation identifiable on dividing each town into sub-areas containing an average of 200 households. A total of twelve different measures of segregation was correlated with violence to discover which gave the best fit, but only three are illustrated in Table 7:3. One of these, the dissimilarity index, is included because it is the most commonly-used measure of segregation in the literature on this subject (Poole and Boal 1973, 23–24; Peach 1975, 2–4), while another, P*, applied to the Catholic population, is included because there are sound theoretical reasons for supposing that this is a measure with direct consequences for inter-ethnic behaviour (Lieberson 1981, 64–70). However, it is the third of the segregation variables illustrated in the table which is the best predictor of the level of violence in a town. This is the number of Catholics living in neighbourhoods which are over 90 per cent Catholic.

In Belfast these neighbourhoods have been referred to by Boal *et al.* (1976, 99) as the 'Catholic city' in order to distinguish them from the 'Mixed city' and the 'Protestant city'. They can also be regarded as the Catholic urban ghettos, and the variable which is so successful in predicting violence can consequently be interpreted as the size of the Catholic ghetto population.[8] Table 7:3 shows that it is the towns with large Catholic ghetto populations which have the high rates of violence. Conversely, towns with very few or none of their Catholics living in this type of neighbourhood have a low level of violence. There is only one exception to this trend, and that is the County Tyrone town of Omagh, which is anomalous because it has a much lower rate of violence than would be predicted from the size of its Catholic ghetto population.

The third group of ethnic variables to be considered involves attributes of the wider territory around each town. Because of the conclusions reached at the end of the inter-regional section about the significance of location with respect to the Border, the distance from each town to the nearest part of the Irish Republic was measured. It was found to be a reasonably good predictor of violence, succeeding in 23 of the 27 towns, but this success-rate is still much lower than that achieved with the best segregation measure. The other variable relating to the wider territory around each town is the Catholic percentage share of the population of the District Council Area in which each town is located. As the final row of Table 7:3 shows, however, this is a rather poor predictor of violence.

Inter-urban and Inter-regional: A Comparison

It therefore clearly emerges that, of all the ethnic variables whose correlation with the rate of fatal incidents per 1,000 people has been examined, there is just one optimal predictor of the level of urban violence. This is the size of the Catholic ghetto population. Since this is basically a variable relating to the ethnic composition of urban neighbourhoods, rather than of the town as a whole or of the wider territory around, we are compelled to arrive at a distinctly different conclusion about the inter-urban variation in violence from that reached at the end of the preceding section on inter-regional variation. In that section, it was concluded that high-violence regions, with the exception of Belfast, were all parts of larger geographical areas composed of adjacent Catholic-dominated regions. The ethnic demography of the wider territory around the high-violence region was therefore perceived as crucial in explaining inter-regional variations in violence.

In the current section, however, it has been concluded that the ethnic demography of a town itself is the key factor in explaining inter-urban variations in violence. This would seem to imply that it is, in fact, rural violence whose location is affected by proximity to the Border. There is insufficient space to develop a full analysis of this topic, but some evidence to support this contention is the discovery that 62 per cent of the rural fatal incidents which have occurred have been concentrated into the six District Council Areas adjoining the Border, especially Newry and Mourne, Dungannon and Fermanagh. In fact, the rate of fatal incidents per 1,000 people for rural areas is 1.38 in these six Border District Council Areas, but only 0.48 elsewhere in Northern Ireland.

Though a contrast has been drawn between the inter-regional finding that distance from the Border is crucial in affecting the level of violence, except in the case of Belfast, and the inter-urban conclusion that the size of the Catholic ghetto population is critical in influencing the rate of violence, these separate discoveries have two features in common. Firstly, in neither case is the ethnic demography of the specific geographical area, whose rate of violence is being measured, of much relevance. For inter-regional variation, it is the wider territory whose ethnic composition is important, while, for inter-urban variation, it is the neighbourhood whose composition is salient. Indeed, this finding can almost certainly be extended to the one area which was exceptional in the context of inter-regional variation, Belfast, for this city is so large that it totally dominates its region. Therefore, it is probably the 'urban factor' of Catholic ghetto-size which is crucial in affecting its regional level of violence.

Secondly, it is suggested that both this urban factor of ghetto-size and the regional or rural factor of distance from the Border are relevant in affecting the rate of fatal incidents because they constitute measures of the absolute size of the Catholic population living in overwhelmingly Catholic places. This is so both in the case of the urban Catholic ghetto population and in the case of the Catholic majority regions adjacent to the massively Catholic territory of the Irish Republic.

Intra-Urban Scale

Ethnic segregation and doorstep murders

The final scale-level to be considered is the intra-urban. There is only one Northern Ireland town whose geographical pattern of political violence at this scale-level has been studied in any depth, and that is Belfast. Intra-urban studies of this city have devoted considerable attention to the relationship between violence and ethnic demography, but, almost without exception, they have evaded the topic of deaths attributable to the Troubles. Instead, they have concentrated on the location either of riots (Day et al. 1971; Easthope 1976, 436–443) or of the refugee movement investigated, as pointed out in the introduction to this chapter, as a demographic effect of intimidation and certain other forms of violence.

This virtual disregarding of Troubles-induced deaths in the research at the intra-urban level makes this scale-level similar, in this respect, to the inter-urban. However, whereas original research has been specially undertaken to fill this void at the inter-urban level, such analysis was not carried out on the location of deaths within towns. This section will, therefore, simply review the limited available literature.

Only one analysis has so far been undertaken of the geographical distribution within Belfast of deaths attributable to the troubles. This was an investigation of a very restricted, but particularly frightening, subset of these deaths, the killing of civilians in their homes, a category referred to as doorstep murders because most victims were shot on answering the door (Murray and Boal 1979, 151–153). There is a very marked concentration of these murders, especially of those carried out by Protestant killers, in north Belfast, for reasons, the authors suggest, connected with the geography of ethnic composition within this area.

The first of these reasons is the complex patchwork pattern, in much of the area, of small segregated Catholic and Protestant housing areas, which are both difficult to defend and easy to penetrate from outside by attackers who can return quickly to the security of their own neighbourhood nearby, which is often one of the larger adjacent segregated areas. The small ghettos thus provide an easy target, while the adjacent larger ghettos provide the best security. The second reason, which Murray and Boal, in fact, regard as more important than the first, is that north Belfast has been subject to much more change in its internal geography of ethnicity since 1969 than the rest of the city, especially in the form of Catholic expansion. This makes it almost unique in the city, for by far the largest part of Belfast has been characterized by a remarkable stability of ethnic composition in both its segregated and its mixed areas for at least several decades (Boal 1982, 254–257). The Catholic expansion in north Belfast, Murray and Boal claim, has made many Protestants feel threatened and resentful at their loss of territory.

It might also be hypothesized that this exodus of Protestants from those areas experiencing Catholic expansion implies that many Protestants are familiar with the lay-out of these particular Catholic areas, thus facilitating penetration to carry out a doorstep murder. This may well be a significant factor in a city where there is so little inter-ethnic contact that one community's familiarity with the territory of the other is normally very low indeed (Boal 1969, 39–47).

Murray and Boal are thus very adamant that there is a relationship between ethnic demography and the location of doorstep murders, but these killings only constituted 4 per cent of all deaths arising from the Troubles in the Belfast high-violence region in their study-period (Murray 1982, 322). They do make reference to other murders, pointing out that many take place in segregated areas, the victim usually having travelled to or through the other ethnic group's territory, but no numerical evidence is provided. In a similarly non-quantitative vein, Murray (1982, 326) claims that most violence occurs in those relatively restricted parts of Belfast where Catholics form the majority of the population: streets of this type, in fact, contain just 18 per cent of the city's households (Boal 1981, 67).

In the absence, however, of quantitative analysis of the location of any but a tiny fraction of the deaths attributable to the Troubles within either Belfast or any other Northern Ireland town, it would be premature to take such limited intra-urban observations as we have been able to make in this section and forward them to our conclusion. This final section of the chapter will therefore draw together our findings at the provincial, inter-regional and inter-urban levels, but ignore the intra-urban.

Conclusion: Scale-level and majority status

In the course of trying to examine the effect of ethnic demography on the geographical variation in the incidence of violence at a number of distinct scale-levels, it has been necessary, not surprisingly, to study the geography of ethnic composition itself at several separate scale-levels. What is much more important, however, is our finding that, at any one scale-level at which the location of violence is examined, it may be necessary to invoke the separate effects of the spatial pattern of ethnic composition at distinctly different scale-levels in order to provide an explanation. This is certainly the case for the inter-regional analysis of violence, where the ethnic composition, not only of each region identified for recording violence, but also, and more importantly, of the wider territory around and of the internal divisions of the region, had to be included in the explanation.

Similarly, the general provincial level of violence, compared with other societies elsewhere, was explained in terms of the double majority model, which involved examining the ethnic composition not only of Northern Ireland but also of the United Kingdom and of the island of Ireland. Indeed, these three scale-levels involved in the double majority model were held to play a part in explaining the ethnic group in which most of the violence originates, which, in turn, affects the location of violence at the inter-regional, inter-urban and, probably, the intra-urban scale-levels, too. There thus emerges a rather complex, multi-tiered hierarchy of geographical scale-levels, the ethnic composition at each of which is relevant in affecting the location of violence at any one scale of investigation.

The specific aspect of ethnic composition which is relevant at all these scale-levels is the identity of the ethnic group which constitutes the majority of the population. The double majority model, for example, emphasizes the paradoxes revealed by varying the scale-level in answer to Lijphart's (1975, 94–95) question, 'Majority of what?', which, he asserts, 'spells trouble for a system with boundaries that are widely questioned'. Similarly, the issue of which ethnic group has majority status is the crucial one with respect to the wider territory around a high-violence region or town, to this high-violence area itself and to the neighbourhoods into which the area may be divided.

There does seem to be a difference amongst these scale-levels, however, in the size of the majority which is important. At the level of Northern Ireland, the United Kingdom and the island of Ireland, it is the mere existence of a majority, no matter how small, which is most important, because there is a crucial difference between majority status and minority status in determining who should exercise power and determine political boundaries in a 'winner take all' democracy. Therefore, the existence of a majority, regardless of how small, provides a precondition for political violence if that majority is frustrated by having its 'democratically justified' objectives thwarted.

On the other hand, at the various smaller scale-levels, there needs to be a much larger majority before the preconditions for violence exist. This is most explicit at the level of the urban neighbourhood, where it was found that areas over 90 per cent Catholic were the most crucial ones. The situation for the wider territories around high-violence regions near the Border is more complicated, but half the wards with Catholic majorities adjoining it on the Northern Ireland side have a Catholic proportion in excess of 75 per cent of their population (Compton 1976, 435; Compton 1978, 5), while all the Rural Districts continguous with it on the Republic of Ireland side are over 75 per cent Catholic (C.S.O. 1977, 10–27).

Even in the case of these Border areas, therefore, and even more so in the case of urban neighbourhoods, it is places with large Catholic majorities, rather than with just bare majorities, which seem to provide an environment conducive to violence. Presumably, it is such overwhelmingly Catholic areas that provide the most secure base for the Catholic guerrilla and which inhibit inter-ethnic contact, and in both these ways they are conducive to political violence (Boal 1972, 167).

If there is any validity in our findings relating to the effect either of the size of the urban Catholic ghettos or of the demographic interpretation of proximity to the Border, then there must be clear policy implications, in terms of both desegregation and repartition, if the reduction of political violence is seen as a desirable goal. Quite apart from the issue of the practicability of these implications, it must be stressed, however, that it is not at this stage desirable to explain and evaluate them in any detail at all, because of the highly preliminary nature of our findings.

It may seem both conservative and conventional to conclude this chapter by calling for more research to confirm or refute these preliminary findings, but this entire subject-area of the relationship between ethnic demography and violent conflict is one which has been so little investigated that such a call is inevitable. In particular, it is suggested that a more sophisticated methodology is required, a careful categorization of deaths is needed whenever fatal incidents form the subject of analysis, and the aspects of violence explored must be broadened and applied consistently at all scale-levels. Such a programme of analysis is surely justified by the severity of the problem of violence still engulfing Northern Ireland so many years after 1969.

Notes

1. This characterization, by Hewitt, of the Northern Ireland conflict as essentially ethnic in nature is by no means a universally agreed one, but there does appear to be strong justification for viewing ethnicity as at least a major component of the division between Protestant and Catholic in the province (Boal et al. 1976, 77–83, 114–122; Darby 1976, 169–174).
2. In one sense, the concept of ethnic composition is not a demographic one at all, for it is not so clearly a part of formal or pure demography as such other aspects of population structure as age, sex or marital status. However, there is a broader and increasingly used definition of demography which includes the study of ethnicity and religion, along with many other socio-economic variables, both in their own right and in relation to group differences in birth rates, death rates and migration (Kirk 1968, 342–343). It is the existence of this broader definition which justifies the use of the term 'demography' in this chapter.
3. The classification of these ethnic groups in Zanzibar and Cyprus as minorities, despite their economic and political privilege before violence occurred, indicates that, in this chapter, we are following Banton (1979, 127) in defining a minority in simple numerical terms rather than in the sense popularized by Wirth.
4. In fact, Jackson seems to have been responsible for the specific term 'double minority' rather than for the concept. For example, virtually the same set of ideas about both minority status and its behavioural consequences was expressed about the same time by Shearman (1970, 45) and by Gibson (1971, 4–5). Moreover, more than a decade earlier, Gallagher (1957, 196–224) had characterized each of Northern Ireland's two ethnic communities as a minority.
5. This 4 per cent figure is estimated from data provided by Jackson (1963, 187), Krausz (1971, 34–36) and Compton (1982, 98).
6. The data on land-area is obtained from N.I.G.R.O. (1975b, 2–13) for wards identified from a comparison of Murray's (1982, 318) map of regions with high levels of violence with the ward-location map presented by Compton (1978, 5–9).
7. The sources of this population data are described in Table 7:1. The set of 27 towns are obtained after amalgamating certain adjacent urban settlements: most importantly, the Newtownabbey, Holywood, Castlereagh and Andersonstown–Dunmurry districts were combined with Belfast, and Brownlow was added to Lurgan.
8. The word 'ghetto' has, it must be admitted, emotive overtones, but it has a cryptic convenience. Moreover, it is commonly used in the academic literature to describe any extreme degree of ethnic residential segregation (Jones and Eyles 1977, 169–170), though a more restricted definition is preferred by some (Boal 1976, 57, 64–75).

8

From Conflict to Violence: The Re-emergence of the IRA and the Loyalist Response

Barry White

It is not only very difficult, but probably highly misleading, to try to see too much of a pattern in the violence which has been the single most consistent factor in Northern Ireland political life since 1969. A relatively small, but long-lived and experienced paramilitary organisation, the Provisional IRA, has been trying, on behalf of a minority of Northern Ireland's Nationalist minority, to bring about radical political change against the expressed wishes of the vast majority of the population, including the local and British-based security forces, supported by the British Government. In these circumstances, the methods used by the IRA—and similar Republican terrorist groups like the Irish National Liberation Army—must involve a considerable degree of violence, along a broad front, in order to try to achieve the short-term objective of intimidating the Catholic and Protestant populations, as well as presenting a credible threat to British Government rule. Of necessity, the intensity and direction of the campaign has to be varied constantly, to counter the superior numbers and firepower of the opposition, as well as to respond to political events, and this makes overall strategy confused and hard to discern. Resourcefulness is perhaps the IRA's most obvious characteristic, ensuring that, despite major setbacks, it has been able to keep up the pressure, at some level.

Broadly speaking, however, the campaign began on the streets, as a follow-up to the Civil Rights demonstrations of 1968-9, in riots and confrontations with the security forces and militant Protestants. It continued in a bombing campaign against commercial, security force and sectarian targets in the early 1970s, at first almost random, but then more selective. From time to time, there have been diversionary bombing attacks in England, or even the Continent, to make a political point or take advantage of the extra propaganda value. But since 1977, when the IRA was reorganised, to improve its resistance to effective new anti-terrorist measures, it has tended to concentrate its attacks on security personnel and military or police targets, with occasional shows of strength in border areas.

The H-Block hunger strike of 1981 provided an opportunity to popularize the IRA cause again, through martyr-like deaths, but the accompanying violence was limited and the beneficiaries were the politicians of Sinn Fein, who gained by the experience of organizing the protest, rather the militants. Out of this evolved the policy of "the Armalite in one hand and the ballot paper in the other" which was to result in the political successes of the Northern Ireland Assembly election in October 1982, when Sinn Fein captured 10.1 per cent of the first preference votes—compared to 18.8 per cent by the SDLP—in their first outing. The low-level violence continued, often reacting to increased pressure by SAS-type police units and supergrasses from within their ranks, but this did not deter young voters, in particular, swinging significantly away from the constitutional SDLP to Sinn Fein. A new phenomenon had arrived in Northern Ireland politics, a potentially powerful revolutionary party, backed by the considerable influence, in terms of physical force and money, of a well-established paramilitary organization.

Meanwhile the Protestant paramilitary organizations, who were responsible for much of the early violence, which revived the IRA, have largely been a reactive force. With their siege mentality, common to most extreme Unionists or loyalists, they regard any challenge to the status quo—even a political one—as subversive, and a cause for retaliation. This has led them not only to indulge in openly sectarian attacks, to terrorise the Catholic population, but to remind the authorities, by direct action, that they hold a veto over radical political change. So their violence can be characterized as part terror and part political, much like the IRA's. Since they are merely defending Protestant and Unionist privilege, rather than working towards a political goal, they have little ideological commitment and therefore work to a less coherent, even more confused plan of campaign. Basically, they think the only way to defeat Republicanism is by force and, although their political theorists argue for independence, there is little evidence that the rank and file has been influenced. Their role will probably continue to be to act as Unionism's strong right arm, ready to strike back at IRA violence when it threatens to overrun the conventional security forces, or to reject any imposed political solution.

Drawing up the Lines: 1965-71

The first hint that the detente in North-South relations begun by Terence O'Neill in 1965 would precipitate violence came a year later, in the Malvern Street murder, in the lower Shankill. The Catholic barman who was killed had no connection with the almost defunct IRA; he had strayed into a Loyalist pub and that was reason enough for his murder, in the over-heated atmosphere brought about by the 50th anniversary commemorations of the 1916 Easter Rising. Fears of a political sell-out had inspired the formation of small fanatical gangs in the lower Shankill, which were not centrally controlled, but became known as the Ulster Volunteer Force, after Edward Carson's original Protestant army in Home Rule days. With this murder, and another in the Falls, the UVF set a pattern for sectarian killing, which already had a long history in Belfast and was to re-establish itself as the Loyalists' primary terror weapon in the 1970s.

The murderers were duly arrested and charged—one of them saying he wished he had never heard of Ian Paisley, then an up-and-coming Protestant demagogue—but the commitment to Protestant paramilitarism survived. When the Civil Rights demonstrators took to the streets in 1968 and O'Neill's government began to surrender to their demands, a reformed UVF was ready, backed by extreme Loyalist politicians, to stage a series of devastating bomb attacks on key electricity and water installations in Spring 1969. The IRA was blamed, the Government's credibility was fatally damaged and O'Neill was forced to resign in April after an inconclusive election.

Meanwhile the civil rights protests around the province showed a degree of organization and discipline which reflected the active participation of the republican movement in this new form of politics. After the failure of the 1956-62 campaign to arouse Catholic support, the IRA turned from violence to community action, forming Republican Clubs—promptly banned in 1967—to further their socialist ambitions. Civil rights was an obvious rallying point for all Catholic dissidents, frustrated by O'Neill's ineffectiveness, but although the republican movement was heavily involved in the formation of the Northern Ireland Civil Rights Association in February 1967, it chose to stay out of the limelight. The only republican in the first executive was Kevin Agnew, a Maghera solicitor; the commanding officer of the IRA declined a nomination. As the Cameron Commission (para. 214) concluded: 'there is evidence that members of the IRA are active in the organization, there is no sign that they are in any sense dominant or in a position to control or direct policy of the CRA'.

Nevertheless, the left-wing republican element was influential in the decision to stage a march to Dungannon in August 1968, and its willingness for confrontation was demonstrated in Derry and elsewhere. By December, the NICRA moderates had called a truce, acknowledging Unionist reforms, but others were ready to test Protestant patience to destruction, culminating in the January 1969 People's Democracy march from Belfast to Derry, which was ambushed at Burntollet. Members of the 'B' Specials, the exclusively Protestant police reserve, were involved in the attack on the student marchers and this was the prelude to days and nights of rioting in Derry—and in Newry a few weeks later—which left permanent scars in both communities. With foresight, the IRA should have expected a violent Protestant backlash, but it had been thoroughly politicized, and was unprepared for what followed O'Neill's downfall.

Tension built up to a dangerous 'marching season'—period between June and August when Protestants and Catholics demonstrate their respective strenghts in marginal areas—and when a weak Government proved unable to stop the annual Apprentice Boys parade in Derry in August, Catholics rioted in resentment at this reminder of their second-class citizenship. The Battle of the Bogside followed, in which Catholics vented their rage on the RUC with bricks and petrol bombs, forcing the Government to call in the British Army for assistance, for the first time since the 1920s. Catholics in west Belfast rioted in sympathy, to divert police attention, but before the Army moved in, a day after Derry, a total of eight had died in violent confrontations, with armed Protestants taking their revenge for months of Catholic agitation in an orgy of destruction.

The arrival of the Army brought an uneasy peace, but already both communities had formed rudimentary defence committees, organized at street level, and these were to be moulded during the summer and autumn into the Provisional IRA and the Ulster Defence Association, which was finally brought together in 1971. By concentrating on leftist politics, the IRA had dropped its basic paramilitary role, as the Catholics' last defence against sectarian attack, and that was its undoing. There were no guns, or gunmen, to repel the Loyalist incursions, and community leaders resolved not to be caught defenceless again. Emissaries went South, capitalizing on the general sympathy for beleagured Nationalist communities and, on a promise that a rival grouping would be formed to challenge the dangerously socialistic IRA, money and resources flowed North, with the blessing of the Fianna Fail Government. The result was the formation of the Provisional IRA, as rival to the Marxist Official IRA, in early 1970, headed by veterans from the 1940s, 1950s and 1960s, with traditional green Republican backgrounds.

At the same time, the Protestants were smarting from the disbandment of the 'B' Special police reserve, which had long been regarded as their most effective anti-terrorist weapon, and anger with this recommendation of the Hunt Committee in October 1969 resulted in the first police death, at loyalist hands, in the lower Shankill. The replacement was the Ulster Defence Regiment, under British Army, rather than local RUC, control and, although it began as a relatively mixed force, against all subversion, it has become almost exclusively Protestant, with a limited, but recognizable loyalist bias. UDA members are not automatically disbarred.

By the summer of 1970, the honeymoon period which marked the early stages of the Army's occupation of Catholic west Belfast was running out; the final break was achieved by the Falls curfew of July, when soldiers sealed off a large area for two days, refusing to let people leave their homes during a house-to-house search. Some arms were found, but the effect was to alienate an entire population and rally support for the Provisional IRA in a campaign that was turning increasingly against the military. Nail grenades were regularly hurled at soldiers and the bombing campaign began in earnest, with one hundred explosions during the year.

The first soldier did not die until February 1971, eighteen months after the Army's deployment on the streets, but the one hundredth victim was killed only sixteen months later, in June 1972. The IRA campaign continued its rapid escalation in 1971, with murders of off-duty soldiers, attacks on the homes of policemen and extensive use of bombs in Belfast. One of these, involving the bombing of a Protestant pub on the Shankill Road, marked the beginning of an openly sectarian campaign, and the Official IRA, which had earlier been engaged in a murderous feud with the Provisionals, denounced them as 'fiendish and sectarian bigots, whose motives are obviously to set the Protestant and Catholic working class at each other's throats'.

Internment: Reaction and Counter-reaction: 1971-72

As the security situation deteriorated on all fronts the Government finally yielded to pressure in August to introduce internment without trial, the traditional and usually effective answer to IRA militancy. But police files were out of date and instead of damping down the violence, the arrest of 300 paramilitary and political activists simply added fuel to the fire. More than 4,000 refugees fled South, where the Taoiseach, Jack Lynch, threatened not to stand idly by, but effectively did. The whole Catholic community united, temporarily, behind the militants, and the sense of grievance was added to by reports of brutal interrogation methods, finally admitted in the Compton report. Extremists exploited the situation by a return to street demonstrations and the result was the confrontation of Bloody Sunday in Derry, January 1972, when British paratroopers, believing they were under fire, shot down 13 civilians after an illegal march.

Again the effect was to unite the Catholic population against the British, providing a flood of IRA recruits and, in the international outcry which followed, the Westminster Government had little alternative but to suspend the Stormont parliament, having failed to obtain consent to a takeover of all security powers. The newly-formed UDA responded by setting up its own no-go areas, following the IRA's lead, and sniping broke out for the first time since 1969 between Protestant and Catholic areas.

Just as internment and Bloody Sunday solidified Catholic opinion, the closure of Stormont had an equally binding effect on Protestants, moderates as well as extremists, as they saw their pre-Troubles world collapse. Five days later the Official IRA declared a cease-fire, acknowledging the dangerous mood of loyalists, but the Provisionals went for the kill, until they finally declared a cease-fire in June, and won inconclusive talks in London with the Ulster Secretary, William Whitelaw.

Whatever hopes they had of British concessions were soon dashed, however, and Bloody Friday, in which 11 were killed in simultaneous bombings in Belfast, ended any thought of detente. In the shocked aftermath, the British were able to occupy the infamous no-go areas of Derry and Belfast, within which the IRA had established itself as a police and defence force, dealing out rough and sometimes fatal justice to its opponents.

The next two years were dominated by frenzied political activity, as the British Government tried to restore some measure of devolution to politicians who were increasingly polarized, like the communities they came from. Hardly a month went by without a new Government initiative, or poll, and the paramilitaries thrived in the atmosphere of uncertainty, in which the province's future appeared to be constantly in the balance. The death rate rose spectacularly, from 174 in 1971, the year of internment, to 468 in 1972, before settling down to 200-300 for the next four years.

The Loyalist Response: 1972-74

At this stage the violence turned nakedly sectarian, with Protestants reacting to the traditional Republican threat in the traditional manner—spreading terror among IRA sympathizers by gunning down innocent Catholics in the street. One of the first of these, in February 1972, was attributed to the Red Hand Commandos, one of the loosely organized gangs which had sprouted up in Protestant areas as the civil rights campaign gained momentum. These briefly centred around the Ulster Protestant Volunteers, a branch of the Rev. Ian Paisley's Ulster Constitution Defence Committee, and were active in the street defence committees of 1969. A year later, the UDA had its beginnings in the Shankill, but it was not until the post-internment chaos that the Protestant vigilante groups saw the need for an organization, distinct from the military-styled UVF, then banned. Just as the Catholic population felt let down, in 1969, by the disarmed IRA, Protestants found the Orange Order ill-equipped to deal with the new situation. 'The Orange Order was never used when the occasion arose against the IRA because its leaders didn't have the guts to turn them into soldiers', said UDA chief, Andy Tyrie, years later.

The Orange leadership was too much a part of the Unionist establishment to dirty its hands in paramilitarism, so the gap was filled by the community's tougher elements, including criminals. There was little co-ordination in the early days and vigilante groups simply affiliated to the Shankill-based UDA, while remaining virtually autonomous in their own areas. As the organization grew in size, however, a 20-man council became too unwieldy, and power struggles broke out periodically between the leading figures in west and east Belfast. Finally, after murders and shoot-outs, a durable compromise candidate emerged in Tyrie, who successfully combined the UDA's twin roles as loyalism's main paramilitary wing and fund raiser.

Many of the most terrible crimes in the early and mid-Seventies were carried out by UDA members, including the bombing of Dublin and Monaghan during the 1974 strike, but the organization managed to avoid proscription by use of a pseudonym, Ulster Freedom Fighters, when claiming credit for assassinations. The sheer size of the organization—at its height it had 15,000 members, compared to an estimated 1,500 in the UVF—made it as difficult to ban as it was easy to infiltrate and therefore the security forces were reluctant to drive it underground. While the IRA had Provisional Sinn Fein to raise funds, which were estimated at £2 million yearly in 1980, the UDA had to perform this function itself, and largely copied IRA methods, ranging from protection rackets to burglaries. But the main providers were the drinking clubs, founded after the destruction of a third of Belfast's pubs, mainly Catholic-owned.

America and the Middle East have provided fruitful sources of arms and ammunition for the IRA, but the UDA has had to rely on less reliable helpers in Canada and Scotland. The number of home-made weapons found in arms caches underlines the problems faced by loyalist groups without a convenient back-door in the Republic and it has been estimated that if Protestants had the same access to explosives as the IRA, the violence would have been even greater and more random, in Catholic areas. As it was, the Shankill-based UVF acquired a reputation for extremism, particularly after the short-lived freedom of Gusty Spence, its jailed leader, left a group of young Turks in charge. Among its more notorious episodes were the Shankill Butcher murders, nineteen killings carried out by a particularly vicious gang between 1975-7, and the 1977 trial in east Antrim, when twenty-six UVF men were given a total of 700 years' imprisonment, including eight life sentences. It also had a habit of mistakenly killing Protestants in its random attacks, unlike the UDA.

In the same way that Unionists have tended, latterly, to greater division in their ranks than Nationalists, Protestant individualism is reflected in the mass of small-scale paramilitary bodies, mainly organized on a geographical basis. In addition to the UDA, the UVF and the Red Hand Commando, regarded as the personal property of an early militant, John McKeague, there were at one time or another at least nine other loyalist groupings.

The main ones were Tara, formed in the late 1960s as 'the hard core of Protestant resistance', with strong Orange and biblical Protestant links, which was reputed to have provided guns for others; Down Orange Welfare, set up under an ex-army colonel and claimed to have 5,000 members; Orange Volunteers, mostly ex-service and reserved for a doomsday situation; Vanguard Service Corps, the military wing of the one-time Vanguard Unionist movement; the Ulster Special Constabulary Association, reserved for ex-'B' Specials.

Attempts were made, with limited success, to co-ordinate the efforts of the paramilitaries, first through the Ulster Army Council, formed in December 1973, and then through the Ulster Loyalist Central Co-ordinating Committee, which grew out of the ad hoc committee which organized the Ulster Workers' Council strike in May 1974. But experience shows that Protestant paramilitaries can only come together effectively in an emergency situation, and their extreme distrust of politicians makes them an unreliable political ally.

'An Acceptable Level of Violence': 1974-82

The interests of the Protestant and Catholic paramilitaries converged during the five months of the power-sharing executive, from January to May 1974, and the IRA's continuing violence was enough to persuade Loyalists that there were no practical benefits—and a lot of possible political disadvantages—from the coalition experiment. (Earlier, the two sides had been brought together informally in well-meaning attempts to establish better understanding of their respective beliefs, but with limited effect). The success of the UWC strike was largely due to loyalist paramilitary involvement, and represents the high point of their campaign, but their inability to capitalize on it underlines their negative rather than positive strength. In short, they proved they could terminate any political development judged to be hostile to loyalist interests, but they were unable to move Government policy in their direction.

If the strike had showed that a British Government could be influenced by loyalist violence, or threats of violence, the Feakle talks which followed it, seven months later, appeared for a time to demonstrate that IRA violence might yet get it to the bargaining table. A group of Protestant clergy and lay people made the running, with a top level IRA delegation, and the discussions were then taken up by the Government, leading to an IRA ceasefire in February 1975. Confusion still surrounds the terms, but what is clear is that the IRA thought much more was on the table than turned out to be the case and the ultimate winners were the security forces, who found it much easier to penetrate the IRA's defences in the new, relaxed atmosphere. By providing Provisional Sinn Fein with 'incident centres' for monitoring the ceasefire the Government gave it a legitimacy which has taken years to wear off, but at the same time the IRA was lulled into a false sense of security. Meanwhile the UVF proscription was lifted, to allow it to fight elections, before being re-imposed five months later. By the year's end, internment was ended, but, this apart, the IRA was no further forward, and as the ceasefire petered out, Protestant sectarian killings were met with the Whitecross massacre, near the South Armagh border, in which ten Protestant workmen were killed. The SAS was called in, the Convention which had been elected to devise a new agreed constitutional settlement ended in failure and battle commenced.

The murder of the new British ambassador to Dublin, Christopher Ewart-Biggs, in July 1976 was a reminder of the IRA's challenge, North and South, and within a month an upsurge of popular feeling against violence led to the formation of the Peace movement, out of a tragic hi-jacked car accident. Equally significant, from the point of view of containing violence, was the arrival of Roy Mason, a new breed of Secretary of State, who eschewed political solutions in favour of economic and security initiatives. Without political distractions, and with the tide of the Peace movement running high, violence fell away, and Ian Paisley badly misjudged the public mood when he led an abortive strike for tougher security measures in May 1977.

The only real effect was to sever the strained links between Paisley and the Protestant paramilitaries, particularly the UDA, who joined the strike in the belief that Paisley was serious about attempting a coup. When he backed away from confrontation with the Government, they were so disillusioned they commissioned their own political solution, which eventually turned out to be independence, with an American-style executive, but failed to get public support.

The Provisionals were also at a turning point for, despite the upsurge of violence in 1976, providing a peak of 297 deaths—second only to 1972—the combination of successful RUC interrogation methods at Castlereagh and the debilitating effect of the ceasefire led to a thorough re-think of policy. Confessions were decimating the old command structure, so the time was ripe for young Northern radicals to gain control of the seven-man Army Council and set it on a new path. Not only was the IRA to be re-organised into four or five-man cells or active service units, in order to minimise the effect of informers, but Provisional politics was to move decidedly to the left, to try to occupy the ground vacated by the Officials. In line with this new thinking, there was no more talk of 'one last heave' to get the British out of Ireland—war weariness was the prevalent mood in the Nationalist community—and instead a 'long haul' strategy was articulated by veteran Republican Jimmy Drumm at Bodenstown in 1977.

The summer was marked by an escalation in Provisional–Official tensions, as frustrated Officials left to join the more active Provisionals, taking their guns with them, and altogether four died and 25 were injured in gun battles. It was an indication of the Government's new confidence that the Queen's Jubilee visit went ahead, and the only alarm was the discovery of a new IRA delayed-action bomb at the New University of Ulster. With the re-arrest of IRA chief of staff Seamus Twomey, after four years on the run, and the interception of an arms consignment from the Middle East, the IRA campaign was at a low ebb at the end of 1977, when deaths fell by nearly two-thirds to 112, the lowest total since 1970.

This improving trend is reflected in the statistics for criminal damage payments, which reached a high of £50 million in 1976-77, but then fell away to hover around £40 million for the next three years. Nevertheless the long war strategy entailed occasional shows of strength, like a New Year blitz on hotels and clubs in 1978, to hit the tourist trade, and increased use of terror weapons like the firebomb—a petrol tin attached to an explosive device—which went disastrously wrong in the La Mon Restaurant attack, killing 12 civilians. A European dimension was added when eight bombs were exploded at BAOR bases in August, implying some German terrorist support. In November and twice in December massive bomb attacks, either in Britain or Northern Ireland, were reminders that the IRA was still in business. The first M16 machine gun, a prestige weapon that was to claim several Army casualties, was put on show in January.

Even so, the death rate fell again—to 81 in 1978—largely because of the more selective nature of the IRA campaign. Despite some spectacular attacks in 1979, resulting in the deaths of Airey Neave, killed by the INLA, a left-wing breakaway faction, in March and Lord Mountbatten in August, the most significant new factor was the increased murder rate of soldiers. Altogether 38 were killed, including 18 at Warrenpoint in August, the highest total for six years. A high proportion of these died in border areas, killed by land mines or—in the case of Warrenpoint—by radio controlled bombs. Especially in South Armagh, terrorists have virtual freedom of movement across the border and only undercover surveillance by the Army and improved cross-border co-operation has helped to minimise the IRA threat. In 1981, South Armagh managed to account for 30 out of the total of 108 murders for the year, as well as 56 attempted murders and 40 explosions.

The ability of the IRA to pick off selected targets in border areas—usually members of the security forces—and either go to ground or escape across the frontier has been a significant factor in keeping the situation on the boil. Protestants see the attacks as proof not only of the Government's ineffectiveness, but of the sectarian nature of the IRA campaign, and their paramilitaries have often reacted in kind in other areas, such as Belfast. In 1981, a series of cross-border assassinations produced the effect of mobilising Protestants behind Ian Paisley's Third Force, nominally to police border areas, as well as uniting loyalist opinion against the Dublin-London talks, equally unpopular with Unionist and Republican extremists.

Another effect of the traumatic killings of August 1979 was to accelerate the process of transferring security responsibility from the Army back to the police, which had run into difficulty since it was first enunciated by the Labour Secretary of State, Merlyn Rees, in January 1977. Relations were strained between the two forces, as the Army resisted surrendering control while its men were at risk, and the former MI6 chief, Sir Maurice Oldfield—who had earlier been an IRA target at his London home—was brought in to mediate. The steady reduction in troop levels continued, as security chiefs agreed that the Army presence in all but the worst areas for violence was merely delaying a return to normality, and locally-recruited forces took up the slack. This Ulsterisation policy saw increased recruitment to both the UDR— 7,500 members by 1982—and the RUC—12,000 part-time and full-time members—while troop levels dropped from the 1972 peak of 21,000 to 13,500 in 1978 and under 11,000 by 1982. The penalty was that the local security forces became the prime targets for the IRA, usually when they were off duty, and the police again took over a front-line role in riot situations, using potentially fatal plastic bullets, in place of CS gas.

The Limits of Violence

Nevertheless the graph of violence, by most calculations, had reached a plateau by the late 1970s which was approaching the 'acceptable level of violence' hoped for 10 years before. Deaths were down to 81 in 1978, less than a third of the 1976 total and there was a consistency about the following three years—113 (1979) 76 (1980) and 108 (1981)—suggesting that the worst was over. Even the tensions of the hunger strike, in 1981, produced nothing like the violence anticipated, although by-election results showed that political attitudes were as polarised as ever. The belief in violence, as a means of changing events, was dying, but not the alienation of which it was the expression. At the same time the quieter mood of the paramilitaries was reflected in the civilian deaths—including sectarian killings. These reached highs of 332 (122 sectarian) in 1972, 216 (144) in 1975 and 245 (121) in 1976, before dropping dramatically to 69 (42) in 1977, down to 50 (26) in 1980.

Accordingly, the numbers of persons charged with serious terrorist offences rose from 531 in 1972 to 1,414 in 1973 and stayed well above the 1,000 mark until 1978, when it fell to 843. In 1980 it was down to 540, almost on a par with 1972, and even the hunger strike year saw the figure only rise to 918. Meanwhile it is a measure of the IRA's continuing concern with internal security that the tally of kneecappings—its usual punishment—has remained high. The number dropped to 67 in 1978, but has since been in the 70-80 range.

The most detailed study of those killed, and by whom, was carried out by Michael McKeown, a Belfast lecturer, who examined the first 2,000 deaths up to January 1980. Comparing the first 500 deaths to the last 500—which brought the total to 2,000—he found that the time scale was broadly similar, 13 a month in the first cycle and 11 a month in the last. (This contrasted sharply with 23 a month during the 43 months August 1972 to April 1976, and even lower rate of 8 a month during 1980 and 1981). The most significant difference was in the groups held responsible for the deaths, showing the diminishing role of the security forces—down from 102 to 30—and the increasing involvement of the paramilitaries. Republican groups were responsible for 260 of the first 500 deaths and 330 of the last 500; Loyalists for 66 and 119.

Looking at the first 2,000 deaths, 554 (27.7 per cent) were members of the security forces, 225 (11.2 per cent) were paramilitaries or subversives, 1,163 (58.2 per cent) were civilians and only 58 (2.9 per cent) unclassified. But of the 225 subversives to die, only 88 were killed by the security forces. The IRA suffered 160 fatalities, including 63 to security forces and 77 to premature explosions. The security forces accounted for 220 deaths (11 per cent), Republicans for 1,024 (51.2 per cent) and Loyalists for 574 (28.7 per cent). But closer examination shows that only 40 per cent of the deaths caused by the security forces were proven subversives and 107 were civilians. If proof were needed that the Catholic areas suffered most from violence the tally of 1,631 deaths of natives of Northern Ireland included 916 Catholics (56.1 per cent) and 715 Protestants (43.8 per cent)—against a Catholic percentage of 35 per cent in the population at large.

Since 1977, the strategy of the IRA has been to plan for a war of attrition, aimed at demoralising the British, through destabilisation of Northern Ireland politics, and respect for their organising ability was demonstrated in a secret Army Intelligence memo, published by the IRA in 1979. The author, General James Glover, concluded that, despite pressure from the Army and the Catholic population, 'the Provisionals' campaign of violence is likely to continue while the British remain in Northern Ireland'. The 'long war' tactics have been to constantly ring the changes in targets, so that from month to month no one can feel safe, be they businessmen, off-duty UDR men, prison warders or prominent personalities, in Northern Ireland or in Britain. Bombing campaigns can be province-wide—such as co-ordinated attacks on hotels, business premises and town centres—or more selective. Discouragement of inward industrial investment has been an important short-term goal. Car bombs were an IRA innovation, now used world-wide, and other methods used to deadly effect include blast incendiaries, car booby traps, radio-controlled bombs—which accounted for 29 of the 86 killings in 1979—home-made rockets, and 'cooked' fertilizer explosives. As soon as the authorities find an effective block, IRA ingenuity finds a way around.

But there is one enemy of the IRA who cannot be eliminated—the informer. The adoption of the cell system and the emasculation of Castlereagh interrogation methods, as a result of the Bennett inquiry, helped to minimise the threat, but important defections in the winter of 1981-2 dealt a severe blow. Arms dumps were turned up on both sides of the border and arrests proliferated as leading IRA men fled to safe houses in the South. In an unprecedented move, the IRA offered an amnesty for all who confessed to informing—an admission that usually would have been suicidal. Even harder hit was the splinter group, INLA, some of whose membership overlapped with the IRA. Pressure from the Southern authorities on the IRA was stepped up after the Mountbatten murder and reached its high point under the FitzGerald coalition, with free exchange of intelligence North and South. The Republic's constitutional inability to permit extradition was a bone of contention, but alternatives continued to be sought.

The Protestant reaction to the more sophisticated IRA campaign in the late 1970s and early 1980s has been to adopt a mainly passive role, avoiding all involvement with loyalist politicians and only striking out at known republicans on rare occasions. The UDA has always claimed to be non-sectarian; 'We do not believe in sectarian violence, but we believe we are justified in making selective attacks on known Republicans and people who lead their campaign, give them orders and supply them with information', said Tyrie, in 1980. This 'terrorise the terrorists' policy has also been used against those whom it regarded as 'cheer-leaders' for the IRA, and that is the explanation for four political ass-assinations in the 1979-80 period, and an unsuccessful murder attempt on Bernadette McAliskey. But the UDA largely involved itself in its commercial activities—raising hundreds of thousands of pounds needed every year to match IRA comforts for serving prisoners— and attempts at establishing negotiated independence as an alternative allegiance for working class Protestants to pro-British Unionism. It was a fruitless exercise, against the tide of history, and demonstrated the extent to which a politically-naive leadership had lost touch with its own community.

One of the beneficial effects, however, of this more thoughtful ap-proach was the UDA's refusal to respond to IRA violence in the wake of the death of the first hunger striker, Bobby Sands, in 1981. The Catholic community was braced, by the IRA, for a loyalist onslaught which never came, not only because the UDA was satisfied with the security forces' handling of the emergency, but because it has learned from experience that mass demonstrations of force are counter-pro-ductive and win no thanks from the Protestant community.

The character of the violence and the threat posed by the para-military organisations has therefore changed considerably over the period of the Troubles, in accordance with the political situation, the Army's response and the mood of their respective communities. Both the Provisionals and the UDA have learned that there are strict limits on the support they can expect for bombings and killings, even in re-taliation, and their reaction has been to switch the emphasis from paramilitarism to politics. On the UDA side, this has met with little success—although it must have helped to save them from proscription—while on the Provisionals' side, the gains for H-Block candidates in the 1981 elections may have been the exception which proves the rule that the Irish will never abandon their gunmen, but won't vote for them. All the more so, because both sets of paramilitaries have drifted far from the traditional conservatism of their communities. This means that the IRA cannot achieve political legitimacy, and therefore will continue to use violence against schemes which exclude it, and leave a British presence. As a result, the UDA is guaranteed a continuing ex-istence as the Protestant equivalent of the IRA, in what Protestants see as their increasingly beleaguered situation, disowned by the British and out-bred by Catholics. The destructive influence of the two organisa-tions will wax and wane, according to Britain's determination to find a political solution through devolution, or an Anglo-Irish approach, but it will not disappear, and must be accounted for in any eventual settlement.

Since both sides accept that there must be limits to their paramilitary activities, or pressures from the security forces or their respective communities will become too great, the violence has never brought ordinary life to a standstill. The nearest to this was during the 1974 Ulster Workers' Council strike, which was accompanied by the threat of force rather than actual violence, and gave Protestants a confidence in their capacity to resist imposition which has been a stabilising factor. Few areas of the province, and few families, have not been touched by the conflict, either through bombing or shooting, but spread over the period since 1969, the effect has not been intense. The troubled areas are well defined, particularly in Catholic Belfast and Derry, and are strictly no-go to those who have no reason to be in them. Even the steady withdrawal of troops, undeterred by sparodic outbreaks of violence, has not altered the balance.

City centre bombing in Belfast in the mid-seventies, widened the field of combat for a time, but the establishment of a security zone, and a military presence, restored confidence. From time to time the IRA has revived its old commercial bombing campaign on the edge of the gated area, to serve as a reminder of its military potential, but the offensive is rarely sustained, and the terror effect soon wears off. Outside these areas, and towns where there is an even sectarian balance, there is a surprising degree of normality, attributable only to the achievement of an acceptable level of violence. Members of the security forces, or ex-members, are special targets, constantly in danger of attack, but retaliation has been minimal from Protestant organisations which themselves do not identify with the forces of law and order. Only two developments could alter what is virtually a stalemate situation—a radical change in the British Government's attitude to the constitution of Northern Ireland, now based on the will of the majority, or an interruption of the flow of British subsidy, up to nearly £2,000 million a year by 1983, which has helped to repair the worst effects of the violence. As long as these are avoided, and each would play into the hands of the extremists, both communities have proved they can live with, and to an extent rely on, the paramilitary organizations in their midst.

9

Reformism and Sectarianism: The State of the Union after Civil Rights

Bill Rolston

Introduction: The Need for Reform

At the base of the Civil Rights struggle of the late 1960s were certain demands. The most vocal of these concerned the need to reform housing allocation and the franchise. Less to the fore, but no less important, were reformist demands concerning public employment, education and local government. These demands were postulated on a political assessment, often meticulously documented and articulated (cf. All-Party Anti-Partition Conference 1954; Jackson 1947; Gallagher 1957; Campaign for Social Justice in Northern Ireland 1969) of the Northern Ireland state, namely, that the Unionist government had no liking for nor commitment to reforming many of the most archaic and sectarian institutions and policies in the society. Many carried that assessment forward to the political conclusion that Northern Ireland was irreformable; but even those who did not share that conclusion (for example, Barritt and Carter 1962) were willing to admit that the Unionist government was not enamoured of a social-democratic style of administration such as was beginning to typify, for example, post-war Keynesian Britain. The fact that most of these latter commentators criticised Stormont, if at all, for its lack of economic reforms (cf. Isles and Cuthbert 1957; Wilson 1965; O'Dowd 1982) does not lessen the importance of the more general conclusion that reformism was not a significant element in the workings of Stormont. In that sense, someone like Brookeborough, Northern Ireland's longest-ruling Prime Minister, was anachronistic, believing in the mid-twentieth century what early American rebels of the late eighteenth century did, that that government is best which govern least.

Given such a philosophy, much of the power in decision-making and the allocation of resources was decentralised in Northern Ireland.

Local government was the key to the daily administration of the society, with its control of health, education, welfare, housing, public employment, etc. So, it is no coincidence that much of the Civil Rights flak was directed towards local government: demands for an end to gerrymandering, for 'one man, one vote', for a fair allocation of public housing, for a fair distribution of local government jobs, for the total restructuring of local government itself.

Some of these demands were conceded by the Unionist government of Terence O'Neill, but the struggle opened a Pandora's box and O'Neill and his cautious reformism were the first victims of the 'ills' which poured out. An interesting question, but not one on which there is time to dwell here, is that of attempting to ascertain what was the main vehicle of the break-up of Unionism which followed on the civil rights campaign. Some would see the Civil Rights demands themselves as the wedge which split the Unionist tree (Devlin 1969); others give pride of place to the entry of monopoly capital and the differing responses of Unionists to that penetration (McCann 1974; Probert 1978); still others see the power struggles within the Unionist camp itself as the major factor in explaining the splintering (Bew, Gibbon and Patterson 1979). Whichever emphasis one wishes to choose, there can be no denying that the Civil Rights campaign was a major worry to Unionists. The Unionist leader who would ignore the campaign risked contributing to its escalation; yet, to concede to any of the demands was to risk one's own position of Unionist leadership. The tight-rope task facing O'Neill—and Chichester-Clark and Faulkner following him—was to get the right balance of reform and repression, keeping the Civil Rights struggle from escalating while not antagonizing Unionists. None of the three Prime Ministers discovered the secret of that correct balance.

One element in their frustration was the increasing intervention of first the Labour government (cf. Callaghan 1973), and later the Tories, in Northern Ireland's affairs. British politicians saw nothing wrong with Northern Ireland that could not be cured by a good strong dose of the same social-democratic reformism that had emerged in post-War Britain. Reforms were 'imported' faster than any Unionist leader could or would have implemented them if the only pressure to reformism had been internal to the society. Ultimately this jeapordised the chances of any Unionist leader remaining in a leadership position, a fact which convinced the British to intervene even more decisively through Direct Rule in 1972.

From the British point of view it could be said that a unitary logic infused its enthusiastic commitment to the initial flurry of reform in Northern Ireland. Where administration was dogged by sectarian practices, the priority was to remove administration from that domain and ground it instead in rational British practice. The eradication of sectarianism was thus paramount, not only in the restructuring of old institutions which administered housing, education, etc., but also, and more obviously perhaps, in some new institutions, such as the Community Relations Commission (CRC) inaugurated to confront directly sectarian practices. Given that, the fact that a second and more substantial logic existed in the reform process was not initially apparent. This latter logic consisted of the importation into Northern Ireland administration of the newest prevailing management ideology and techniques already well on the way to being established in Britain itself. Throughout the 1960s local government management in Britain was transformed. Managers 'geared up to govern', as Cockburn (1977) puts it, changing their techniques to match the needs of late twentieth century capitalism. Now, the reforming of Northern Ireland may have meant the relative hobbling of local government, but there was no reason, according to this 'progressive' logic, why similar principles should not infuse the practices of whatever institutions took over those tasks in Northern Ireland which were carried out by local government in Britain. The rise of this new managerialism meant the demise of the initial reformist logic. Reforms were seen as necessary and efficient in themselves, rather than instituted in order to eradicate sectarianism. Of course, the technocratic logic as applied to Northern Ireland did rest on an assessment of sectarianism. Technocracy by definition is rational and therefore non-sectarian. The new managerialism was seen as linked in a see-saw manner with sectarian administration: the rise of one was the inevitable fall of the other. Of course, institutions would be necessary in the transition period to mop up the residual elements of sectarian practice, but in the long run technocracy needed no reformist institutions directly geared towards eradicating sectarianism.

So because of a number of factors—the persistence of the Civil Rights activists, the splintering of Unionism and the pressures exerted by the British—the years between 1968 and 1972 saw a number of major changes in Northern Ireland. Many of these were in the realms of emergency laws, and the growth of security personnel, technology and training (cf. *Belfast Bulletin* 1982)—what I will collectively call 're-pression'. But the 'reforming of repression' (cf. Tomlinson 1980a) will not be the concern of this chapter. (For a critical look at analyses of the growth of state power in Ireland, north and south, see Rolston and Tomlinson 1982). Instead, the concentration will be on those changes which can more easily be termed 'reforms'. In short, within the four years mentioned, the major demands of the Civil Rights struggle were conceded. Yet, by 1972 it was also apparent that such concessions had not served to lessen the escalation of violence. This has led some observers to declare with retrospective exasperation that the civil rights activists got what they wanted: what more can they want? Why did the violence increase? An obvious, but incomplete, reply would be that the reforms were too little, too late; such an answer does not of itself explain why the violence has continued for well over a decade; it postulates too direct a relationship between the original demands and violence. It also presumes that all the violence emanates from one source, namely, from Civil Rights activists and their successors. That presumption comes to the fore in some of the pieces of 'historical revisionism' now beginning to emerge which will be examined later in this chapter.

A more valuable starting point is not to ask why the violence did not stop once the reforms were instituted, but to seriously examine what it was that was 'won' in terms of reforms. What has been the substance in the establishment of the Northern Ireland Housing Executive, the institution of the CRC and the Fair Employment Agency, the reforming of local government, the establishment of non-elected Health and Social Services and Education and Library Boards? More fundamentally, in what way is Northern Ireland in 1983 a 'normal' social democratic reformist state? If it is such, does this mean that sectarianism has been eradicated? In short, how successful has been the union between contemporary capitalist reformism and traditional sectarian division in Northern Ireland?

At most some of these reforms have dealt with symptoms only and did not come near to touching the fundamental causes. Or, to use a geographical rather than a medical metaphor, they have operated at the level of the epicentres of trouble, but have been unable to penetrate to the structural faults underneath. Reformism and sectarianism can happily coexist; they are not mutually antagonistic. This means that not only have the reforms not necessarily eradicated sectarian division, but they have often reconstituted that division in new and often more pervasive ways than before. Reforms do not occur in the abstract. The process and consequences of introducing reforms in a social democracy are not the same as those which emerge when the same reforms are instituted in a society where sectarian class relations prevail.

Assessing the Reforms

In a sense, everything that has been written about Northern Ireland since Civil Rights days has touched in one way or another, inadvertently or otherwise, on the questions of reform and sectarianism. Yet, paradoxically, remarkably little has been written which directly tackles the relationship between reformism and sectarianism in the last decade.

In an attempt to establish some order out of the copious literature, it is perhaps useful to arrange what has been written into four categories, as follows:

1. Description

Description has been by far the most common approach to the recent past in Northern Ireland. Some pieces in this genre have been superficial, even opportunistic. At the other extreme have been substantial pieces of work. The rapid changes in politics, the decline of the economy, the social conditions and the policies of the state all require careful charting if any valid analysis is to be undertaken. Hence the value of many of the descriptive accounts.

Within this category, journalists' accounts predominate—from the daily copy of local journalists and those doing tours of duty on behalf of British media, through semi-autobiographical considerations of the problem of being a journalist in Northern Ireland (cf. Bell 1972; Hoggart 1973; Winchester 1974; Holland 1981) to substantive pieces of research which are indispensible in drawing an accurate picture of post-Civil Rights Northern Ireland. In the last category have been such books as the Sunday Times Insight Team's (1972) investigation of the origins of the Troubles and Robert Fisk's (1975) incisive account of the Ulster Workers' Council strike in 1974.

Some journalists have attempted to use their knowledge through a different medium, the novel, with varying degrees of success. The most critically acclaimed has been Kevin Dowling's *Interface Ireland* (1979). Even the least successful novel allows journalists to reveal in slightly disguised fiction what they could not otherwise state in factual reporting. There are limits to such revelations, however. Dowling's novel was withdrawn from circulation after a threatened suit from a politician less than enchanted by his fictional other self.

To an even greater degree than journalists, participants in the events of Northern Ireland during Civil Rights and after are in a unique position to give the 'inside story'. On the other hand, there are many obstacles preventing them going into print. Public figures, for example, may be constrained by law or protocol from revealing all. Moreover, the task of writing requires one to stand back at least momentarily from events, a feat for which not every participant has time or ability. Consequently, participants' accounts cover a wide spectrum as regards quality and accuracy. This has not prevented a substantial number of participants from taking the plunge, however. Civil Rights activists have written of their involvement, notably McCann (1974), Devlin (1969) and Farrell and McCullough (1974). Others have used their experience to more academic ends, such as Arthur (1974) in his account of People's Democracy. In contrast to the reticence of earlier politicians, recent politicians in Northern Ireland have been prepared to write either memoirs (O'Neill 1972; Faulkner 1978), or accounts of key events in their experience (Devlin 1975). The earlier reticence may have derived from an unwillingness to reveal the mechanisms of patronage in Northern Ireland. Those who would see a new-found willingness of politicians to write books as a sign of the death of patronage would do well to recall that there is much that remains unsaid, despite these autobiographical meanderings.

If that is true of politicians' accounts, it is even more so of civil servants' autobiographies. Sworn to secrecy all their working lives, civil servants in retirement are unable to reveal much about anything except themselves. Their accounts thus become perhaps the most idiosyncratic of all participants' accounts. The prime example here is the tale of the ex-head of the Civil Service at Stormont, John Oliver (1978). More useful, if not for titbits of government secrets, at least about the psychology of a Catholic top civil servant at Stormont, is Paddy Shea's (1981) story.

Some participants have heard the same siren call as some journalists, and been drawn onto the rocks of fiction, with perhaps even more disastrous results. Notable here is the novel of ex-Stormont Minister of Commerce Roy Bradford (1981), with its mixture of partial fact, fiction and sheer fantasy.

Like journalists and participants, many academic researchers have turned their attention to description. To categorise their work thus is not to belittle it, but is to stress that their over-riding task has been to describe accurately the present nature of Northern Ireland society, with fundamental theoretical analysis a secondary, even minor, element in their work. Much of this work has been crucial in unravelling the mysteries of present social policy (cf., for example, Birrell and Murie 1972 and 1980; Morrissey and Ditch 1979), and specifically of housing (Kennedy and Birrell 1978; Birrell, Hillyard, Murie and Roche 1971), poverty (Evason 1978 and 1980; Ditch and McWilliams 1982; Black *et al.* 1980), and others. To the best of my knowledge, no academic researcher has as yet turned to the novel form!

2. Fiction

The Troubles in Northern Ireland have provided the subject matter for a number of television plays, to take just one form of fiction, among them Stewart Parker's *Catch Penny Twist* (December 1977), Colin Welland's *Your Man From Six Counties* (BBC 1, October 1976), Caryl Churchill's *Willie: the Legion Hall Bombing* (BBC 1, August 1978; the script was based on the transcript of an actual trial), and Jennifer Johnston's *Shadows on Our Skin* (March 1980; originally a novel). In addition, the Troubles have found their way to varying degrees into television series, notably *Spearhead* and *The Professionals*. In some cases the violence of Northern Ireland has been the background (for example, in Graham Reid's *Too Late to Talk to Billy*), though in most cases it has been central. Such centrality seems to require most of the authors to distance themselves quickly from the violence and present a moral judgment through drama. In as far as the public nature of their art requires them to choose in the struggle between 'good' and 'evil', in this case between 'terrorism' and 'democracy', it could thus be suspected that these authors' opposition to violence is simultaneously an acceptance of reform in Northern Ireland. Be that as it may, reform and its institutions have not been a direct subject for any dramatic author.

The same conclusion may be drawn from a consideration of live drama within Northern Ireland that deals with the Troubles. Plays such as John Boyd's *The Flats,* Martin Lynch's *The Interrogation of Ambrose Fogarty,* etc., have concentrated on the violence of Northern Ireland, not the question of reformism. This is not to say, however, that the concern of many playwrights in Northern Ireland, in as far as they set out to condemn violence, is at base a reformist one.

Elliot, Murdock and Schlesinger (1981) point out that, despite a powerful constraint towards upholding dominant definitions in drama, fictional television allows some scope for 'oppositional' definitions.

As one example they cite David Leland's *Psy-Warriors* (BBC 1, May 1981), a play with very direct and critical conclusions about army inter-rogation techniques in Northern Ireland. Beyond that one example, it is possible to find a good deal of evidence to support their general con-clusion in television drama as a form of fiction. However, another form of fiction, the novel, would appear to be much more monolithic in its approach. Elsewhere I have noted that a spate of novels for teenagers about the Troubles focus on their heroes' need to escape from Belfast (Rolston 1978). In their inability to come to terms with violence, these heroes display qualities and moral conclusions more fitting to the novelist as outsider than to the insider in Northern Ireland. A remarkably similar conclusion has been reached by McMinn (1981) in his consideration of adult novels. Compared to the dramas, the opposi-tional assessment seems to have even less outlet in novels. The novels thus, even more emphatically than drama, confirm the superiority of 'good', and consequently can be seen as being on the side of reform in Northern Ireland, even though never directly taking up the question.

3. Analysis: Reformability versus Irreformability

Those who go beyond description usually divide quickly and clearly into two camps—those who argue that the Northern Ireland state is irreformable and those who argue the converse.

The first position is in many ways a logical successor to much of the civil rights literature. Some activists who held in the 1960s that Northern Ireland needed reforms also hoped that those reforms could be delivered. However, their delivery as part of a package which also included increased repression convinced many that the reforms were a sham. It was a relatively short step from this to the belief that even the sincerest reformer would have little chance in Northern Ireland, and the conclusion that Northern Ireland is irreformable. Other Civil Rights activists believed from the beginning that the state was beyond reforming and have found no reason to question that conclusion in the intervening years. Given these two roads to the same point, the irreformability thesis has been evident not only from an early stage in the Troubles (De Paor 1970), but also in most nationalist and repub-lican and some socialist literature since (McCann 1974; O'Hearn 1981; Revolutionary Communist Group 1978; Revolutionary Communist Tendency 1978). The strongest and most coherent statement of this position is in the work of Farrell (1976).

Similarly, there are old-guard and newly-arrived protagonists of reformability. There were those who held at the time when O'Neill was cautiously wooing sections of the Catholic bourgeoisie through reforms that Civil Rights demands were part of a republican plot against Ulster. (This conclusion was well caught by the few researchers who examined Protestant consciousness in the first half of the 1970s; cf. Nelson 1975 and 1979; Wright 1973). Recently, a second and more sophisticated variant of the position has appeared. The past need for reforms is conceded, but it is argued that these reforms have been established and Northern Ireland is to all intents and purposes a proper bourgeois democracy. If the reforms are not operating as fully or successfully as they might, that is due in large part to the continuing irredentist claims of reactionary nationalists and the Left republicans who tail-end them (Bew, Gibbon and Patterson 1979 and 1980; Morgan 1980). What is needed is to forget such 'side issues' (Devlin 1981) as the supposed 'outstanding national question' (as well as, for some, the supposed repression that is rife in Northern Ireland; cf. Byrne 1980, 43) and get on with the task of 'proper class politics' in Northern Ireland (Devlin 1981; Gibbon 1977).

It should be obvious that specific sets of politics follow from these contrary analytical positions. Without exploring the intricacies of each position, it is possible to typify them. The irreformability thesis has lead at various times to tactics such as armed struggle, mass action and abstentionism. The goal of socialist supporters of this position, as much as republicans, is the dissolution of the Northern Ireland state. The reformability thesis has at various points espoused trade union activity, community action and the provision of a 'viable socialist alternative' to voters. The socialist variant of the position may be summed up by stating that sections of the Left in Northern Ireland have taken to heart the admonition of Boserup (1972, 27):

> It needs to be recognised that the destruction of the Orange system and its replacement by the 'welfare state' of managerial capitalism is historically necessary and historically progressive.

4. Analysis: The Reproduction of Sectarian Class Relations

It is possible—and, as I have argued elsewhere with others (cf. O'Dowd, Rolston and Tomlinson 1980), necessary—to begin with neither of the above two positions. There are practical reasons for this, not least the fact that pro-reformists and anti-reformists can often spend much of their time pirouetting in a sort of moral pas-de-deux. In short, abandoning *a priori* positionalism is a necessary first step on the path to analysis. However, it is not of itself sufficient. It is also necessary to examine in close detail the actual effects of the operations of the British state in Northern Ireland in order to accurately answer the questions: How far are reforms merely superimposed on a society that remains basically as sectarian as ever? Have reforms meant a substantial dismantling of sectarianism?

One preliminary piece of definition is necessary. The word 'sectarianism' is not used in a narrow sense to connote merely a set of attitudes. It refers to a material reality, reconstructed and hence perpetuated in everyday life. If 'sectarianism' is taken in the narrow sense of a set of attitudes only, then it can refer to the attitudes of both the dominating and the dominated. But in a structural sense of the word, it can only be fully applied to the activities of the dominating. This approach to the analysis of sectarianism has respectable links with analyses of other ideologies, for example, racism (Downing 1981) and sexism (Barrett 1980). By analogy, if racism exists only at the level of attitudes, then blacks who hate whites can be said to be as racist as whites who hate blacks. Many state policies to supposedly counteract racism are built on that assessment. But, if racism is a phenomenon at the structural level, then it is only institutions and policies designed and managed by powerful whites that can properly be said to be racist in as far as they perpetuate the domination of blacks. In this sense, even those institutions and policies designed to counteract racist attitudes can themselves be racist.

Our analysis of the operations of the British state in Northern Ireland led us to conclude that there were many ways in which changes had occurred in Northern Ireland, especially since Direct Rule. Policies have changed, technocracy predominates, the rhetoric of fairness and impartiality prevails at governmental level, many laws have been updated, repression has been refined, and traditional class alignments have been disjointed to the point where, ten years after the imposition of Direct Rule, concrete and lasting realignments have not as yet emerged. In fact, it can be said that the last few years of Direct Rule have seen the struggle between, on the one hand, British politicians intent on a new class alliance of centre bourgeois parties on a non-sectarian basis, and on the other, Paisley of the Democratic Unionist Party and Molyneaux of the Official Unionist Party locked in what John Hume of the Social Democratic and Labour Party once neatly titled a 'virility contest' to determine who will be patriarch of 'the Unionist family'. In short, many things have changed in Northern Ireland.

However, the basic structures of Northern Ireland's inequality remain remarkably undented despite these changes. Not only does sectarianism remain—a phenomenon which could be explained in terms of past legacies, or residue—but also the combined actions of capital and the British state in Northern Ireland serve to reconstitute sectarianism in new ways. We have shown how this process operates as regards regional policy, housing, trade unions, community politics, local councils and repression. Hence the conclusion that 'the UK state is not "above" the NI problem, it is an integral part of that problem' (O'Dowd, Rolston and Tomlinson 1980, 208).

Some may partially accept that statement, seeing the state as being partly benign and partly malign. British repression may thus be seen as part of the problem, but British reformism as part of the solution. However, it must be stressed that both are actions of the same state, and, despite contradictions and anomalies within that state, must be seen as having an underlying unity of effect. Repression and reformism can happily coexist as twin elements of British technocracy in Northern Ireland.

Similarly, reformism and sectarianism can coexist. More, technocracy can reproduce sectarian division. To give two examples: one may devise the most rational procedures in which to guarantee the hiring of the best skilled manual person for a job, thus eradicating traditional forms of patronage. But, in a society where that skilled manual person is more likely to be Protestant, such rational procedures contribute to the perpetuation of inequality. Furthermore, capital has a tendency to go where capital is established, for reasons of proven profitability, existing infrastructure, etc. In Northern Ireland such areas are in the predominantly Protestant East of the Bann area. Thus, even in the absence of sectarian intentions or traditional patronage, the influx of capital can easily perpetuate sectarian division. Capitalism in Northern Ireland has simultaneously class and sectarian biases.

To be 'fair' in the midst of inequality is not enough. Politically, then, it is logical to argue for policies of reverse discrimination. This, however, is not an acceptable official logic within Northern Ireland. Technocracy is seen to be fair and non-sectarian by definition. Sectarianism is consequently seen as residual, requiring a 'mopping up' exercise by a few quite low-level institutions. It is on those institutions that I will focus in what follows. The assumption that technocracy reproduces sectarianism is taken as given, and the task at hand is to examine the successes and failures of these institutions in the light of that assumption.

Reforming Sectarianism

In 1969 the Community Relations Commission (CRC) was established to bring Catholics and Protestants together. Modelled on the similar CRC in Britain it was, however, placed under the wing of a completely new Ministry, the Ministry of Community Relations. The British CRC was under the Home Office, but placing the Northern Ireland CRC under the equivalent Ministry of Home Affairs would not have been politically wise. The CRC was put forward as a response to civil rights demands, although the establishment of such a body had never been mooted in civil rights circles. It would have been impossible to put it forward in such a manner if it had been placed in the same Ministry with that other area of responsibility which was under close scrutiny as a result of civil rights pressure, that is, the police. Other than overseeing the CRC, the Ministry of Community Relations' only reason for existence initially was the administration of Social Needs legislation, whereby money was distributed to areas of special social need.

The CRC instituted a community development programme, arguing that the surest way to bring about a deep-rooted meeting of the Catholic and Protestant working class was to encourage both to organise independently on issues of immediate local concern, such as redevelopment and motorways. The argument was that both would then see that the solution to such issues could not be at the local level alone and would come together to organise jointly on issues of common concern (Hayes 1971). Eventually this argument led the Commission's community development team to demand much greater autonomy and resources, a demand which the Ministry did not concede. Instead the Ministry built up its responsibilities and staff over time, until the point where Ivan Cooper, SDLP Minister of Community Relations in the 1974 power-sharing Executive, abolished the CRC, arguing that now the Catholic community, through the SDLP, had a stake in power, there was no need for an independent community relations body (cf. Rolston 1976 and 1978). The demise of the CRC resulted not merely from the empire-building moves of the Ministry and the consequent confrontation between it and the Commission, as Griffiths (1974) argues, but from the establishment of technocratic administration in Northern Ireland and the consequent British withdrawal from policies directly seeking to eradicate sectarianism (Rolston 1980). Only such an assessment can make sense of the fact that when Direct Rule was re-established later in 1974, the British not only confirmed the closure of the CRC, but disbanded the Ministry of Community Relations as well.

A similar retreat from the initial enthusiasm regarding direct attacks on sectarianism can be seen in the case of the Prevention of Incitement to Hatred Act (1970). Again modelled on similar British practice (the Race Relations Act 1965, from which Northern Ireland had initially been excluded at the request of the Stormont government), the law in Northern Ireland allowed for the prosecution of people for stirring up sectarian emotions. But such legislation operates in a most nebulous legal area. There are problems of assessing intentionality, of judging the effects of a statement or publication, of making links between causes and effects—all of which had led to extreme caution. Only one prosecution has ever occurred under the legislation, that of the late John McKeague and two other men for the publication of a book of Orange Loyalist Songs in 1971, and specifically for a song titled 'I was Born Under a Union Jack'. Sung to the tune of 'I Was Born Under a Wandering Star', the lyrics included the aphorism that the only good Catholic was one with a bullet in his back. The three men were acquitted. Those who have concluded in the years since that there have been many—including notable politicians—who might equally deservedly be charged under the Act might take consolation from the anomaly of British practice where an Act ostensibly to protect blacks from the racism of dominant white Britain has been used more often against black people than white (Dickey 1972).

One other institution which emerged from the early days of reform and which was initially inspired by the then dominant logic of eradicating sectarian administration was the Ombudsman. Initially there were two Ombudsmen, the Northern Ireland Commissioner for Complaints and the Parliamentary Commissioner for Administration (cf. Benn 1973). But for some years both posts have been held by the same person, who has thus had overall responsibility for investigating individual complaints of maladministration by local government, central government departments and public bodies. Although originally the Ombudsman saw his brief as subsuming complaints of religious discrimination, a more recent practice is to pass on most of these complaints to the Fair Employment Agency (FEA). The Ombudsman's task has been then the more mundane one of handling complaints of what might be termed non-sectarian maladministration, for example, where a person disagrees with the outcome of a planning decision of the Department of the Environment, or with the Department of Health and Social Services regarding social security payments. Of the 149 complaints against government departments received in 1980, 108 (72 per cent) concerned the above mentioned Departments. 109 cases were rejected as being outside the Ombudsman's jurisdiction, 4 were discontinued after partial investigation and 22 were still in progress at the end of the year. In short, investigations were completed in only 34 cases. In most of these cases no finding of maladministration was made. A less severe attrition rate emerged as regards complaints against local government and public bodies. In 1980 there were 593 complaints, the vast majority of which were against the Northern Ireland Housing Executive. 452 cases were investigated, but of these a judgment of maladministration was made in only 23 cases. (5 per cent). All in all, the Ombudsman's task is seen as that of safety net. The number of complaints each year is few, and the number of findings of maladministration miniscule. The Ombudsman's Annual Reports therefore bear testimony to the belief that technocracy is working rationally and efficiently.

Finally, mention needs to be made of the Standing Advisory Commission on Human Rights. Superficially this statutory body, set up in 1973 as a result of the Northern Ireland Constitution Act, seems to fit into the logic of a direct attack on sectarianism. In fact its *raison d'etre* is entirely different. The Commission's relevance from the British state's point of view is not internal to Northern Ireland. Its primary purpose is not that of pressure group to force the British government to be more concerned about human rights in Northern Ireland, no matter how much the commissioners themselves should judge that to be their task. Thus, the Commission's agonised deliberations on emergency legislation, its advice to government on divorce and gay rights legislation and its commitment to a Bill of Rights (cf. Standing Advisory Commission on Human Rights 1976; Campbell 1980) are of little immediate concern to British politicians and administrators. The value of the Commission is external. Faced with international concern and even opposition over its management of the Northern Ireland problem, especially in the midst of the H-Blocks crisis of 1981, and of its continual derogation from the European Convention for the Protection of Human Rights and Fundamental Freedoms (of which it is a signatory) in order to continually implement emergency legislation in Northern Ireland, Britain can point to the Commission as proof of its concern about human rights in Northern Ireland. The Commission's function becomes that of showpiece, or shield to deflect some international flak. As to the Commission's space to be a vital pressure group, Secretary of State Humphrey Atkins put the matter clearly in perspective at the annual renewal of the Emergency Provisions Act in Parliament in 1979; commenting on arguments such as those sometimes put forward by the Commission, he said:

> I am well aware that there is a contrary view: that, in fact, the temporary powers are an irritant rather than an emollient, tending to enhance the opposition to the forces of law and order, and to encourage disrespect for the law. I recognise that this is no frivolous argument . . . But the hard fact is that the powers which I asked the House to renew need to be available (NI Information Service, Press Release, 11.12.79).

The Possibilities of Reforming Sectarianism: the Case of the Fair Employment Agency

The FEA is the major reformist body in existence in 1983 whose task is to specifically counter sectarianism. It was established as a result of the Fair Employment (NI) Act 1976

> to promote equality of opportunity in employment and occupations between people of different religious beliefs . . . and to work for the elimination of religious and political discrimination in employment and occupations.

It was envisaged that the FEA's tasks would include the investigation of individual complaints of discrimination, the investigation of the practices of specific employers and organisations, the carrying out of research, and a cluster of tasks (such as holding conferences, running training courses) which might collectively be termed 'education'. In assessing the success of the FEA, it is essential to examine each of these functions.

Section 24 of the Act empowers the FEA to investigate individual allegations of discrimination. However, there are a number of problems involved in this task. Much as many crimes are not 'known to the police', many cases of discrimination never reach the point of beginning the perilous path through the legislative labyrinth, a fact which the FEA itself acknowledges (FEA 1979, 19). Furthermore, many individual complaints are not investigated, either because they fall outside the FEA's jurisdiction, or because there is not enough evidence to warrant investigation. If a *prima facie* case is thought to exist, evidence is collected by conciliation officers (documentary evidence, or verbal evidence, the latter taken under oath) in order that the officers can make a report to a sub-committee of the FEA. It is the whole Agency itself which finally judges whether a case of 'unlawful discrimination' has occurred.

The sheer quantity of hurdles involved means that many complaints do not last the course. In addition are qualitative problems: how is one to judge whether discrimination has occurred or not, or if there was a religious or political motive in the victimisation of the complainant? It would seem that, on the basis of experience, the FEA has come up with a number of rules of thumb. For example, if the person actually appointed was of the same religion as the complainant, it is unlikely that a finding of discrimination will be made (cf. case number 8; FEA 1979, 47). On the other hand, the non-appointment of a candidate for possibly unfair, but not discriminatory (as defined), reasons is not judged as discrimination (cf. case number 3; FEA 1979, 39). Lastly, even the initial declaration of the employer that the reason for not hiring the candidate was his/her religion will not necessarily lead to a judgment of discrimination if the employer later claims that this was an excuse to cover up more fundamental reasons for not hiring the candidate (cf. case number 10; FEA 1979, 52).

While conceeding the difficulty of ascertaining intentional bias in such cases, McCrudden (1982) in his confidential examination of the FEA, is severely critical of such rules of thumb.

> I recommend there should be increasing reliance on making inferences of discrimination on the basis of 'harder' evidence of this (statistical) type, and a decreasing reliance on intuitive judgment based on the 'feel' of a case (McCrudden 1982, 20).

The overall effect of relying on such rules of thumb seems to be that the benefit of doubt is given to the respondent rather than the complainant. This may be due in great part to the backgrounds of the Agency members themselves, middle-of-the-road political types, businessmen, trade unionists, etc., all of them government-appointed, and most of them appointed on the basis of their respectibility . Such people are undoubtedly inclined to move in the same ideological and political (not to mention social) space as many of the respondents with whom they deal. There is thus an inbuilt tendency for them to behave in a rational manner with the respondents, seeking to solve difficulties in a 'gentlemanly' manner, rather than to use the might of their quasi-legal muscle on behalf of the complainants. (For allegations of one notable case of caution and pro-respondent bias, cf. McConnell 1978).

As a result of these quantitative and qualitative factors, very few findings of 'unlawful discrimination' have been made by the FEA, as table 9:1 shows.

Table 9:1

COMPLAINTS ON WHICH DECISIONS HAVE BEEN TAKEN BY THE FEA, 1 APRIL 1977 TO 31 MARCH 1982

(Source FEA Annual Reports)

	Discrimination	No Discrimination
Government Departments	0	24
Local Authorities	6	9
Education and Library Boards	0	16
Health and Social Services Board	2	15
Other Public Bodies	0	14
Food, Drink and Tobacco Industry	1	12
Chemical and Allied Industries	0	2
Engineering Industries	0	13
Textiles and Clothing	1	8
Manufacturing Industries	1	6
Construction Industry	2	6
Transport	0	2
Distributive Trades	0	9
Other businesses	0	8
Total	13	144

Even a finding of discrimination is not the end of the matter. The FEA's finding has the force of law, requiring the respondent to compensate the complainant. An appeal against a finding of discrimination thus goes through the Courts. In the Courts, four of the FEA's first six findings of discrimination were overturned. Disagreeing with their very first finding of discrimination against the Northern Ireland Civil Service Commission, Judge Topping concluded that the FEA,

> probably convinced that this attitude was expected of it, appears to have gone to considerable lengths to reach a finding that unlawful discrimination had taken place (FEA 1979, 35-5).

Furthermore, although respondents found 'guilty' of discrimination may be required to pay compensation, they frequently do not, thus requiring the FEA to bring *them* to court for the money. As a result, only one of the cases where a finding of discrimination has been upheld has to date led to compensation in the complainant's hand.

In short, the investigation of individual complaints is a costly task in terms of both time involved and in finances. Only a Department of Manpower Services concession whereby legal costs above and beyond the FEA's budget are met by the Department prevents the FEA reaching the point already reached by the Equal Opportunities Commission of finding that the cost of considering individual complaints has left little by way of finances to engage in other tasks.

Section 12 of the Act empowers the FEA to investigate specific employers or industries to ascertain the religious composition of their workforces. This task can be thwarted by employers' reluctance to cooperate, often justified in quite plausible terms. The most notorious case of a formal investigation being blocked is that of the Civil Service investigation, where opposition to FEA 'snooping' reached to the highest level, to Ministers of State themselves (cf. Moloney 1979). It is telling that, faced with such lofty opposition, the Agency did not use its full legal weight to win the compliance of a Department of a government supposedly committed to supporting equality of opportunity unreservedly, but sought to smooth matters over in a conciliatory manner.

Even if an investigation is completed, further criticisms can be made. Some of the more publicly contentious investigations have been noted, even summarized, in FEA Annual Reports (for example, the Civil Service investigations in FEA 1981, and Cookstown and part of the Engineering investigation in FEA 1982). But six years into the life of the Agency, only one of the investigations has been published, that into the Northern Ireland Electricity Service (FEA 1982b). But, for detailed information about Cookstown and Civil Service investigations, one has had to rely on well-informed press coverage. The same holds true for the cluster of individual investigations which comprise the FEA's formal investigation of the engineering industry: Ford Motor Co., Davidson & Co. (Sirocco), James Mackie, Short Brothers, Harland & Wolff, Standard Telephone and Cables, Hughes Tool Co., Hugh J. Scott and Co., Tilley Lamp Co., Grundig and Strathearn Audio. It is of paramount important to note the findings of these investigations, for they constitute the little evidence there is (outside of the FEA's own research reports) to enable one to judge whether sectarian division in employment persists. In the case of the Northern Ireland Electricity Service, the evidence is damning:

> It is evident that the numbers of management staff who could be classified as Roman Catholic were very small both at the highest level and perhaps more surprisingly at the next most important levels . . .

(This) coupled with a promotion policy which gives first preference to in-house candidates must result in a very slow rate of change in the higher echelons of management from a pattern which may have initially been influenced by prejudice. (NI Electricity Service investigation, paragraphs 6.1 and 6.4).

Similarly, in the case of the engineering industry:

In all the companies visited the predominance of Protestants in the craftsmen engineering trades confirmed the census figures. In two companies it was not disputed that the skilled fitters and similar tradesmen (in both cases, workforces of three figure strength were involved) employed almost certainly did not include a Catholic. If there were any Catholics, one employer told the Agency, they would be 'sleepers'. (Engineering Investigation and Report, 3).

Given these conclusions and the FEA's reluctance to publish them, it is evident that the potential for public debate on the question of continuing discrimination in employment in Northern Ireland is lessened by the self-imposed secrecy of the FEA.

What is the purpose of these formal investigations in the view of the FEA? It would seem that they are regarded as an element in their task of gently pressuring employers to mend their ways. In other words, they are not seen in the first place as a contribution to public debate. Their target audience is not the public, but the employers investigated, and the investigations thus become part of the refined and 'gentlemanly' discourse between employers and Agency members. They could be much more than that. Just as they sometimes grow out of individual complaints against the firm or sector investigated, a further link could be made between investigation and research. However, that link is not made, leaving the FEA's researchers to rely on already published statistics, such information as may be made available by government departments, and information gathered by the researchers, for example, through questionnaires. The non-publication of formal investigation findings is thus one factor contributing to a strong tendency towards narrow empiricism and a frequent lack of imagination as regards both the scope and the methods of the research conducted. At the same time some of the reports (cf. FEA 1978a; Miller 1978; Osborne and Murray 1978; Miller 1979; Cormack, Osborne and Thompson 1980; Murray and Darby 1980) have helped to lift the debate on discrimination above the most simple level of direct one-to-one intentional bias to that of structures within employment, and by extension education, which reproduce sectarian division.

The difficulty, however, is imagining what the FEA might do to operationalize this latter understanding of inequality in its daily work. There is, in short, a major disjunction between the logic of the Research Reports and the exigencies of the FEA's daily casework task, the latter looking for evidence of direct one-to-one bias. This is a point to which I will return in the final section of this chapter.

The only other major task pursued by the FEA is that of having employers sign a Declaration of Principle and Intent, thus supposedly committing themselves to the pursuit of fair employment. But signing the Declaration does not necessarily mean one is actually or even potentially a fair employer. In the absence of any link between the Declaration and any of the Agency's other tasks, especially its right to conduct formal investigations, the Declaration becomes innocuous. No candidate seeking to sign is subject to investigation to see if the firm does in fact practice fair employment. Conversely, Shorts for years refused to sign. When the firm eventually got around to signing, the FEA permitted it to do so, even though its own formal investigation of the firm revealed a massive inbuilt sectarian imbalance in the firm's workforce. Only a total failure to link the various elements of its strategy could account for the fact that when it came to acquiring a printer to print their *Guide to Manpower Policy and Practice,* they did not choose a firm which was a signatory to their Declaration of Principle and Intent! Recently the FEA has made much of a government policy change which the Agency has been advocating for some time. From 1982

> the government have decided that tenders for government contracts will not normally be accepted from firms . . . unless they hold an equal opportunity employer certificate issued by the Fair Employment Agency following the signing of the statutory declaration of principle and intent (Mr John Patten, House of Commons, 10.12.81.)

One can confidently expect a rush of firms to sign the Declaration, including firms which have consistently refused to do so in the past. But, will such a rush prove that these firms are in fact any less discriminatory, or that their workforces are likely to be any more balanced than at present?

Instead of linking tactics the FEA has been content to pursue the more nebulous strategy of 'educating' employers. It has compiled (as instructed under the Act, Section 5), a *Guide to Manpower Policy and Practice;* but few employers have gone out of their way to implement the recommendations of the Guide (cf. FEA 1981, 7). The FEA has increasingly involved itself in advice services and training sessions for employers.

But these are puny weapons indeed with which to fight structural inequality. They all exist in the grey area of cajolery and appeals to employers' consciences. In addition, it is not improbable that increased dialogue with employers will enhance the chances of Agency members also being 'educated' into 'seeing the employers's point of view' and 'not stepping on the toes' of someone providing precious jobs.

It is often said of organizations such as the FEA that they lack teeth. But this is not true of the FEA. As a quasi-legal body with the force of law to back it up, it has some potentially formidable weapons. That it does not use them, or use them enough, is at least partially its fault. Unable to deal with structural inequality, it concentrates on individual grievances. Unwilling to force, it is reduced to cajolery and gentlemanly persuasion. Knowing that changing attitudes is not enough, it does not pursue any other consistent strategy than attempting to change attitudes. As McCrudden (1982, 36) concludes:

> The experience of the legal enforcement of the Fair Employment Act, thus far, is a depressing picture of a massive task, of the possibility of change, but of an Agency which failed to meet that challenge. A complete overhauling of the FEA is necessary . . . It is by no means certain that the Act will then prove successful. What *is* clear, however, is that without such changes the ideals which the Act was meant to achieve stand little chance of success.

The Politics of Reform

> The FEA is a baby which should have been strangled at birth. (Mrs. Dorothy Dunlop, Belfast City Council; cited in *Belfast Telegraph,* 26.4.77).

> The sooner they are Thatcherized, the better. (Mr. Paddy Newell, Belfast businessman; cited in *Belfast Telegraph* 16.12.80).

The FEA, no less than the other reformist institutions which have existed to directly counter sectarianism, does not exist in a vacuum. It is not possible to comment on its potential or actual success in isolation from the fact that there is a politics of reform in Northern Ireland. Within that politics the FEA has few adamant supporters. Reformists have tended to accept the dominant characterization of the task of such bodies as the FEA as residual, namely, mopping up the remaining vestiges of sectarianism. Given that, they have concentrated their support (sometimes critical, sometimes not) on the supposedly non-sectarian technocratic bodies such as the Northern Ireland Housing

Executive. On the other hand, the FEA has had its opponents. For example, the Northern Ireland Chamber of Commerce and Industry opposes the FEA from a base of local bourgeois conservatism; in an oddly non-sectarian sort of way they are opposed to *all* reformist bodies.

> In our view the Equal Opportunities Commission and the FEA have not had a useful effect on industrial relations. The EOC has experienced internal dissension; its existence has stimulated female workers to take action against their employers, while the FEA is considered by many to have operated to the detriment of business. (Memorandum to Adam Butler, Minister of State, February 1981).

But the most vocal of the FEA's opponents have been loyalists of various shades. Loyalist councillors in 1977 led a sustained attack on the FEA's Declaration of Principle and Intent. As a result few of Northern Ireland's 26 District Councils signed. Various reasons were voiced for this refusal: Councillor Jack McKee of Larne, having publicly torn up the Declaration, stated the most commonly articulated objection to signing.

> To sign the Act would only give credence to the old republican propaganda cries about '50 years of misrule' which are proven unfounded (cited in *East Antrim Times,* 4.2.77).

The opposition, in short, is to the very existence of the FEA itself. That existence is seen as a

> capitulation by the British government to a minority of people in Northern Ireland who have clamoured for certain things to put them in a place of privilege above the majority (Councillor George Willey of Craigavon Council, 8.2.77).

The policy that follows is therefore one of non-cooperation and a call for the disbandment of the Agency altogether.

Inconsistently, loyalist politicians seem to have at times sought the best of both worlds, dismissing the FEA while demanding that it also investigate discrimination against Protestants. For example, Martin Smyth, head of the Orange Order and MP for South Belfast, called for the FEA's disbandment on the ground that it has been kept busy doing virtually nothing at enormous cost (cited in *Belfast Telegraph,* 16.2.80). Later in the same speech he went on to demand that the FEA investigate recruitment to the health service, where, he alleged, discrimination against Protestants was rife.

Loyalist opposition to the FEA, and indeed any similar reformist body, has from time to time received a fillip from an apparently unusual source, namely, from academics. In 1980 Paul Compton singled out the FEA's research reports for criticism. They had all failed, he claimed, to include one vital factor in their quantification of inequality, the relationship between religion and fertility. The persistence of Catholic disadvantage therefore should not be attributed to discrimination (as is argued by the FEA), but 'in considerable part to the structure of the Roman Catholic community itself' (Compton 1980; cf. also his elaboration of these arguments in Compton 1981; cf. also the reply to the original piece by Osborne and Miller 1980). There is much in this argument that is reminiscent of traditional loyalist disclaimers of discrimination, and indeed of a standard right-wing dismissal of the poor. More specifically, the approach rightly rejects a concentration solely on 'discrimination', but equally narrowly judges the Catholic community apart from all the other elements in Northern Irish society. Compton sees a 'structural' approach as a counter to the inadequacy of relying on the concept of 'discrimination', but reduces his concept to refer to certain demographic characteristics of the Catholic community. A truly structural approach must see the interconnection of many factors in the reproduction of sectarianism, of which sectarian intentions and Catholic behaviour patterns are but two.

Similar criticisms of reductionism and narrowness of definition can be made of what might be described as the recent historical revisionist approach to the civil rights struggle. Although the academics here do not consider the FEA as such, their conclusions have repercussions for an assessment of contemporary reformism in general and institutions formed to combat sectarianism in particular. Hewitt has concluded as follows:

> Supposedly the civil rights demonstrators wanted reforms. Yet the violence was not reduced in the slightest by a 'one man one vote' franchise, the redrawing of local council boundaries, a massive housebuilding programme and an allocation system for housing that favoured Catholics. There are two reasons for this: first since the old system was not particularly inequitable, reforms could not have much impact, second the nationalists who predominated in the movement were not really interested in reforms (Hewitt 1981, 377).

Despite its concentration on history, Hewitt's piece is really a statement about the present, as the above quotation reveals. Yet he produces no evidence for his conclusions about the present effectiveness and impartiality of reforms. His evidence for the supposed absence of discrimination in the past is presented, but it is weak. For example, he argues that many Protestants were disenfranchised by the lack of 'one man, one vote', and that gerrymandering was less widespread than civil rights activists maintained. In short, democracy was more alive and well than 'nationalist mythology' would have it. But, in concluding that he fails to investigate the ways in which democracy—that is, majority rule—in a sectarian setting has sectarian effects and leads to the perpetuation of sectarian division in ways not captured by quantification.

In fact, it is to the most dubious of statistical methods that he turns in order to prove his corollary conclusion, that Catholics were not interested in reform. For example, one piece of 'evidence' is that Catholics in the 1960s consistently voted 'nationalist', a category which is obtained only by subsuming every party for which Catholics could reasonably vote, with the exception of the Northern Ireland Labour Party, under one undifferentiated label. Similar reductionism is required in his pursuit of an 'objective' measure of the relationship between 'nationalism' and violence.

Much more sophisticted, but no less revisionist, is Whyte's reassessment of the civil rights campaign with the benefits of hindsight. He examines allegations of discrimination in six areas under the Unionist government. His conclusion is that those allegations have differing degrees of merit, allowing him to rank the levels of discrimination in descending order as follows: electoral practices, public employment, security, private employment, public housing and regional policy (Whyte 1981, 40). But even the amount of discrimination in the area of electoral practice is less than is normally suggested. Hence,

> the most serious charge against the Unionist government is not that it was directly guilty of widespread discrimination, but that it failed to restrain a portion of its followers who were. By that failure, it provoked the reaction which eventually brought the whole Unionist regime crashing down (Whyte 1981, 41).

The argument is clear, but its major flaw is in the narrowness of the definition of 'discrimination'. It is a concept most often used in an intentional sense; that was how it was used by Civil Rights activists. Taking that same usage, Whyte concludes that there was less 'discrimination' than was believed at the time.

In the light of arguments put forward earlier in this chapter, it can be said briefly that the major flaw in Whyte's analysis is in his unarticulated, but operational, definition of the concept 'discrimination'. He defines it in intentional, even conscious, terms, thus not only ignoring the ways in which apparently non-sectarian actions can have sectarian effects, but also failing to move beyond the level of interaction to a consideration of structural inequality and disadvantage. For example, he concludes at one point that 'the Housing Trust has generally been exonerated of all *conscious desire* to discriminate' (Whyte 1981, 26; my italics.) Yet it is entirely possible to prove that at least two 'rational' policies of the Housing Trust—that is, allocating houses to more 'responsible' tenants, and building estates near new factories for skilled workers—had, given the sectarian balance of skill and wealth in Northern Ireland, markedly sectarian consequences, even in the absence of intentional bias (cf. Tomlinson 1980b, 123-131).

To return to the FEA, academic arguments such as the above indirectly and in some cases inadvertently add fuel to opposition to the Agency. However, it must be stressed that the FEA's greatest antagonists need no such rational arguments to assure them that the Agency should not exist. In the face of all this opposition, then, it should not be surprising that FEA members are easily tempted to proceed with caution. Their fears are real, not imaginary. The problem is, however, that their caution lends support to their opponents. In short, by hobbling themselves FEA members play into the hands of those who seek to hobble it. One example will perhaps portray the weakness of the FEA's response to criticism. The Reverend Martin Smyth, in the speech already cited, called for the FEA's dissolution on financial grounds; the Agency cost £80,000 per annum to run, he said, with next to nothing to show in terms of results. In reply Bob Cooper, Chairperson of the FEA, could have pointed out that the task of delivering equal opportunity for Catholics and Protestants in Northern Ireland could not be fulfilled at the mere cost of £80,000 per annum. Instead he argued that the original estimates for the FEA were for 40 staff and a budget of £280,000. He went on:

> In fact, the FEA is now costing £80,000 a year and has a staff of 12. I challenge Mr. Smyth to name any organisation which costs such a small fraction of the cost ancitipated. (cited in *Belfast Telegraph*, 16.2.80).

But surely this is winning a battle only to lose the war. In effect the Chairperson is boasting about the FEA's weakness, and in doing so is giving credence to Smyth's claim that the Agency has no real purpose.

Compare this to the comments of Christopher McCrudden to the effect that if the FEA is to being to be serious about its task it must at very least use its original budget to the full (McCrudden 1982, 16). For

McCrudden the FEA's failure to do so is one sign of its overall failure to work at full capacity. Hence he urges a commitment on the FEA's part to 'affirmative action' for fair employment. He hastens to add (McCrudden 1982, 29) that he is not advocating 'positive discrimination'. In stating this, he is recognising the fact that the FEA is bound, not only specifically by the Act, but also, apparently, by the ideology of the Department of Manpower Services-appointed Agency members themselves, to a position of staunch opposition to any notion of 'positive', 'reverse', or 'benign discrimination'—that is, it will not countenance the countering of structural inequality by a policy of hiring people on the basis of their religious background. In fact, one of the successful FEA findings of unlawful discrimination was in the case of Newry and Mourne District Council, which hired a Protestant for its sports staff because it had no Protestants thus employed. Finding for the Catholic refused a job, the FEA concluded that 'it is wrong that an individual should suffer because of possible prejudice in favour of his or her section of the community in the past' (FEA 1980, 61). It is true that Bob Cooper did at one point seem to come close to arguing for a form of positive discrimination, namely, a system of quotas in employment. Although there are 'substantial moral objections' to such an approach, he said, 'if we are unable to deal with this major social problem, then the argument for quotas will surface very strongly indeed' (Cooper 1979, 6). But as he does not seem to have returned to the suggestion publicly at any later date, it would seem that he was doing no more than flying a kite briefly. Those with experience of attempts at positive discrimination as regards black people and women in the U.S. would surely argue that such a strategy is by no means an instant panacea. The point regarding Northern Ireland is that it is a strategy ruled out in advance.

The paradox is that McCrudden's notion of 'affirmative action' sounds remarkably close to a policy of positive discrimination. He argues that the FEA must work towards the point that in the future employment patterns in Northern Ireland more or less reflect the sectarian balance in the wider society. Such a policy would require taking on, not only those who have a conscious stake in continued sectarian imbalance, but also the technocratic institutions themselves. It is imperative to spell out what 'taking on technocracy' in the pursuit of fair employment would in fact mean. The problem is not just that technocrats are not amenable to formal democratic influence. This is an argument with which even the Right can easily agree. In doing so they can even appropriate the rhetoric of their political rivals, as when loyalist councillor Esmond Thompson of Maghera claimed that the present powerless local councils were merely a facade for British colonial rule in Northern Ireland (cited in *Belfast Bulletin* 1981, 33).

Nor does the problem of technocracy derive only from the fact that technocracy is not amenable to popular pressure, for all that this is probably true. O'Dowd and Tomlinson (1980) have illustrated the confrontation between popular pressure groups and planners on the issues of housing and urban motorways in Belfast (as regards motorways, cf. also Community Groups Action Committee 1980), and have shown that, despite the verbal commitment to democracy through the medium of public inquiries, the processes whereby technocrats arrive at their decisions are remarkably impervious to popular pressure. More studies of this sort are required, not least because they illustrate that for all their opposition to technocrats on the grounds of formal democracy, the Right is often in no doubt as to where it stands when the choice must be made between supporting technocratic versus popular control of decision-making.

'Taking on technocracy' must rest on the realization that technocracy enables the reconstitution of sectarian imbalance in Northern Ireland. Given that, the task of the FEA is far from residual, but entails a full-frontal attack on the structures within Northern Ireland. 'Affirmative action' in practice requires confronting not only loyalist patronage, but also the logic of technocracy. Three predictions can be made about such a strategy: Firstly, on the basis of the past practice of Agency members, there is no possibility of such a militant strategy being pursued by the FEA. Secondly, this strategy would lead to an incredible amount of opposition from both loyalists and technocrats, such as would make the FEA's previous encounters with Martin Smyth and Ministers of State pale into insignificance. On the positive side, it should be added that as the FEA is going to experience opposition anyway, it might as well do something to earn that opposition. Thirdly, while it is highly unlikely that such a strategy would be pursued, or, if pursued, be successful, any success could be expected to contribute to destabilisation, for it would practically call into question the whole logic at the basis of British management of Northern Ireland in the past decade. Whether the British state could weather such a criticism of its management, in other words, the extent to which such a policy of positive discrimination would in fact be destabilizing, is, if not a hypothetical question, at least one too massive to be answered here.

Reformism is not the counter to sectarianism. A real strategy for elimination of sectarianism would quickly lead to a confrontation with reformism. For this reason it is far-fetched to imagine the British state sponsoring such a strategy. It has not even been able to sponsor such a strategy as regards racism on its home front. Peter Newsam, Chairperson of the Commission for Racial Equality in Britain, recognized this fact, and was thus implicitly criticizing his employer, the state, when he said, 'the real problem, after all, is with the white community. If it wasn't, we wouldn't have a problem' (cited in *Guardian* 17.1.82.). The relationship between the FEA and the British state in Northern Ireland, between reformism and the elimination of sectarianism, is perhaps illustrated in no better way than imagining the unlikely: what would be the consequences of an equivalent statement emanating from the Chairperson of Northern Ireland's FEA?

10

The Logistics of Enquiry:
A Guide for Researchers
John Darby

There has never been a shortage of myths about the Irish conflict, and the renewed demand for information since 1969 has added to the total. Some of them are based on an element of truth. During the early 1970s, for example, the evening cluster of visiting reporters in the bar of the Europa hotel in Belfast did lend some support to the popular view that its bar provided a more frequent source of news stories than the dangerous streets outside; since then, of course, this picture has been embroidered by apocryphal stories of gullible reporters and mickey-taking Irishmen. Gullibility was also a characteristic of some academics. Few locally-based researchers in Northern Ireland during the early 1970s can have avoided meeting carpetbagging American researchers, in transit to Cyprus, the Lebanon or other troubled spots, who were visiting Ulster for a fortnight to collect data for a comparative analysis of community conflict. Most departed, disappointed.

The research scene has changed considerably since those heady days when Northern Ireland, for a brief and unaccustomed few years, was academically fashionable for conflict research. While the rate of publications may have diminished slightly, their substance has improved. A body of theory, as distinct from polemic, has emerged; more empirical studies have been carried out, and more time has been spent on them; the province's academic institutions have become more concerned with the problems, and better equipped to tackle them. At every level, from undergraduate dissertation to major research project, a more serious approach has been adopted to the conflict.

At all these levels remains the problem of where a research investigation might be started. In this chapter, despite the risks in providing a tourists' guide to the Northern Irish conflict, the more modest aim is to consider what information is available to serious researchers, whether undergraduates or established academics, and to suggest possible starting points for their inquiries.

Basic References: Registers, Bibliographies and Chronologies

The preliminary information required by social scientists varies little between different settings. What research is being carried out, and by whom? Has it been published, and when? Is it possible to establish reliably when particular events took place? Until the early 1970s these questions could not be answered without considerable inconvenience. However, as the amount of social research increases, so do the research tools required to carry it out.

Two registers of research dealing exclusively with the Irish conflict have been published since the current violence began in 1969 (Darby 1972; Darby, Dodge and Hepburn 1981). Apart from providing information about individual researchers and their projects, they allow comparison between the strengths and weaknesses of conflict research at the two dates. Registers of a more general nature are produced by public bodies north and south of the Irish border—by the Policy, Planning and Research Unit at the Department of Finance in Northern Ireland, and by the Economic and Social Research Institute in Dublin; both deal with social and economic research, and the latter includes details of research being conducted in all Irish institutions. At a more specialized level, four registers of research on educational themes have been published by the Northern Ireland Council for Educational Research, which are unusual in that they include undergraduate dissertations. Equally specialised is the register of 71 projects into mental illness (Roche and Williamson 1977). However, most specialised projects are also described in the *Register of Social and Economic Research on Northern Ireland* sponsored by the SSRC (Darby *et al* 1983).

Research registers are primarily concerned with the present and the future, and are designed to inform researchers or other scholars working in similar fields. To find out what books, pamphlets, articles and ephemera have been printed in the past, one must go to the numerous bibliographies on the conflict. These are essentially parasitic publications, each one absorbing its predecessors, so some earlier bibliographies now have only limited value (Rose 1972; Deutsch 1975; Darby 1976). The two most comprehensive bibliographies of Irish materials have been published by the Library Association in London, and both contain many references to the conflict: Eager's *Guide to Irish Bibliographical Material* contains more than 9,000 entries, and Shannon's *Modern Ireland* has more than 5,000 (Eager 1980; Shannon 1982). Rather more accessible, if less complete, is *A Bibliography of the United Kingdom* (Pollock and McAllister 1980). The difficult task of collating all social and economic references to Northern Ireland since 1945, and making them available in computer readable form, is being attempted by a group of social scientists in Belfast, but its completion date is uncertain.

Most bibliographers include details of some unpublished theses, and the few conflict-related ones written before 1968 are detailed in *Theses Related to Ireland* (Institute of Irish Studies 1968). Undergraduate dissertations are more difficult to track down, and require visits to individual departments; this is occasionally worth the journey.

The review pages of all Irish newspapers are characterized by instinct rather than method, and they are uncertain guides to new publications. Two specialist publications are more thorough: *Irish Booklore* which is printed irregularly in Belfast, and *Books Ireland,* a monthly review printed in Dublin since 1976.

Chronologies, especially of events since 1969, are included in many of the more general books on the conflict. Most of these may be waived by serious students in favour of more detailed chronologies. In particular, the three volumes of *Northern Ireland: A Chronology of Events* (Deutsch and Magowan 1973-5) cover the period 1968 to 1974 on a daily basis. These are carefully researched, have excellent indices and appendices, and are indispensible for more modern investigations. For events during the previous half century, Richard Mansbach's 1973 chronology may be consulted. The post-1974 period causes greater difficulties, but the most useful references are the annual chronologies printed in *Hibernia* until its closure in 1980, and in the *Irish Times;* these are produced at the turn of each year. *Northern Ireland: A Political Directory 1968-79* also contains a chronology for the period, as well as useful reference material (Flackes 1980), and at least three general books on terrorism include chronological references to Northern Ireland (Sobel 1979, Vols. 1 and 2; Micholus 1980).

Official Publications

The quantity of information published by official bodies often seems to have an inverse relationship to its usefulness. Certainly there is no shortage of government publications. A cyclostyled paper compiled by the Policy, Planning and Research Unit at the Department of Finance, *Northern Ireland Sources for Social and Economic Research* (PPRU 1981) details 58 separate themes, each with up to sixteen references. Guidance is needed through this mountain of paper, and some is supplied by the Stationery Office catalogues (HMSO Occasional) and by a useful breviate of Northern Ireland government publications (Maltby 1974).

Some of the more general publications contain sufficient information to provide a statistical backcloth. The *Ulster Year Book* and *Facts at Your Fingertips* are general descriptions of broad social and economic trends, and may be supplemented by other regular publications such as *Social and Economic Trends in Northern Ireland,* the *Annual Abstract of Statistics (Northern Ireland)* and the *Digest of Statistics (Northern Ireland).* Command papers published by both Westminster and Stormont are usually more analytical examinations of specific issues, and a number of them are directly concerned with the conflict. The Northern Ireland *Census of Population* is also published every decade, but only in the form of secondary analyses by counties, religion, etc.; for more interpretive examinations it is necessary to look to academic researchers, and the 1971 census, for example, has been broken down by geographical distribution (Compton 1976) and by occupations (Aunger 1975). The Registrar-General, at his discretion, may provide more detailed tables.

Many government departments also issue their own publications. The Department of Education, for example, issues annually two volumes of *Northern Ireland Education Statistics,* which contain information on many aspects of the school population, with the notable and characteristic omission of their religions. The monthly analysis of unemployment statistics produced by the Department of Manpower Services also has interest for social scientists. Social and economic research conducted from within the civil service is mainly the responsibility of the Policy, Planning and Research unit at the Department of Finance, and from 1983 it began the publication of some of its own—mainly internal—research papers. It welcomes visits by serious researchers.

Annual reports from a number of public bodies contain relevant material. These include the Royal Ulster Constabulary, the Northern Ireland Housing Trust and, later, Housing Executive, the Community Relations Commission (until 1974), the Fair Employment Agency, the Northern Ireland Commissioner for Complaints and Parliamentary Commissioner, and the Standing Commission on Human Rights.

Local government is less well served by published reports. Financial returns are printed, and minutes of meetings of the 26 District councils are available for consultation. So are annual reports of the Health and Social Services Boards, and the Education and Library Boards, which took over some of the main functions of local authorities in 1973. However, apart from a chapter in the annual financial report of the

Department of the Environment, no synthesis of local government data is provided officially. Birrell has examined, by means of a survey, how councillors and their work were effected by the 1973 reorganization (Birrell 1981), and McAllister has carried out a study of councillors belonging to the Alliance party (McAllister 1977). Beyond these, very little is available.

History

For the Irish, according to ATQ Stewart, 'all history is applied history' (Stewart 1977, 16), unconsciously underlining the importance of its study for social scientists. The marked increase in the number of general histories since the 1960s, however, has not made it any easier to prepare a selective bibliography for the general reader. The specialist, on the other hand, has a number of historiographies as convenient starting points. J. Carty's two earlier *Bibliographies of Irish History* (1936 and 1940) deal with the period 1870-1921, while E. Johnston's *Bibliography of Irish History* (1969) includes more modern references. Joseph Lee's *Irish Historiography 1970-79* (1981) is a sequel to *Irish Historiography 1936-70* (Moody 1971); and an annual bibliography entitled 'Writings on Irish History', previously printed in *Irish Historical Studies,* is now available on microfiche by the Irish Committee of Historical Sciences. Closer to ground level is a checklist of books and articles on local history in Northern Ireland (City of Belfast Public Libraries 1972).

These may be augmented by general books of historical reference. Hickey and Doherty's *Dictionary of Irish History since 1800* (1980) is a substantial research aid, and the *Atlas of Irish History* (R. Dudley Edwards 1981) adds a geographical perspective. Recently, too, collections of historical documents have become more accessible: the Northern Ireland Public Record Office, for example, have published a series of Educational Facsimiles—collections of documents on such themes as the 1798 Rebellion and the Famine, with brief introductions—which have an obvious educational function. The violence in Northern Ireland during the 1970s has also led to the publication of extracts from conflict-related papers. Hepburn's *Conflict of Nationality in Modern Ireland* (1980) and Magee's *Northern Ireland: Crisis and Conflict* (1974) both help to place the violence within an historical context, while a collection of documents on the Ulster Troubles by Carlton (1977) was printed in the United States. European interest in the conflict is affirmed by the publication of no less than three separate collections of documents in German (Vogt 1972; Schilling 1972; Hermle 1976).

Any advice for the general reader is inevitably more subjective. Books by Beckett (1952 and 1966) and Lyons (1971) are standard references, and the Gill series on Irish history maintains a good standard. On the more detailed history of Northern Ireland, a wide range of interpretations have recently become available: Buckland (1979) and Stewart (1977) adopt traditional forms of historical analysis, while Farrell (1976) and Bew, Gibbon and Patterson (1979) approach the issue from different Marxist interpretations. Shearman has written one of the few histories which is strongly sympathetic to the Unionist administrations in Stormont (1971).

Access to primary data is obviously more difficult for the historian. Depending on the subject under study, a visit to the Public Record Offices in Belfast or Dublin will almost certainly be necessary. Under the 1867 Public Record (Ireland) Act, the holdings in many Irish repositories were centralised in Dublin, and annual reports were printed between 1869 and 1921. On June 30 1922 the main record repository in the Four Courts building was destroyed by bomb and fire as the Irish Civil war began. Fortunately indexes and catalogues were saved, and many records have subsequently been copied and are now available for consultation in Dublin.

The Public Record Office of Northern Ireland (PRONI) was set up in 1924, and attempted to replace some of the materials relating to Northern Ireland which had been destroyed in the fire. For many years PRONI's most valuable holdings were the private collections which it obtained through purchase or donation. Since the early 1970s, however, records of many of the old local authorities have been deposited, and the Office has become responsible for the records of the Northern Ireland Government, which were previously unavailable. Access to the latter is restricted to files which are more than 30 years old, although some earlier government material is also withheld from public scrutiny. In some cases this amounts to a serious obstruction to research. PRONI is generally well-regarded by researchers, and has excellent facilities and staff in Belfast.

Newspapers and Periodicals,

Newspapers and periodicals are the starting point for most social reporters, and for some the complete race. It is appropriate, therefore, to consider the value of the media for researchers. To some extent this depends upon whether they are interested in the events reported in the newspapers, or in the way the media report them. There has been a growing research interest in the treatment of Northern Ireland by the British press, and one major analysis of newspaper coverage (Elliott 1977). Those wishing to look at the coverage of the violence by Northern Ireland's three daily newspapers will find a terrain which has been largely uncharted. However readership figures are available for all the main publications read in the province (Research Services Limited 1970), and some interesting subjective descriptions of the local press have been written (see, for example, Firth 1971 and Winchester 1974).

The use of newspapers as a source of information on events in Northern Ireland since 1969 is complicated by their variety. Within the province, the *Belfast Telegraph,* which crosses the sectarian barriers, has a larger readership than that of the two daily morning newspapers, which do not; for purposes of record it is the most useful local newspaper. All three Dublin morning newspapers have offices in Belfast, but only the *Irish Times* has consistently devoted much space to events in Northern Ireland, and some of its reporting has been excellent. British media coverage has been very inconsistent: the interest of the popular press declined as the violence became repetitious, leaving the field to more serious newspapers. The *Observer* and *Times* have taken a close interest in the issue, and the *Sunday Times* has conducted useful, if occasionally flashy, investigations. The most consistent and reliable British coverage has undoubtedly been supplied by the *Guardian.*

Periodicals in Ireland have always struggled to keep their heads above the ground financially, but two are essential references for researchers. *Fortnight,* produced regularly in Belfast between 1970 and 1976, and thereafter with a fitfulness which belies its name, provides an important commentary on events, adopting a liberal stance. The Dublin magazine *Hibernia,* if more unreliable on details, performed a similar function from a republican perspective until its closure in 1980. Occasionally major investigations concerning Northern Ireland have been carried out by *Magill,* which is produced in Dublin.

A strangely underused, and very valuable, source of information are the underground and political newspapers which flourished especially in the early 1970s. These were produced by a wide variety of loyalist, republican, socialist and community organisations in an almost equally wide variety of formats. Some lasted only for a few issues; others have been published regularly for decades—notably the *United Irishman* since 1931; a few transmogrified with bewildering rapidity, closing down to reemerge under another name and format. Fortunately tracks through this complicated minefield have been charted by a number of librarians: the Northern Ireland branch of the Library Association published a catalogue of *Northern Ireland Newspapers 1737-1979* (Adams 1980), with details of where copies can be located. Small-format political papers are not included in this catalogue, but some of the more important of these have been described elsewhere (Gracey and Howard 1971; Howard 1972; *Sunday News* 1981). The most useful guide to alternative newspapers and periodicals, with brief descriptions, was compiled by the Belfast Workers Research group (*Belfast Bulletin* Spring 1979).

It is not possible to consult all these newspapers and periodicals under a single roof. Belfast's Central Library has the fullest collection, but other libraries also have some, and a small number of libraries also have partial collections of political newspapers. Nowhere in Northern Ireland is it possible to examine the back files of British popular newspapers, even in the Belfast offices of these newspapers; for this thankless task it is necessary to visit the British Library newspaper archives at Colindale in London. There are also microfilm copies of, among others, the *Irish Times, Belfast Newsletter, Guardian, Sunday Times, Observer* and London *Times*. Most important, the Linenhall Library in Belfast has produced microfiche copies of political newspapers for the years 1973-75, under the general categories of republican press, loyalist press and socialist press. These include some of the most extreme political expressions to be found in any newspapers, and are a valuable research tool.

Ephemeral and Audio-visual Materials

The production of political newspapers is not the only literary accompaniment to periods of violence and instability. Pamphlets, broadsheets, campaign buttons, posters, graffiti, songs and poetry—these are the ephemera of unrest. They share the qualities of being essential for anyone interested in political and social attitudes, and extraordinarily elusive. By their very nature ephemeral materials are intended to have an immediate impact, and have a short life. Retrospective collection is notoriously difficult, so there is a particular debt to those institutions which had sufficient prescience to build up contemporary collections.

By far the most important of these is the Linenhall Library, which has been operating in some form since 1792. Its Irish collection of historical publications is excellent, and many of these were the ephemera of earlier periods of violence. It was natural, therefore, for the Linenhall to begin a new collection during the Civil Rights campaigns of the mid-1960s. The real strength naturally lies in its Northern Irish ephemera, although Southern material is also well represented. Unfortunately the library's endemic financial problems has prevented the cataloguing of most of the material.

There are other ephemeral collections within Northern Ireland's libraries, although none to compare with the Linenhall's. The Central Library in Belfast started its ephemeral collection in 1977, relying on purchasing existing materials, and is particularly strong on papers relating to the People's Democracy. Its holdings, described in the Library's own *Guide to the Irish and Local Studies department* (1976), include 88 indexed cuttings books from local newspapers since the turn of the century, and an expanding photographic archive. There is also a small uncatalogued collection in the Ulster Museum. Outside Belfast, the New University of Ulster begn assembling ephemera in 1980, and purchased an important collection for 1968 to 1974, which has subsequently been augmented by other purchases and donations; an Archive committee, jointly initiated by the Centre for the Study of Conflict and the University Library, is beginning to build on these holdings. There is also a small, recently catalogued, collection of materials, mainly relating to Londonderry, at NUU's Magee University College campus. The Library of Queen's University Belfast also has a well catalogued collection, which includes a number of foreign items.

In the Irish Republic the largest archive is housed in Trinity College Dublin which, as a copyright deposit library, includes much of the relevant material printed in Britain. Its holdings of Dublin-produced ephemera are also good, although its collection of materials produced north of the border is less comprehensive. The National Library in Dublin also holds some relevant publications.

An increasing demand for audio-visual materials has been largely unsatisfied. Propaganda films aimed at public opinion in Europe and North America have been produced both by the Provisional IRA and by the British government. Television and radio, however, constitute the great bulk of material. On television alone, and not counting news broadcasts, 162 programmes wholly or primarily devoted to Northern Ireland have been identified between 1968 and 1978 (*Belfast Bulletin* 1979). It is not easy to secure access to these programmes. BBC news bulletins on national television, which include items on Northern Ireland, may be consulted in the British Film Archive in London, but programmes produced in Northern Ireland are not normally available to researchers. Nevertheless, exceptions have been made in the past. Apart from these sources, the History Film and Sound Archive at the New University of Ulster includes some valuable sound and visual records.

Politics and Religion

Two of Northern Ireland's political parties—the Official Unionists and the Social Democratic and Labour Party—have been the subjects of books (Harbinson 1973; McAllister 1977); the others await their Boswells. In the meantime, the most useful introductions to the issues and personalities in Northern Irish politics are W. D. Flackes' *Political Directory* (1980) and Rose and McAllister's *United Kingdom Facts* (1982), and there are biographical notes in Farrell (1976) and Harbinson (1973).

The mutations which most Northern Irish political parties have undergone since 1969 are reflected most clearly in the literature which they produce themselves. Curiously, until recently neither of the main unionist parties—the Official Unionist and Democratic Unionist parties—had a regular publication, relying respectively on duplicated local newsheets and on the *Protestant Telegraph* (circulation 7,000), which in fact closely reflected DUP political views; In 1982 both launched new newspapers, the Official Unionist *Unionist '82* (10,000 monthly) and the DUP *Voice of Ulster* (10,000), which replaced the *Protestant Telegraph*. Other parties became conscious of the need for publicity earlier. The Ulster Defence Association has had a monthly magazine since 1972, and recent issues of *Ulster* (13,000) make it possible to examine the process by which the UDA decided to become involved in elections. The largest of the political newspapers, *An Phoblacht* (circulation 44,000) is produced weekly by Sinn Fein and circulates widely outside Northern Ireland. However the Social Democratic and Labour Party has had a much more unsettled history: the *Social Democrat* was printed for a time in the 1970s but by 1982 had been replaced by the twice yearly *SDLP News* (13,000). Straddling the sectarian fence is *Alliance* (formerly *Alliance Bulletin*) which has been produced since the Alliance party was formed in 1971; in 1982 7,000 copies were printed each month.

In addition to these regular publications, most of the parties produce other literature, especially during election campaigns. More to the point, it is now at least theoretically possible to contact most party offices by telephone, an improvement since 1969.

A number of other bodies with a direct concern about the prevalence of violence also produce publications. The Peace People produce *Peace by Peace* (2,000 monthly), and publications have also been issued by Protestant and Catholic Encounter (*Pace Journal*), the Quakers and the Corrymeela Community. *Dawn* (2,000), an Irish journal of non-violence, is produced in Belfast, and issue 38-39 has a description of Irish peace groups since the 1930s.

Clearly the churches also have an interest here, but have published little. *Violence in Ireland* was written by a joint group on social questions, which was appointed by the Catholic hierarchy and the Irish Council of Churches in an attempt to find a cross-confessional approach to community violence. Apart from this, the Catholic church has been responsible for very few publications, though some papers, especially on peace education, have been issued by the Irish Council of Churches. The best guide to publications by the main churches may be found in the bibliography of *Christians in Ulster* (Gallagher and Worrall 1982).

Public Opinion: Elections and Surveys

With three tiers of elected bodies for most of its existence—Westminster, Stormont, and local councils—Northern Ireland is potentially a psephologist's paradise. The reality is different. While it is relatively easy to find the election returns for the twelve Westminster seats, it has been necessary until recently to assemble the results from other elections from unreliable newspaper reports. This problem has been partly resolved by the publication of *Northern Ireland Parliamentary Election Results* (Elliott 1973), a meticulous summary of election results for the Stormont parliament from 1921 until its prorogation in March 1972.

The political controversies of the 1970s rekindled academic and political interest in elections, and some of the more significant elections during this period have been the subject of specific studies: the 1969 Stormont election which saw the eclipse of the old Nationalist party and the emergence of Paisleyism was examined by Boal and Buchanan (1969) for its demographic implications; the 1973 Assembly elections were analysed by both Knight (1974) and Lawrence *et al* (1975), while Knight (1975) and McAllister (1975) published papers on the elections to the 1975 Constitutional Convention. Northern Ireland's first elections to the European parliament, when the entire province comprised the constituency, were described in a book by Elliott (1980). Nor has the activity been confined to academics. The Ulster Unionist party published two papers in 1975, on the 1973 Assembly elections and the 1974 Westminster elections, and on the 1975 Convention elections. The poverty of election studies of the 1960s has been replaced by almost an embarrassment of riches.

Local election returns pose the greatest problems of all, although Elliott has monitored the elections of 1977 and 1981. In most other cases researchers must go to the newspapers for the raw material on local elections.

It is equally difficult to secure access to the raw data from academic and private public opinion surveys, or even to their published results. In only a few cases have findings been published in sufficient detail to allow a proper assessment of methodology, or permit replication. Of these the most important is Rose's 1969 survey (1971), which has also been the basis for follow-up research by Moxon–Browne and others. Other academic surveys have never been fully analysed, and some not even published. A similarly unsatisfactory situation applies to the surveys and polls which have been conducted for the *Belfast Telegraph*, *Fortnight* and other newspapers.

There is no central depository for such data in Northern Ireland, although the Centre for the Study of Public Policy in Strathclyde keeps a file of public opinion data. John Coakley has built up an archive at the National Institute for Higher Education in Limerick but, with the exception of the Eurobarometer surveys, the survey data there relates exclusively to the Irish Republic. The Social Science Research Council archive at the University of Essex contains relevant materials, but it is necessary to examine its periodic Bulletins to find them. Clearly expense is the main obstacle to establishing and maintaining a data archive for Northern Ireland, which would include both academic research data and the raw material from commercial surveys. Its absence is a major problem which is only likely to be resolved by co-operation between funding bodies and all the institutions of higher education in the province.

Quantifying the Violence

The level of violence since 1969 is undoubtedly the main reason for the subsequent avalanche of research and publications on Northern Ireland, so there has been a constant demand for reliable information on its effects. Such information as is available comes from a variety of primary and secondary sources, but virtually none of them has been accepted universally as indisputable.

Most basic information on the course of the violence comes from the Royal Ulster Constabulary. The Chief Constable's report, published annually since 1970, has an appendix on terrorist crimes, which records, among other statistics, the number of murders, explosions and security incidents. For a more detailed breakdown it is necessary to consult the security statistics which are issued each month by the RUC Press Office.

Beyond these published data, the RUC Press Office occasionally provides additional facilities to what it describes as 'the serious academic researcher who is pursuing a reasonably "benign" thesis'.* Each request is judged on an *ad hoc* basis.

The closeness of the 'information' and 'propaganda' roles implied in this quotation is inevitable during periods of violence, and is equally evident in the activities of the Army Information Office. The importance of this office as a course of information to the press is well illustrated in the observation of Simon Hoggart from the *Guardian*:

> When the British press prints an account of an incident as if it were an established fact, and it is clear that the reporter himself is not on the spot, it is a 99 per cent certainty that it is the army's version that is being given. (Hoggart 1973).

Although security statistics are available from the Army Information Office, they are regarded as 'principally for the use of the press'.* This may help explain why so little of the information has been used by researchers. One exception, however, perhaps explained by the 'benign thesis' assessment, are the four volumes on the British army in Ulster by David Barzilay (1973-81).

A major limitation in the official data is their lack of detail. Although the RUC statistics identify general categories of victims, for example, they do not discriminate between different groups of civilian casualties. Consequently it is not possible from the statistics to analyse the 2,000 plus deaths since 1969 on the basis of religion, or to discover which groups of individuals were responsible for them. Analyses of this sort have been carried out, however, mainly from newspaper files and personal research: Dillon and Lehane tried to explain the patterns of violence and the reasons behind them by classifying the deaths caused by the IRA, Protestant paramilitaries and the British army (Dillon and Lehane 1974). McKeown also examined the groups responsible for fatalities, and the backgrounds of the victims themselves—discovering, for example, that 62 per cent of the casualties who could be classified accurately were 'civilian noncombatants'; he also provides interesting insights into the problems involved in this type of research (McKeown 1977).

The wide variations in the incidence of violence between different regions of Northern Ireland are often underestimated by commentators and researchers. Darby and Williamson (1978) attempted to demon-

* Correspondence with the author, April 27 and April 15 1982.

strate the special distribution of different types of violence by extracting all recorded incidents during an arbitrary sample period for each year from 1969 to 1975; during these periods 72 per cent of deaths and 91 per cent of injuries resulting from civil disorder took place in Belfast or Londonderry. A more systematic study of Schellenberg (1977) further substantiated the uneven pattern of violence in the province.

Some bases for comparing the violence of the 1970s with earlier outbreaks is possible from official reports. A number of Parliamentary papers published since 1969 include data on the civil disturbances. The Cameron report (1969), for example, considered evidence of the long-term and immediate causes of the violence, and the published reports of the Scarman (1972) and Widgery (1972) Tribunals are also important. Transcripts of the evidence taken by the Scarman Tribunal are also available in the Province's two university libraries. These reports, and the newspaper debates accompanying them, provide some basis for comparison with earlier riot reports, notably those into the 1857 and 1866 Belfast riots. The nineteenth century reports include evidence on intimidation and enforced population movement, subjects which have been examined in closer detail during the more recent disturbances (Darby and Morris 1974; Boal, Murray and Poole 1976).

No previous riots have lasted as long as the post-1969 violence. One effect of this is that the violence itself, and its effects, has become a subject for study while still going on. The economic cost of such sustained destruction, a highly difficult research task, has been attempted by Davies and McGurnaghan (1975) and by Rowthorn (1981). The effects of violence on Northern Ireland's social institutions—education, health and social welfare services, policing, housing and community action—was the subject of a book by Darby and Williamson (1978). The papers in the book illustrate the extent to which private research was necessary to fill the gaps left by official statistics, and how many gaps still remain.

Centres for Conflict Study in Ireland

Study of the Irish conflict has been greatly boosted by recent developments within Northern Ireland's two universities. The Centre for the Study of Conflict at the New University of Ulster in Coleraine was formed in 1977, and became a formal part of the university's structure in 1980. Its activities include the development and maintenance of a resource collection on the conflict, the publication of research papers, conferences and seminars. It also provides facilities for visiting researchers, who may apply for honorary fellowships at the Centre. The Centre's emphasis is on comparative and cross-disciplinary research, and there are regular meetings within the university of those involved in conflict studies.

The Institute of Irish Studies at Queen's University Belfast has been in operation since 1970, and offers fellowships to visiting academics. Its interests include Irish literature, langue, history and other branches of Irish studies, including conflict studies.

In the Irish Republic, the School of Irish Studies in Dublin was formed in 1969. While it provides courses in Irish literature, history and culture for students from abroad, it functions mainly at undergraduate and graduate levels, and is not primarily concerned with conflict studies.

Outside Ireland

There has been an extensive, if fluctuating, interest in the Northern Irish conflict outside Ireland—educationalists interested in its segregated school system, churchmen in the apparently denominational basis of the conflict, students of violence and its effects, medical researchers examining the emergency procedures and surgical techniques in its hospitals. Of 151 research projects on the conflict detailed in 1981 (Darby, Dodge and Hepburn), 23 per cent were being carried out in Britain, and 7 per cent outside the British Isles. The findings of many of these researchers are often unknown or ignored in Ireland.

In Britain there are recognisable centres of interest in the conflict, sometimes encouraged by the work of individual researchers. The School of Peace Studies at Bradford University has long had Irish connections, and published *Contemporary Irish Studies* in 1983. Many of the *Studies in Public Policy,* produced from the Centre for the Study of Public Policy at the University of Strathclyde, reflect Richard Rose's interest in Northern Ireland and its politics; the Centre itself maintains a bibliography of United Kingdom politics and a life of machine-readable surveys about public opinion in Northern Ireland. The Centre for Mass Communications Research in Leicester has also initiated research into the media and the conflict (Elliott 1977).

North American interest in Irish matters is more traditional. The American Committee for Irish Studies produces a regular newsheet for its members which contains book reviews, and has also commissioned an important *Guide to Irish Studies in the United States* (Murphy 1978). Its annual conference, and that of the Canadian Committee for Irish

Studies, often includes papers on Northern Ireland, but really demonstrate that the predominant American interest in Ireland is literary or historical. *Eire-Ireland,* the quarterly publication of the Irish American Cultural Institute in St. Paul Minnesota, also has a literary bias, but has published papers on the conflict. A substantial number of American colleges and universities have developed links with Irish universities, and some have built up collections of Irish materials. Most of these are on the east coast, but there is also an interest in Ulster-Scots studies in the Carolinas, and Stanford University in California has an Irish collection. As a general observation, there is no recognisable centre on the conflict in North America, but quite a substantial amount of individual research.

Outside North America, most foreign research on Northern Ireland has come from Europe. The level of interest in Germany between 1969 and 1976 is reflected in the publication of three collections of documents in German, and in the devotion of an entire issue of *Das Parlament,* the German parliamentary paper, to the theme (August 11, 1973). The Dutch churches have supported research into the conflict, and this concern has been maintained. In France, the Centre d'etudes et de recherches irlandaises at the University of Lille is an important centre of study and, though its main focus is literary, there have been articles on the conflict by Richard Deutsch and Pierre Joannon in its journal *Etudes Irlandaises.* Other centres of interest are Rennes and Caen. The Centre d'etudes irlandaises at the Sorbonne has become increasingly concerned with Northern Ireland, and publishes papers on this and related themes. Indeed French academic interest in the conflict shows distinct signs of revival in the 1980s.

Problems of Co-ordination

If the two published Registers of Research into the Irish conflict are accurate reflections of research activity, they record an increase in the number of projects from 92 in 1972 to 153 in 1981. During that decade basic data have become more readily available to researchers; a body of reference has been built up; the growth of interest both inside Northern Ireland and elsewhere is reflected in a variety of associations, centres, study groups and other forms of research collaboration; more subjectively, the depth of scholarship has also improved. These improvements have brought with them both challenges and opportunities. In effect a relatively simple set of primary problems has been replaced by more complex and potentially more serious ones. In 1969 the key obstacle to the pursuit of research was shortage of information; by 1983 the obstacles had become those of co-ordination.

1. Co-ordination of Data

One of the most encouraging changes in conflict research during the 1970s has been the growing recognition of how important it is to collect ephemeral materials at the time of their production, and make them available to researchers. The lone furrow ploughed by the Linenhall library for so many years has become the model for other institutions, some of them developing particular specialisms. For political and social scientists, however, the difficulty of securing access to public opinion data is a continuing frustration. Sidney Elliott's work on election results and the Strathclyde collection of survey data have improved matters, but the need for a data archive to include material from commercial and academic surveys becomes greater as the number of surveys increases. The two major obstacles to the establishment of such an archive are lack of finance, and inter-disciplinary and inter-institutional suspicion. These can only be overcome by an initiative which co-ordinates the interests of the institutions of higher education, libraries and other interested bodies, to establish and maintain a depository for public opinion materials, and to make them readily accessible to researchers. It is an initiative which could only be introduced by a major funding body or, better still, a combination of funding bodies.

2. Co-ordination of Researchers

The passage of time has also underlined the need for more effective co-ordination between researchers in Northern Ireland and those from outside the province. The latter group constituted 38 per cent of the research projects described in the 1981 Register, and there are signs of a growing schism between them and local researchers. The effects of the low level of co-ordination are different for the two parties: for those outside Northern Ireland who are interested in its conflict, the main difficulties are finding out who is doing related research, and how to get access to data; local researchers, on the other hand, are often ignorant of the extent and nature of foreign study. The point may be illustrated by comparing the references in articles and books on the two sides of the Atlantic: publications in Northern Ireland are usually dominated by local references, while in American publications references typically include the more standard Irish references, but also lean heavily on the American literature. Indeed the chauvinism is multilateral rather than bilateral. Apart from the core sources, French researchers rely as exclusively on French references as the American ones do on their own. The danger, therefore, is that a series of independent reference islands will continue to drift apart, each sharing the same agreed set of central references, but ignoring the more specialist work in the other islands. This issue has become more serious as interest in the conflict has grown outside Northern Ireland. Co-ordination between the different parties can only be organised effectively by the institutions within Northern Ireland itself, and the time appears to be right for such an initiative.

3. Co-ordination between Research and Policy

Mutual suspicion between policy-makers and independent researchers is both inevitable and healthy. It is rooted in the intrinsic secrecy of the former and the intrinsic scepticism of the latter. Whatever the justification, the effect has been an unwillingness by policy-makers to trust external research, and a relative failure by researchers to provide decision makers with directions for their policy. Of course this is too sweeping a judgment, but it has more than a grain of truth in relation to conflict research. Equally true, however, is the fact that some researchers, whatever their ideological view of the conflict and the value they place on their own independence, have an important contribution to make in the field of policy. One example is the research which has been carried out into the enforced population movements during the early years of the Troubles, which has important implications for housing and educational planning, as well as monitoring the major demographic changes in some parts of the province. Another is the research into segregated schooling: whatever their views on the issue of integration, almost every serious researcher in the field has reached the conclusion that it is not realisable in the short term; if this is accepted, the question of how relationships between the two separate school systems might be improved then becomes a researchable issue, and one where policy-makers and researchers might usefully find some degree of common ground. Many similar examples might be cited. For them to materialise, some avenue between research and policy-making must be constructed. Of the three forms of co-ordination detailed in this conclusion, this is likely to be the most difficult.

I would like to record my gratitude to the individuals and organizations who provided information about their resources and activities. My particular thanks are due to Stephen Gregory, Tony Hepburn and John Whyte for their advice and suggestions.

Bibliography

Ackroyd, C., Margolis, K., Rosenhead, J. and Shallice, T., *The Technology of Political Control*, London, Penguin, 1977.

Adams, J. R. R., *Northern Ireland Newspapers*, Library Association, N.I. Branch, N.D.

Akenson, D. H., *Education and Enmity: The Control of Schooling in Northern Ireland 1920–50*, London, David & Charles, 1973.

Alcorn, D., 'Who Plans Belfast?' *Scope*, 52, 4–6, 1982.

All Party Anti-Partition Conference, *Discrimination: A Study in Injustice to a Minority*, Dublin, 1954.

Amnesty International, *Report of an Amnesty International Mission to Northern Ireland*, London, Amnesty International, 1978.

Amnesty International, *Report of an Inquiry into Allegations of Ill-treatment in Northern Ireland*. London, Amnesty International, 1975.

Amnesty International, *Report on Torture*. London, Duckworth, 1975.

Annual Abstract of Statistics, London, H.M.S.O.

Arthur, P., *The People's Democracy*, Belfast, Blackstaff, 1974.

Arthur, P., *The Government and Politics of Northern Ireland*, London, Longman, 1980.

Association for Legal Justice, *Torture—The Record of British Brutality in Ireland*, Belfast, ALJ, 1971.

Aunger, E. A., 'Religion and Occupational Class in Northern Ireland', *Economic and Social Review*, 7, 1, 1975.

Baker, S. E., 'Orange and Green: Belfast, 1832–1912' in Dyos, H. J. and Wolff, M., (eds.), *The Victorian city: images and realities*, London, Routledge and Kegan Paul, 1973, 789–814.

Banton, M. P., 'Minority', in G. D. Mitchell (ed.), *A New Dictionary of Sociology*, Routledge and Kegan Paul, London, 1979.

Barrett, M. *Women's Oppression Today*, London, Verso, 1980.

Barritt, D. P. and Carter, C. F., *The Northern Ireland Problem: A Study in Community Relations*, Oxford, Oxford University Press, 1962.

Barrow, J., *Tour Round Ireland*, London, John Murray, 1836.

Barzilay, D., *The British Army in Ulster* (4 Volumes), Belfast, Century Services, 1973–81.

Bax, Mart, *Harpstrings and Confessions*, Assen, Netherlands. Van Gorcum, 1976.

Beckett, J. C. and Glasscock, R. (eds.), *Belfast: The Origin and Growth of an Industrial City*, London, BBC, 1967.

Beckett, J. C., *A Short History of Ireland*, London, 1952.

Beckett, J. C., *The Making of Modern Ireland*, London, Faber, 1966.

Beckett, J. C., *The Ulster Debate*, London, The Bodley Head, 1972.

Belfast Bulletin, 9, 'Still Crazy After all These Years: A Look at the Unionist Local Councils', Belfast, Workers' Research Unit, 1981, 24–33.

Belfast Bulletin, 10, 'Rough Justice: The Law in Northern Ireland', Belfast Workers' Research Unit, 1982.

Belfast Central Library, *Guide to Irish & Local Studies Department*, B.C.L., 1970.

Bell, J., 'Relations of Mutual Aid Between Ulster Farmers', *Ulster Folklike*, 24, 1978, 48–58.

Bell, M., 'Views', *The Listener*, 6 January 1972.

Benn, J. *A Commissioner's Complaint*, New University of Ulster, Coleraine, 1973.

Bennett Committee, *Report of the Committee of Inquiry into Police Interrogation Procedures in Northern Ireland*, Cmnd. 7497, London, HMSO, 1979.

Bew, P. and Norton C., 'The Unionist State and the Outdoor Relief Riots of 1932', *Economic and Social Review*, 10, 3, 1979, 255–65.

Bew, P., Gibbon, P. and Patterson, H., *The State in Northern Ireland*, Manchester, Manchester University Press, 1979.

Bew, P., Gibbon, P. and Patterson, H., 'Some Aspects of Nationalism and Socialism in Ireland, 1968–1978', in Morgan, A. and Purdie, B. (eds.) 1980, 152–171.

Birrell, W. D., Hillyard, P. A. R., Murie, A. S. and Roche, D. J. D., *Housing in Northern Ireland*, London, Centre for Environmental Studies, 1971.

Birrell, W. D. and Murie, A. S., 'Social Policy in Northern Ireland', in Jones, K., (ed.), *The Year Book of Social Policy in Britain*, London, Routledge and Kegan Paul, 1972, 134–155.

Birrell, W. D. and Murie, A. S., *Policy and Government in Northern Ireland: Lessons of Devolution*, Dublin, Gill and Macmillan, 1980.

Black Committee, *Report of the Working Party for Northern Ireland: The Handling of Complaints against the Police*, Cmnd. 6475, Belfast, HMSO, 1976.

Black Review Group, *Report of the Children and Young Persons Review Group*, Belfast, HMSO, 1979.

Black, B., Ditch, J., Morrissey, M. and Steele, R., *Low Pay in Northern Ireland*, London, Low Pay Unit, 1980.

Black, R., 'Flight in Belfast', *Community Forum*, 2.1, 1972, 9–12.

Black, R., Pinter, F. and Ovary, B., Flight: *A Report on Population Movement in Belfast during August 1971*, Northern Ireland Community Relations Commission, Belfast, 1971.

Blacking, J. A. R., and Holy, L., *Situational Determinants of Recruitment in Four Northern Irish Communities*, Report to SSRC; retained by British Library Lending Division, 1978.

Boal, F. W., and Buchanan, R., 'The 1969 Northern Ireland Election', *Irish Geography*, 6, 1, 1969, 22–29.

Boal, F. W., 'Territoriality on the Shankill–Falls Divide in Belfast', *Irish Geography*, 6, 1, 1969, 30–50.

Boal, F. W., 'Social Space in the Belfast Urban Area', N. Stephens and R. E. Glasscock, (eds.), *Irish Geographical Studies*, Belfast, Queen's University, Belfast, 1970.

Boal, F. W., 'Territory and Class: A Study of Two Residential Areas in Belfast', *Irish Geography*, 6, 1973, 229–248.

Boal, F. W., 'The Urban Residential Sub-community: A conflict Interpretation', *Area*, 4, 1972, 164–168.

Boal, F. W., 'Ethnic Residential Segregation', in Herbert, D. T., and Johnston, R. J., (eds.), *Social Areas in Cities, 1. Spatial Processes and Form*, Chichester, John Wiley, 1976, 41–79.

Boal, F. W., 'Residential segregation and mixing in a situation of ethnic and national conflict: Belfast', in Compton, P. A., (ed.), *The contemporary population of Northern Ireland and population-related issues*, Institute of Irish Studies, Queen's University of Belfast, 1981, 58–84.

Boal, F. W., 'Segregation and mixing: space and residence in Belfast', in Boal, F. W., and Douglas, J. N. H., (eds.), *Integration and division: geographical perspectives on the Northern Ireland problem*, London, Academic Press, 1982, 249–280.

Boal, F. W., Murray, R. C., and Poole, M. A., 'Belfast: the urban encapsulation of a national conflict', in Clarke, S. E., and Obler, J. L., (eds.), *Urban ethnic conflict: a comparative perspective*, Institute for Research in Social Science, University of North Carolina, Chapel Hill, 1976, 77–131.

Boehringer, G. H., 'Beyond Hunt: A Policing Policy for Northern Ireland', *Social Studies*, 2, 4, 1973.

Bonnet, Gerald, *The Orange Order*, Paris, unpublished University of Paris III Ph.D. thesis, 1972.

Boserup, A., *Who is the Principal Enemy?* London, Independent Labour Party, 1972.

Bowyer Bell, J., *The Secret Army*, London, Sphere, 1972.

Boyd, A., *Holy War in Belfast*, Tralee, Anvil, 1969.

Boyle, John W., 'The Belfast Protestant Association and the Independent Orange Order, 1901–10', *Irish Historical Studies*, 13, 1962, 113–52.

Boyle, K., 'The 'Minimum Sentences' Act', *Northern Ireland Legal Quarterly*, 21, 4, 1970, 425–441.

Boyle, K., Chesney, R. and Hadden, T., 'Who are the Terrorists?', *New Society*, 36, 1976, 709.

Boyle, K., Hadden, T. and Hillyard, P., *Law and State: The Case of Northern Ireland*, London, Martin Robertson, 1975.

Boyle, K., Hadden, T. and Hillyard, P., *Ten Years on in Northern Ireland: The Legal Control of Political Violence*, London, Cobden Trust, 1980.

Boyle, K. and Hannum, H., 'Ireland in Strasbourg', *Irish Jurist*, 7, New Series, 1972, 329–348.

Bradford, R., *The Last Ditch*, Belfast, Blackstaff, 1981.

Brady, B., Faul, D. and Murray, R., *Corruption of Law: Memorandum to the Gardiner Committee*, Dungannon, 1974.

Brady, B., Faul, D. and Murray, R., *British Army Murder: Leo Norney (17 Years)*, Dungannon, 1975.

Brady, B., Faul, D. and Murray, R., *British Army Terror Tactics, West Belfast, September–October 1976*, Dungannon, 1977.

Browne, V., 'H-Block Crisis: Courage, Lies and Confusion', *Magill*, August 1981.

Buckland, Patrick, *Ulster Unionism and the Origins of Northern Ireland, 1886–1922*, Dublin, Gill and Macmillan, 1973.

Buckland, Patrick, 'The Unity of Ulster Unionism, 1886–1939', *History*, 60, 1975, 211–23.

Buckland, Patrick, *The Factory of Grievances: Devolved Government in Northern Ireland 1921–1939*, Dublin, Gill and Macmillan, 1979.

Buckland, Patrick, *A History of Northern Ireland*, Dublin, Gill and Macmillan. 1981.

Buckley, A. D., *The Gentle People: A Study of a Peaceful Community in Ulster*, Ulster Folk Museum, 1982.

Bunyan, T., *Political Police in Britain*, London, Quartet Books, 1977.

Burton, F., *The Politics of Legitimacy: Struggles in a Belfast Community*, London, Routledge and Kegan Paul, 1978.

Burton, F., 'Ideological Social Relations in Northern Ireland', *British Journal of Sociology*, 30, 1974, 61–80.

Burton, F. and Carlen, P., *Official Discourse: On discourse analysis, government publications, ideology and the state*, London, Routledge and Kegan Paul, 1978.

Byrne, D., *Theorising Northern Ireland*, Unpublished Paper, Department of Sociology and Social Administration, University of Durham, 1980.

Cairncross Review, *Review of Economic and Social Development in Northern Ireland*, Cmd. 564, 1971.

Callaghan, J. *A House Divided*, London, Collins, 1973.

Calvert, H., 'Special Powers Extraordinary', *Northern Ireland Legal Quarterly*, 20, 1, 1969, 1–18.

Cameron Commission, *Disturbances in Northern Ireland*, Cmd. 532, Belfast, HMSO, 1969.

Campaign for Social Justice in Northern Ireland, *The Mailed Fist*, C.S.J., Dungannon, 1971.

Campaign for Social Justice in Northern Ireland, *Northern Ireland: The Plain Truth*, C.S.J., Dungannon, 1969.

Campbell, C. M., *Do We Need a Bill of Rights?*, London, Maurice Temple Smith, 1980.

Campbell, J. J., *Catholic Schools: A Survey of a Northern Ireland Problem*, Dublin, Fallons, 1964.

Carlton, Charles (Ed.), *Bigotry and Blood: Documents on the Ulster Troubles*, Chicago, Nelson-Hall, 1977.

Carroll, W. D. 'Search for Justice in Northern Ireland', New York, *University Journal of International Law and Politics*, 6, 28, 1973, 28–56.

Carty, J., Bibliography of Irish History 1911–1921, Dublin, 1936.

Carty, J., Bibliography of Irish History 1870–1911, Dublin, 1940.

Central Citizens Defence Committee, *Black Paper: The Story of the Police*, Belfast, CCDC, 1973.

Central Statistics Office, *Census of Population of Ireland 1971*, Vol. 9, Religion Stationery Office, Dublin, 1977.

Cockburn, C., *The Local State*, London, Pluto, 1977.

Community Groups Action Committee, *Roads to Destruction*, Belfast, 1980.

Compton Committee, *Report of the Enquiry into Allegations against the Security Forces of Physical Brutality in Northern Ireland arising out of Events on the 9th August, 1971*, CMND. 4823, London, HMSO, 1971.

Compton, P. A., 'Religious Affiliation and Demographic Variability in Northern Ireland', *Transactions of the Institute of British Geographers*, 1, 1976, 433–452.

Compton, P. A., *Northern Ireland: A Census Atlas,* Dublin, Gill and Macmillan, 1978.

Compton, P. A., 'The Other Crucial Factors Why Catholics don't get more Jobs', *Belfast Telegraph*, 28th October, 1980.

Compton, P. A., *The Contemporary Population of Northern Ireland and Population-related Issues*, Institute of Irish Studies, Queen's University of Belfast, 1981.

Compton, P. A., 'The demographic dimension of integration and division in Northern Ireland', in Boal, F. W., and Douglas, J. N. H., (ed.), *Integration and division: geographical perspectives on the Northern Ireland problem*, London, Academic Press, 1982, 75–104.

Compton, P. A., and Boal, F. W., 'Aspects of the Intercommunity Population Balance in Northern Ireland', *Economic and Social Review*, 1, 4, July 1970, 455–476.

Conway, Cardinal William, *Catholic Schools*, Dublin, Catholic Communications Institute of Ireland, 1971.

Coogan, T. P., *Ireland Since the Rising*, London, Pall Mall, 1966.

Coogan, T. P., *On the Blanket: The H-Block Story*, Dublin, Ward River Press, 1980.

Cooper, B., 'Responsibility is the Key to Success', *Fair Employment in Action*, 2, Fair Employment Agency, Belfast, 1979.

Cormack, R., Osborne, R. and Thompson, W., *Into Work? Young School Leavers and the Structure of Opportunity in Belfast,* Belfast, Fair Employment Agency, Research Paper 5, 1980.

Crawford, C., *Long Kesh: An Alternative Perspective*, M.Sc. Degree Thesis, Cranfield Institute of Technology, 1979.

Criminal Law Revision Committee, *Eleventh Report*, Cmnd. 4991, London, HMSO, 1972.

Darby, J., *Register of Research into the Irish Conflict*, Northern Ireland Community Relations Commission Research Paper, Belfast, 1972.

Darby, J., 'History in the School', *Community Forum, 4, 2, 1974.*

Darby, J. and Morris, G., *Intimidation in Housing,* Northern Ireland Community Relations Commission, Belfast, 1974.

Darby, J., *Conflict in Northern Ireland: The Development of a Polarised Community*, Dublin, Gill and Macmillan, 1976.

Darby, J., et al, *Education and Community in Northern Ireland: Schools Apart?,* New University of Ulster, Coleraine, 1977.

Darby, J., 'Northern Ireland: Bonds and Breaks in Education', *British Journal of Educational Studies*, XXVI, 3, 1978, 215–223.

Darby, J. and Williamson, A., (eds.), *Violence and the Social Services in Northern Ireland*, London, Heinemann, 1978.

Dash, S., *Justice Denied: A Challenge to Lord Widgery's Report on Bloody Sunday*, London, NCCL, 1972.

Davies, R. and McGurnaghan, M., 'Northern Ireland, The Economics of Adversity', *National Westminster Bank Review*, May 1975.

Day, M. C., Poole, M. A. and Boal, E. W., 'The Spatial Distribution of Disturbances in Belfast, 1969–71', Paper read at the Conference of Irish Geographers in Coleraine, May 1971 (summarised in Poole, M. A. and Boal, F. W., 'Religious Residential segregation in Belfast in mid-1969: a Multi-Level Analysis', in Clark, B. D. and Gleave, M. B. (eds.), *Social Patterns in Cities*, London, Institute of British Geographers, 1973, 1–40).

Dent, G. I., *The Law of Education in Northern Ireland and the influence of English Law*, Unpublished Ph.D. thesis, University of London, 1965.

De Paor, L., *Divided Ulster*, Middlesex, Penguin, 1970.

Deutsch, R., *Northern Ireland 1921–1974. A Select Bibliography*, Garland, 1975.

Deutsch, R. and Magowan, V., *Northern Ireland: Chronology of Events* (3 Volumes) Belfast, Blackstaff, 1973–75.

Devlin, B., *The Price of my Soul*, London, Pan, 1969.

Devlin, P., *The Fall of the Executive*, Belfast, Author, 1975.

Devlin, P., 'The Politics of Class', *Left Perspectives*, 1, 3, 1981, 20–23.

Dickey, A., 'Anti-Incitement Legislation in Britain and Northern Ireland', *New Community*, 1, 2, 1972, 133–128.

Digest of Statistics, Belfast, H.M.S.O., Annual.

Dillon, M. and Lehane, D., *Political Murder in Northern Ireland*, London, Penguin, 1973.

Diplock Commission, *Report of the Commission to consider Legal Procedures to deal with Terrorist Activities in Northern Ireland*, CMND. 5185, London, HMSO, 1972.

Ditch, J. and Morrissey, M., 'Recent Developments in Northern Ireland's Social Policy', in Brown, M., Baldwin, S. (eds.) *The Year Book of Social Policy in Britain 1979*, London, Routledge and Kegan Paul, 1979.

Ditch, J. and McWilliams, M., *The Supplementary Benefits System in Northern Ireland, 1980–1981*, Belfast, Northern Ireland Consumer Council, 1982.

Douglas, J. N. H. and Boal, F. W., 'The Northern Ireland Problem', in Boal, F. W. and Douglas, J. N. H., (eds.), *Integration and Division: Geographical Perspectives on the Northern Ireland Problem*, London, Academic Press, 1982, 1–18.

Dowling, K., *Interface Ireland*, London, Barrie and Jenkins, 1979.

Downing, J., *The Media Machine*, London, Pluto, 1980.

Dudley Edwards, R., *An Atlas of Irish History*, London, Methuen, 1973.

Eager, A. R., *A Guide to Irish Bibliographical Material*, London, Library Association, 1980.

Easthope, G., 'Religious War in Northern Ireland', *Sociology*, 10, 1976, 427–450.

Economic and Social Research Institute, *Register of Current Social Science Research in Ireland*, Dublin, E.S.R.I., Occasional.

Egan, B. and McCormack, V., *Burntollet*, London, LRS Publishers, 1969.

Elliott, P., 'Reporting Northern Ireland' in O'Halloran, J. et al., (eds.), *Ethnicity and the Media*, Paris, UNESCO, 1977.

Elliott, P., Murdock, G. and Schlesinger, P., *The State and 'Terrorism' on British Television*, Paper delivered to Festival Dei Popoli, Florence, Italy, 1981.

Elliott, Sydney, *Northern Ireland Parliamentary Election Results, 1921–72*, Chichester, Political Reference Publications, 1973.

Elliott, Sydney and Smith, F. J., *The Northern Ireland Local Election Results of 1977*, Belfast, Queen's University of Belfast, 1977.

Elliott, Sydney, *The Northern Ireland local government elections 1981*, Queen's University Belfast, 1981.

European Commission of Human Rights, *Ireland against the United Kingdom, Application No. 5310/71, Report of the Commission* (Adopted 25 January, 1976) Strasbourg, 1976.

European Commission of Human Rights, *McFeeley v United Kingdom, Application No. 8317/78*, (Partial Decision, adopted 15 May 1980), Strasbourg, 1980.

Evason, E., *Family Poverty in Northern Ireland*, London, Child Poverty Action Group, 1978.

Evason, E., *Ends That Won't Meet*, London, Child Poverty Action Group, 1980.

Fabian Society, *Emergency Powers: A Fresh Start*, London, Fabian Society, 1972.

Fahy, P. A., 'Some Political Behaviour Patterns and Attitudes of Roman Catholic Priests in a Rural Part of Northern Ireland', *Economic and Social Review*, 3, 1, 1971, 1–24.

Fair Employment Agency, *First Report of the FEA for Northern Ireland, 1 September 1976-31 March 1977*, Belfast, FEA, 1978a.

Fair Employment Agency, *An Industrial and Occupational Profile of the Two Sections of the Population in Northern Ireland*, Belfast, FEA, Research Paper 1, 1978b.

Fair Employment Agency, *Second Report of the FEA for Northern Ireland, 1 April 1977-31 March 1978*, Belfast, FEA, 1979.

Fair Employment Agency, *Third Report of the FEA for Northern Ireland, 1 April 1978-31 March 1979*, Belfast, FEA, 1980.

Fair Employment Agency, *Fourth Report of the FEA for Northern Ireland, 1 April 1979-31 March 1980*, Belfast, FEA, 1981.

Fair Employment Agency, *Sixth Report of the FEA for Northern Ireland, 1 April 1981-31 March 1982,* Belfast, FEA, 1982a.

Fair Employment Agency, *A Final Report of the Fair Employment Agency for Northern Ireland into the Employment Practices of the Northern Ireland Electricity Service*, Belfast, FEA, 1982b.

Fair Employment Agency, *Engineering Investigation and Report*, Unpublished, Belfast, FEA, n.d.

Farrell, M., *Northern Ireland: the Orange State*, London, Pluto, 1976.

Farrell, M. and McCullough, P., *Behind the Wire*, Belfast, People's Democracy, 1974.

Farrell, Michael, *Arms Outside the Law: Problems of the Ulster Special Constabulary 1920-22*, Glasgow, Unpublished University of Strathclyde Msc. dissertation, 1978.

Farrell, M., 'The Establishment of the Ulster Constabulary', in Morgan, A. and Purdie, B., *Ireland: Divided Nation Divided Class*, London, Irish Links, 1980.

Faul, D. and Murray, R., *British Army and Special Branch RUC Brutalities, December 1971-72*, Cavan, 1972.

Faul, D. and Murray, R., *Whitelaw's Tribunals: Long Kesh Internment Camp, November 1972-January 1973*, Dungannon, 1973.

Faul, D. and Murray, R., *Flames of Long Kesh*, Belfast, 1974.

Faul, D. and Murray, R., *Castlereagh File*, Belfast, 1978.

Faul, D. and Murray, R., *The British Dimension: Brutality, Murder and Legal Publicity in Northern Ireland*, Dungannon, 1980.

Faulkner, B. *Memoirs of a Statesman,* London, Weidenfeld and Nicolson, 1978.

Firth, G., 'Polar Press', *Fortnight*, 14 May 1971.

Fisk, R., *The Point of No Return: The Strike which broke the British in Ulster*, London, Deutsch, 1975.

Flackes, W. F., *Northern Ireland: A Political Directory*, Dublin, Gill & Macmillan, 1980.

Foy, Michael, *The Ancient Order of Hibernians: An Irish Political-Religious Pressure Group, 1884-1976*, Belfast, Unpublished Queen's University MA Thesis, 1976.

Gallagher, E, and Worrall, F., *Christians in Ulster 1968-1980*, Oxford, 1982.

Gallagher, F., *The Indivisible Island*, London, Gollancz, 1957.

Gardiner Committee, *Report of a Committee to consider, in the Context of Civil Liberties and Human Rights, Measures to Deal with Terrorism in Northern Ireland*, CMND. 5847, London, 1975.

Geraghty, T., *Who Dares Wins: The Story of the SAS 1950-1980*, London, Fontana, 1980.

Gibbon, P., 'Some Basic Problems of the Contemporary Situation', in Miliband, R. and Saville, J. (eds.), *The Socialist Register*, London, Merlin, 1977, 81-87.

Gibson, N. (Ed.), *Economic and Social Implications of the Political Alternatives that my be Open to Northern Ireland*, Coleraine, New University of Ulster, 1974.

Gibson, N., 'The Northern Problem: Religious or Economic or What?', *Community Forum*, 1, 1, 1971, 2-5.

Government of Northern Ireland, *Census of Population 1971*, Preliminary Report, Belfast, HMSO., 1971.

Government of Northern Ireland: Department of Commerce, *Facts and Figures on the Northern Ireland Economy*, Survey Prepared for the Department of Commerce, October 1980.

Government of Northern Ireland: Department of Education, *Northern Ireland Education Statistics*, Annual.

Government of Northern Ireland: Department of Finance, *Northern Ireland Sources of Social and Economic Research*, Policy, Planning and Research Unit, No Date.

Government of Northern Ireland: Department of Finance, *Register of Research*, Policy, Planning and Research Unit, 1973.

Government of Northern Ireland: Department of Manpower Services, *Northern Ireland Unemployment Figures*, D.M.S., Monthly.

Government of Northern Ireland, *Proposals for Further Discussion*, Cmd. 7950, London, HMSO., July 1980.

Gracey, J. and Howard, P., 'Northern Ireland Political Literature: 1968-70', *Irish Booklore*, 1, 1, 1971.

Graham, John, *The Consensus Forming Strategy of the Northern*

Ireland Party, 1949–68, Belfast, Unpublished Queen's University MSSc Thesis, 1972.

Greer, D., 'The Admissibility of Confessions Under the Northern Ireland (Emergency Provisions) Act', *Northern Legal Quarterly*, 31, 3, 1980, 205–238.

Greer, J., *A Questioning Generation*, Belfast, Church of Ireland Board of Education, 1972.

Griffiths, H., *Community Development in Northern Ireland: A Case Study in Agency Conflict*, Coleraine, New University of Ulster, 1974.

Griffiths, H., 'Community Reaction and Voluntary Involvement', In Darby, J. and Williamson, A. (eds.), *Violence and the Social Services in Northern Ireland*, London, Heinemann, 1978, 165–194.

Hadden, T. and Hillyard, P., *Justice in Northern Ireland: A Study in Social Confidence*, London, Cobden Trust, 1973.

Hall Report, *Report of the Joint Working Party on the Economy of Northern Ireland*, Cmnd. 1835, 1962.

Harbinson, John F., *A History of the Northern Ireland Labour Party, 1884–1949*, Belfast, Unpublished Queen's University MSc. Thesis, 1966.

Harbinson, John F., *The Ulster Unionist Party*, 1882–1972, Belfast, Blackstaff, 1973.

Harbinson, R., *No Surrender*, London, Faber & Faber, 1960.

Harris, R., *Social Relations and Attitudes in a Northern Ireland Rural Area: Ballybeg*, University of London, Unpublished M.A. thesis, 1954.

Harris, R., 'The Selection of Leaders in Ballybeg, Northern Ireland', *Sociological Review (N.S.)*, 8, 1961, 137–149.

Harris, R., *Prejudice and Tolerance in Ulster: A Study of Neighbours and 'Strangers' in a Border Community*, Manchester, Manchester University Press, 1972.

Harris, R., 'Religious Change on Rathlin Island', *Pace*, 6, 1974, 11–16.

Harris, R., 'Community Relationships in Northern and Sourthern Ireland: A Comparison and a Paradox', *Sociological Review*, 27, 1979, 41–53.

Harris, R., 'Myth and Reality in Northern Ireland: An Anthropological View', in McWhirter, L. and Trew, K., (Eds.) *The Northern Ireland Conflict: Myth and Reality; Social and Political Perspectives*, Ormskirk, Planned Publication Date 1983.

Harvey, R., *Diplock and the Assault on Civil Liberties*, London, Haldane Society, 1981.

Hayes, M., *Community Relations and the Role of the Community Relations Commission in Northern Ireland*, London, Runnymede Trust, 1971.

Hepburn, A. C., (ed.) *The Conflict of Nationality in Modern Ireland*, 1980.

Hermle, R., (ed.), *Konflikt und Gewalt: Texte Zur Lage in Nordirland, 1972-74*, Munich, Kaiser, 1976.

Hewitt, C., 'Majorities and Minorities: A Comparative Survey of Ethnic Violence', *Annals of the American Academy of Political and Social Science*, 433, September 1977, 150-160.

Hewitt, C., 'Catholic Grievances, Catholic Nationalism and Violence in Northern Ireland During the Civil Rights Period: A Reconsideration', *British Journal of Sociology*, 32, 3, 1981, 362-380.

Hezlet, B., *Fermanagh 'B' Specials*, London, Tom Stacey, 1972.

Hickey, D. J. and Doherty, J. E., *A Dictionary of Irish History Since 1800*, Dublin, Gill & Macmillan, 1980.

Hillyard, P., 'From Belfast to Britain: The Royal Commission on Criminal Procedure', in *Law, Politics and Justice*, London, Routledge and Kegan Paul, 1981.

Hillyard, P., *The Media Coverage of Crime and Justice in Northern Ireland*, Cropwood Conference Paper, 1982.

Hoggart, S., 'The Army PR Men in Northern Ireland', *New Society*, 11 Actober, 1973.

Holland, J., *Too Long a Sacrifice: Life and Death in Northern Ireland Since 1969*, N.Y., Dodd, Mead and Co., 1981.

Howard, P., 'The Paper War', (Three Articles), *Fortnight*, 11 January, 25 January, 8 February 1974.

Howard, R., *The Movement of Manufacturing Industry in the United Kingdom, 1945-65*, HMSO, 1968.

Hunt Committee, *Report of the Advisory Committee on Police in Northern Ireland*, Cmd. 535, Belfast, HMSO, 1969.

Hull, R. H., *The Irish Triangle: Conflict in Northern Ireland*, Princeton, N.J., Princeton University Press, 1976.

Information on Ireland, *The British Media and Ireland*, London, Information on Ireland, 1980.

Institute of Irish Studies, *Theses Related to Ireland*, Belfast, Institute of Irish Studies, Queen's University Belfast, 1968.

Irish Council of Churches, *Violence in Ireland*, Dublin, Christian Journals Ltd., 1976.

Irish Historical Studies, *Writings on Irish History*, Microfiche, 1983.

Isles, K. S. and Cuthbert, N., *Economic Survey of Northern Ireland*, Cmd. 475, Belfast, HMSO, 1957.

Jackson, H., *The Two Irelands: A Dual Study of Inter-group Tensions*, London, Minority Rights Group, London, 1971.

Jackson, J. A., *The Irish in Britain*, London, Routledge and Kegan Paul, 1963.

Jackson, T. A., *Ireland Her Own*, London, Lawrence and Wishart, 1947.

Jenkins, R., 'Doing a Double', *New Society*, 44, 1978, 121.

Jenkins, R., 'Thinking and Doing: Towards a Model of Cognitive Practice', in Holy, L. and Stuchlik, M., (eds.), *The Structure of Folk Models*, London, Academic Press, 1981a.

Jenkins, R., *Young People, Education and Work in a Belfast Housing Estate*, Cambridge University, Ph.D. Thesis, 1981b.

Johnston, E., *Irish History: A Selected Bibliography*, Historical Association Pamphlet, 73, 1969.

Jones, E., 'The Distribution and Segregation of Roman Catholics in Belfast', *Sociological Review*, 4, 1956, 167–189.

Jones, E. and Eyles, J., *An Introduction to Social Geography*, Oxford, Oxford University Press, 1977.

Kennedy, S. and Birrell, W. D., 'Housing', in Darby, J. and Williamson, A. (eds.), *Violence and the Social Services in Northern Ireland*, London, Heinemann, 1978, 98–116.

Kirk, D., 'The Field of Demography', in Sills, D. L. (ed.), *International Encyclopaedia of the Social Sciences*, 12, Macmillan, 1968, 342– 349.

Kirk, T., *The Religious Distribution in Lurgan*, Queen's University Belfast, Unpublished M.A. Thesis, 1967.

Kitson, F., *Low Intensity Operations: Subversion, Insurgency and Peace-keeping*, London, Faber and Faber, 1971.

Knight, J., *Northern Ireland: The Elections of 1973*, London, Arthur McDougall Fund, 1974.

Knight, J., *Northern Ireland: The Election of the Constitutional Assembly*, London, Arthur McDougall Fund, 1975.

Krausz, E., *Ethnic Minorities in Britain*, London, MacGibbon and Kee, 1971.

Laver, Michael, (1976), *The Theory and Practice of Party Competition: Ulster, 1973–75*, London, Sage Contemporary Political Sociology Series 06–014, 1976.

Law Enforcement Commission, *Report to the Minister for Justice of Ireland and the Secretary of State for Northern Ireland*, Prl. 3832, Dublin, Stationery Office, 1974.

Law Officers' Department, (1974), *Prosecutions in Northern Ireland: A Study of Facts*, London, HMSO, 1974.

Lawrence, R. J. et al, *The Northern Ireland General Election of 1973*, London, HMSO, 1975.

Lee, J., *Irish Historiography 1970–1979*, Cork, Cork University Press, 1981.

Leyton, E., 'Conscious Models and Dispute Regulation in an Ulster Village', *Man* (N.S.), 1, 1966, 534–542.

Leyton, E., 'Spheres of Inheritance in Aughnaboy', *American Anthropologist*, 72, 1970a, 1378–1388.

Leyton, E., 'Death and Authority in the Fishing Authority', *Resurgence, 3, 1970b, 12*–13.

Leyton, E., 'Opposition and Integration in Ulster', *Man* (N.S.), 9, 1974a, 185–198.

Leyton, E., 'Irish Friends and 'Friends': the Nexus of Friendship, Kinship and Class in Aughnaboy', in Leyton, E. (ed.), *The Compact: Selected Dimensions of Friendship*, St. John's Newfoundland, Institute of Social and Economic Research, Memorial University, 1974b.

Leyton, E., *The One Blood: Kinship and Class in an Irish Village*, St. John's Newfoundland, Institute of Social and Economic Research, Memorial University, Newfoundland Social and Economic Studies, 15, 1975.

Leyton, E., 'Studies in Irish Social Organisation: the State of the Art', Dublin, *Social Studies*, 6, 1977.

Lieberson, S., 'An Asymmetrical Approach to Segregation', in Peach, C., Robinson, V. and Smith, S. (eds.), *Ethnic Segregation in Cities*, London, Croom Helm, 1981, 61–82.

Lijphart, A., 'The Northern Ireland Problem: Cases, Theories, and Solutions', *British Journal of Political Science*, 5, 1975, 83–106.

Lindsay, K., *The British Intelligence Service in Action*, Dundalk, Dundrod, 1980.

Linenhall Library, *Northern Ireland Political Literature* 1973–74 (2 vols), 1975 (1 vol), Irish Microform, ND.

Lowry, D. R., 'Legislation in a Social Vacuum: the Failure of the Fair Employment (Northern Ireland) Act 1976 and Alternative Solutions', *New York University Journal of International Law and Politics*, 9, 3, 1977, 345–388.

Lyons, F. S. L., *Ireland Since the Famine*, London, Weidenfeld & Nicholson, 1971.

McAllister, Ian, *The 1975 Northern Ireland Convention Election*, Glasgow, Survey Research Centre Occasional Paper No. 14, 1975a.

McAllister, Ian, 'Political Opposition in Northern Ireland: The National Democratic Party, 1965–70', *Economic and Social Review*, 6, 3, 1975b, 353–66.

McAllister, Ian, *The Northern Ireland Social Democratic and Labour Party*, London, Macmillan, 1977.

McAllister, Ian and Wilson, Brian, 'Bi-confessionalism in a Confessional Party System: The Northern Ireland Alliance Party', *Economic and Social Review*, 9, 3, 1978, 207–25.

McAllister, Ian and Nelson, Sarah, 'The Modern Development of the Northern Ireland Party System', *Parliamentary Affairs*, 32, 3, 1979, 279–316.

McCafferty, N., *The Armagh Women*, Dublin, Co-op Books, 1981.

McCann, E., *War and an Irish Town*, Middlesex, Penguin, 1974.

McConnell, J., 'The Michael Farrell Case: Discrimination in Belfast's College of Technology', *Hibernia*, 21 December, 1978.

McCracken, J. L., 'The Political Scene in Northern Ireland, 1926–37' in McManus, F. (ed.), *The Years of the Great Test, 1926–39*, Dublin, Mercier, 1967.

McCrudden, C., *A Report to the Fair Employment Agency*, unpublished, February 1982.

McElligott, T., *Intermediate Education and the Work of the Commissioners 1870–1922*, Trinity College Dublin, Unpublished M.Litt. Thesis, 1969.

McFarlane, W. G., *Gossip and Social Relations in a Northern Irish Village*, Queen's University, Belfast, Unpublished Ph.D., Thesis, 1978.

McFarlane, W. G., ''Mixed' Marriages in Ballycuan, Northern Ireland', *Journal of Comparative Family Studies*, 10, 1979, 191–205.

McFarlane, W. G., 'Social Life in Northern Ireland', *Social Science Research Council Newsletter*, 42, 1980, 12–13.

McKeown, M., *The First Five Hundred*, Belfast, Irish News Ltd., 1972.

McKeown, M., 'Considerations on the Statistics of Violence', *Fortnight, 151, July 1977,* 4–5.

McGuffin, J., *The Guineapigs*, Middlesex, Penguin, 1974.

McGuffin, J., *Internment*, Tralee, Anvil Press, 1973.

McMahon, B. M. E., 'The Impaired Asset: A Legal Commentary on the Report of the Widgery Tribunal', *The Human Context*, VI, 3, 1974, 681–699.

McMinn, J., 'Contemporary Novels on the 'Troubles'', *Etudes Irlandaises*, 5, 1980.

Magee, J., 'The Teaching of Irish History in Irish Schools', Belfast, *The Northern Teacher*, 10, 1, 1970.

Magee, J., *Northern Ireland, Crisis & Conflict*, London, Routledge and Kegan Paul, 1974.

Maltby, A. *The Government of Northern Ireland*, Shannon, Irish University Press, 1974.

Mansbach, R. (ed.) *Northern Ireland: Half a Century of Partition*, New York, Facts on File, 1973.

Marquand, J., *Measuring the Effects and Costs of Regional Incentives*, London, Government Economic Service Working Paper 32, 1980.

Matthew Report, *Belfast Regional Survey and Plan*, Cmd. 451, Belfast, HMSO., 1963.

Micholas, E., *International Terrorism: A Chronology of Events, 1968–1979*, London, Aldwych, 1980.

Miller, David W., *Queen's Rebels*, Dublin, Gill and Macmillan, 1978.

Miller, R., *Attitudes to Work in Northern Ireland*, Belfast, Fair Employment Agency, Research Paper 2, 1978.

Miller, R., *Occupational Mobility of Protestants and Roman Catholics in Northern Ireland*, Belfast, Fair Employment Agency, Research Paper 4, 1979.

Mitchell, J. K., 'Social Violence in Northern Ireland', *Geographical Review*, 69, 1979, 179–201.

Mogey, J. McF., *Rural Life in Northern Ireland: Five Regional Studies made for the Northern Ireland Council of Social Services*, London, Oxford University Press, 1947.

Mogey, J. McF., 'The Community in Northern Ireland', *Man*, 48, 1948, 85–87.

Moloney, E., 'Dirty Tricks in the North's Fair Employment Agency', Dublin, *Hibernia*, 26 July 1979.

Monaghan, C. M., *Coping with Mixed Marriage among a Group of Professional People in Belfast*, Queen's University Belfast, Unpublished B.A. dissertation, 1980.

Moody, T. W. (ed.) *Irish Historiography 1936–70*, Dublin, Irish Committee of Historical Studies, 1971.

Morgan, A., 'Socialism in Ireland: Red, Green and Orange', in Morgan, A. and Purdie, B. (eds.), 1980, 172–225.

Morgan, A. and Purdie, B. (eds.), *Ireland: Divided Nation, Divided Class*, London, Ink Links, 1980.

Morrisey, M. and Ditch, J., 'Social Policy Implications of Emergency Legislation in Northern Ireland', *Critical Social Policy*, 1, 3, 1982, 19–39.

Moxon-Browne, E., 'The Water and the Fish: Public Opinion and the Provisional IRA in Northern Ireland', in Wilkinson, P. (ed.), *British Perspectives on Terrorism*, London, George Allen and Unwin, 1981.

Moxon-Browne, E., 'Terrorism in Northern Ireland: The Case of the Provisional IRA', in Lodge, J. (ed.), *Terrorism: A Challenge to the State*, London, Martin Robertson, 1981.

Murphy, M., *Irish Studies in the United States*, ACIS, 1979.

Murray Inquiry, *Report into Proposed Compulsory Acquisition of Land at Maghaberry for Prison Accommodation*, Belfast, HMSO, 1975.

Murray, D. and Darby, J., *The Vocational Aspirations and Expectations of School Leavers in Londonderry and Strabane*, Belfast, Fair Employment Agency, Research Paper 6, 1980.

Murray, D., *The Character and Culture of Protestant and Catholic Primary Schools in Northern Ireland*, New University of Ulster, Unpublished Ph.D. Dissertation, 1983.

Murray, R., 'Political Violence in Northern Ireland 1969–1977', in Boal, F. W. and Douglas, J. N. H. (ed.), *Integration and Division: Geographical Perspectives on the Northern Ireland Problem*, London, Academic Press, 1982, 309–331.

Murray, R., and Boal, F. W., 'The Social Ecology of Urban Violence', in Herbert, D. T. and Smith, D. M. (eds.), *Social Problems and the City: Geographical Perspectives*, Oxford, Oxford University Press, 1979, 139–157.

Murray, R. C. and Boal, F. W., 'Forced Residential Mobility in Belfast 1969–1972', in Harbison, J. and Harbison, J. (Eds.), *A Society under Stress: Children and Young People in Northern Ireland*, Somerset, Open Books, 1980, 25–30.

Murray, R., Boal, F. W. and Poole, M. A., 'Psychology and the Threatening Environment', *Architectural Psychology Newsletter*, 5, 4, December 1975, 30–34.

Nairn, T., *The Break-up of Britain: Crisis and Neo-Nationalism*, London, New Left Books, 1977.

National Council for Civil Liberty, *The RUC: A Report on Complaints Procedure*, London, NCCL, 1975.

National Council for Civil Liberty, *The Special Powers Act of Northern Ireland*, (First Edition, 1935), London, NCCL, 1972.

Nelson, S., 'Discrimination in Northern Ireland: The Protestant Response', in Veenhoven, W. A. (ed.), *Case Studies on Human Rights and Fundamental Freedoms: A World Survey*, The Hague, Martinus Nijhoff, 1976a, 404–429.

Nelson, S., 'Developments in Protestant Working Class Politics', Dublin, *Social Studies*, 5, 1976b, 202–224.

Nelson, S., *Ulster's Uncertain Defenders: A Study of Protestant Politics, 1969–75*, University of Strathclyde, Ph.D. Thesis, 1980.

Northern Ireland Council for Educational Research, *Register of Research in Education*, Belfast, NICER, Occasional.

Northern Ireland Development Programme 1970–75, Report of the three Consultants, Professor T. Wilson, Professor J. Parkinson and Professor Sir Robert Matthew, HMSO, 1970.

Northern Ireland Development Programme, 1970–75, Government Statement, Cmd. 547, Belfast, HMSO, 1970.

Northern Ireland Police Authority, *The First Three Years, 1970–73*, Belfast, NIPA, 1973.

Northern Ireland General Register Office, *Census of Population 1971: Religion Tables*, Belfast, HMSO, 1975a.

Northern Ireland General Register Office, *Census of Population 1971: Summary Tables*, Belfast, HMSO, 1975b.

Northern Ireland General Register Office, *Census of Population 1971: County Reports*, Belfast, HMSO, 1973–4.

Northern Ireland Housing Executive, *Seventh Annual Report: 1st April 1977 to 31st March 1978*, Belfast, NIHE, 1978.

Northern Ireland Information Service, *Facts at Your Fingertips*, Belfast, NIIS, Irregular.

O'Boyle, M. P., 'Torture and Emergency Powers under the European Convention on Human Rights', *American Journal of International Law*, 71, 4, 1977.

O'Donnell, E. F., *Northern Irish Stereotypes*, Dublin, College of Industrial Relations, 1977.

O'Dowd, L. and Tomlinson, M., 'Urban Politics in Belfast: Two Case Studies', *International Journal of Urban and Regional Research*, 4, 1, 1980, 72–95.

O'Dowd, L., Rolston, B. and Tomlinson, B., *Northern Ireland Between Civil Rights and Civil War*, London, CSE Books, 1980.

O'Dowd, L., *Intellectuals on the Road to Modernity: Aspects of Social Ideology in the 1950s*, Paper delivered to Sociology Association of Ireland Annual Conference, Ballyvaughan, Co. Clare, April 1982.

O'Fearghail, S., *Law (?) and Orders: The Belfast Curfew of 3rd–5th July, 1970*, Belfast, Central Citizens' Defence Committee, 1970.

O'Hearn, D., 'Accumulation and the Irish Crisis', *Monthly Review*, 32, 10, 1981, 31–44.

Oliver, J., *Working at Stormont*, Dublin, Institute of Public Administration, 1978.

O'Neill, T., *Ulster at the Crossroads*, London, Faber, 1969.

O'Neill, T., *Autobiography*, London, Hart-Davis, 1972.

Osborne, R. and Murray, R., *Educational Qualifications and Religious Affiliation in Northern Ireland*, Belfast, Fair Employment Agency, Research Paper 3, 1978.

Osborne, R. and Miller, R., 'Why Catholics Don't Get More Jobs—A Reply', *Belfast Telegraph*, 14 November 1980.

Osborne, R., 'Fair Employment in Northern Ireland', *New Community*, 8, 1–2, 1980, 129–137.

Osborne, R., 'Voting Behaviour in Northern Ireland 1921–1977', in Boal, F. W., Douglas, J. N. H., (ed.), *Integration and Division: Geographical Pespectives on the Northern Ireland Problem*, London, Academic Press, 1982, 137–166.

Palley, C., 'Evolution, Disintegration and Possible Reconstruction of the Northern Ireland Constitution', *Anglo–American Law Review*, 1, 1972.

Park, A. T., 'An Analysis of Human Fertility in Northern Ireland', *Journal of Statistical and Social Inquiry Society of Ireland*, 21, 1, 1962–63, 1–13.

Parker Committee, *Report of the Committee of Privy Counsellors Appointed to consider Authorised Procedures for the Interrogation of Persons Suspected of Terrorism*, Cmnd. 4901, HMSO, 1972.

Patterson, H., 'Review of Burton 1978', *Sociological Review*, 27, 1979, 582–583.

Paxton, J. (ed.), *The Stateman's Yearbook: Statistical and Historical Annual of the States of the World for the Year 1981–1982*, London, Macmillan, 1981.

Peach, C., *'Introduction: The Spatial Analysis of Ethnicity and Class'*, in Peach, C. (ed.), *Urban Social Segregation*, London, Longman, 1975, 1–17.

Pollack, A., 'Overhaul of Northern Ireland Job Agency Urged', *Irish Times*, 29 March, 1982.

Pollock, Laurence and McAllister, Ian, *A Bibliography of United Kingdom Politics: Scotland, Wales and Northern Ireland*, Glasgow, University of Strathclyde Studies in Public Policy, III, 1980.

Poole, M. A., 'Riot Displacement in 1969', *Fortnight*, 22, 6–31 August 1971.

Poole, M. A., 'Religious Residential Segregation in Urban Northern

Ireland', in Boal, F. W. and Douglas, J. N. H., (eds.), *Integration and Division: Geographical Perspectives on the Northern Ireland Problem*, London, Academic Press, 1982, 281-308.

Poole, M. A. and Boal, F. W., 'Religious Residential Segregation in Belfast in mid-1969: A Multi-level Analysis', in Clarke, B. D. and Gleave, M. B. (eds.), *Social Patterns in Cities*, London, Institute of British Geographers, 1973, 1-40.

Poulantzas, N., *State, Power and Socialism*, London, NLB, 1978.

Pounce, R. J., *Industrial Movement in the United Kingdom, 1966-75*, London, HMSO, 1981.

Probert, B., *Beyond Orange and Green: The Political Economy of the Northern Ireland Crisis*, London, Zed Press, 1978.

Quigley Review Team, *Economic and Industrial Strategy for Northern Ireland, Report by Review Team*, Belfast, HMSO, 1976.

Radzinowicz, L. and Hood, R., 'The Status of Political Prisoners in England: The Struggle for Recognition', *Virginia Law Review Association*, 65, 8, 1979, 1421-1481.

Rauche, E., 'The Compatability of the Detention of Terrorists Order', *New York Journal of Internal Law and Politics*, 6, 1, 1979.

Red Cross, *Report on the Visits Carried out by Delegates from the international Committee of the Red Cross to Places of Detention in Northern Ireland, July 1973*, Geneve, Comite International de la Croix-Rouge, 1973.

Regional Physical Development Strategy 1975-1995, Discussion Paper, London, HMSO, 1975.

Research Services Limited, *Readership Survey of Northern Ireland*, London, RSL, 1970.

Revolutionary Communist Group, 'Ireland: Imperialism in Crisis, 1968-1978', *Revolutionary Communist*, 8, 1978, 5-33.

Revolutionary Communist Tendency, 'British Imperialism and the Irish Crisis', *Revolutionary Communist Papers*, 2, 1978, 3-20.

Roberts, David, A., 'The Orange Order in Ireland: A Religious Institution?', *British Journal of Sociology*, 22, 3, 1971, 269-282.

Robinson, A., *A Social Geography of Londonderry*, Queen's University Belfast, M.A. Thesis, 1967.

Robinson, A., 'Education and Sectarian Conflict in Northern Ireland', *New Era*, 52, 1, January 1971.

Roche, D. and Williamson, A., *Register of Recent Research into Mental Illness and Handicap in Ireland*, Coleraine, N.U.U., 1977.

Rolston, B., 'Reforming the Orange State: Problems of the Northern

Ireland Community Relations Commission', in Downing, J., Smyth, J. and Rolston, B., *Northern Ireland*, Thames Papers in Social Analysis, Series 1, Thames Polytechnic, London, 1976, 56–85.

Rolston, B., *Community Development and the Capitalist State: The Case of the Northern Ireland Community Relations Commission*, Queen's University Belfast, Ph.D. Thesis, 1978.

Rolston, B., 'Escaping from Belfast: Class, Ideology and Literature in Northern Ireland', *Race and Class*, 20, 1, 1978, 41–62.

Rolston, B., 'Community Politics', in O'Dowd, L. Rolston, B. and Tomlinson, M., 1980, 148–177.

Rose, Richard, 'The Dynamics of a Divided Regime', *Government and Opposition*, 5, 2, 1970, 166–92.

Rose, Richard, *Governing Without Consensus*, London, Faber, 1971.

Rose, Richard, 'Discord in Ulster', *New Community*, 1, 2, 1972, 122–27.

Rose, Richard, *Northern Ireland: A Time of Choice*, London, Macmillan, 1976.

Rose, Richard, 'Is the United Kingdom a State? Northern Ireland as a Test Case', in Madgewick, P. and Rose, R. (eds.), *The Territorial Dimension in United Kingdom Politics*, London, Macmillan, 1982.

Rose, R., McAllister, I. and Mair, P., *Is There a Concurring Majority about Northern Ireland?*, Centre for the Study of Public Policy, University of Strathclyde, 1978.

Rose, R, and McAllister, Ian, *United Kingdom Facts*, London, Macmillan, 1982.

Rowthorn, W., 'Northern Ireland: An Economy in Crisis', *Cambridge Review of Economics*, 1981, 5.

Royal Ulster Constabulary, *Chief Constable's Report*, Belfast, R.U.C., Annual.

Royal Commission on Criminal Procedure, *Report*, Cmnd. 8092, London, HMSO, 1976.

Rumpf, E. and Hepburn, A. C., *Nationalism and Socialism in Twentieth Century Ireland*, Liverpool, Liverpool University Press, 1977.

Rutan, Gerard, F., 'The Labour Party in Ulster: Opposition by Cartel', *Review of Politics*, 29, 4, 1969, 326–35.

Russell, J., *Some Aspects of the Civic Education of Secondary Schoolboys in Northern Ireland*, Belfast, Northern Ireland Community Relations Commission, 1972.

Sacks, Paul, *The Donegal Mafia*, New Haven, Conn., Yale University Press, 1977.

Savage, D. C., 'The Origins of the Ulster Unionist Party, 1885–1886', *Irish Historical Studies*, 12, 1961, 185–208.

Scarman Tribunal, *Report of Tribunal of Inquiry into Violence and Civil Disturbances in Northern Ireland, 1969*, Vol. 1 and 2, Cmd. 566, Belfast, HMSO, 1972.

Schellenberg, J. A., 'Violence in Northern Ireland, 1965–1975', *International Journal of Group Tension*, 6, 1976, 6–21.

Schellenberg, J. A., 'Area Variations of Violence in Northern Ireland', *Sociological Focus*, 10, 1977, 69–78.

Schilling, F. C. (ed.), *Lokaltermin in Belfast: Die Kirchen im Nordirischen Konflikt*, Eckart (GFR), 1972.

Schools Cultural Studies Project, *The (1982) Director's Report*, Coleraine, New University of Ulster, 1982.

Scorer, C. and Hewitt, P., *The Prevention of Terrorism Act: The Case for Repeal*, London, NCCL, 1981.

Shallice, T., 'The Ulster Depth Interrogation Techniques', *Cognition*, 1, 4, 1973.

Shannon, M. O., *Modern Ireland: A Bibliography for Research, Planning and Development*, London, Library Association, 1982.

Shea, P., *Voices and the Sound of Drums,* Belfast, Blackstaff, 1981.

Shearman, H., *Northern Ireland 1921–1971*, Belfast, HMSO, 1971.

Shearman, H., 'Conflict in Northern Ireland', *Year Book of World Affairs*, 24, 1970, 40–53.

Sheehy, M., *Divided We Stand*, London, Faber and Faber, 1955.

Simpson, J., 'The Finances of the Public Sector in Northern Ireland, 1968–78', *Journal of the Statistical and Social Inquiry Society of Ireland, 1981*.

Smith, P., *Emergency Legislation: The Prevention of Terrorism Acts*, European Group for the Study of Deviance and Social Control, Working Paper No. 3, 1982.

Sobel, L. (ed.), *Political Terrorism*, Oxford, Clio Press, Two Volumes, 1979.

Spense, W., *The Growth and Development of the Secondary Intermediate School in Northern Ireland Since the Education Act of 1947*, Queen's University Belfast, M.A. Thesis, 1959.

Spilerman, S., 'The Causes of Racial Disturbances: A Comparison of alternative explanations', *American Sociological Review.* 35, 1970, 627–649.

Spjut, R., 'Executive Detention in Northern Ireland: The Gardiner Report and the Northern Ireland (Emergency Provisions) (Amendment) Act 1975', *Irish Jurist*, 10, 1975, 272–299.

Spjut, R., 'Torture under the European Convention' *American Journal of International Law*, 73, 2, 1979.

Standing Advisory Commission on Human Rights, *Bill of Rights: A Discussion Paper*, Belfast, 1976.

Starling, S., *The Sociology of Voluntary Organisations in Belfast*, Queen's University Belfast, Unpublished Dissertation, 1971.

Stewart, A. T. Q., *The Narrow Ground: Aspects of Ulster, 1609–1969*, London, Faber and Faber, 1977.

Sunday News, Belfast, 16 August 1980.

Sunday Times Insight Team, *Ulster*, London, Penguin, 1972.

Taylor, D., *Power and Prayer: A Cast Study of Religious and Political Convergence*, Paper Presented to British Sociological Association Conference on 'Sociology of Religion', London, 1979.

Taylor, D., *Militant Fundamentalism: Ulster's Debt to America*, Paper Presented to British Sociological Association Conference on 'Sociology of Religion', Birmingham, 1980.

Taylor, D., *'No Surrender': An Ethnographic View, of Ian Paisley's Ideological Rhetoric*, Paper presented to Conference of Irish Sociological Association, Limerick, 1981.

Taylor, L. and Nelson,S. (eds.), *Young People and Civil Conflict in Northern Ireland*, Belfast, 1977.

Taylor, P., *Beating the Terrorists? Interrogation in Omagh, Gough and Castlereagh*, Middlesex, Penguin, 1980.

Tomlinson, M., 'Housing, the State and the Politics of Segregation', in O'Dowd, L., Rolston, B. and Tomlinson, M., 1980a, 119–147.

Tomlinson, M., 'Reforming Repression', in O'Dowd, L., Rolston, B. and Tomlinson, M., 1980b, 178–202.

Tomlinson, M., 'Policing the Periphery—Ideologies of Repression in Northern Ireland', *Bulletin on Social Policy*, 5, 9–26, 1980c.

Treasury, H.M., *Needs Assessment Study*, London, H.M. Treasury, 1979.

Twining, W., *Emergency Powers: A Fresh Start*, Fabian Tract 416, London, Fabian Society, November 1972.

Ulster Unionist Party, *The Assembly Elections (1973) and the 1974 United Kingdom General Election*, Belfast, U.U.C., 1975.

Ulster Unionist Party, *The Convention Elections 1975*, Belfast, U.U.C., 1975.

Ulster Year Book, Belfast, HMSO, Annual.

Vogt, Hermann (Ed.), *Nordirland: Texte zu einen Konfessionellen, Politischen und Sozialen Konflikt*, Evang. Missionsverlag, 1972.

Walsh, B. M., *'Religion and Demographic Behaviour in Ireland*, Dublin, Economic and Social Research Institute, 1970.

Walsh, D., *The Diplock Court Process: Today and Tomorrow*, Paper presented to the Conference of the Administration of Justice, Belfast, 24th April, 1982.

Whyte, J., 'Intra-Unionist Disputes in the Northern Ireland House of Commons, 1921–72', *Economic and Social Review*, 5, 1, 1973, 99–104.

Whyte, J., 'Recent Writing on Northern Ireland', *American Political Science Review,* 70, 2, 1976, 592–596.

Whyte, J., 'Interpretations of the Northern Ireland Problem: An Appraisal', *Economic and Social Review*, 9, 4, July 1978, 257–282.

Whyte, J., 'How Much Discrimination Was There Under the Unionist Regime, 1921–68?', Unpublished Paper, Department of Political Science, Queen's University, Belfast, 1981.

Widgery Tribunal, *Report of the Tribunal Appointed to inquire into the Events on Sunday, 30th January 1972, which led to Loss of Life in Connection with the Procession in London on that day*, HC 220, London, HMSO, 1972.

Williams, T. (ed.), *Secret Societies in Ireland*, Dublin: Gill and Macmillan, 1974.

Wilson, T., *Economic Development in Northern Ireland*, Cmd. 479, Belfast, HMSO, 1965.

Winchester, S., *In Holy Terror: Reporting the Ulster Troubles*, London, Faber, 1974.

Workers Research Unit, *Repression*, Bulletin No. 2, Belfast, 1977.

Workers Research Unit, *The Law in Northern Ireland*, Bulletin No. 10, Belfast, 1982.

Wright, F., 'Protestant Ideology and Politics in Ulster', *European Journal of Sociology*, 14, 1973, 213–280.

Wright, S., 'New Police Technologies: An Exploration of the Social Implications and Unforseen Impacts of Some Recent Developments', *Journal of Peace Research*, XV, 4, 1978, 305–322.

Wright, S., 'Your Unfriendly Neighbourhood Bobby', *The Guardian*, 16th July, 1981.

Wright, S., 'An Assessment of the New Technologies of Repression', in Hoefnagels, M., (ed.), *Repression and Repressive Violence*, Amsterdam, Swets and Zeitlinger, 1977.

Index